Kristopher Karl Woofter teaches on the American Gothic, horror and the "Weird tradition" in literature, cinema and television at Dawson College, Canada, and is Associate Editor of *Slayage: The Journal of Whedon Studies*. He is also Editor of *MONSTRUM*, the Journal of the Montréal Monstrum Society, and his publications include work on Joss Whedon in *Slayage: The Journal of Whedon Studies* and *Reading Joss Whedon* (2014), on 1940s horror in *Recovering 1940s Horror Cinema: Traces of a Lost Decade* (2014), and on the intersection of the Gothic and documentary in the journal, *Textus: English Studies in Italy*.

Lorna Jowett is Reader in Television Studies at the University of Northampton, UK, where she teaches horror, science fiction, and television, sometimes all at once. Her most recent book is *Dancing With the Doctor: Dimensions of Gender in the New Doctor Who Universe* (2017, I.B.Tauris): she is also author of *Sex and the Slayer: A Gender Studies Primer for the Buffy Fan* (2005), and co-author with Stacey Abbott of *TV Horror* (2012, I.B.Tauris).

JOSS WHEDON VS. THE HORROR TRADITION

The Production of Genre in
Buffy and Beyond

Edited by
Kristopher Karl Woofter and
Lorna Jowett

BLOOMSBURY ACADEMIC
LONDON • NEW YORK • OXFORD • NEW DELHI • SYDNEY

BLOOMSBURY ACADEMIC
Bloomsbury Publishing Plc
50 Bedford Square, London, WC1B 3DP, UK
1385 Broadway, New York, NY 10018, USA

BLOOMSBURY, BLOOMSBURY ACADEMIC and the Diana
logo are trademarks of Bloomsbury Publishing Plc

First published in Great Britain by I.B. Tauris 2019
Paperback edition published by Bloomsbury Academic 2021

ISBN: HB: 978-1-7883-1102-1
PB: 978-1-3502-0122-4
ePDF: 978-1-7867-3541-6
ePub: 978-1-7867-2541-7

Typeset by OKS Prepress Services, Chennai, India

To find out more about our authors and books visit
www.bloomsbury.com and sign up for our newsletters.

For George A. Romero (1940–2017) and
Tobe Hooper (1943–2017), horror superheroes

Contents

Contents

List of Illustrations

Figures

List of Illustrations

Table

Acknowledgments

Kristopher would like to thank Lorna, a fantastic editor, and the contributors to this collection for their insightful work. Thanks also to inspiration and support from Jenna Bates, Lynn Bowser, Tanya Cochran, Dawson College, Concordia University's Mel Hoppenheim School of Cinema, Mario DeGiglio-Bellemare, Maddy Hamey-Thomas, Alysa Hornick, Jodie Kreider, Cory Legassic, Tim Minear, the instructors and students of the Montréal Monstrum Society, Patricia Pender, the Whedon Studies Association, Rhonda Wilcox, Meghan Winchell, Tim Woofter, and Joni Woofter (my first horror buddy).

Lorna would like to thank Kristopher for conceptualizing this collection and taking the lead in putting it together; its breadth and depth are testament to his vision and rigor. Thanks also to the contributors for their hard work, enthusiasm and scholarship. My own work on this owes a debt to students and staff at the University of Northampton, the Whedon Studies Association, and, as ever, Stacey Abbott and Bronwen Calvert, plus many other horror fans and feminist killjoys.

INTRODUCTION

Whedon Studies and the Ghost of Horror

Kristopher Karl Woofter and Lorna Jowett

"I want to invade people's dreams."[1]

— Joss Whedon

The Whedonverse is a haunted house. Haunted, that is, not only in its many conjurings of uncanny spaces, troubled psyches, monsters, and monstrous potentialities, but also by the avowed purpose of grappling with the excesses of a horror tradition that, in many ways, gives it substance and impact. Beyond more straightforward interrogations of the 1980s slasher-film tradition in *The Cabin in the Woods*, Joss Whedon's projects have borrowed heavily from moving image and literary horror. From *Buffy the Vampire Slayer*'s monster-of-the-week format, to *Dollhouse*'s weekly monstrous-human-puppet scenarios—an inspired updating of that trope; and from the soulfully tormented Gothic-inspired monsters of *Buffy* and *Angel*, to *Firefly*'s abject, raping, and devouring Reavers—Whedon's productions work both within and against popular (mis)conceptions of horror.

Ghostliness as a "conceptual metaphor" is meant here to indicate rupture, residual trauma echoing forth, demanding to be encountered.[2] The ghost renders the present (or, the object) uncanny with potential revelation, creating a state of critical paranoia, where otherwise would be complacency, denial. The ghost's power is that it disrupts assumptions; its

1

weakness is that it is (presumed) dead, only a faint repetition. The Whedon text is often framed as a kind of resurrection, a repurposing of genre diminished through repetitive formula into a mere echo of the original form. Yet, horror texts maintain the ghost's "unruliness."[3] In the words of *Firefly* Captain Malcolm Reynolds, horror texts "aim to misbehave." In doing so, they reveal cracks in cultural and scholarly discourse, allowing monstrous truths and possibilities to seep—or gush—into awareness. Horror has endured as a genre in part because it acknowledges the place of the body—visceral emotions and physical sensations—in how we experience reality. Horror makes us uncomfortable, brings us into physical and emotional places that are fascinating, dreadful, and shocking to contemplate. Horror courts all the senses, not only vision with its privileged link to enlightened thought (seeing clearly)—but also hearing, touch, smell, and taste. Horror's frank acknowledgment of the full human sensorium, a thinking-by-and-in-feeling, and the mixture of dis/pleasure it evokes, is another reason the genre is often dismissed as exploitative— something targeted by the Whedon-brand stance against genre excess and exhaustion.

This book investigates the unruly ghost of horror haunting Whedon's (and his collaborators') work on the series *Buffy the Vampire Slayer* (1997–2003), *Angel* (1999–2004), *Firefly* (2002–2003), and *Dollhouse* (2009–2010), and the films *Buffy the Vampire Slayer* (Fran Rubel Kuzui, 1992), *Serenity* (Joss Whedon, 2005), and *The Cabin in the Woods* (Drew Goddard, 2012). The fifteen chapters situate these Whedon productions within three contexts. One is the horror conventions, tropes, and formulae within and against which these texts operate; a second is horror production and prior genre work that informs and demarcates the creative and critical landscape of Whedon productions; and a third is a challenge to a particular tendency in scholarly discourse positioning Whedon's engagement with horror as uniquely revisionist (i.e., intelligent, subtle, suggestive, reflexive).

From the start, the Whedon "vision" has perpetuated the notion that horror conventions are the rot and dust of corpses—something in need of reanimation. Framing *Buffy* as reinventing horror tropes like the slasher's "Final Girl," for example, implicitly announces its horror genre targets as degenerative, defunct, dead.[4] "You've been here before," it says, when a pretty, blond girl breaks into a high school at night for a tryst with a horny boy. And so—rather than becoming innocent fodder for his flesh-cravings (figuratively sexual, vampirically literal)—the blond girl sprouts fangs and sucks the boy dry. This preamble to Whedon's first hit series is startling and humorous, playing as it does against expectations (generic and cultural) of female victim, male aggressor. It is also highly self-conscious. First, the ostensibly hallowed halls of academia suggest the audience is being *schooled*. It says, just-this-side-of-mockingly: "you've been here before, yes... but this time it's different. Take notes."

And perhaps we should. But what are we meant to learn? A key characteristic of horror *is* just this kind of self-consciousness. Horror relies on intertextuality and built-in allusion to its own conventions to celebrate, reinvent, and subvert them (see Figure I.1). The House of Whedon is haunted by inconsistencies in its scholarly analyzes (and prominent statements by Whedon and his collaborators) that frame Whedon productions as constant innovators in a genre that risks degenerating into cliché. In this critical context, "formula" connotes corpselike stasis. Genre formula, however, is more constructively understood as certain tropes that

Figure I.1 Being Schooled: Classic horror imagery at Sunnydale High opens "Welcome to the Hellmouth."

structure a set of texts—without which, there would be no genre to adhere to, or to subvert. The very spaces that horror returns to again and again are, then, both a comfort and a burden. Genre fans and scholar-fans want to see something familiar subverted or transformed. They want, in other words, an *uncanny* experience of genre—shocking violations, pleasing innovations, but also the comfort of classic formula. In this respect, all genres dance the razor-thin edge of convention-versus-invention. Production contexts are key to forming genres, certain characteristics being molded into form(ula) because of prior success, and thus the idea of repetition, and certainly sequelization, can seem to merely exploit formula, as Peter Hutchings (2004) has noted.[5] Horror sequels are often seen as symptomatic of creative bankruptcy, merely pandering to the market. Yet Hutchings also argues that "so far as an understanding of genre history is concerned, the follow-up films are more important than the films that spawned them inasmuch as they reveal patterns of generic development not immediately apparent from just looking at the initial work."[6] Sequels and remakes are, then, crucial to the development of a generic discourse. Horror film sequels of the 1940s, for example, crystallize many tropes of the "classical" period, 1930s horror cinema, represented by *Dr. Jekyll and Mr. Hyde* (Rouben Mamoulian, 1931) and *Bride of Frankenstein* (James Whale, 1935). Even in this revered period, films like *The Mummy* (Karl Freund, 1932), *The Wolf Man* (George Waggner, 1941), and arguably *Cat People* (Jacques Tourneur, 1942) attempted to replicate the success of *Dracula* (Tod Browning, 1931).[7] For the horror fan, the horror scholar, and the horror artist alike, convention in the form of repeated returns sets the rules by which genre statements are made, and against which genre texts are measured as original, while remaining consistent. Herein lies the dilemma: genre is a specter. Horror's forms and conventions are powerful haunters, but to be ghostly is also to be constantly on the verge of disintegration—an echo that reverberates into the future with diminishing force. Discussions of the work of Whedon and his collaborators are most often framed within a context of such diminishing returns, yet this forgets that the ghost is a shifting, boundary-challenging *hybrid*.

If anything can be said to be the primary characteristic of the work of Joss Whedon, it is its attempt to hybridize and reinvent genres that the writer-director-producer sees as worn out, degenerating, or even defunct.

Buffy (both film and series) and *Cabin* parody or tackle horror, *Angel* the crime genre and film noir cycle, *Firefly* and *Serenity* the western, *Dr. Horrible's Sing-Along Blog* the musical and social media performance, and *Dollhouse* Gothic-inflected science fiction. Within these series, audiences find a great degree of generic hybridity, including moments of horror, comedy, melodrama, musical, fairy tale, and other styles; indeed, appeal to a genre-savvy fandom seems to be a key ingredient in this modal stew. *Buffy* the series, for example, contends with the post-*Scream* (Wes Craven, 1996) environment where a "savvy" horror audience is built into the film's reflexivity. And, as Kristopher Woofter has argued vis-à-vis *Cabin*,[8] a hesitancy as to whether that canny fandom should be addressed as skeptical or adoring of sacrosanct genre tropes risks undercutting the creative verve. Are Whedon and company perpetual re-inventors of the genres within which they work, or practitioners adept at manipulating those genres? The degree to which both apply is a central drive informing this collection.

Genres, because they are discursive, are also complex. Rick Altman argues that "genres are not inert categories shared by all [...], but discursive claims made by real speakers for particular purposes in specific situations. Even when the details of the discourse situation remain hidden, and thus the purpose veiled," he continues, "we nevertheless do well to assume that generic references play a part in an overall discursive strategy."[9] Neither audiences, nor artists consider genre to be a stable entity that resists hybridity or change; in fact, hybridity is one element audiences have come to expect of horror (or perhaps any genre). As Mark Jancovich observes,

> each new text cannot be a simple reproduction of an existing model but is always engaged in a *process of negotiation and transformation*, and this process works both within and between periods. [...] [G]enre history is a complex process of assemblage, in which each new text is only ever constructed through the articulation of existing elements, a process that necessarily reworks the meanings of these elements.[10]

The ghost haunting Whedon's work and its critics is just this: genre is a complex "process of negotiation and transformation" in conversation with industry, artists, fans, and scholars. Let's further uncover the inconsistencies inherent to the myth of horror and the work of Joss Whedon.

On the perennial importance and endurance of horror, Whedon has stopped just short of a judgment call regarding horror's attractions:

> Why do we need horror stories? And I don't mean enjoy, I mean NEED. Because we do. We revel in them. [...] If there's one constant I've found in my work, it's the devastating and necessary human capacity for conflict of interest. We are always at war with ourselves. Our darkness and our better angels. Our desire to achieve and our desire to succumb. Our capacity for self-destruction, or at least self-sabotage. Watching horror, identifying and objectifying, rooting for and against both sides, is a particular thrill, a sleigh ride into that inner conflict. And it's fucking fun.[11]

The "conflict of interest" against "our better angels" identified by Whedon in a companion book to *Cabin* is key to understanding Whedon's oblique stance on horror. His framing elides a good deal of the productive and complex relationship between the horror object/text and its reception. The ostensibly perverse pleasures and cathartic release horror offers a deeply repressed (and oppressed) audience—what Stephen King calls horror's power to "keep the gators fed"—are only two among myriad possible explanations for horror's draw.[12] Additionally, catharsis presupposes that emotions need purging, when emotions are exactly what audiences of horror (and other "body" genres)[13] seek out. The foundational work in horror scholarship since the late 1970s (see Appendix II) has shown the genre to have endured not only because of its psychoanalytical underpinnings and its metaphorical adaptability to the zeitgeist, but also because of its aesthetic complexity, its political capacity to challenge institutionalized oppression, its ability to move its audience viscerally and profoundly, its inherent reflexivity and hybridity, its collapsing of binaries and challenging of categorical thinking, and its aesthetic and epistemological engagement with sublimity. The degree of agency that these scholarly conclusions most often grant to audiences, whether stated directly or not, is critical. Horror fans and horror artists *expect* a ghostly return of formal, thematic, and theoretical precedent.

This collection testifies to how the Whedonverse is haunted by the following broad concepts in horror.

Repetition and Return

In horror, (most) everything returns, especially it if has been buried in an attempt to forget, forego, deny—or, in psychoanalytic terms, *repress*. Edgar Allan Poe's economical short story "The Tell-Tale Heart" (1843) might be the most feverishly allegorical treatment of the theme: its narrator butchers a loved friend, covers up the heinous crime, and then betrays the deed to the authorities in a perverse, staged performance of unconscious guilt. Whedon evokes his own monstrous unconscious in an interview, on the eve of Donald Trump's election to the office of U.S. President, where he discusses a new "historical fiction slash [/] horror" script he is working on:

> I'm in the middle of a screenplay that I am extremely passionate about, and I'm going to be extremely passionate about it again on November 9. It's definitely a departure from the things I'm known for. It's as dark as anything I've ever written. [...] I just said, 'OK, id, your turn'. I would write scenes and be like, 'Oh this is great! I shouldn't be allowed near people.'[14]

History repeats itself, with fears (by now more or less realized) that the potential Trump presidency would be an uncanny reenactment of past terror of World War II, "when the world was going insane."[15] But Whedon's own history repeats itself here, too: the writer-director—now with some clout after the success of two box-office-topping *Avengers* films (2012, 2015) behind him—is able to turn back to the genre that gave his first series its basic concepts.

Repetition in horror also comes in the form of convention, as suggested above, and this collection begins with the Whedonverse's various derivations from key horror conventions and concepts. Essays in the opening section, "(Under)Groundwork: Horror Concepts and Conventions in the Whedonverse," place Whedon productions in terms of their adherence to and deviations from horror tropes. In Chapter 1, Clayton Dillard examines stylistic and thematic parallels between *Buffy* and perhaps the most canonical slasher film, *Halloween* (John Carpenter, 1978). Rather than a wholesale reinvention of the slasher cycle, *Buffy*, Dillard claims, essentially reenacts its tried-and-tested tropes in a number of revealing ways, particularly in its first seasons. Selma A. Purac takes up the silent era of horror in Chapter 2, explicitly examining the *Buffy*

7

episode "Hush" and arguing that while scholarship has tended to note Whedon and company's subversion of horror, this episode is a striking homage to silent horror. Unpacking the ways in which "Hush" returns to, rather than revises, techniques of silent-era horror, Purac makes a strong case for Whedon working *with* key conventions and established strategies of the genre. Mario DeGiglio-Bellemare in Chapter 3 situates a key Whedon-directed episode of *Buffy*, "The Body," within several important scholarly, media, and aesthetic traditions, from Noël Carroll's influential study of horror's "disclosure narratives" around a monstrous entity, to more recent scholarship on embodiment, affect, and the long tradition of non-narrative, attractions-based cinema in horror from early cinema into the twenty-first century. In Chapter 4, Anne Golden addresses another attractions-based genre, the musical, illuminating the parallels between the two genres via a case study of "Once More, with Feeling," and what she calls the "melancholy musical." In Chapter 7, Stephanie Graves situates one of Whedon's most cynical collaborations, *The Cabin in the Woods*, within a wider context of postmodern horror cinema. For Graves, Whedon and Drew Goddard's film can be placed *within* a tradition of self-reflexive horror rather than (re-)initiating that tradition, as many critics would have it.

Along with repetition, horror is associated with return, most particularly with what Robin Wood calls the "surplus repression" caused by oppressive ideological forces.[16] The dread and sudden awareness of resurfacing surplus repression is the power Freud sees as generating a sense of the uncanny. In Wood's Marxist-Freudian framework, American horror cinema performs the same function as nightmares, confronting us with an awareness of the terrible exigencies of bourgeois, hetero-normative, patriarchal capitalism.[17] Drawing on Wood, Cynthia Burkhead in Chapter 5 traces the horrifying prophecy of dreams in *Angel* and *Buffy*. Focusing primarily on the "ensouled" vampire Angel, Burkhead distinguishes between dreams that draw upon the anxieties of the characters, and those that tag the audience's collective anxiety. In Chapter 6, Bronwen Calvert examines a later series, *Dollhouse*, via foundational psychoanalytical concepts such as abjection and haunting. Calvert's study treats space and place in *Dollhouse* as intensely Gothic, resonating with the dreadful suggestion of the uncanny, as well as the powerfully visceral confrontation of the abject. *Dollhouse*, Calvert argues, both upholds and updates horror's "haunted house" trope in illuminating ways that may go unnoticed in this under-seen show.

Repetition and return are also characteristic of the Whedon production context, as attested to by the collection's second section, "Mutant Enemies: TV Horror, Industry and Influence." Here, Jerry Metz, Stacey Abbott, and Erin Giannini explore production contexts that inform and influence the aesthetic attributed to Whedon and his collaborators' work. Both Metz in Chapter 8 and Abbott in Chapter 9 are concerned with the degree to which production restraints, particularly around ratings systems and a reserved climate for horror in the 1990s, were integral to the form and style of Whedon's earlier productions. Metz's chapter focuses on what is for many a kind of pariah text, the film version of *Buffy the Vampire Slayer*, directed by Fran Rubel Kuzui from a script by Whedon in 1992. The film's failure to "bite" has been attributed to either Kuzui's vision straying too far from Whedon's conception, or her inept direction, or both. Metz's fresh look at the film examines an interstitial period in Hollywood horror cinema, with the introduction of the PG-13 rating, and all the expectations (and limitations) this new rating brought with it. In this context of possibility and restraint, the *Buffy* film becomes part of a PG-13 horror sub-genre or cycle, periodizing the film and looking beyond its reputation as a missed opportunity. Abbott traces the Whedon aesthetic against the backdrop of television horror production prior to the recent horror "boom," represented by visceral US network shows such as *Hannibal* (2013–2015) and popular cable series like *The Walking Dead* (2010–present). Before these and other successes, Abbott identifies a production context where constraint was a priority, leading to the more nuanced or subtle aspects of the Whedon aesthetic.

In Chapter 10, Erin Giannini implicitly addresses repetition and return in her genealogy of television horror and crime hybrids, also providing an example of the discursive nature of genre, as outlined by theorists like Altman, Rick Worland, Hutchings, and Mark Jancovich. Focusing on three hybrid shows—*Forever Knight* (1992–1996), *Angel*, and *Supernatural* (2005–present)—Giannini traces similarities in narrative, themes and production contexts that demonstrate clear development from one North American series to the next, looking at intertextuality through casting to shed light on the complex interactions between production, reception, and genre now characteristic of contemporary horror TV.

Monstrosity, Sublimity, and Radical Otherness

One integral aspect in the body of horror-related work produced by Whedon and his collaborators is the degree to which it acknowledges the broad, complex nature of the "monster."[18] Jeffrey Jerome Cohen, in his preface to *Monster Theory: Reading Culture* (1996), tells us "that the monster is best understood as an embodiment of difference, a breaker of category, and a resistant Other known only through process and movement, never through dissection-table analysis."[19] Cohen's focus on the monster's liminality, its "propensity to shift," informs many chapters in this collection.[20] Several chapters in the third section, "'It's About Power': Revisiting Whedon's 'Revisionist' Horror," engage with these concerns head-on, including Kristopher Woofter's positioning of monstrous sublimity in *Buffy* and *Firefly* between the Gothic and Weird traditions in Chapter 12. Woofter demonstrates hesitation in Whedon productions between the Gothic's hauntological mode of resurfacing trauma and psychically charged, metaphorical landscapes, and the Weird tradition's configurations of monstrosity as resisting even the unsettling familiarity of the uncanny, radically confronting the subject with confounding unknowns. Woofter argues that these characteristics are often situated or collapsed into the figure of the hero, and Brenna Wardell notes in Chapter 13 that even the seemingly superficial fairy tale tropes and allusions in a series like *Buffy* reveal that the monster is "not necessarily a marker of evil but of difference," a breaking-down of binaries of self/other.

In Chapters 11, 14, and 15, Lorna Jowett, Karen Herland, and Alanna Thain, respectively, raise this discussion within the wider context of feminist horror. Jowett tracks the feminist framing of Whedon's work, examining possible contradictions or tensions between production and reception within a broad canvas that identifies several characteristics of the horror genre in Whedon productions, and suggests how horror is, potentially, moving away from traditionally masculinist tropes and approaches to attract female and queer viewers. Jowett suggests that feminist horror is glimpsed in the fantastic spaces between mundane and supernatural, the generation of physical and emotional effects, and the centrality of female protagonists. Herland links the borders and frontier spaces of two series, *Firefly* and *Westworld* (2016–present), to the way these western/sci-fi/horror hybrids confront the body itself as an uncanny frontier. For Herland, both series generate unease around individual agency and the vulnerability of bodies, particularly the interaction between the monstrous-masculine and the female body. Alanna Thain's concluding chapter explores the "horror of dispossession" that marks Whedon's work, with a particular focus on the wiping and repurposing of bodies central to *Dollhouse*. From the reconstituted bodies in *Frankenstein* (1818) to the sublime implications of cloning, Thain situates the series within an enduring horror and science-fiction tradition of bodily dispossession, arguing that "*Dollhouse* is a dark vision of the creeping horror of social control," and a radical take on the body in the place of what she calls a "media ecological sublime."

This collection's breadth of subject matter and critical approach—from convention, to production, to new ways of understanding the genre's revisions and revisionism—will hopefully be a significant contribution to the already rich and broad scholarship on the work of Joss Whedon and his collaborators, and of particular inspiration and use to those scholars wishing to investigate these works in relation to horror.

A Final Revenant

At the time of writing, Whedon is under fire from fandom, journalism, and scholarship. His self-proclaimed feminism has been challenged by his ex-wife, Kai Cole, in a public letter revealing Whedon's fifteen years of infidelity and "us[ing] his relationship with [her] as a shield" to maintain his feminist cred.[21] The letter was published online on August 20, 2017, and by the next day, Whedon's "feminism" had been labeled a sham; the website, *Whedonesque*,[22] an important resource for news of Whedon, had shut down;[23] and at least one publisher had stalled publication of scholarly work on Whedon.[24] Popular opinion has severely judged the man, whose regrettable personal mistakes are magnified into the transgressions of, ostensibly, a poser and power-player, using his branding as a feminist to advance his career. This collection stands as an investigation of the work. All the contributors are acutely aware of the complex factors (industrial, personal, aesthetic, and commercial) that impact the reception and reputation of a genre that, throughout its history, has been denigrated and defended in equal measure. Several timely chapters in this collection deal explicitly with Whedon's feminism through the lens of horror, the western, folklore, and embodiment (Jowett, Herland, Wardell, Thain). In the spirit of continued open debate and critique of Whedon and his collaborators' work, these essays are of perhaps added importance to this collection.

Notes

1. Joss Whedon, interviewed by Emily Nussbaum, "Must-See Metaphysics," *The New York Times Magazine*, September 22, 2002. www.nytimes.com/2002/09/22/magazine/must-see-metaphysics.html. Thanks to Karen Herland for pointing us to this article.
2. See Mieke Bal's notion of "traveling concepts," cited in María del Pilar Blanco and Esther Peeren, "Introduction: Conceptualizing Spectralities," *The Spectralities Reader: Ghosts and Haunting in Contemporary Cultural Theory*. Ed. María del Pilar Blanco and Esther Peeren (London: Bloomsbury, 2013), 1.
3. See Maria del Pilar Blanco and Esther Peeren, "Introduction: Conceptualizing Spectralities," *The Spectralities Reader: Ghosts and Haunting in Contemporary Cultural Theory*. Ed. María del Pilar Blanco and Esther Peeren (London: Bloomsbury, 2013), 9.
4. The term, "Final Girl," the tomboyish, studious/pensive young woman who survives horrific events through sheer ingenuity and perseverance, was coined by theorist Carol Clover, in relation to the slasher cycle of the late 1970s to mid-1980s. See Carol Clover, "Her Body, Himself: Gender in the Slasher Film," *Representations* 20 (Special Issue: Misogyny, Misandry, and Misanthropy, Autumn 1987), 187–228.
5. Peter Hutchings, *The Horror Film* (Harlow and London, UK: Pearson Longman, 2004), 16.
6. Ibid., 16.
7. David J. Skal, *The Monster Show: A Cultural History of Horror* (New York: Faber and Faber, (1993) 2001), 168.
8. Kristopher Karl Woofter, "Watchers in the Woods: Meta-Horror, Genre Hybridity and Reality TV Critique in *The Cabin in the Woods*," *Reading Joss Whedon* (Syracuse, NY: Syracuse University Press, 2014), 277–8.
9. Quoted in Hutchings, ibid., 8.
10. Mark Jancovich, "Pale Shadows: Narrative Hierarchies in the Historiography of 1940s Horror," *The Shifting Definitions of Genre: Essays on Labeling Films, Television Shows and Media*. Eds. Lincoln Geraghty and Mark Jancovich (Jefferson, NC and London: McFarland, 2007), 27, emphasis added.
11. Joss Whedon, "Afterword," in Joss Whedon, Drew Goddard, and Abbie Bernstein, *The Cabin in the Woods: The Official Visual Companion* (London: Titan Books, 2012), 172.
12. Stephen King, *Danse Macabre* (New York: Everest House, 1981), 175.
13. See Linda Williams, "Film Bodies: Gender, Genre, and Excess," *Film Theory and Criticism*. Ed. L. Baudry and M. Cohen (New York: Oxford University Press, 2004), 727–41.

14. Frazier Tharpe, "*Avengers* Director Joss Whedon Wants to Make a *Star Wars Movie*," *Complex*, October 20, 2016. http://uk.complex.com/pop-culture/2016/10/joss-whedon-interview. Accessed July 31, 2017.
15. Ibid.
16. Wood, Robin, "An Introduction to the American Horror Film," *Planks of Reason: Essays on the Horror Film*. Eds. Barry Keith Grant and Christopher Sharrett (Lanham, MD: Scarecrow Press, 2004), 108.
17. Ibid., 108.
18. One of the most significant studies to acknowledge this complexity is Elizabeth Rambo, James B. South, and Lynne Y. Edwards' edited collection, *Buffy Goes Dark: Essays on the Final Two Seasons of* Buffy the Vampire Slayer (Jefferson, NC and London: McFarland, 2008).
19. Jeffrey Jerome Cohen, "Preface: In a Time of Monsters," *Monster Theory: Reading Culture*. Edited by Jeffrey Jerome Cohen (Minneapolis, MN: University of Minnesota Press, 1996), x.
20. Jeffrey Jerome Cohen, "Monster Culture (Seven Theses)," *Monster Theory: Reading Culture*. Ed. by Jeffrey Jerome Cohen (Minneapolis, MN: University of Minnesota Press, 1996), 5.
21. Kai Cole, "Joss Whedon is a 'Hypocrite Preaching Feminist Ideals,' Ex-Wife Kai Cole Says" (Guest Blog), *The Wrap* (20 August, 2017), Online. www.thewrap.com/joss-whedon-feminist-hypocrite-infidelity-affairs-ex-wife-kai-cole-says/. Accessed August 25, 2017. Despite the title suggesting an interview with, or report on, Cole's comments, it is a "Guest Blog" written entirely by Cole.
22. The 21 August post at *Whedonesque* reads, "So farewell then. 15 years is a long time and a lot of water has flowed under the bridge. But now it's time to say goodbye. No more threads after this one, we're closing down. The site will at some stage become a read only site. So if you want to leave your contact details in this thread for other posters to get in touch that would be great otherwise email us at whedonesque@gmail.com." The post is quoted here as it appeared, without correction. Source: http://whedonesque.com/comments/36482. Online. Accessed August 25, 2017.
23. Beatrice Verhoeven, "Joss Whedon Fansite Shuts Down After Ex-Wife's Explosive Essay," *The Wrap* (August 21, 2017), Online. www.thewrap.com/joss-whedon-fan-site-shuts-ex-wife-explosive-essay/. Accessed August 25, 2017.
24. In a Facebook post on the Whedon Studies Association page, scholar Don Macnaughtan writes: 'Unfortunate fallout from Whedon's recent troubles ... I had an essay on Whedon due for imminent publication at OUPBlog, the academic blog for Oxford University Press. They have just told me it has been delayed: 'Due to the nature of this story, as it develops, our Social Media team has decided to delay publication of this piece for the time being'. I hope more of us will not hear this reaction in our publishing efforts, which would be very discouraging!' (August 25, 2017).

PART I

(Under)Groundwork: Horror Concepts and Conventions in the Whedonverse

1

The Slasher Template: *Buffy the Vampire Slayer* vs. John Carpenter's *Halloween*

Clayton Dillard

The first season of *Buffy the Vampire Slayer* (1997–2003) begins with two teens—a boy and a girl—sneaking into their high school late at night. It's a familiar sort of scene to scholars and fans of horror films, almost comical in its naked appeal to the creaky castles of Gothic horror. Yet, the outcome is unanticipated; rather than either of the teens falling victim to a lurking killer or monster, as would be typical, the young woman, Darla, morphs into a vampire and kills her companion. Is this opening a feminist rebuke to the gender politics of the slasher film? Or, is this brief scene less a radical act of practice-as-scholarship than a realigning of viewer expectations within the narrative template of the slasher sub-genre? This chapter favors the latter option by illustrating how creator Joss Whedon refers to the slasher film within the first season of *Buffy* to utilize John Carpenter's *Halloween* (1978) as both a narrative and production model for crafting a playful, low-budget television series capable of privileging and melding elements of horror, comedy, and melodrama.

The most prominent accounts of Whedon's series, in which a young heroine faces weekly challenges from a legion of vampires and monsters, posit its revision of certain archetypes, ranging from quest narratives to vampirism, as the show's central attraction. These accounts necessarily focus on Buffy, who is positioned as a heroic figure from the show's first episode. In a paradigmatic account of the series that focuses on Buffy's placement "within a narrative of the disorderly rebellious female," Frances H. Early argues that Whedon offers "a fresh version of the classic quest myth in Western culture."[1] Such a reading compliments A. Susan Owen's sense of the series' depiction of Buffy's body as "signifying toughness, resilience, strength and confidence," which derives from Buffy "experiencing intense pleasure in physically challenging encounters with various monsters."[2] The tough female character, in these accounts, is both a woman warrior and fully in charge of her body and mind; as Owen concludes: "The series reconfigures some of the relations of power in the body rhetorics of horror and action by relocating narrative agency from masculine to feminine."[3]

Part of these accounts stems from Whedon's statement that his idea for the series was sparked by an image inherent to many slasher films of a young blonde woman being murdered in a dark alley by a killer.[4] For Whedon, this imagery demonstrates that the slasher film characteristically positions the woman as victim; in *Buffy*, he wants to turn the female victim on her head, thereby making her into a hero. Those familiar with scholarly writing on the slasher film may automatically notice an issue here, specifically regarding the "Final Girl" as theorized by Carol J. Clover. The Final Girl, according to Clover, is a trope of slasher films that designates one member within a larger group of potential victims as the main character; she is more alert and aware than her peers and, in some cases, either virginal or more removed from sexual activity. She is the one who will face the killer near the film's conclusion. Therefore, she is not simply a victim, but a "victim-hero," who gains agency through confrontations with the killer over the film's duration, so that she may, ultimately, appropriate the killer's own (usually phallic) weapons and, if not outright kill him, defer his threat until another day (or the next installment).[5]

Clover and Barbara Creed are often cited by film scholars as having written the inaugural monographs on the topic of gender and sexuality in the horror film.[6] Clover's *Men, Women, and Chainsaws: Gender in the Modern Horror Film* (1992) and Creed's *The Monstrous-Feminine: Film, Feminism, Psychoanalysis* (1993) each give a respective face to femininity within horror filmmaking—specifically the slasher film of the 1970s and

1980s—through the tripartite construction of the monster, victim, and hero: all subject positions variously occupied by female protagonists.[7] While each of these studies theorizes femininity within the horror film, the placement and role of the female spectator, either theoretically or practically, receives little to no attention. In *Passionate Detachments: An Introduction to Feminist Film Theory*, Sue Thornham reaches similar conclusions about each of Clover and Creed's work, saying that their studies of male fears and desires yield "little consideration of the position of the *female* spectator—so important in earlier feminist film theory."[8] In Thornham's eyes, these canonical contributions to the contemporary horror and slasher film stop short of engaging women outside the screen.

Whedon's revisionism in the form of Buffy as a psychologically developed and well-rounded protagonist implicitly appeals to female spectators by acknowledging the lack of such a figure within many horror films from the 1970s and 1980s. Buffy is developed into a Final Girl who is not a victim, nor even a victim-hero, but simply a hero, capable of dispatching the threat posed by a weekly villain because she's versed in the mythology of vampires and navigates the challenges of adolescence—whether social, physical, or emotional—with a certain amount of consideration. It's not that she is thinly defined by heroic acts, however; her actions are not determined by a singular mode of thought or behavior. Whedon addresses this in reference to "Innocence" (2.14), an episode he wrote and directed during the second season, which depicts the rocky aftermath of Buffy's first sexual encounter with Angel. When an interviewer asks Whedon whether or not he intends to tell young people to abstain from sex, Whedon responds, "Absolutely not … it was about what happens when a guy stops calling you. What happens if you give him what he wants and he starts treating you like shit."[9] In other words, Whedon wants to convey what he perceives the slasher film to omit through its focus on killers and hero-victims: the *logic* of character emotions. By giving Buffy and her cronies lives beyond the eyeline of a killer, Whedon imagines how such characters handle themselves—and their emotions—in those moments when the killer is not lurking around the corner. The Final Girl, in particular, ceases to be "abject terror personified," as Clover says, and more like a personification of growing pains both evil and domestic. As a television series, then, *Buffy* implements exposition and prolonged character mythology where slasher films might typically have machete stabs and post-coital decapitations.

A narrative question ("what happens if . . .") defines *Buffy*'s blend of episodic and serialized television, where characters return week after week to face new trials and tribulations, and with sporadic reference to the previous episodes' events. Films, even franchises, on the other hand, must confine their narrative to a strict temporal block, where only one "story" can be told, no matter how many overlapping characters or subplots are present throughout its duration. Films may, of course, have scenes and events that happen over a prolonged period of time and afford characters varying degrees of reflection and contemplation, but they nevertheless constitute a single work. Slasher franchises, in particular, have proven beholden to this model, where it is not typically victims and Final Girls that recur throughout the films, but the killers.[10] For example, in the opening scene of *Friday the 13th: Part 2* (Steve Miner, 1981), Alice, the surviving Final Girl of the inaugural film, is killed. The scene has little to do with the subsequent events of the film itself; instead, it literally severs ties with the victims of the first film and allows Jason Voorhees, rather than his victims, to emerge as the emblem for the franchise.

Once the focus shifts from killers to victims/victim-heroes/heroes, as it does in *Buffy*, the series less resembles the traits of a slasher franchise than, say, a horror-tinged version of *Party of Five*, the teen television drama that ran on Fox from 1994 to 2000, which follows a family of orphaned teenagers as they grapple with the deaths of their parents. That is, just as *Party of Five* tracks the emotional and romantic entanglements of their characters through a semi-serialized format that requires viewers to be knowledgeable of the plot details from past episodes, so too does *Buffy* comingle "saving the world" with the standard-issue conflicts of adolescence. Yet we would be remiss to think of the serialized teenage melodrama as *Buffy*'s origin point. Its bifurcated interest in the lives of high schoolers and their dealings with actual monsters and killers that hope to cause them harm bears a sharper resemblance to *Halloween,* which has been cited alongside *Black Christmas* (Bob Clark, 1974) as the first film in the inaugural teen slasher cycle.[11]

Rather than arguing for Whedon as a commercial artist who is doubling as a feminist film and television theorist, a more productive line of inquiry looks to Whedon's engagement with the slasher template as a simultaneously commercial and artistic venture that could appeal to female spectators. In doing so, Whedon consulted existing templates for such dual success; the slasher genre, with its typically low-budget production model and intersection with the lives of teenage characters, provides a narrative space to create psychologically defined characters and entice viewers to revel in the confrontations between those heroic teenagers and the evil monsters that crop up in each new episode.

Buffy's prototypical first season is not a direct remake of or homage to Halloween: the narratives of Halloween and Buffy are only nominally similar. However, each features ideas about horror's function that revolve around the same set of issues, where the prospect of facing evil is mirrored by the equally daunting challenge of conquering the social and sexual demands of high school, and, in later seasons, college and adult life. In Halloween, we might be tempted to read the deteriorating American suburbs—places that house teenage sex, are prone to home invasions, and conceal the presence of shadowy stalkers—in the wake of a preceding decade that put a damper on nationalist notions of U.S. supremacy. Although David A. Cook doesn't explicitly make such an argument for Halloween in his monograph Lost Illusions: American Cinema in the Shadow of Watergate and Vietnam, 1970–1979, he says we should read Carpenter's film as a continuation of Wes Craven's The Last House on the Left (1971) and The Hills Have Eyes (1977), in which "a reflexive indictment of America's high tolerance for violence" is carried out by "compulsive" villains who "set the standard for the slasher films that followed."[12] On the other hand, Buffy uses vampires as a framework for its central characters' uncertainties about their own bodies and desires within the constraints of a hip television series; as such, vulnerable characters are routinely lured into treacherous places in pursuit of either sexual attention or curiosity, though violent death or graphic sexual assault is necessarily excluded. The pilot "Welcome to the Hellmouth" (1.01), written by Whedon, in which Willow follows an unknown teenage boy-cum-vampire into a darkened graveyard, epitomizes this tendency. In Halloween, Laurie is shy and reticent; her angst initially derives not from Michael Myers, the lurking killer, but an upcoming dance in which she might finally admit her crush on a male classmate. While Whedon's writing dispenses with Carpenter's minimalist suspense in favor of comedic overtones, the metaphoric potential to understand teenage years spent in suburbia as a living hell—one that resonates with comparably adolescent, middle-class spectators—resounds through each's work.[13]

Rather than merely pursue the narrative similarities between *Halloween* and *Buffy*, I assert that Whedon, having endured a series of compromized projects while writing screenplays for Hollywood, looked to models of independent auteur filmmaking within familiar genres for guidance.[14] *Halloween* can therefore be understood as both a narrative *and* production model for *Buffy*: as a guiding light to the artistic autonomy that both Whedon and Carpenter hold in high regard. In making this claim, I draw upon recent work by Jeff Menne, who argues that the auteur theory should be understood in its historical contexts less as "the individual's messianic overcoming of the stubbornly profit-minded corporation" than as "a form of business-management theory" that helps to "reconfigure corporate capital."[15] Carpenter has spoken at length about his preference for smaller budgets so long as he is afforded final cut. In the case of *Halloween*, Carpenter (and producing partner Debra Hill) made the film for $300,000 using independent funds and created what became one of the most profitable independently produced films ever made. Whedon has alluded to his appreciation of Carpenter's work; in a 2012 interview following the release of *The Cabin in the Woods*, Whedon says he is "a John Carpenter, Wes Craven kind of guy" when it comes to slasher films and goes on to bemoan the "devolution of the horror film" that began with *Friday the 13th*, which was, according to Whedon, "a series of killings and not a film."[16] Thus, Whedon's engagement with slasher films begins with *Buffy*'s first season adopting Carpenter's use of minimal setting (during season one, the majority of scenes are set within a sparsely decorated Sunnydale High), revealing dialogue exchanges, and gender-focused takes on contemporary sexual politics. Moreover, Whedon echoes *Halloween* as an object lesson in horror production and storytelling execution, where narrative tension and character emphases, rather than gore and a focus on drawn-out and/or graphic murder sequences, illuminate the sociological aspects of the slasher sub-genre.

The alignment of Whedon and Carpenter questions the notion that Whedon produced *Buffy* as an explicitly feminist act, especially as one that can be readily likened to feminist film theory, such as that of Clover. However, the direct alignment of Whedon and Clover has already been made; in "Buffy in the 'Terrible House'," Holly G. Barbaccia evaluates *Buffy* in light of Clover's writings on the Final Girl and through Freudian theoretical models. Barbaccia guesses that Whedon has read both Clover and Freud, though no evidence is provided for this assertion, and concludes an introductory passage by saying that, "[Whedon] and Clover come to the slasher aesthetic with what looks like similar projects: to recuperate horror for women."[17] Such a mistaken appropriation of Clover's text likely derives from her argument's emphasis on gender fluidity, where sex proceeds from gender, and in her departure from Laura Mulvey's strict understanding of cinematic identification as tied to gender identities in the canonical essay "Visual Pleasure and Narrative Cinema," in which Mulvey argues that the sadistic male gaze renders the woman an object of spectacle.[18] Clover's book asks readers to understand the slasher template as a set of conventions that rearrange gender dynamics through microcosmic shifts in character types and attitudes, but *not* macrocosmic shifts from, say, heteronormative to homosexual or feminist forms of expression. If the Final Girl is "boyish," as Clover describes her, it is not a gesture of "recuperation" in any feminist sense, but an adaptation to changing social strata that also coincides with shifting target demographics. As Richard Nowell argues, the emergence of the Final Girl (Nowell prefers the term "Final Woman") should be understood less as a viable conduit for the adolescent male than "an invaluable instrument with which to attract females, on the basis that a projection of female empowerment promised to resonate with female ticket buyers."[19] Barbaccia's claim is therefore fundamentally incorrect on two levels. Throughout her book, Clover makes clear that the Final Girl's function within the slasher film is as "a congenial double for the adolescent male."[20] In no portion of the text does Clover devote substantial analysis to female spectatorship or remark upon the slasher film as a cycle of recuperation for women. Barbaccia has mistaken Clover's analysis of women and their roles within slasher films as an endorsement of their feminist potential—a claim that oversimplifies Clover's more nuanced consideration of the slasher film's complex gender dynamics.[21] In a second error, Barbaccia's equating of Whedon and Clover's "projects" overlooks the fact that Whedon's creation of a television program and Clover's authoring of a monograph for an academic press are significantly different forms of cultural production. *Buffy* exists as a commodity tied to consumption and corporate support; its debut on The WB, a television network launched in 1995 as a joint venture between Time Warner and Tribune Broadcasting, necessarily situates the show within a commercial, capitalist platform. It is thus imperative that scholars be more accurate in their discussion of Whedon in relation to gender and film theory. Even if Whedon is familiar with the literature, one cannot proffer *Buffy* as akin to an act of critical theory without overlooking a number of dubious assumptions and argumentative potholes.

Whedon's vaunted status as a commercial artist doubling as a feminist film and television theorist should therefore be reformed to realize Whedon's engagement with the slasher template as a simultaneously commercial and artistic venture that could appeal to female spectators. Here is where Carpenter comes in; throughout his career, Carpenter has consistently directed low-budget genre productions that cannot be separated from their socio-political implications. Although critics and scholars have consistently pointed out that the sexually active characters are killed in *Halloween*, while Laurie, a virgin, survives the series of assaults, Carpenter maintains that this reading overlooks the broader matter of Laurie's hyper-awareness of her surroundings.[22] The issue at stake here is not whether arguments for *Halloween*'s punishment of characters that have sex is right or wrong, it's that interpretation is a fluid entity that should not be reduced to a singular perspective. Such was especially the case in film exhibition of the 1970s, when a film's distribution and reception were equally matters of space and time. Word of mouth travelled slowly, through newspaper outlets, television broadcasts, and watercooler conversations. As Carpenter explains, an initial round of reviews in 1978 despised *Halloween*—it was only later, after a few favorable reviews were published, that critics began a revaluation in 1979 and helped make the film into an unprecedented financial success. By the mid-'90s, the burgeoning instantaneity of the Internet gave film—and especially television—a new means to reach fans and consumers. Whedon was among the first television showrunners to recognize this potential; with *Buffy*, he created a show featuring characters in a genre setting that made allusions to archetypes by then familiar for many viewers, ensuring a welcoming, even rabid reception from a starved portion of the pop-culturally inclined youth market. A taste for self-aware genre fare featuring attractive teenage characters was already in the air; Wes Craven's *Scream* debuted in US theaters four months before *Buffy* premiered in April 1997. *Scream* became the highest-grossing slasher film of all-time—a feat it still holds as of this publication—helping pave the way for *Buffy* to become a successful take on the slasher template for television.

Buffy, Vampires, and Female Spectatorship

Recall Whedon's stated preference for films by Craven and Carpenter over the rest of the slashers, the lot of which amounts to "a series of killings and not a film." In effect, Whedon agrees with critics Siskel & Ebert's trashing of the sub-genre and the resulting narrative: the slasher cycle is a pile of refuse that is only redeemed by a few gems.[23] But Whedon's claim begs the question: what is it about *Halloween* that makes it a film rather than a series of killings? Whedon's preference might have us look to character development and style: it seems he appreciates Carpenter's balance between scares and the emotional investment placed in Michael's teenage victims. Another reason to affiliate Whedon and *Buffy* with Carpenter and *Halloween*, though, is their usage of identification with the female protagonist through shot construction and direct address. Film scholar Brigid Cherry explains how the shot construction in *Halloween* in fact allows the spectator to empathize with Laurie rather than Michael, so that scenes where Laurie is in danger are consistently executed from her point of view (see Figure 1.1).[24] Of course, the same cannot be said for the film's

Figure 1.1 The camera identifies with Laurie Strode, who looks at Michael from her window in *Halloween*.

opening I-camera long take, which places the spectator into the subjective perspective of an unseen assailant, who is subsequently revealed as an adolescent boy. Cherry has an answer for this: "The intent is quite clearly to additionally shock the spectator out of any sense of identification via the killer's point-of-view shot later in the film."[25] In addition to Cherry's perceptive reading, we can see that a direct identification with the killer is already built into the scene's visual construction. As Michael approaches his sister, sound effects rather than visuals announce the knife's piercing of her flesh. The clown mask worn by Michael obscures the spectator's view of any such mutilation. Most significantly, the camera turns, as if to mimic Michael's gaze, to look at his own hand as it stabs the knife forward, thus refusing the spectator any direct visual access to the murder. The obscuring of vision for the spectator, particularly that of Michael as an ocular conduit, is thus accomplished through these visual and aural choices.

Identification through the camera's perspective is more complex than simply identifying with whichever character's perspective it holds. Whedon plays with this notion at the beginning of "Prophecy Girl" (1.12), another episode he wrote and directed, in which Xander sits inside a bar. As the camera pans across and finds Xander's face, he's mid-sentence and seemingly confessing his secret love for Buffy, whom the spectator likely assumes is sitting opposite him. After a suspenseful hold on Xander's face, a reverse shot reveals not Buffy, but Willow, soaking up what turns out to be a trial run for a real confession meant for Buffy at a later date. The prolonged shot of Xander makes knowing the recipient of his gaze part of the joke; the spectator becomes aware of off-screen space in this moment just as she might when she's anticipating a jump scare. Suspense is built through the withholding of identity—a possibility omitted in strictly sadistic readings of spectatorial identification. Though not as elaborate as the disembodying of spectatorship in *Halloween*, Whedon's implementation of implied subject positions reveals that, in the world of *Buffy*, spectatorship is a significant component of its comedic postmodern menu, one arguably inherited, at least in part, from the '80s slasher films Whedon disavows.

Cherry's essays on female spectatorship have contributed to an understanding of horror in ways that had previously only been speculated on. For all of the foundational analysis offered by Creed and Clover, it is Cherry and Isabel Cristina Pinedo, whose *Recreational Terror: Women and the Pleasures of Horror Film Viewing* was published in 1997, who provide the first works devoted exclusively to the ways women watch horror films.[26] Pinedo acknowledges, like Clover, that horror can be pleasurable for both male and female audiences, but she takes the discussion further by considering other facets of genre, like the way comedy "serves a double, paradoxical function in horror films" by creating "both distance and proximity."[27] Pinedo discusses how comedy became an integral component of the slasher template, so that by the time of *Friday the 13th Part VI: Jason Lives* (Tom McLoughlin, 1986), a character says, "I've seen enough horror films to know this means trouble." These postmodern elements enable a certain multiplicity to take shape within the horror genre, which speaks to female spectatorship's complicated relationship with identification, violence, and pleasure. Pinedo claims that such "shifting of identifications is not a 'problem' for the audience; on the contrary, it is at the heart of the experience and pleasure of the genre."[28] By the premiere of *Buffy* in 1997, the groundwork for the spectator's expectation of such identificatory fluidity—especially in the mode of self-aware slasher films derived from *Halloween*'s model—had been laid. The most immediate entry in this sense is *The Slumber Party Massacre* (Amy Holden Jones, 1982), which makes the phallic proportions of the killer's weapons into part of the film's self-knowing dimension. In sum: postmodern play with genre elements and gender identification was already a component of the slasher film (and as shown in the previous section, the proto-iterations of the cycle) well before *Buffy*'s debut.

Cherry's other writings on horror's multidimensionality for female viewers provide an even starker framework with which to situate *Buffy*'s placement within a particular tradition. "Gothics and Grand Guignols: Violence and the Gendered Aesthetics of Horror Cinema" (2008) makes the case that numerous horror films from the latter decades of the twentieth century can not only be understood as transgeneric, but should also be traced to the theatre of the Grand Guignol, where "the mixing of comedy, melodrama, horror, and violence" defined its run from the late eighteenth century through the mid-twentieth century.[29] *Buffy* contains all of these elements in nearly equal measure and deploys them evenly throughout its prototypical first season, as Buffy, Willow, and Xander come to grips with the reality of their world-saving predicament (which begets the horror and violence), all while navigating the complexities of transitioning from adolescence to adulthood (comedy and melodrama). In addition, Whedon takes the aesthetics of the Grand Guignol and applies them to the slasher template, where the same band of teens face a new monster or stalker each week, so that the narrative beats of the slasher film are ingrained within the diegesis. Postmodern play becomes postmodern slay; once again, the winking and referential logic of *Buffy* announces Whedon's personal imprint on comedy, horror, and melodrama. Thus, the slasher template becomes integrated within the sandbox for Whedon's games.

Let's return to the opening of "Welcome to the Hellmouth" (1.01), in which two teens—a boy and a girl—sneak into their high school late at night. If this were a teen drama or comedy, we might expect some sort of intimacy or witty exchange; since it's unfolding within the realm of horror, we automatically fear for the girl's safety, if only because generic conventions dictate such an expectation. Instead, it turns out that our concerns are misplaced: when the girl suddenly transforms into a vampire and bites her male companion, we realize, through a comedic reversal of violence, that an archetype has been altered in order to produce, per Cherry, a sense of distance and proximity (see Figure 1.2). That the potential female victim becomes not only the aggressor but also the assailant indicates how Whedon alters character types within the framework of genre by suspending viewer expectations. Yet deeming these suspensions as "feminist" or even more basically socially progressive miscalculates the effect of such a semiotic maneuver. To expand upon an earlier point, the effect of simultaneous distance and proximity can only produce a microcosmic shift within its generic confines (say, from fear to laughter) because it occurs within the framework of cultural ritual. Akin to an aesthetic sacrifice, we might follow René Girard, who says that "sacrifice is primarily an act of violence without risk of vengeance."[30] Whedon, then, doesn't so much commit a vengeful act against genre conventions as he sacrifices viewer expectations without fear of reprisal.

One point of Cherry's remains certain: "We need to take into account the fact that the horror genre is extremely heterogeneous and horror texts offer a wealth of elements that appeal to women."[31] *Buffy*'s first season in particular makes explicit recognition of this truth by constructing episodes that make reference to gender-specific components of other horror films— mostly slasher films—that do indeed reveal Whedon's sense of himself as "a John Carpenter, Wes Craven kind of guy." The episode "Nightmares"

Figure 1.2   Darla, hardly a victim, transforms into a vampire in "Welcome to the Hellmouth."

(1.10), for which Whedon receives a story credit, can be read as a direct allusion to *A Nightmare on Elm Street* (Wes Craven, 1984), as several characters begin to have waking nightmares that blend fantasy and reality. Once again, Whedon performs a reversal, so that the nightmares more resemble fears and anxieties relating to social decorum than serving as platforms for slaughter, with the most emblematic being a sequence where Xander appears naked in a Sunnydale High classroom. That Xander is a virgin highlights how his nudity at school conveys an insecurity and vulnerability regarding his own body and reinforces how the series' defining of sexual uncertainty reaches across genders, to the effect that the female spectator may recognize the representation of Xander's predicament as one more typically occupied by female victims.

Sunnydale High provides a locus for these feelings of social dread across episodes, where the intersection of potential violence, sexual maturation, and intellectual pursuit routinely coincide. The episode "Out of Mind, Out of Sight" (1:11), provides the most direct reference to

29

Halloween, where this mixture of feelings also takes root. While in class, Cordelia answers a question about "being an outcast in society" as it relates to Shakespeare's *The Merchant of Venice*. Cordelia's response is useful; she compares Shylock's suffering to a time she ran over a girl on her bike and bemoans that her own subsequent trauma, *not* the girl's injuries, should be the key issue. In short, Cordelia can only understand literature as a myopic means to diagnose herself—she reads for literal rather than any potential metaphoric or allegorical meaning. Contrast this with a comparable scene in *Halloween*, where Laurie answers a question about fate by discussing the text at hand through an appropriate comparative analysis with another text. Laurie's intelligible answer makes her into a model student, but on the other hand, it offers no visible weight to her social status, whereas Cordelia's nonsense comparison reveals her ineptitude at institutional academic thought—a trait that nonetheless bolsters her popularity outside of those confines. In this scene, *Buffy* nods to *Halloween*'s template for contrasting feminine pursuits of institutional clout; it's probable that Cordelia is modeled after Lynda from *Halloween*, not least because Whedon has expressed admiration for the character/actress. Lamenting how other horror films treated her character type, Whedon says: "Seeing the trend of the blonde girl who always got killed, like P.J. Soles in *Halloween*, who was cute, had sex, was bouncy and frivolous, always got her ass killed. I just felt really bad for her."[32] One might be led to conclude from Whedon's assessment that he used Lynda's archetype as a model for Buffy, but that isn't quite right, though the fact that Buffy is a cheerleader makes any direct mapping of character types from *Halloween* to *Buffy* impossible and, more to the point, undesirable; Buffy contains traits taken from Lynda, but is not simply a replication of her "bouncy and frivolous" traits in hero form. In fact, Lynda's statement of outright distaste for knowledge provides Cordelia a more distinct corollary: "I always forget my chemistry book and my math book and my English book ... well, who needs books anyway?" Lynda's throwaway refrain ("totally") to various statements made by her peers further cements her as a prototype for the "valley girl" that found primarily comedic prominence in subsequent films like *Valley Girl* (Martha Coolidge, 1983) and *Clueless* (Amy Heckerling, 1995). While Buffy fakes knowledge of Emily Dickinson and is ribbed by Giles for her lack of studiousness in "Never Kill a Boy on the First Date" (1.05), she's by no means "frivolous." The range of feelings towards intelligence among female characters indicates Whedon's approach to representing femininity and, by extension, attracting female viewers, as one with hybridity. Buffy constitutes the middle ground between Willow, an intellectual, and Cordelia, a narcissist. The range of types also uses *Halloween* as a basis, where Annie provides a third female character type; her sarcastic tone and disregard for the rules set by adults distinguishes her from both Lynda and Laurie. It is evident through this comparison that Whedon is by no means reinventing the model for these characters, but conceiving of and deploying their individual traits in a slightly altered manner. Such is the nature of operating within genre; changes occur that may create differences in type and tone, but the generic template remains intact.

When *Buffy* abandons the slasher template in later seasons, especially the "monster of the week" format that helps define the first, it is in keeping with Whedon's utilizing and referencing of multiple subgenres for a renewed sense of textual play. Yet the first season of *Buffy* remains firmly within the traditions of the horror genre by taking the slasher template and calibrating it to suit the aims of Whedon's female-inclined textuality. Buffy's status as a hero is less revisionist than in concert with the spirit of the Grand Guignol in its self-aware shifting of roles, types, and identifications. For several film scholars, this precise sort of multiplicity between subject positions is what gives the horror film its appeal. Whedon has even made this point himself, albeit in a joking manner; when asked in 2009 if he's been surprised by the attention his work has received from women, he responds: "No. Everyone knows there is a little girl inside of Joss. I literally grew up wishing that I were a woman ... I've always felt a great affinity for women on various levels."[33] Moreover, Whedon's stated interest in women should be read equally in financial terms, not just textual. As the marketplace has expanded to recognize female spectators, Whedon continues to pursue series and films that are indeed inclusive of a range of subject positions. His own recognition of such transgender capabilities is not literal, but figurative; just as the Final Girl is "boyish," we might say that Whedon acknowledges a certain "girlishness" in his work. But it is still, nonetheless, a response to preceding models of auteur-based success within horror filmmaking, building a brand not from scratch or in defiance of a form, but firmly within its historically contextualized generic confines.

Notes

1. Francis H. Early, "Staking Her Claim: Buffy the Vampire Slayer as Transgressive Woman Warrior," *Journal of Popular Culture* 35.3 (2001), 12–13.
2. A. Susan Owen, "Vampires, Postmodernity, and Postfeminism: Buffy the Vampire Slayer," *Journal of Popular Film and Television* 27.2 (1999), 25.
3. Ibid., 30.
4. Commentary track for "Welcome to the Hellmouth," *Buffy the Vampire Slayer: The Complete First Season* (1997; Burbank, CA: Warner Home Video, 2002), DVD.
5. Carol J. Clover, *Men, Women, and Chainsaws: Gender in the Modern Horror Film* (Princeton, NJ: Princeton University Press, 2015), 21–64.
6. Daniel Humphrey, "Gender and Sexuality Haunt the Horror Film," in *A Companion to the Horror Film*, ed. Harry M. Benshoff (Oxford: Wiley Blackwell, 2017), 38.
7. Clover, *Chainsaws*, 4. Clover begins her book by discussing Carrie White from *Carrie* (Brian De Palma, 1976) as occupying all three positions at different points throughout the film.
8. Emphasis original in Sue Thornham, *Passionate Detachments: An Introduction to Feminist Film Theory* (London: Arnold, 1997), 106.
9. James Longworth, "Joss Whedon, Feminist," *Joss Whedon: Conversations*. Eds. David Lavery and Cynthia Burkhead (Jackson, MS: University of Mississippi Press, 2011), 57–8.
10. Clover, *Chainsaws*, 30.
11. Richard Nowell, *Blood Money: A History of the First Teen Slasher Cycle* (New York: Continuum, 2011), 105.
12. David A. Cook, *Lost Illusions: American Cinema in the Shadow of Watergate and Vietnam, 1970–1979* (New York: Macmillan Library Reference, 2000), 231–2. Cook cites *Halloween* as the central inheritor of this lineage.
13. See Tracy Little, "High school is Hell: metaphor made literal in *Buffy the Vampire Slayer*," *Buffy the Vampire Slayer and Philosophy: Fear and Trembling in Sunnydale*. Ed. James B. South (Peru: Open Court, 2003), 282–93; Sara Magee, "High School is Hell: The TV Legacy of *Beverly Hills, 90210*, and *Buffy the Vampire Slayer*," *The Journal of Popular Culture* 47, no. 4, (2014): 877–94; Kara M. Kvaran, "'You're All Doomed!' A Socioeconomic Analysis of Slasher Films," *Journal of American Studies* 50, no. 4 (2016), 953–70.
14. Tasha Robinson, "The Onion A.V. Club Interview with Joss Whedon," *Joss Whedon: Conversations* (Jackson, MS: University of Mississippi Press, 2011), 25–7. Whedon has expressed varying degrees of frustration over creative control with his screenplays throughout the 1990s on films such as *Speed* (1994), *Twister* (1996), and, in particular, *Alien: Resurrection* (1997).
15. Jeff Menne, *Francis Ford Coppola* (Champaign-Urbana, IL: University of Illinois Press, 2013), 8–9.

16. "Joss Whedon Explains Why We Fear and Need Horror Films, and How He Knew *Cabin in the Woods* Had a Star in Chris Hemsworth," *The Huffington Post UK*, September 25, 2012, www.huffingtonpost.co.uk/2012/09/25/joss-whedon-avengers-cabin-in-the-woods_n_1912148.html.

17. Holly G. Barbaccia, "Buffy in the 'Terrible House'," *Slayage* 1, no. 4 (2001), n.p.

18. Thornham, *Passionate*, 115.

19. Nowell, *Blood Money*, 131.

20. Clover, *Chainsaws*, 51.

21. Ibid., 64. Clover concludes her opening chapter by saying: "One is deeply reluctant to make progressive claims for a body of cinema as spectacularly nasty toward women as the slasher film is, but the fact is that the slasher does, in its own perverse way and for better or worse, constitute a visible adjustment in the terms of gender representations."

22. Audio Commentary by John Carpenter and Debra Hill, *Halloween*, directed by John Carpenter (1978; Anchor Bay: 2007), Blu-ray.

23. Though Siskel and Ebert championed *Halloween*, the critics despised the films that followed in its wake. In a 1980 broadcast titled "Women in Danger," which examines more recent slasher films, Siskel claimed that "the movies are played almost so that they're in favor of the killer." *Siskelandebert.org.* "Women in Danger (SP/1980)." http://siskelandebert.org/video/N5SUHUORRKB9/Women-In-Danger-SP1980 (accessed September 8, 2017).

24. Brigid Cherry, *Horror* (Abingdon: Routledge, 2009), 135.

25. Ibid.

26. Isabel Cristina Pinedo, *Recreational Terror: Women and the Pleasures of Horror Film Viewing* (New York: SUNY Press, 1997).

27. Ibid., 46.

28. Ibid., 80.

29. Brigid Cherry, "Gothics and Grand Guignols: Violence and the Gendered Aesthetics of Horror Cinema," *Particip@tions* 5, no. 1 (2008), n.p.

30. Renée Girard, *Violence and the Sacred* (Baltimore, MD: Johns Hopkins University Press, 1979), 13.

31. Ibid.

32. Longworth, "Joss Whedon, Feminist," 53.

33. S.F. Said, "Joss Whedon—About *Buffy*, *Alien*, and *Firefly*," *Joss Whedon: Conversations* (Jackson, MS: University of Mississippi Press, 2011), 138.

2

The Sonic Horror of "Hush"

Selma A. Purac

As Professor Walsh indicates at the beginning of "Hush" (4.10), this *Buffy the Vampire Slayer* (1997–2003) episode revolves around the question of communication. In the opening sequence, the professor stands before a full class, lecturing on the difference between language and communication: "Not the same thing," she proclaims.[1] Walsh turns our attention to the limitations of language here, but as she does so, her speech becomes imprecise and difficult to follow. Her lecture both engages with the issue and exemplifies it; language is a flawed tool of communication. Accordingly, in the first act of "Hush," we watch as the show's characters struggle to express themselves verbally.

Joss Whedon, who both wrote and directed the episode, claims that it was motivated by "the idea that when people stop talking, they start communicating."[2] This idea is enacted through the episode's central premise: the mysterious Gentlemen arrive in town and steal the voices of Sunnydale's residents, rendering their victims incapable of crying for help. Having lost the ability to speak, the mute townspeople are forced to find alternative means of communicating. Though Sunnydale dwindles into chaos under the mute menace of the Gentlemen, silence is often shown to help rather than hinder one's ability to connect with others. In this respect, "Hush" stands as an often poignant meditation on the nature of inter-personal communication.

Unsurprisingly, numerous critics have explored the episode's focus on language. For instance, Karen Overbey and Lahney Preston-Matto look at how "Hush" disrupts *Buffy*'s positioning of the spoken word as a weapon, Patrick Shade examines how the loss of language weakens the community, and Kelly Kromer considers the relationship between language and the Symbolic Order in the episode.[3] Such works recognize the complex ways in which language intersects with communication; I propose, however, that "Hush" ultimately explores how horror itself is communicated.

Fourteen minutes into the forty-four-minute episode, the characters are silenced and the show is stripped of one of its central features: the witty dialogue that critics have long identified as the cornerstone of *Buffy*'s success.[4] This silence defamiliarizes the series, but it also draws our attention to the mechanics of horror. In considering the question of how horror is communicated, "Hush" looks to models of early horror, most notably silent cinema. Musical cues, pantomime, and sight gags play a significant role in the episode. The scene of Giles' slideshow—complete with "title cards" and classical soundtrack—signals the work's engagement with these conventions, as does the design of the Gentlemen, which draws on the iconography of pre-sound era horror films such as F.W. Murnau's *Nosferatu* (1922) and Paul Leni's *The Man Who Laughs* (1928). These elements, borrowed from silent horror cinema, work together to create an atmosphere of heightened fear.[5]

That Whedon should look to an early model of horror is significant in part because it demonstrates his indebtedness to the genre's conventions. This idea is especially important given the common positioning of Whedon as an auteur known for disrupting the horror genre. Allison McCracken, for instance, notes his "revisionism, particularly in relation to the horror genre";[6] David Graeber similarly asserts that "Joss is responsible for subverting the message of the horror genre."[7] Others have noted the varied ways in which Whedon works to challenge horror film conventions, from Janet K. Halfyard's handling of the show's theme music to Jason Middleton's consideration of the Slayer as a re-envisioned Final Girl.[8] Indeed, Whedon himself points out that Buffy's origins are rooted in overturning the horror "trend of the blonde girl who always got killed."[9] Such comments point to the postmodern project of subversion and deconstruction, which often dominates discussions of Whedon's output;

however, more critical attention needs to be given to his work *within* the horror tradition.

"Hush" deliberately stages a return to—rather than a revisioning of—early horror conventions. In doing so, it resists what Linda Hutcheon identifies as a key strategy of postmodernism: the critical revisiting of the past. For Hutcheon, postmodern works are "always a critical reworking, never a nostalgic 'return'."[10] "Hush," however, is tinged with nostalgia, from its Victorian aura to its use of fairy tales and nursery rhymes, but most prominent is its return to the techniques of silent film. This cinematic past is not evoked for the purpose of a critical return, in the vein of postmodernism, but in order to inspire fear in the audience. "Hush," then, stands as a particularly strong example of Whedon's work within the horror tradition, forcing us to reconsider his relationship to the genre.

"Hush" as Horrific Pastiche: From Fairy Tales to Silent Film

Whedon admits that he sought to challenge himself by quieting the snappy dialogue for which the show is known.[11] In doing so, he moves against not only audience expectations, but also the expectations of the medium in which he works. As Katy Stevens points out, "it is the human voice which bears the weight of hailing and retaining the television audience."[12] "Hush" subverts the sonic conventions of both the series and the television medium itself; however, even as he contests these conventions, Whedon celebrates those of silent horror. This pattern of both challenging *and* celebrating convention is symptomatic of Whedon's work, as "Hush" demonstrates.

The Gentlemen act as a regressive force in Sunnydale, returning its residents to a pre-linguistic state of childlike vulnerability.[13] Accordingly, Rupert Giles, the resident adult of the group that assists Buffy in her slaying (known as the Scoobies), is reduced to communicating through childish, hand-drawn illustrations. Given the infantilizing influence of the Gentlemen, it is no surprise that they are identified as "fairy tale monsters"[14] and that Giles' research is compiled from a leather-bound tome entitled *Fairy Tales*. Normally, the texts to which the Scooby Gang refer in their research are taxonomies of monstrosity: works that identify and classify creatures firmly grounded in the diegetic reality of the

Buffyverse. The Gentlemen, however, are not grounded in this reality; indeed, they literally float above it. These are fictional bogeymen made real.

In fact, their fairy tale status, alongside the nursery rhyme associated with them, gestures towards Whedon's engagement with horror tropes, as both fairy tales and lullabies have long been a staple of the horror genre. These juvenile works act as a window into the viewer's own childhood fears of unknown monsters lurking in the dark; they are therefore often incorporated in horror works to further unsettle the audience. In his commentary on "Hush," Whedon points out that the original *A Nightmare on Elm Street* (Wes Craven, 1984) used this trope most effectively, thereby revealing his own work to be something of an intertextual response to the film.[15] From classic horror movies such as *Rosemary's Baby* (Roman Polanski, 1968) and *The Exorcist* (William Friedkin, 1973) to more recent works like *The Conjuring 2* (James Wan, 2016) and *IT* (Andy Muschietti, 2017), nursery rhymes and lullabies are conventions that often signal our entry into a sinister world. Because they evoke childhood, such stories and songs represent a return to a state of greater vulnerability, which is exploited by horror. "Hush" borrows this technique in order to fulfill Whedon's stated goal for the episode: "to traumatize children."[16]

Silent film plays a significant role in achieving this goal. In fact, the Gentlemen themselves seem to be exiles from the early silent era. They are visually coded as Victorian figures, evoking the very period in which cinema emerged. That their first appearance in town is preceded by a close-up shot of a vintage clock face signals this association with the past—a link that is strengthened by the clock house in which they reside. Silent themselves, and relying upon gestures to communicate, the Gentlemen are the spectres of silent film come to haunt Sunnydale.

"Hush" is commonly identified as one of the most frightening of the show's 144-episode run. Rhonda Wilcox calls it "dead scary,"[17] Kromer calls the Gentlemen "the scariest monsters of the series,"[18] and Ben Lane identifies them as "some of the creepiest villains on TV."[19] These responses point to Whedon's successful deployment of silent horror techniques; he revisits the icons and strategies that succeeded so well in terrifying an earlier generation of cinephiles.

Murnau's silent masterpiece *Nosferatu* holds a notable place in the history of vampire cinema as the earliest existing adaptation of Bram Stoker's

Dracula. From its unsettling low-key lighting to the famously disquieting image of the vampire's shadow slinking across a wall, *Nosferatu* created a visual vernacular not just for the vampire but for horror film. Indeed, "Hush" demonstrates that *Nosferatu*'s legacy extends into the world of television as well. Though the Gentlemen are not vampires, they are nighttime predators, and in appearance they owe a great deal to Max Schreck's iconic depiction of the gaunt and otherworldly bloodsucker. Like their cinematic predecessor, Whedon's villains blend the grotesque and the civilized. Both Count Orlok and the Gentlemen—as their titles suggest—are coded as smartly dressed members of the upper class. Orlok's trim military-style frock coat, slim black trousers, and leather dress shoes stand in contrast to the peasants depicted in *Nosferatu.* Similarly, the Gentlemen are dressed in fine suits, but in both instances, fine clothes are offset by the desiccated appearance and unnatural movements of the villains. This visual dissonance makes the monsters of both works especially unsettling.[20]

Whedon himself comments on the influence of Murnau's horror classic. He says of the Gentlemen's design, "I was drawing on everything that had ever frightened me ... *Nosferatu*, Pinhead, Mr. Burns. Anything that gave that creepy feel."[21] This idea is reiterated in the script, where one of the Gentlemen is described as "old, bone white, bald—*Nosferatu* meets *Hellraiser* by way of the Joker. Actually, he looks kind of like Mr. Burns, except that he can't stop his rictus-grin."[22] The description is telling. First, it explicitly highlights the influence of Murnau's film, which Whedon stresses once more when he comments on a later scene. He says that his direction to one of the actors playing a villain was, "'Give me *Nosferatu* on the hand.' Up it came, curled like a spider; he knew exactly what I meant when I said that."[23] The iconography of the film is integral to his vision. Second, the description demonstrates that Whedon's debts extend well beyond the scope of a single movie. He notes the influence of four separate works here—two of which are horror films. "Hush," then, is a pastiche of horror influences. Moreover, the "rictus-grin" to which he refers recalls yet another silent horror film: Paul Leni's *The Man Who Laughs.*

The title character of this film, portrayed by Conrad Veidt, is disfigured when outlaws carve a permanent grin into his face. The grotesque smile transforms Veidt's character, Gwynplaine, into a horrifying spectacle that is exploited both by the visual medium of film and by the narrative, which positions him as a sideshow attraction (see Figure 2.1). This technique of

Figure 2.1 Conrad Veidt in *The Man Who Laughs* (Paul Leni, 1928).

Figure 2.2 The Gentlemen as Whedon's horrifying pastiche.

placing a physically distorted figure at the center of the production was widely practised in horror films of the silent era, most notably by the "Man of a Thousand Faces" himself, Lon Chaney.[24] Because the absence of diegetic sound intensifies the role of visual storytelling, striking disfigurements were a common means of inspiring dread in the audience. As Roger Ebert notes, "Silent films, like black-and-white films, add by subtracting. What they do not have enhances what is there, by focusing on it and making it do more work."[25] The appearance of the Gentlemen, which borrows heavily from the silent monsters that precede them, functions similarly in that their silence underscores their striking appearance. The monsters of "Hush" never speak, even before they steal the voices of Sunnydale's citizens; like Gwynplaine, they are, quite literally, silent smiling monsters forced to communicate visually (see Figure 2.2).

The Sound of Silence: Amplifying Fear

Because "Hush" earned the series its only Emmy nomination—for "Outstanding Writing for a Drama Series"—the episode has received a good deal of critical attention. I have already noted the focus that is often placed on the issue of communication and language in the episode. However, critical work on "Hush" tends to fall into another broad, but overlapping category: considerations of the work's sonic experimentation. Jacqueline Bach, Katy Stevens, and Gerry Bloustein, for instance, have examined the varied ways in which the episode's soundtrack compensates for the characters' muteness.[26] Given the premise of the episode, such focus is hardly surprising.

It is important to stress, however, how the episode's use of sound contributes to the construction of fear. Sound design is central to the expression of horror in "Hush" partly because it pushes the work into the territory of silent film. In his consideration of *Nosferatu*, Ebert claims that the movie is more frightening *because* it is silent. He writes that its "characters are confronted with alarming images and denied the freedom to talk them away. There is no repartee in nightmares. Human speech dissipates the shadows."[27] Accordingly, the muteness of the characters in "Hush" amplifies the horror of events. Nowhere is this more evident than in the first attack of the episode.

In this scene, two Gentlemen slowly glide through the hallways of a college dorm before settling on a particular door. A knock is heard as the camera cuts to the inside of the room where we see a shadowy bedroom, the window casting a venetian blind effect on the wall. The young male occupant, who is awoken by the knock, groggily makes his way to the door. As he opens it, a POV shot reveals two Gentlemen in a medium close-up, grinning directly at us. The camera focuses on the boy's horrified face as two Footmen force him back on to the bed, his open mouth making no sound. His terror is seen but not heard. To silence him in this way is to further disempower him. But the scene isn't entirely silent. Diegetic sounds that emphasize his status as a victim are amplified; we hear the boy struggling against the Footmen, the clasp of the medical bag opening, and the scalpel slicing into his chest. Paired with low-angle POV shots that place viewers in the position of the silent victim, the scene conveys a powerful sense of helplessness made all the more moving by his muteness. The boy's silence serves a participatory function. Because the screams of the victim are not heard, they resonate only in our imagination, thereby intensifying any fear we might feel. The sequence illustrates perfectly Whedon's claim that "silence is the essence of horror."[28]

What is clear from this scene is that while the dialogue is hushed in the episode, it is anything but silent. The accompaniment of a non-diegetic soundtrack aligns "Hush" with silent films, which were commonly played alongside live music and effects. Stevens writes, "From major movie palaces with their permanent orchestras to the traveling roadshow and its solo pianist, the cinema has always been an audiovisual spectacle."[29] The lack of dialogue in silent film therefore shifts the emphasis not only on to the movie's visuals, but on to its music as well. Accordingly, in "Hush," we find a greater reliance on Christophe Beck's non-diegetic score to engage the audience emotionally; the music must speak where the characters cannot. In the first attack scene, then, the music that is layered over the visuals intensifies the dread one feels, but it also gestures towards the work's appropriation of sonic conventions.

As the Gentlemen glide down the dorm hallway past rooms of sleeping students, the music is ethereal and eerily childlike. Beck's affective score engages with common codes of musical signification; like Whedon, he is working *within* conventions here rather than against them. Thus, the music that is associated with the Gentlemen is a dark, fairy tale-styled theme very much in keeping with Danny Elfman's collaborations with Tim Burton. The bell-like quality of the celeste, the ethereal choral singing, and the sighing strings show that Beck engages with well-established musical codes.

When the Gentlemen choose their target, however, the music swells to a deeper and more menacing climax, before it stops entirely, thereby isolating the sound of the knock at the door. The quiet is broken by loud dissonant strings that accompany the POV shot of the victim's monstrous visitors; the music acts as a substitute for the boy's surprised gasp. Similarly, when the Footmen hold him down, woodwinds blare on the soundtrack, intensifying his panic and conveying a sense of urgency. The tinkling fairy music resumes, however, once the Gentlemen float into the room, creating an unnerving sonic contrast that plays through the remainder of the sequence. The musical dissonance expertly augments the horror of the scene—made more troubling due to the victim's mute vulnerability. What the sequence achieves is an effect like that of silent horror film wherein muteness and music work together to disturb the audience. Murnau himself was aware of this fact when he subtitled his vampire film *A Symphony of Horror*. "Hush" offers a similar symphony; music and horror, it would seem, go hand in hand.

Overtures and Overheads: TV *as* Silent Film

Perhaps the scene that best exemplifies the episode's engagement with silent horror conventions is Giles' slideshow. The setting itself is cinematic: a darkened lecture theatre in which the audience sits silently, staring at the bright projection screen that dominates the front of the room. In preparation for the entertainment, Anya, like any practised movie patron, enjoys popcorn. Giles then cues the music and the show begins.

Lacking dialogue, this expositional sequence relies upon the written word to convey information that is difficult to express otherwise.[30] In this respect, the slides of Giles' presentation act as intertitles, transforming the sequence into a miniature silent film embedded within the larger homage to silent cinema that is "Hush." The presentation unfolds in a series of fourteen slides that convey crucial information about the Gentlemen; we learn, for instance, that they have come to Sunnydale to steal seven hearts from their silenced victims and that only the scream of a "princess" can kill them.[31] Brad Chisholm notes that intertitles of the silent era "could be vital to the narrative strategy of a film. Expository intertitles informed, delayed, dismissed, amused, and even misled."[32] In keeping with this idea, Giles' slides do more than simply inform: they reflect and comment upon the episode's formal experimentation.

Only two of the slides contain text alone; these are the slides that pose questions regarding the nature of the villains: "Who are the Gentlemen" and "What do they want."[33] The majority of the slides—ten in total—contain illustrations alongside text. Thus, the image and the written word are positioned as parallel communicative modes. In a mute world, where the visual dominates, words are visualized rather than spoken; they become images rather than sonic expressions. The "intertitles" of "Hush" therefore emphasize the dominance of visual communication in a silent community. However, these slides also comment on the articulation of horror.

Of the fourteen slides, two contain no words at all: the slides that focus on the gruesome extraction of the victims' hearts. We are first informed that the Gentlemen steal the voices of the townspeople so that none can scream; the next slide depicts a single smiling Gentleman primly poised on the edge of the frame and the word "then."[34] This slide creates a momentary pause in the visual narrative; Giles builds suspense and anticipation by manipulating the pacing of his presentation. The slide that follows contrasts this straight-laced depiction. We see a Gentleman with a blade standing over the bed of his bloodied victim. The next slide transitions to only a few moments later: the Gentleman has extracted the heart and now holds it over his victim. This image is nearly identical to the one that precedes it, but for the heart and a greater abundance of blood, which covers the face of both the victim and villain, drenches the bed, and pools on the floor. Unlike the slides before it, which are framed in medium shots so that we can see both the slide and Giles' manipulation of the projector, this slide appears in a close-up, framed so that we see the violent image alone[35] (see Figure 2.3). By highlighting the image in this way and by placing these wordless slides back to back, Whedon—and, of course, Giles—draws out the violence to emphasize its impact. A reverse shot demonstrates that the two images have had their intended effect: both Buffy and Willow convey expressions of disgust and discomfort. In the presentation, as in the episode itself, the horror of the

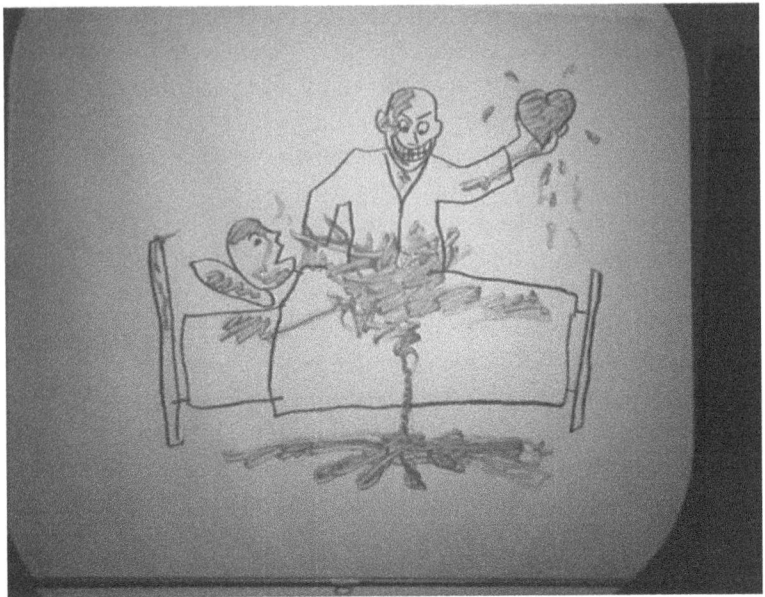

Figure 2.3 Wordless horror: The extraction of the heart.

Gentlemen is best conveyed without words; the visuals accent the grim nature of the threat.

Like Murnau before him, Giles understands that music can intensify visuals. Accordingly, to highlight his slideshow, he chooses a pre-existing musical work: Camille Saint-Saen's *Danse Macabre*.[36] During the brief musical introduction, Giles prepares himself, flexing his fingers like a conductor before a performance. Indeed, from his choice of music to his timing, Giles reveals himself to be something of a maestro. As the first violin punctuates the track, the first slide appears onscreen, perfectly timed; the music reaches its orchestral climax with the most striking of Giles' images: the Gentleman's bloody removal of the victim's heart. The pivotal revelation that no sword can kill them is paired with a similar musical crescendo.[37] The original track, which is seven minutes long, is strategically manipulated into a two-and-a-half-minute piece that coordinates with the onscreen action. In effect, it is equivalent to the non-diegetic live music that so often accompanied silent movies. Moreover, Christopher Wiley identifies the composition as "a standard piece with which to represent the diabolical and otherworldly";[38] once more, then, we find that "Hush" is working within sonic traditions.

Laughing to Death: Horror and Humor

In "Hush," Whedon expertly uses the techniques of old silents to evoke both fear *and* laughter. At first glance, comedy and horror may seem to be antithetical genres. In their introduction to *The Laughing Dead*, Cynthia J. Miller and A. Bowdoin Van Riper explain, "If comedy is best achieved through detachment, as Bergson claims, horror relies on engagement for its maximum effect, suggesting that the two are not only dramatically opposed, but biologically, psychologically, and philosophically, as well."[39] Fear and laughter are drastically different emotional responses, but the means through which such reactions are evoked are surprisingly similar: "At their most basic level, both comedy and horror depend on the shock of the unexpected: the subversion of the audience's expectations."[40] The horror-comedy genre relies upon this shared strategy.

Fear and laughter are visceral responses; a work that effectively inspires these reactions is a work that manages to reach its audience on an almost instinctual level. When Pauline Kael famously claimed that "scary-and-funny must be the greatest combination for popular entertainment," in part, she was referring to this emotional investment: the "teasing style" of works that mix "comedy and horror and tension," pulling viewers between radically different emotional poles in a manner that keeps them stimulated.[41]

Laughter also has a cathartic distancing effect; the sudden intrusion of humor in a horrifying narrative is a subversion of expectation that momentarily breaks the tension. As Isabel Cristina Pinedo writes, humor in such works provides "the proverbial comic relief, cessation of terror, thus providing the requisite distance to stave off terrorism at strategic points."[42] Cumulatively, this fluctuation from fear to laughter, and back again, has a destabilizing effect, resulting in a world that is always ready to unravel. Thus, the narrative is never static and the viewer is never disengaged. The horror and humor of "Hush" is similarly choreographed.

For example, humor features heavily in the sequence that introduces Sunnydale's muteness—but only *after* the seriousness of the condition has been established. The town wakes to find itself silenced in a series of three scenes: Buffy and Willow panic in their dorm, Xander blames Spike for the ailment, and both Riley and Forrest rush to the Initiative for guidance. As each of the sequences begins, we watch familiar characters overcome with confusion and panic. This helplessness is tempered by the incorporation of humor into the latter half of each scene. I have already noted that the muteness of the characters emphasizes their vulnerability, making the episode especially unnerving. These humorous moments allow for a temporary relief from the panic of well-loved characters. Similarly, Buffy's intense final battle with the Gentlemen is crosscut with Xander's amusingly misguided attack on Spike—this intrusion allows for comic distancing of the kind that keeps viewers swinging between emotional extremes. Perhaps somewhat surprisingly, the technique also points towards the episode's references to silent cinema.

The horror-comedy genre originates in the silent period with such films as D.W. Griffiths' *One Exciting Night* (1922), Roland West's *The Monster* (1925), and Paul Leni's *The Cat and the Canary* (1927). The funny moments of this hybrid genre follow the techniques of straight comedies of the time wherein humor tends to be conveyed either physically in the form of sight gags or screwball sequences, or through text via tongue-in-cheek intertitles or diegetic notes and letters. Together, these techniques form the visual vocabulary of the silent era's comedies.

Without the guidance or the distraction of diegetic sound, visuals occupy an elevated role; thus, physical humor becomes dominant. The work of Charlie Chaplin and Buster Keaton is a sign of this strategy's success; their humor is built upon a foundation of pantomime and sight gags. Naturally, silent horror-comedies incorporate the same technique. In Leni's film, for instance, the bumbling character Paul Jones provides much of the comic relief. A series of screwball sequences outlining his exaggerated terror exemplify the film's carefully choreographed comedy, but these sequences are incorporated with the horror genre in mind; they break the film's suspense at key points, keeping the viewer swaying between fear and laughter.

Jones' fear is evident even in the movie's intertitles, where the shaky lines of his stuttered dialogue visualize his weakness. In the absence of spoken dialogue, silent film developed a complex visual language of its own. Visualized text is one way in which these works convey not only plot points and information but also emotional cues. Lingering shots of diegetic letters or newspaper headlines supplement the most common technique: non-diegetic intertitles. In silent horror-comedies, title cards are sometimes used to deliver punch lines or to humorously comment on events or characters. West's *The Monster*, for example, begins with an unsettling scene: the night-time abduction of John Bowman, a wealthy resident of Danburg. The disquieting scene is followed by a light-hearted title card that reads, "Bowman's disappearance was Danburg's biggest thrill since the milkman eloped with the bootlegger's wife."[43] Text is incorporated to add levity and humor to the film, and very often occurs after more unnerving moments as a means of easing tension.

The funniest moments of "Hush" occur *after* Sunnydale has been silenced; in other words, humor notably reaches its height during the "silent" sequences. As Phil Dyess-Nugent puts it, "Amazingly effective as this episode is as nightmare fuel, it may be even more impressive for demonstrating how funny this show could be when the actors didn't have access to the series' crackling, semi-invented teen slang and wild tempest of pop-culture references."[44] Humor is transferred from the show's dialogue to the physical comedy and humorous text that features so prominently in horror-comedies of the silent era. Moreover, given the theme of communication, the muteness of the characters contributes to the miscommunications that are so often central to comedy. In "Hush," silence is not only golden, but hilarious, too.

Once more, we return to Giles' presentation – the sequence that perhaps most closely resembles a silent film. It is worth noting that the funny scene is preceded by one of the episode's most frightening: the Gentlemen's attack of the college boy. The slideshow scene therefore helps to break the tension of the previous sequence, not only by providing a potential solution to the threat of the Gentlemen, but also through humor.

Pantomime and writing are prominent in the sequence, as they are the primary means through which the characters communicate, or humorously fail to do so. Despite his careful attention to timing, Giles begins his presentation with a mistake. The first slide, which he places dramatically onscreen in time to the music, is backwards, but he doesn't realize the error until it is pointed out to him. His commanding performance is immediately deflated through humor, and this humor is conveyed, in part, via writing. Just as Paul Jones' fear is expressed through the intertitles of *The Cat and the Canary*, Giles' uncertainty is expressed through this initial error. He might present himself as a figure of authority here, but he is prone to mistakes and miscommunications like all the rest.

The scene also showcases physical comedy through pantomime, particularly in terms of double entendre and sexual innuendo. For instance, in response to a slide that asks, "What do [the Gentlemen] want," Willow enthusiastically points to her chest—a gesture that Xander evidently misinterprets when he mouths the word "boobies."[45] He is soon corrected, but the annoyed looks on the faces of his female companions add to the humor of the misunderstanding. Similarly, in response to the question, "How do we kill them?," Buffy gestures with her hand in a way that suggests male masturbation.[46] The discomfort of her friends is alleviated when she repeats the gesture with a stake in her hand, making her meaning clear. Through gestures and sight gags, the episode conveys humor without a single spoken word. What the episode demonstrates, then, is that the strategies of silent cinema can be used not only to inspire fear in a contemporary audience, but laughter as well. Whedon's debt to the techniques of the silent era allows him to produce the great entertainment of which Kael writes.

The slideshow presentation allegorizes what the episode itself does as a whole: it uses the lack of spoken dialogue to its own advantage. In watching "Hush," we sit in the darkened theatre alongside the Scooby Gang, and we, like them, are both terrified and amused by what we see. This episode showcases Whedon's storytelling skills by transforming television into silent film. What Whedon experiments with here is not just how to tell a tale without words, but also how to frighten an audience without them. The answer, in part, is found in silent cinema. With its monsters that pay homage to the work of Murnau and Leni, and the way in which it engineers both fear and laughter, "Hush" demonstrates an indebtedness to silent film, but Whedon does not restrict himself to early film alone. Indeed, this episode is evidence of his tendency to borrow icons, tropes, and techniques already established in the horror genre. From its incorporation of fairy tales and nursery rhymes to its use of sonic codes to build tension and fear, this episode is an excellent example of Whedon's work within horror traditions. Despite its lack of dialogue, then, "Hush" echoes with influence.

Notes

1. "Hush," *Buffy the Vampire Slayer*, directed by Joss Whedon (1999, Los Angeles, CA: 20th Century Fox, 2003), DVD.
2. "Commentary: Hush," *Buffy the Vampire Slayer*, directed by Joss Whedon (1999, Los Angeles, CA: 20th Century Fox, 2003), DVD.
3. Karen Overbey and Lahney Preston-Matto, "Staking in Tongues: Speech Act as Weapon in *Buffy*," in *Fighting the Forces: What's at Stake in Buffy the Vampire Slayer*. Ed. by Rhonda V. Wilcox and David Lavery (Lanham: Rowman & Littlefield, 2002), 73–84; Patrick Shade, "Screaming to be Heard: Reminders and Insights on Community and Communication in 'Hush'," *Slayage* 6, no. 1 (2006): 1–10; Kelly Kromer, "Silence as Symptom: A Psychoanalytic Reading of 'Hush'," *Slayage* 5, no. 3 (2006): 1–8.
4. Perhaps the most comprehensive handling of *Buffy*'s language is Michael Adams' *Slayer Slang: A Buffy the Vampire Slayer Lexicon*. However, see also Rhonda Wilcox's chapter on language in *Why Buffy Matters* and Karen Overbey and Lanhey Preston-Matto's "Staking in Tongues: Speech Act as Weapon in *Buffy*."
5. Despite its importance in the episode, the topic of silent film has not been handled in any great detail. A few websites dedicated to popular culture, such as *Talk Film Society* and *AV Club*, have covered the topic in passing. In her consideration of sonic codes in *Buffy*, Katy Stevens does consider the link between "Hush" and silent cinema, but her focus is largely on the soundtrack's affective dimensions.
6. Allison McCracken, "At Stake: Angel's Body, Fantasy Masculinity, and Queer Desire in Teen Television," in *Undead TV: Essays on Buffy the Vampire Slayer*. Ed. by Elana Levine and Lisa Parks (Durham: Duke University Press, 2007), 119.
7. James Longworth, "Joss Whedon, Feminist," in *Joss Whedon Conversations*. Ed. by David Lavery and Cynthia Burkhead (Jackson, MS: University Press of Mississippi, 2011), 46.
8. Janet K. Halfyard, "Love, Death, Curses, and Reverses (in E minor): Music, Gender, and Identity in *Buffy the Vampire Slayer* and *Angel*," in *Music, Sound, and Silence in Buffy the Vampire Slayer* (Farnham: Routledge, 2008); Jason Middleton, "Buffy as *Femme Fatale*: The Cult Heroine and the Male Spectator," in *Undead TV: Essays on Buffy the Vampire Slayer* (Durham: Duke University Press, 2007).
9. James Longworth, "Joss Whedon, Feminist," in *Joss Whedon Conversations*. Ed. by David Lavery and Cynthia Burkhead (Jackson: University Press of Mississippi, 2011), 53.
10. Linda Hutcheon, *A Poetics of Postmodernism: History, Theory, Fiction* (New York: Routledge, 1988), 4.
11. "Commentary: Hush," *Buffy the Vampire Slayer*, directed by Joss Whedon (1999, Los Angeles, CA: 20th Century Fox, 2003), DVD.

12. Katy Stevens, "Battling the Buzz: Contesting Sonic Codes in *Buffy the Vampire Slayer*," in *Music, Sound, and Silence in Buffy the Vampire Slayer*. Ed. by Paul Attinello, Janet K. Halfyard, and Vanessa Knights (Farnham: Ashgate, 2008), 82.
13. In "Hush," Buffy is a figure on the verge of adulthood. The final slide of Giles' presentation contains a breadcrumb regarding her liminal status: the text is consistently written in capital letters – but for Buffy's name. The final slide reads, "BUFFY WILL PATROL TONIGHT" – Buffy's name, combining both upper case and lower case letters, visualizes a transitional state somewhere between childhood and adulthood – a notion that is suitable given her status in the episode as both the Slayer *and* the princess of the fairy tale.
14. "Hush," *Buffy the Vampire Slayer*, directed by Joss Whedon (1999, Los Angeles, CA: 20th Century Fox, 2003), DVD.
15. "Commentary: Hush," *Buffy the Vampire Slayer*, directed by Joss Whedon (1999, Los Angeles, CA: 20th Century Fox, 2003), DVD.
16. "Commentary: Hush," ibid.
17. Rhonda Wilcox, *Why Buffy Matters: The Art of Buffy the Vampire Slayer* (New York: I.B.Tauris, 2005), 147.
18. Ibid., 4.
19. Ben Lane, "Joss Whedon, The Silent Era, and 'Hush'," *Talk Film Society*, last modified December 1, 2016, www.talkfilmsociety.com/articles/joss-whedon-the-silent-era-and-hush.
20. The parallels between these works are numerous. In both, the monsters are liminal figures, often positioned near barriers such as windows and doorways, and their attacks are erotically charged. Both works incorporate a medical discourse, complete with simian straight-jacketed minions, and the demise of the monster is linked to sound; a crowing rooster signals the sunrise and the vampire's doom in Murnau's film, and in "Hush," it is the scream of the symbolic princess that kills the Gentlemen.
21. "Commentary: Hush," *Buffy the Vampire Slayer*, directed by Joss Whedon (1999, Los Angeles, CA: 20th Century Fox, 2003), DVD.
22. "Shooting Script: Hush," *Buffy the Vampire Slayer*, directed by Joss Whedon (1999, Los Angeles, CA: 20th Century Fox, 2003), DVD.
23. "Commentary: Hush," *Buffy the Vampire Slayer*, directed by Joss Whedon (1999, Los Angeles, CA: 20th Century Fox, 2003), DVD.
24. His depictions of Quasimodo in *The Hunchback of Notre Dame* (1923), Erik in *Phantom of the Opera* (1925), and the Hypnotist in *London After Midnight* (1927) relied upon facial and physical deformity. Indeed, Gwynplaine's grotesque grin in *The Man Who Laughs* famously served as the inspiration for DC's Joker – whom Whedon mentions as an influence in his "Hush" script.
25. Roger Ebert, "Great Movie: *The Man Who Laughs*," *RogerEbert.com*, last modified January 18, 2004, www.rogerebert.com/reviews/great-movie-the-man-who-laughs-1928.
26. Jacqueline Bach, "Not Just Another Love Song: *Buffy*'s Music as Representation of Emerging Adulthood," in *The Truth of Buffy: Essays on Fiction Illuminating*

Reality. Ed. by Emily Dial-Driver, Sally Emmons-Featherston, Jim Ford, and Carolyn Anne Taylor (London: McFarland, 2008), 38–54; Katy Stevens, "Battling the Buzz: Contesting Sonic Codes in *Buffy the Vampire Slayer*," in *Music, Sound, and Silence in Buffy the Vampire Slayer*. Ed. by Paul Attinello, Janet K. Halfyard, and Vanessa Knights (Farnham: Routledge, 2008), 79–89; Gerry Bloustein, "And the Rest is Silence: Silence and Death as Motifs in *Buffy the Vampire Slayer*," in *Music, Sound, and Silence in Buffy the Vampire Slayer*. Ed. by Paul Attinello, Janet K. Halfyard, and Vanessa Knights (Farnham: Routledge, 2008), 91–108.

27. Roger Ebert, "Great Movie: *Nosferatu*," *RogerEbert.com*, last modified September 28, 1997, www.rogerebert.com/reviews/great-movie-nosferatu-1922.

28. Gerry Bloustein, "And the Rest is Silence: Silence and Death as Motifs in *Buffy the Vampire Slayer*," in *Music, Sound, and Silence in Buffy the Vampire Slayer*. Ed. by Paul Attinello, Janet K. Halfyard, and Vanessa Knights (Farnham: Ashgate, 2008), 102.

29. Katy Stevens, "Battling the Buzz: Contesting Sonic Codes in *Buffy the Vampire Slayer*," in *Music, Sound, and Silence in Buffy the Vampire Slayer*. Ed. by Paul Attinello, Janet K. Halfyard, and Vanessa Knights (Farnham: Ashgate, 2008), 82.

30. See Alice Jenkins and Susan Stuart's "Extending Your Mind: Non-Standard Perlocutionary Acts in 'Hush.'" The authors point out that because speech is silenced in the episode, acts of writing are uniquely privileged.

31. "Hush," *Buffy the Vampire Slayer*, directed by Joss Whedon (1999, Los Angeles, CA: 20th Century Fox, 2003), DVD.

32. Brad Chisholm, "Reading Intertitles," *Journal of Popular Film and Television* 15, no. 3 (1987): 137.

33. "Hush," *Buffy the Vampire Slayer*, directed by Joss Whedon (1999, Los Angeles, CA: 20th Century Fox, 2003), DVD.

34. "Hush," ibid.

35. The only other slide framed in a close-up shot reveals information essential to the plot: it identifies how to kill the Gentlemen.

36. Based upon the poem by Henri Cazalis, where Death calls forth the dead from their graves to dance as he performs a midnight concert, the piece suits the mood of the slideshow. Moreover, given its association with the British mystery series *Jonathan Creek*, which began airing the same year as *Buffy*, the music carries with it associations of mystery and magic that are successfully called upon in the scene.

37. In "Theorizing Television Music as Serial Art: *Buffy the Vampire Slayer* and the Narratology of Thematic Score," Christopher Wiley makes a similar point when he notes that "Giles' last slide, and specifically Buffy's reaction to his drawing of her, coincides with the solo violin music of the work's coda, which relates to the point in Cazalis's poem at which the cockerel crows to indicate daybreak – thereby identifying Buffy with the deathly protagonist of *Danse Macabre* and hinting that she, rather than the Gentlemen, will ultimately be the one to bring about the demise of the other" (44).

38. Christopher Wiley, "Theorizing Television Music as Serial Art: *Buffy the Vampire Slayer* and the Narratology of Thematic Score," in *Buffy, Ballads, and Bad Guys Who Sing: Music in the Worlds of Joss Whedon*. Ed. by Kendra Preston Leonard (Lanham: Scarecrow Press, 2011), 44.

39. Cynthia J. Miller and A. Bowdoin Van Riper, "Introduction," in *The Laughing Dead: The Horror-Comedy Film from Bride of Frankenstein to Zombieland*. Ed. by Cynthia J. Miller and A. Bowdoin Van Riper (Lanham: Rowman & Littlefield, 2016), xiv.

40. Ibid., xiv.

41. Pauline Kael, "The Curse," in *When the Lights Go Down* (New York: Holt, Rinehart, & Winston, 1980), 208.

42. Isabel Cristina Pinedo, "Postmodern Elements of the Contemporary Horror Film," in *The Horror Film*. Ed. by Stephen Prince (New Jersey: Rutgers University Press, 2004), 111.

43. *The Monster*, directed by Roland West (1925; Los Angeles, CA: MGM, 2010), DVD.

44. "When the Gentlemen stole the voices (and hearts) of BtVS," *AV Club*, last modified October 9, 2013, http://tv.avclub.com/when-the-gentlemen-stole-the-voices-and-hearts-of-buf-1798241106.

45. "Hush," *Buffy the Vampire Slayer*, directed by Joss Whedon (1999, Los Angeles, CA: 20th Century Fox, 2003), DVD.

46. "Hush," ibid.

3

"The Body" That Will Not Sit Up: Shock, Stasis, and the Negative Space of the Horror Genre

Mario DeGiglio-Bellemare

Joss Whedon's "The Body" (*Buffy the Vampire Slayer* 5.16) has received much attention for its frank and realistic portrayal of death and grief. Some discussions focus on how television seriality helps produce this episode's emotional intensity by building up character identification and emotional context over many episodes. Arguably, following Noël Carroll's classic model for horror, the general framework of a *Buffy* episode falls squarely into "the complex discovery plot," which turns on the gradual revelation of an impossible monster.[1] In Carroll's reading, narrative is central to horror's appeal. Yet I argue that "The Body" diverges from the traditional revelatory plot in important ways. This chapter focuses on affective materiality in "The Body," especially its production of intensity through corporeal shock. The dreadful immobility of Joyce's fleshy corpse is key; unlike the vampire lying in the morgue with her at the episode's end, Joyce's body will not sit up.

Infecting Windows

I begin this heterogeneous entry into the world of *Buffy* through my parallel exposure to another vampire story—focused not on a slayer, but on a sympathetic vampire (possibly the first on screen), Barnabas Collins (Jonathan Frid). The iconic Gothic vampire soap opera, *Dark Shadows*, which aired in North America from 1966 to 1971, became hugely successful in its second year, after creator Dan Curtis and his team introduced Barnabas, a vampire posing as a cousin of the Collins family from Britain. The term "heterogeneous" is meant to highlight how my entry into *Dark Shadows* parallels my discovery of *Buffy the Vampire Slayer* when I watched "The Body," independent of the rest of the series, upon the insistence of a friend. I was knocked over by "The Body," and it is this eventful knocked-overness that interests me. I want to discuss the episode specifically in relation to this reception. While I watched every season after initially viewing "The Body," I lack the loyalty to the series that many *Buffy* fans have. Television is popularly called a writer's medium and *Buffy*, like much television, is often discussed in terms of plotting and narrative; television studies generally tends to focus on story, and the extended space television offers for complex narratives. My loyalty as a fan to a narrativized vampire story begins with *Dark Shadows* and I believe analyzing my reception of that series is an interesting starting point from which to discuss issues of narrativity. This is not because I believe "The Body" is best considered outside the series' narrative context, but focusing on the materiality of the episode's attractions reveals important ways that Whedon works with horror.

Joyce's corpse in "The Body" has a weighty materiality in Sunnydale, where staked vampires typically vanish into dust. In *Dark Shadows* the vampire's creeping corporeality drew many new fans to Collinsport: "children, teenagers, and young adults of both sexes, as well as housewives."[2] Harry Benshoff's discerning study of the show focuses on its micro- and macro-narratives and suggests that the show was short-lived (for a soap!) because the writers ran out of Gothic plot-lines from classic novels, observing that "its dependence on story lines from classic Gothic novels was perhaps its greatest strength as well as its biggest weakness."[3]

Feminist research suggests that soap opera's reception was rather complex. Tania Modleski argues that for women in the domestic realm,

TV-watching, especially soap opera, should be understood in terms of "rhythms of reception" where work and leisure overlap, where distraction and attraction are blurred.[4] My most vivid memory of my southern Italian mother watching soaps (and I watched many with her on summer break), is of her folding laundry as she watched or ironing as she listened. In *Make Room for TV*, Lynn Spigel notes that "early soaps, with their minimum of action and visual interest, allowed housewives to listen to dialogue while working in another room."[5] Spigel reminds us here of the importance of sound in early soaps (and TV's derivation from radio). Daytime TV was not only about story, but about filling the domestic space: "the networks put enormous amounts of money and effort into variety shows when they began to compose daytime program schedules."[6] Television is not monolithically a medium of story, though it is often discussed in this way. My experience of *Dark Shadows* challenges the over-emphasis on narrative in television generally, and in *Buffy* specifically.

I situate my examination of "The Body" within a television history that does not revolve around story and narrative.[7] Television viewing cannot be understood outside the context of both public and private spectator reception. Television history evidences a productive fluidity between outside/public and inside/domestic divisions. With the advent of motion pictures, Spigel argues, the noisy, interactive crowds of vaudeville theatres were disciplined into silent, well-mannered (and apparently absorbed) crowds by bourgeois "good taste."[8] In "the postwar era, this theatrical experience [of disciplining] was being reformulated in terms of television experience" in domestic spaces. In the living room, the television spectator was physically isolated, an experience often emphasized as a new attraction.[9] Hence, the term "window" onto the world was often invoked to talk about the postwar television experience, invoking documentary-like realism. But this view forgets the immediacy of attractions. Spigel notes that *Variety*'s "Harry Hershfield complained, 'Overnight our homes have taken over the burdens carried by outdoor strolling minstrels, park gatherings and stadiums. Previously, every man's home was supposedly his castle'."[10] With the television window came fear of infection, especially the contagion of lowbrow attractions—"minstrels," "parks," and "stadiums." "Don't watch too much TV", my aunt Cécile would tell me as I sat down to watch a Creature Double Feature from Boston's WLVI-56 on Saturday afternoons, "you will ruin your eyesight." I was the provincial Canadian cousin who spent his summers in New Hampshire and this was her way of warning me against consuming too much "junk TV." I brokered a deal with my aunt: I would watch only one film from the double feature, then "go outside to get some sun." At this time I discovered *Dark Shadows* being replayed in syndication. Its "macro-narrative" of a Gothic stranger insinuating himself into the small New England town of Collinsport had a profound effect on me, as I, like the vampire, thrived on my time out of the sunshine of reason and good judgement.

I, of course, identified with Barnabas, but it was more than identification, it was contagion, paradoxically and monstrously terrifying and appealing. My engagement with Barnabas was not predicated on representational verisimilitude or empathy, but with his intensities, viscerality, and movement. Notwithstanding narrative, the quiet intensity of the vampire engaged me, the very visceral power he held over the people of Collinsport—especially his keeper Willie Loomis (John Karlen)—and how he physically moved surreptitiously among them. In addition, the show's fetishistic focus on Barnabas' cane and large ring released dreadful tactility, as in the now-iconic moment when Willie opens an old coffin hoping to find jewels, but unleashes the vampire instead (episodes 210–211). Vampiric infection was in the movement of Barnabas' jewelled hand, grabbing Willie by the neck. And because *Dark Shadows*, like much early TV, was taped live, this intensity was uncannily repeated in the next episode as the moments leading up to the previous episode's cliff hanger were mimetically reproduced by the actors the next day.[11] This combination of movement and stasis, immediacy and stylistic excess, careful mimesis and accident, engenders a corporeal infection of attraction repeated in Joyce's immobile body. Moreover, for this pre-teen who did not quite understand his bisexuality, Barnabas' intensities (not coincidentally performed by a gay actor) sparked sexual attraction. *Dark Shadows* was thus not only the story of a vampire; it was corporeal vampiric infection. This is the dangerous and passionate relation to the televisual window that my aunt's "good judgment" feared. It not only ruined my eyesight, it was a deeply passionate and embodied event that disturbed the rational (insight). The body of Barnabas, like Joyce's corpse, infected materially, literally, directly.

In this way, I aim to draw out heterogeneous mappings that link *Buffy* and *Dark Shadows* materially and generically through corporeal attractions. Like Lawson Fletcher's incisive "Is She Cold: Telaesthetic Horror and Embodied Textuality in 'The Body'," my approach takes a "post-representational" framework for textual analysis, focusing on the episode's fleshy and aural materiality,[12] the materiality of generic infection. Barnabas Collins' infectious nature evidences the corporeal materiality of *Dark Shadows* as exploding into the living rooms of millions. My focus is on "the affective, sensory, and embodied dimensions of the viewing experience."[13]

As Tom Gunning remarks "the cinema of attractions persists in later cinema...[;] it provides an underground current flowing beneath narrative logic and diegetic realism, producing a moment of cinematic *dépaysement* beloved by the surrealists."[14] The still-fleshy corporeality of "The Body" moves beyond the realism vs. supernatural dichotomy that underscores some responses to the episode. Joyce's body *dépayse*—that is, it disorients and defamiliarizes spatially insofar as the French *dépayse* has the word *pays* (meaning country) and *paysage* (meaning landscape) within it. The verb to *dépayser* means to remove from its country/landscape/context producing uncanny (defamiliar) disorientation and shock that is not simply about character identification or narrative contexts. By design, the episode rejects stylistic markers that would reduce it to realism. A kind of spatial negativity is promoted with respect to the corpse. When Dawn (Michelle Trachtenberg) is told about her mother's death, she is in art class with a friend. The teacher instructs the students, "We are not drawing the object—we're drawing the negative space around the object. The space in-between." Negative space resonates around the body in reactions to Joyce's death, but also in how the *dépaysement* of her corpse encourages a stickiness of affect between bodies and the production of powerful emotions surrounding a loved one's death—especially within a world where dead bodies, vampires, sit up or reach out from a coffin like Barnabas Collins. I use the word "affect" not as a catchy new way to discuss emotion, but because an affective focus of the senses and the body is deeply important for the experience of fear, dread, and disgust in the horror genre. Following Baruch Spinoza, Brian Massumi explains that "affect is the capacity to affect and be affected."[15] In this sense, affect always involves mutuality and interrelation. Affect is a pre-personal unformed intensity distinct from emotion, which is its public performance. For Massumi, "affect is one creative factor entering into the constitution of events."[16] By emphasizing "events" Massumi moves away from semiological approaches that often forget the mutuality between the audience and the screen outside of subject/object relations. Although the turn to genre studies was a turn from auteurs to audiences, these studies still operate in either ideological-psychoanalytical (Robin Wood), or phenomenological (Carroll) registers, as representational text-based analyzes.[17] Because affect is interrelational, always about connection and encounter; applied to horror TV it suggests reception as less a window onto the world than an infectious invasion of domestic space.

In horror, televisual infection is a central theme, from the visceral sadomasochism of David Cronenberg's *Videodrome* (1984), to Hideo Nakata's televisual hauntings in *Ringu* (1998) the corporeal image literally links up to—and often viscerally touches or penetrates—the audience through the window of television, seemingly infecting the world. These films present fleshly, material interaction between medium and audience—as when *Videodrome's* Max Renn (James Woods) develops a vaginal opening for inserting videocassettes in his stomach, or when Tomoko (Yûko Takeuchi) climbs out of the TV screen to visceral effect in *Ringu*. The medium is not only the message, to echo Marshall McLuhan's famous phrase; the medium infects the space of reception (and the bodies that inhabit it). My contention here is that "The Body" infects like the disruptive body of Barnabas in Collinsport, with corporeal attractions through shock. The stillness of Joyce's corpse in "The Body" *dépayse* the usual mobility of bodies in *Buffy*, becoming a kind of infection. In other words, Joyce's body, in its material stillness, contrasts vampiric bodies that sit up—and return.

Corporeal Shock and *Dépaysement*

Rhonda Wilcox's discussion of "The Body" is attentive to the corporeal: "'The Body' leads viewers to experience death in consciously physical terms."[18] Even more acutely, Wilcox points out, "[s]ense after sense is engaged in the horror."[19] Her emphasis on engagement speaks to the ways both living and dead bodies shock in the episode. Attention is paid to the "so-called" lower senses, often forgotten in discussions of the audio-visual arts—Wilcox highlights the smelling of flowers, the seeing of Joyce's body, the hearing of her body's bones cracking, the touch of a cold dead body, and Buffy's vomiting. However, Wilcox's treatment of the senses is apprehended within an understandably apologetic redress of anti-genre elitism that seeks to prioritize the natural (realism) over the supernatural (non-realistic content) in critical discussions of "Quality TV series."[20] She notes, "[c]ritics often remarked on the instance of the vampire's appearance in the closing act as a single flaw in an otherwise uninterrupted realistic surface."[21] Wilcox concludes her chapter with a thoughtful discussion of the "intrusion of unreality in the shape of a vampire."[22] She argues that the supernatural functions here in terms of thresholds: in the episode's final scene, the (un)dead threshold-breaking vampire sitting up metaphorically links to Buffy's physically breaking through the doors to save an unsuspecting Dawn, who has gone to the hospital morgue to be with her mother's body. I do not want to situate "The Body" as an episode that stands outside of narrative; season five uses Joyce's surprisingly non-supernatural illness to question how Buffy and others think about death. Rather, I want to flesh out a context additional to narrative, one that highlights a negative space between stasis and movement, between bodies that sit up and bodies that do not.

Many *Buffy* episodes fit the narrative model proposed by Carroll in his highly influential book, *The Philosophy of Horror*.[23] Carroll's structuralist account of horror is problematic,[24] particularly in its essentialist notions of horror narrative as revolving around the "iterated disclosure" of a supernatural monstrous entity.[25] Yet his study is important for horror scholarship in various ways. First, though Carroll does not distinguish emotion from "affect,"[26] he is nonetheless attentive to the corporeal and emotional, focusing on disgust as central to the pleasures of horror. Second, he moves beyond psychoanalytical theory, which dominated horror scholarship for decades. Third, his account of horror is reception-friendly, crucial for a genre made for, and by, fans. And fourth, Carroll's account is a defense of genre as formula, challenging the high-art bias that emphasizes originality over mimesis.[27] I bring Carroll's ideas to bear on TV studies as a means of challenging narrative and serialization as dominant in the study of horror TV. Vampiric formula has more to do with infectious embodiment than the hook of story.

A classic "monster of the week" *Buffy* episode, for example "Hush" (4.10), operates within what Carroll labels the "complex discovery plot" of horror.[28] This structure has four movements or functions, which Carroll lays out as "onset, discovery, confirmation, and confrontation."[29] Onset comes when "the monster's presence is established,"[30] which in a typical *Buffy* episode occurs in the pre-credit sequence. According to Carroll, discovery is always linked to doubt or skepticism about the monster's existence, and is when "an individual or group learns of its existence."[31] This is, for Carroll, what makes the genre so popular: love of knowledge, curiosity, and disclosure, and especially of deduction.[32] Carroll suggests that "horror stories are often protracted series of discoveries," and this is true of the majority of *Buffy* episodes. In Carroll's model, research and deduction bring us to the third stage of horror narrative: confirmation of the monster's existence, along with convincing others of this, and coming up with a plan of action to defeat it. The last is confrontation, which may involve a victory over the monster—or not! When watching *Buffy* it is tempting to see the show as perennially organized in this way: that it has Carroll's "deep narrative structures."[33] Apologia colors Carroll's treatment as he is decidedly, for the period (1990), defending aspects often used to deride the horror genre, such as repetition and predictability: "[a]nyone familiar with the genre of horror knows that its plots are very repetitive"[34]; yet he argues that this plotting is part of the "pleasures" of horror, as are the various iterations required to identify and learn about the monstrous entity.[35] Carroll's structures are found in "The Body" and Joyce's corpse can easily be taken as the monster of the week that Buffy and Dawn discover and confront. But this does not do justice to Carroll's theory. According to Carroll, art-horror requires the "thought" that an impossible being, like a supernatural vampire, is indeed possible.[36] Joyce's corpse does not function in the way The Gentlemen do in "Hush," her corpse is not an impossible monster, as Carroll notably reduces the monster to a supernatural entity, become possible through discovery, but all-too-real death infecting life. Joyce's immobile corpse shocks with its overwhelming presence throughout the episode. It is simply there, not there to be discovered as the monster is discovered. However, when the corpse is initially discovered in the first scene, Buffy vomits. This is where Carroll's championing of emotions, especially around disgust, is pertinent: "horrific beings are often associated with contamination—sickness, disease, and plague."[37] For him, emotions are centrally linked to dangerous threat and contaminating disgust. They are the "particular object[s] the emotion can focus upon."[38] The act of vomiting literalizes the definition of emotion discussed by Carroll as a moving out. I think about infection and shock as this inner agitation directed outward. The episode's corpse is not an impossible monster requiring discovery; rather it is death, infecting the frame and viscerally shocking the audience.

This study is interested in surfaces and infection rather than deep structures—in the place of the corpse as it *dépayse* and infects the home and the morgue. As such, I am interested in Joyce's body's reception by first Buffy and then Dawn, at the beginning and end of the episode. These scenes work to promote shock. Walter Benjamin was the first to theorize affect, shock, and the senses (especially tactility) in the mid-1930s. Benjamin argues that the "distracted mass absorbs the work of art."[39] Even more importantly, Benjamin argues that cinema promotes "reception in a state of distraction" through shock by putting "the public in the position of the critic" and as such challenging the very concept of art.[40] As early as 1935, Benjamin challenged fears like my Aunt Cécile's that a window onto the world of Collinsport, or Creature Double Features, would distract me from "getting enough sun," or "ruin my eyes." He argued that audiences created filters to protect themselves from modernity's shocks, and "the film with its shock effect meets this mode of reception half way."[41] Taking the reins from Dadaism, Benjamin argued that cinema can shock into meaning, that distraction is part and parcel of the experience, not something to be avoided or feared, and more importantly, not producing passivity in audiences. Benjamin's profound theorizing on shock is key for staging corporeal and affective readings. Buffy's vomiting is not simply a moment that reveals shock under the surface; it viscerally works on the surface, as the paper towel she uses to clean up her vomit reveals. Shock has a materiality. What "The Body" reveals or discovers is the shocking materiality of the corpse, of everyone's becoming-corpse.

Joyce's corpse is seen only twice in the pre-credit sequence: once out of focus in the background as Buffy calls out to her, and once in a delicate track-in for a mere three seconds (Figure 3.1). The post-credit scene begins with a flashback to the Scooby gang having Christmas dinner. The sense of abundant life contrasted to death is not only thematically stated around talk about food, being stuffed, and "barfing," it also operates around the movement of Buffy and Joyce's reaction to a burnt pie. Buffy attempts to remove the burnt crust and they drop the pie to the floor. Whedon cuts in a disorienting fashion from this moment in the past to a close-up of the face of Joyce's corpse for three seconds. Static. Confrontational. Eyes staring

Figure 3.1   The corpse of Joyce in the living room.

and lifeless. Whedon then cuts on movement again as Buffy moves towards the body on the couch. These contrasts between movement and stasis, life and death are where the shock of the episode resides. The disorienting out-of-context corpse comes back again and again during the episode. Joyce's corpse is the "monster of the week," but its shock comes from the placement of the body within the living room. The difference here between thematic meaning and the impact of shock can be related to the placement of Christ's body in two different paintings: "The Body of the Dead Christ in the Tomb" by German painter Hans Holbein (the Younger) (circa 1521) and "The Lamentation of Christ" (circa 1480), by the Italian painter Andrea Mantegna (Figures 3.2 and 3.3, respectively). In the Holbein painting, Christ's dead body is shown from the side in an enclosed tomb, completely divorced from its original context, creating the sense of *dépaysement*: staring eyes, open mouth, terrifyingly stiff body, and half-clenched hand suggest the shock of the moment of death. Mantegna's painting is a frontal shot of Christ's dead body, laid out on a marble slab with an ornate pillow, with mourners (mother and disciples) to the left.

Figure 3.2 *The Body of the Dead Christ in the Tomb,* Hans Holbein (the Younger), circa 1521.

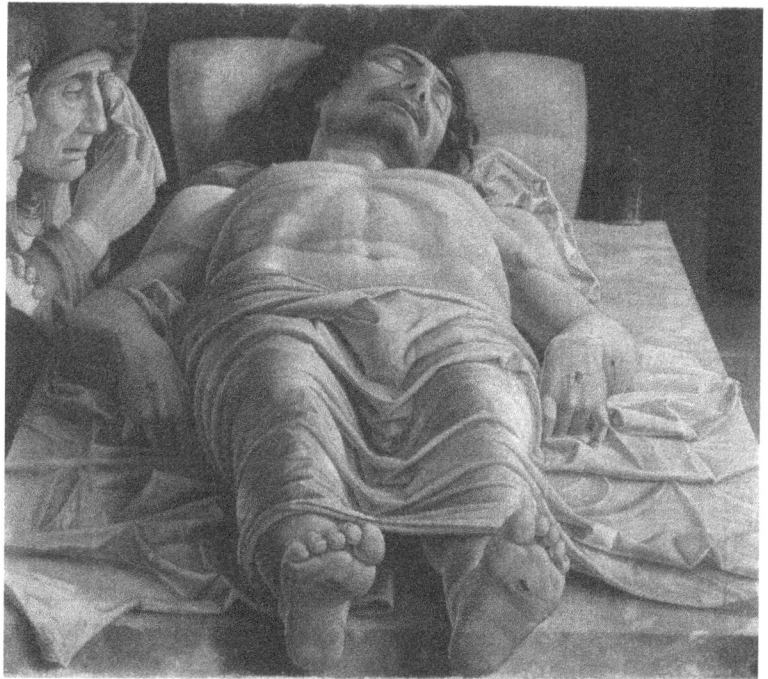

Figure 3.3 *The Lamentation of Christ,* Andrea Mantegna, circa 1480.

The contexts of separation from life and attachment to life in the two paintings is stark and can be appreciated in the framing of the body and its context. In Fyodor Dostoyevsky's novel *The Idiot* (1869), Prince Myshkin declares that the Holbein painting has the power to make a viewer lose one's faith. In Christian terms, the shock of Holbein's Dead Christ is fear of losing hope in the resurrection. In material terms, the body's stasis shocks the viewer into new knowledge of decaying corporeality. Holbein's Dead Christ is literally *dépaysé*, as is Joyce's corpse.

As the opening scene progresses, Whedon carefully keeps Joyce's body ambiguously between life and death, maybe sleeping, or dead as in the Mantegna painting. Buffy asks her questions: "Mom? What are you doing? Mom? Mom? Mommy?" A close-up shows Buffy's response as the emotional weather shifts in the move from "mom" to "mommy." Cut to black. Buffy is uncannily with Joyce in this moment, the Joyce who lived in that home, but not quite her. After the flashback, Buffy sees she is not responding, rushes to the couch, and attempts to give mouth-to-mouth. And it is sound that alerts Buffy to her mother's fragility and otherness, as well as Buffy's own Slayer strength. A rib cracks. When the medics arrive, Buffy delicately and disturbingly pulls down her mother's skirt, because Joyce should be treated respectfully. This is not the response Buffy offers Dawn at the end of the episode when asked if Joyce is cold: "It's not her!" In the first scene this body could be her. We are still in the uncanny spatial arena of Joyce's everyday. The intensity of the moment is emphasized by Buffy vomiting. The corporeal knowledge that this is no longer Joyce is viscerally affective and contrasts with the opening flashback with the Scooby Gang feeling they have eaten too much, and talking mundanely about "barfing." The body has its own grammar, as Eric Shouse remarks, and the emphasis on barfing and vomiting speaks to the way our bodies create meaning with matter.[42] Giles arrives. Whedon keeps the body in the background or in long-shot for most of the scene except for a few medium-shots of Buffy trying to resuscitate her. Only at the end of the scene is the body seen in lifeless close-up as in Holbein's isolation of Christ from all other life. Here, otherness is registered through the pale corpse that is divorced from her home, her life. The close-up cuts Joyce off from her world. This is not only great direction; it is a marker of attention to the centrality of the body that is integral to the horror genre. As Giles calls out continually, "Joyce! Joyce!" Buffy's words pierce the moment with intensity: "We are not supposed to move the body!" This powerful moment often brings tears to my eyes. Not only because I've known Joyce for five seasons, but because Buffy's words affectively circulate around the intensity of the moment: the reality that this is a body. Like the movement from "mom" to "mommy," the reality of death strikes the audience through the registers of Buffy's voice. The scene stages a very corporeal understanding of death that is central to body genres.[43] After this, Whedon effectively cuts from Joyce's pale, lifeless body to black. The next cut is to the dreadful sound of a plastic body bag, Joyce's new "home."

The power of this opening scene resides in its material elements and *dépaysement*. Joyce's body is never at the center of the scene, only the affect circulating around Buffy's responses. In the body bag, Joyce's corpse is quickly removed from Buffy's world. There are no moments of characters engaging the body in grief, in ways common in Western Christian art, such as the Lamentations where Mary is straddling Christ's dead body.[44] Gunning suggests that "[c]onfrontation rules the cinema of attractions in both the *form* of its films and their mode of exhibition. The directness of this act of display allows an emphasis on the thrill itself—the immediate reaction of the viewer."[45] Joyce's corpse is confrontational in this sense of attractions cinema; it is not simply a display of death and resulting grief. The body infects the space, the scene, and the space of reception with multiple and conflicting possibilities and sensations. Gunning's focus on form here is crucial to "The Body," as the opening scene is not an attempt to represent grief, it is staging shock. The body is motionless. The eyes are vacant. The ribs crack. Buffy vomits. The body should not be moved. And then the shredding sound of the zipper on a body bag.

Negative Space and Attractions

I want to return to Dawn's art lesson before engaging the episode's attractions-like climax in the morgue. Early cinematic audiences experienced films like a window. Gunning challenges to the possibly mythical, but nonetheless powerful, anecdote of the gullible and credulous spectators who ran out of the screening of the Lumière brothers' *Arrivée d'un train à la Ciotat* ("Arrival of a Train at La Ciotat") (1895). The moment shows a double pleasure: both delight and shock in the "magic trick" of the cinema. Gunning suggests that "pleasure derives from the *energy* released by the play between the shock caused by this illusion of danger and delight in its pure illusion."[46] The kind of "energy" that Gunning highlights here is what I call "affect." The corporeal and affective aspects of "The Body" set it apart from *Buffy*'s typical "monster of the week" episodes. The body in "The Body" weighs down on the audience: the staging of shock operates around its static materiality. This resonates quite clearly with Dawn's final words, "Is she cold?" as her hand moves to finally touch the body[47] that she has been asking "to see" throughout the episode. Refracted through Dawn's experience, the episode takes on a different hue: she is clearly interested in Joyce's corpse as a *body*. Dawn is in fact the "the Key" in human form, a tool allowing passage to another dimension that must be protected by Buffy. But I want to suggest that Dawn—once a kind of negative space herself—is also the key to a kind of negative space of the horror genre, the negative space of attractions.

There are of course other *Buffy* episodes that operate in terms of attractions. The musical episode, "Once More, with Feeling" (6.7), with its non-narrative moments of direct address and performative display, stands out as an obvious example.[48] Gunning remarks that attractions-based "cinema addresses and holds the spectator, emphasizing the act of display."[49] Horror cinema is, of course, a cinema of display. Indirect and suggestive imagery are still a form of display, even in earlier eras, when displays of violence had to be handled delicately, like the shower sequence in Alfred Hitchcock's *Psycho* (1960), a moment of shockingly effective editing and sound design. Because display is associated with sight, attractions are understood in scopocentric terms. The classic lines of the carnival "barker" are, "Step this way and see with your own eyes!" The Italian giallo films and, later, American slasher films in large part inspired by them are subgenres where attractions are key, to the point of filmmakers wanting to outdo the elaborate set-pieces or special make-up effects of previous films. In the Italian giallo, even the titles are attractions, reaching excess such as in Sergio Martino's *Your Vice Is a Locked Room and Only I Have the Key* (1972).[50] The baroque opening murder in Dario Argento's *Suspiria* (1977), where a woman is stabbed repeatedly and thrown through a stained-glass ceiling to hang, is not only a brilliant executed set piece of excessive violence, it is corporeal attractions cinema *par excellence*. Movement is key to the effect. Not only the movement of bodies (stabbing, falling) through editing, direction, and camera work, but the material movement of the music by progressive rock band, Goblin. As Hitchcock understood when he watched the shower sequence from *Psycho* without Bernard Herrmann's piercing score, the music in *Suspiria* does not *accompany* the image but drives it viscerally forward. The opening of *Suspira*, like the musical, is obvious attractions cinema. "The Body" operates on this level of corporeal attractions. In contrast to *Suspiria*'s driving music and movement, bodies being and hung and stabbed, the corporeal attractions of "The Body" occur through lack of motion, a dreadful stillness in shocking contrast to other bodies in the series—particularly the bodies of vampires constantly shown fighting, kicking, thrashing, and dramatically turning to dust. The monster de(monstr)ates return, unlike Joyce's corpse. The scenes of attraction from *Suspiria*, or *Psycho*, are not simply virtuoso filmmaking moments. They assault and clash through their materiality.

In the final scene, Joyce's corpse in the Holbein style of *dépaysement* mentioned above shocks again. The abrupt cut to black in the first scene is now rendered less abrasive. Yet the harsh overexposure of light suggests a new, clinical home for Joyce's corpse: the morgue. The audience has by now adapted to these shots and now Joyce's corpse is in its rightful place. Whedon cuts to the physician covering the body, and a single, long Steadicam traveling take moves from Joyce's corpse in the depths of the morgue to the bright waiting room where the Scooby Gang convenes for the first time since Joyce's death. The corpse' stasis here contrasts with the uninterrupted movement of the previous shot. Contrasts abound—darkness/light, quiet/noisy—but touch/distance dominate this final scene. The sequence operates as haptic visuality, discussed by Laura Marks, where "the eyes themselves function like organs of touch."[51] Marks argues that haptic cinema is not evoked simply by shots of hands touching things, predicated upon identification with a character. Instead, she suggests that the "haptic bypasses such identification and the distance from the image it requires"[52] through the use of filmic techniques, such as speeding up or slowing down the image, enlarging film grain, *mise-en-abyme* constructions often seen in found-footage films, the use of close-ups, and, as I argue here, the use of contrasts, motion, and *dépaysement*. Unlike the body in the living room with its proximity to Buffy, now Joyce's corpse is far removed from contact. This distance is emphasized in the long traveling take, which cuts to shots where the camera moves over the gesturing bodies of friends and family experiencing grief, hugging each other with emotional deliberation. The audience identifies with the grieving family and friends but the affect of the scene circulates around the corporeal materiality of characters, their interrelation with each other, the separation of their space of togetherness from Joyce's space of repose, and the scene's audio-visual design.

As the physician speaks to Buffy, Giles and Dawn, the shots are very static. Dawn seems frozen in position with her arms crossed below the chest, a posture that can suggest relaxation, but here implies Dawn blocking out or buffering herself in a strained gesture. After Dawn goes to the bathroom, at approximately thirty-six minutes into the episode, a static medium-long-shot of Buffy and Tara (Amber Benson) discussing the impact of death on their lives holds for fifty seconds, a very long take by the editing and pacing standards of mainstream TV. This scene, like the rest of the episode, is edited joltingly, awkwardly juxtaposing moments of movement and stasis, emphasizing the difficulties of grief and mourning. Yet, in this extended take the shot is structured in a way that promotes hapticity. Buffy and Tara are motionless and sitting apart from one another; conveying distance and isolation. Yet the shot's design also materially embodies how Dawn is feeling about her "mother's body," as it is called earlier by the physician. After the doctor says he has examined the body, Dawn responds: "can we see her?" Buffy immediately dismisses her, "Dawn, not now!" The later static two-shot ends with a cut to Tara in close-up, revealing to Buffy the loss of her own mother. Buffy asks Tara if her mother's death was sudden. Tara's words are revealing: "no . . . and yes! It's always sudden." This sense of suddenness is embodied in the final scene. Dawn leaves the bathroom and surreptitiously makes her way to the dark room where her mother's corpse rests among a host of other dead bodies. A combination of static shots and moving POVs from Dawn's perspective heighten the suspense as she goes to a forbidden place. Genre fans know that they are in horror territory here; they have seen this scene many times. Attractions cinema operates by displaying well-known conventions as much as displaying familiar content. Quiet pervades the scene. This is true of the whole episode (which uses no music to move the audience), but it is also a convention of the horror genre—the quiet before the storm. What was shocking in the opening scene has become dreadful in the final scene. If dread is usually understood as fear of the face-to-face encounter—fear without a clear object—here tactility, emphasis on the desire for touch, promotes dread. Dawn moves towards her mother's body slowly, her right hand rising, wanting to touch her. But she hesitates. Her hand moves back down. At the forty-minute mark, in a medium-shot with Joyce's body in the foreground covered by a sheet, an unknown body sits up in the background, also covered by a sheet. Here the audience may hesitate, the body sitting up in the background may be Dawn's mother's. There have, after all, been moments previously in the episode that visualize a more hopeful outcome, daydream-like moments, as in the first scene where the paramedics bring Joyce back to life, only for us to abruptly return to the horrid sight of her corpse. In the morgue, an unknown vampire is coming to life. It is, in the show's supernatural terms, a threat like any other in Sunnydale.

In a moment that takes me back to Barnabas Collins reaching out of his coffin, grabbing his eventual servant, Willie, by the neck and sitting up, a vampire sits ups and looks menacingly in Dawn's direction. In the waiting room, Buffy notices that Dawn has been absent and makes her way to the autopsy room. She forcibly breaks open the door her sister locked when she entered. Seeing that the vampire threatens Dawn, Buffy engages it in battle. In Carroll's terms, this would constitute the *confrontation* moment of a complex discovery plot. Yet instead, this vampire-threat finale is an attraction in the way Gunning understands it, and in a double sense: the shock of the magic trick and the shock of the magician's skill. The attractions sensibility of the episode also operates in a double sense: the shocking display of Joyce's unmoving corpse is dreadful (actual shock) in relation to the vampire who comes back to life (genre shock). In that negative space between Joyce's unmoving corpse and the moving vampire we find the very tactile frisson of mortality. As mentioned above, some have argued that this scene takes away from the episode's realism, really suggesting that low-art genre elements are infecting high-art realism. *Infection* is the point here. Genre infection. Vampiric infection. Corporeal infection. And affective infection. The contrast between movement and stasis, and the unrealized tactility of Dawn's hesitation about touching a corpse, is where dread resides. The second-to-last shot moves from Buffy's post-fight position on the floor to Dawn confronting, and confronted by, Joyce's corpse. Dawn says: "Is she cold?" Buffy responds: "It's not her. It's not her. She's gone." "Where'd she go?" Dawn wonders. The last shot is of a disembodied hand finally approaching the corpse in medium-shot. The audience realizes that not only has Dawn finally gotten to *see* her mother's body, she is about to find out that it is, indeed, cold. Yet the episode, too, hesitates. It cuts to the final credits before Dawn's hand makes fleshly contact. The episode ends in a "negative space," the negative space of hapticity. Dawn's fear resides in the question, "is she cold?" Buffy's answer signals the grim reality that the horror genre brings; not greater realism, but the negative space of genre as attractions. Joyce's corpse is not simply cold; the corporeal encounter with the vampire shows that Joyce is indeed dead. Dawn's realization is clear: it is not her mother, but a body. Dawn is shocked into this knowledge like the shock of the vampire's attack. The episode's ending on the movement of Dawn's hand toward the stilled body, produces *dépaysement*. The fact that the dead body is not touched is chilling. This frisson comes not only from identifying with a character who will no longer touch her mother, but through *dépaysement*, the still, material body itself confronts and infects the audience with the sublime and dreadful ambiguity of death.

Notes

1. Noël Carroll, *The Philosophy of Horror or Paradoxes of the Heart* (New York: Routledge, 1990), 99.
2. Harry M. Benshoff, *Dark Shadows: TV Milestones Series* (Detroit: Wayne State University Press, 2011), 2.
3. Ibid., 25.
4. Tania Modleski, "The Rhythms of Reception: Daytime Television and Women's Work," in *Regarding Television*. Ed. by E. Ann Kaplan (Los Angeles, CA: The American Film Institute, 1983), 67–75.
5. Lynn Spigel, *Make Room for TV: Televison and the Family Ideal in Postwar America* (Chicago: University of Chicago Press, 1992), 78.
6. Ibid., 78.
7. Helen Wheatley, *Spectacular Television: Exploring Televisual Pleasure* (New York: I.B.Tauris, 2016).
8. Ibid., 116.
9. Ibid., 116.
10. Ibid., 117.
11. Part of the fun of watching *Dark Shadows* on DVD is spotting how the actors replayed the ending slightly differently when asked to replay the scene live for the next day's broadcast. Those who first encounter the show on DVD complain that it is repetitive, re-broadcasting the previous cliff-hanger endings in the opening scene of the next episode. But this daily mimesis is not simply

uncanny; it added to the show's intensity when I saw it originally, and when I watch it now on DVD.

12. Lawson Fletcher, "Is She Cold: Telaesthetic Horror and Embodied Textuality in 'The Body'," *Slayage: The Journal of the Whedon Studies Association* (9.1, 2011), 1.

13. Ibid.

14. Tom Gunning, "An Aesthetic of Astonishment: Early Film and the (In)Credulous Spectator," in *Film Theory and Criticism (Sixth Edition)*. Ed. by Leo Braudy and Marshall Cohen (New York: Oxford University Press, 2004), 870.

15. Brian Massumi, *Politics of Affect*, (Cambridge: Polity Press, 2015).

16. Ibid., 63.

17. Robin Wood and Richard Lippe (Eds), *American Nightmare: Essays on the Horror Film* (Toronto: Festival of Festivals, 1979); Carroll, 1990.

18. Rhonda Wilcox, *Why Buffy Matters: The Art of Buffy the Vampire Slayer* (London: I.B.Tauris, 2005), 186.

19. Ibid.

20. Ibid., 174.

21. Ibid., 176.

22. Ibid., 187.

23. Carroll, 97–157.

24. See, for example, Matt Hills's critique in "An Event-Based Definition of Art-Horror" in *Dark Thoughts: Philosophic Reflections of Cinematic Horror*. Ed. by Steven J. Schneider and Daniel Shaw (London: Scarecrow, 2003).

25. Carroll, 182.

26. Ibid., 14–15.

27. Michael Taussig, *Mimesis and Alterity: A Particular History of the Senses* (New York: Routledge, 1993).

28. Carroll, 99.

29. Ibid.

30. Ibid.

31. Ibid., 100.

32. Ibid., 102. Carroll does not discuss Poe in relation to this term.

33. Ibid., 97.

34. Ibid.

35. Ibid., 98.

36. Ibid., 27–8.

37. Ibid.

38. Ibid., 28.

39. Walter Benjamin, "The Work of Art in the Age of Mechanical Reproduction," in *Film Theory and Criticism (Sixth Edition)*. Ed. by Leo Braudy and Marshall Cohen (New York: Oxford University Press, 2004), 809.

40. Ibid.

41. Ibid.

42. Eric Shouse, "Feeling, Emotion, Affect," in *A Journal of Media and Culture*. (Volume 8, Issue 6, 2005) http://journal.media-culture.org.au/0512/03-shouse. php (accessed July 23, 2017).
43. Williams, Linda. "Film Bodies: Gender, Genre, and Excess," in *Film Theory and Criticism* (Sixth Edition), Ed. by Leo Baudry and Marshall Cohen (New York: Oxford University Press, 2004.
44. Classically represented in Roberto Rosselini's *Roma Città Aperta* (1945) when Pina (Anna Magani) is killed by the Germans while running after the truck of prisoners that includes her fiancée. Her body is straddled by the priest (Aldo Fabrizi) like the dead Christ. It is also a shocking early death of a major star in the film made fifteen years before Alfred Hitchcock did it with Janet Leigh in *Psycho*.
45. Gunning, 869–70 (emphasis mine).
46. Ibid., 876 (emphasis mine).
47. I had a similar experience when I was called by the hospital to inform me that my dear ninety-two-year-old nonno (grandfather) had died during the night. When I arrived at the hospital, I was alone with his body in his room, I had an overwhelming urge to touch his body, but also hesitated, afraid to encounter him in this dreadful changed state.
48. See Anne Golden's chapter in this collection for an extended discussion of "Once More, with Feeling" as hybrid horror.
49. Gunning, 869.
50. The original title is: *Il tuo vizio è una stanza chiusa e solo io ne ho la chiave*.
51. Laura U. Marks, *The Skin of the Film: Intercultural Cinema, Embodiment, and the Senses* (Durham: Duke University Press, 2000), 162.
52. Ibid., 171.

4

The Melancholy Musical: Horror and Avant-Garde Strategies in "Once More, with Feeling"

Anne Golden

In 1940, over forty musical films were released. In 1970, there were just four.[1] Even though the genre is no longer sustained by a significant number of releases each year, artists regularly engage with some of the touchstones of the musical. One important example is found in *Buffy The Vampire Slayer*, when Sweet, a demon summoned inadvertently by Xander Harris, takes over the citizens of Sunnydale, including members of the Scooby Gang, urging them to sing their innermost anxieties and desires. "Once More, with Feeling" (6.07) is both a tale of demonic possession and a remarkable mash-up of allusions to musicals and musical styles. While the episode functions in close proximity to the musical, comedy, and horror genres, its gleeful plundering and pastiche are strategies and formal tactics used in avant-garde films, particularly its staging of the spectacular and aestheticizing of dreamlike trance states. Like these other forms, the episode often diminishes narrative and causality to focus on an emotionalized reality as a series of attractions. For Tom Gunning (1986), a "cinema of attractions" originates in silent cinema strategies such as direct address, tableau, and prioritizing of spectacle over narrative, and he argues that these elements survive in avant-garde practices.[2] Horror, musical *and* avant-garde films regularly foreground and make spectacles of physicality, psychology, dream, desire, and the build-up and release of emotions. Horror films, for example, regularly halt the narrative with scenes of abjection, bodily torment and trauma, and extreme emotional distress. Musicals incorporate choreographed dance sequences that mirror the extreme physicality of bodies experiencing a rush of physical and emotional expression. And avant-garde films include poetic sequences where subjects in wander trance-like through spaces and events designed to resemble, or follow the logic of, dreams or nightmares. Horror, musicals, and avant-garde works are also highly reflexive, particularly aware of their often sensational nature. "Once More, with Feeling" adopts this reflexivity, featuring characters simultaneously inhabiting tropes of the musical and self-consciously questioning those very tropes. They are often aware of being manipulated into releasing their emotions through music, casting a sideways glance, or offering an eye-roll when succumbing to the urge to sing. The episode's lyrics are also self-reflective, and often belie the conventionally giddy tone of classical musicals. The result is a complex cauldron of hybridity in the episode, and an uncanny performance of sudden self-awareness for the characters. Musical films of all kinds inspire the postmodern grab bag that this episode celebrates, while horror genre and avant-garde strategies inform each carefully timed step, underlining the commonalities that link musical, horror, and experimental film. The result is a mixture of gloom and glee, pathos and humor, dread and verve, that render "Once More, with Feeling" a melancholy musical.

The thrilling, staged spontaneity featured in most musicals, where characters erupt into song, becomes treacherous in "Once More, with Feeling," where the impulse to sing and perform one's feelings can cause one literally to burst into flame. Here, Buffy, Xander, Spike, Dawn, Anya, Tara, Giles, and to some extent Willow, all risk emotional exposure to the point of immolation (the parallel between spontaneous bursting into song and spontaneous combustion has not escaped Whedon and company). Here, the sudden exposure of pent-up emotions can be deadly. Jane Feuer discusses the myth of spontaneity in musicals,[3] noting how certain characters—stars, mostly—access spontaneity more easily than secondary or supporting characters.[4] For example, in *Singin' In The Rain* (Gene Kelly, Stanley Donen, 1952), Gene Kelly's character Don Lockwood expresses an impromptu ease while Lena Lamont (Jean Hagen) is depicted as being unable to master lines easily—her handicap, a lack of looseness and spontaneity. "Once More with Feeling" democratizes this spontaneity so that each Sunnydale resident has the potential to star in their own private musical. In a musical, the spontaneity demonstrated by characters is expected and understood. In "Once More, with Feeling," the very idea of being spontaneous is fraught with peril, as it threatens to reveal emotions carefully concealed by the Scooby Gang. The impulsive expression of emotion yields to a musical abandon that threatens characters with annihilation, underlining the parallels between musical spontaneity and emotional release, bodily abjection and horror. The episode upholds the tradition of musical comedy in that the action progresses via singing and dancing, humorously out of place in the world of the vampire Slayer. But "Once More, with Feeling" undercuts the humour with a lurking fear that reality has been compromised by a sinister, puppeting force using an otherwise light-hearted genre as a weapon.

Through analysis of specific musical numbers in "Once More with Feeling," I argue that the episode both sustains and subverts musical comedy idioms, moving closer to the dreadful attractions of avant-garde and horror.[5] These genres often intertwine in their emphasis on the spectacle of bodily excess, where a surfeit of sensations leads to excessive movement. The musical's expressions of excess physicality, dancing and singing, become, in a horror film, running, squirming, and screaming. In highlighting such parallels, the episode "deconstruct[s] ... the musical's myths of desire" as akin to "delusion," as Diana Sandars and Rhonda V. Wilcox have argued.[6] This is not to say that popular musicals have nothing to offer but whimsy and wholesomeness. Key examples featuring the more dreadful elements associated with horror are *The Wizard of Oz* (Victor Fleming, 1939), *Fantasia* (1940), *The Red Shoes* (Powell and Pressburger, 1948), and *The Phantom of the Paradise* (De Palma, 1974). Robin Wood (1976, 1986) famously suggested that *Meet Me in St. Louis* (Vincente Minnelli, 1944) includes sequences that are precursors to contemporary horror films.[7] The mix of horror and musical is key to the emotional effect of *Meet Me In St. Louis* in two sequences featuring the youngest child, Tootie Smith. A song even triggers Tootie's violence in one scene. After her sister (Judy Garland) has sung "Have Yourself a Merry Little Christmas" to Tootie, the latter runs from her bedroom and out of the house. Wielding an axe, she destroys a snowman in a proto-slasher action. Later horror films such as *Alice, Sweet Alice* (Alfred Sole, 1976) foreground similar violent acts by young protagonists, but it is revealing that such scenes may have roots in the musical. Wood identifies this sequence in *Meet Me in St. Louis* as a precursor to family horror, blurring the line between actions appropriate for a musical and those more fitting for a horror film. In another sequence, Tootie 'kills' Mr Brokoff, by throwing flour in his face on Halloween night. The throwing of flour at a foe had been equated with 'murder' earlier in the film by Tootie and her young friends. Additionally this latter sequence signals horror with eerie lighting, uncanny Halloween costumes (the kids wear fake noses and disguises suggesting skewed versions of adulthood), and a haunted house. "Once More, with Feeling" shares this shrewd comingling of horror and musical tropes by undercutting the incredible release of repression in its musical numbers with a sense of dread.

In "Once More, with Feeling," Xander has summoned the demon Sweet. As the episode's supernatural monster, Sweet is also the character who most embodies the quintessential musical performer, his big number in the episode's finale demonstrating that he is an accomplished tap dancer in a chic zoot suit. His singing offsets the more amateur vocals of other characters who, with the exception of Giles, seldom find themselves compelled to sing. Sweet is introduced as a monster in the first shot featuring him. "That's entertainment!" he exclaims, invoking the 1974 film of the same name. In fact, the different styles of music and sub-stories within the overarching narrative of "Once More, with Feeling," are not unlike *That's Entertainment!* (Jack Haley, Jr.), a clip-pastiche of musical numbers from four decades of MGM films. "Once More, with Feeling" similarly cycles through many musical styles and trends from the history of the genre, including vaudeville, jazz, and folk traditions. Sweet not only curses people through song and dance, his spell is responsible for this excessive pastiche of styles, "reflecting the multiplicity and complexity of desires" of the characters who perform them.[8]

Sweet is introduced in an upward pan from feet to head. He is positioned in the right of the frame, shot from the back in three-quarter profile. The red zoot suit he wears is associated with the 1940s, locating him at least sartorially within the golden age of musical film (1930s–1950s). On the left, lower frame of the medium-long shot featuring Sweet, a corpse billows smoke from recent spontaneous combustion due to excessive tap dancing. Death and dancing here signal a brutal collision of the musical and horror genres. Furthering this collision are allusions to horror convention. It is night. Rising smoke from the body suggests fog. As the camera tilts up, we see Sweet's hand/claw. Sweet's elongated chin juts out, as in classic representations of Satan. The dominant colors of this sequence are deep blue and vivid red, a nod to the vibrant colors associated with grand musicals such as *An American in Paris* (Vincente Minnelli, 1951) and *The Pirate* (Minnelli, 1948), and with Italian giallo films such as *Blood and Black Lace* (Mario Bava, 1964) and *Suspiria* (Dario Argento, 1977)—but also, importantly, to another musical that blends avant-garde and horror strategies to associate dancing with death, one to which "Once More, with Feeling" owes a great debt: *The Red Shoes*, directed by Michael Powell and Emeric Pressburger.

Based on Hans Christian Andersen's tale of the same name, *The Red Shoes* features a demonic shoemaker who offers a young woman the "gift" of dancing via a pair of shoes. The gift becomes a curse; the young woman's uncontrollable dancing propels her into poverty and alienation. This story informs "The Red Shoes" ballet production number in the Powell and Pressburger film, but the curse also operates in the "real" life of the film's ballet-dancer main character, Victoria Page (Moira Shearer), who ultimately dances over a balcony in a kind of suicide, though it is implied that the red shoes have made her a victim-puppet. In the film, the ballet begins with an extreme-long shot of a stage on which the dance will be performed. The first figure we see is the shoemaker. As the ballet unfolds, the camera is closer to the action on stage, encouraging the sense that we are in the audience watching a performance. A similar distancing conceit appears in the opening credits of "Once More, with Feeling," one of only two instances in *Buffy* that the episode title appears onscreen.[9] As Sandars and Wilcox argue, this direct confrontation signals the spectator, not the other characters, as the primary audience for the episode's musical confessions.[10] *The Red Shoes* breaks with distancing effects; by the end of the sequence, medium-long shots and close-ups dominate, drawing the audience into a claustrophobic relationship to the evolving nightmare world of the female dancer, who is tossed from one group of men to another in a carnivalesque setting that acts as a simultaneous augmentation and psychological projection of her terror.

The parallels between the staging of the "Red Shoes" ballet and the finale of "Once More, with Feeling" are undeniable. Sweet, too, appears on a stage, dancing with Dawn, controlling her balletic movements like a puppet-master. Sweet's curse is also similar in that his victims are affected with excessive performativity. They have no control over their actions, which are fuelled as much by pent-up emotions as by the curse itself. In this way, the characters are linked to *The Red Shoes*, but also to demonic possession horror films such as *The Exorcist* (William Friedkin, 1973), in which the twisting, probing, and manipulation of young Reagan's (Linda Blair) body by both demonic forces and the doctors trying to diagnose her, gradually reveal corruption through extreme, even impossible, abject physicality. Excessive style and content link horror and musicals; both share a necessary staging of surplus emotions and physicality. In "Once More, with Feeling," the horror is that the characters are powerless to stop their singing and dancing even as they bare their souls. This trope also appears in *Singin' in the Rain*, where the refrain "Gotta sing, gotta dance" is an expression of joy and the need to express feelings, but also suggests that characters are *compelled* to sing and dance.

"Once More, with Feeling" is both musical and anti-musical in that it serves up song and dance while subverting the classical musical's goal to unify. While works of horror also tend to use localized spaces and communities—a small town, a neighborhood, a house, a family—*dis*unity is often the catalyst for conflict. "Once More, with Feeling" suggests disunity by focusing on the internal degeneration of interrelationships among characters—through their open questioning of each other's motives (as Tara does with Willow's increasing reliance upon magic), their silence and emotional remove (exemplified by Xander and Anya's "I'll Never Tell" number), their isolation (sometimes self-imposed, like Buffy's; sometimes forced upon them, as with Spike), and the feeling that they all have limited choices. In musical films from the 1940s and 1950s, while there may be conflicts and setbacks, the final number is about looking to the future in harmony and with optimism. *Oklahoma!* (1955), for example, ends with a reprise of the title song, whose lyrics are an ode to the beauty of Oklahoma and the promise of a grand future: "We know we belong to the land and the land we belong to is grand." As Amy Bauer suggests, "Once More, with Feeling" "conflates the utopian fantasy of the musical with the dystopian fantasy of the *Buffy*verse."[11] The episode's final number directly subverts

Oklahoma's brand of American positivism and positivity, asking continually, "Where do we go from here?" without ever answering the question. There is also a marked disunity of tone in the episode. The songs are in diverse styles, adopting pop, jazz, rock and folk idioms, among others. Some songs are disrupted, cut off in mid-line or -word, leaving characters isolated at an emotional cliffhanger, or impasse. Every character's signature song finds them in crisis, or questioning their future, and often in a musical style that clashes with other big numbers associated with individual characters. The degree to which "Once More, with Feeling" focuses on disunity places the episode in the American Gothic tradition's exploration of the internal collapse of systems meant to secure and protect: family, friends, and community primary among these.

Despite their differences in tone and overall goal, there are significant links between "Once More, with Feeling" and *Oklahoma!* that gesture towards the shared tropes of the musical and horror as critiquing American idealism. Even though *Oklahoma!* offers a generally positive vision of the pioneer spirit, there are moments of rupture. In classic musicals, the need to dance is often portrayed as an act of exuberance and/ or a way to channel surplus energy. *Oklahoma!* features an uncanny dream sequence, the Dream Ballet, that follows this tradition. In the Dream Ballet, however, there is a sort of corrosion present in how performance is staged, particularly in the appearance of several doppelgangers, an inspired use of stand-ins for the film's non-dancing lead performers. Choreographed by Agnes Demille, the ballet requires a level of dance ability well above the capabilities of its singer-actor stars, Shirley Jones (Laurey) and Gordon MacRae (Curly). In the scene, after falling asleep and singing "Out of My Dreams," Laurey, now dreaming, moves to meet her double, a dancer that will represent her, like the passing of a baton. Laurey and Dream Laurey (Bambi Linn) touch palms and circle each other. Jones then backs away and out of frame to cede the role to her double. MacRae briefly appears behind his own double, Dream Curly, who moves forward and, in a sense, becomes him. Adding to this uncanny supplanting of the film's stars, some supporting performers in the scene express an intentionally eerie, lifeless quality, as if they are marionettes manipulated by an unseen hand. The effect is not unlike the balletic dance sequence in "Once More, with Feeling," where an entranced Dawn has a wordless dance-duet with Sweet, who manipulates her every move in a sinister version of the "lead" in a romantic dance coupling (he seeks to make Dawn his bride, after all). In *Oklahoma!*, the dream becomes a nightmare as Jud Fry (Rod Steiger) pursues Dream Laurey while she searches for Dream Curly. Jud eventually kills Curly against an intense, impressionistic Todd-AO-painted artificial backdrop of dark skies and storm clouds. While things in *Oklahoma!* end well for Laurey and Curly outside the dream, as they begin their life together, the Dream Ballet remains a startling, uneasy centerpiece, suggesting something rotten in the middle of so much positivity.

In "Once More, with Feeling," a similar unease undercuts even the more exuberant and comical numbers, often suggested by compartmentalization of dancing from singing, which the episode uses to great effect in offsetting otherwise "realistic" events. In one shot, as Anya, Giles and Xander walk and talk in a left-to-right tracking shot, they encounter—and are aurally overtaken by—a woman singing mournfully to a police officer about a parking ticket, and then by two sets of dancers. The shot is unbroken and elaborate, the conversation among the three leads often drowned out by singing and music occurring in the musical scenes they encounter. First, the three pass in front of a couple performing a routine with ballet elements, in keeping with choreographies meant to suggest budding romance. Soon after, the three pass in front of three "janitors" treating their brooms like canes. The dancers are not so much there to support the main players as to offset their conversation—highlighting the episode's musical style as incongruous with reality. Other extras pass behind Anya, Giles and Xander and in front of the dancers. The three characters don't participate or even seem to notice these mini-musicals, a conceit that occurs even in the duet with Anya and Xander, who sing with, but *not to*, each other; and in Giles's ballad expressing fears about, but *not to*, Buffy. (I discuss these scenes in more detail below.) These are interior moments—a kind of interior monologue presented to the *spectator*, not as open communication between characters. These scattershot moments—where excessive expressions coexist with "normal" actions, such as walking and talking—are part of an overall aesthetic association of music and dance with the unconscious, and dialogue with acts of denial and repression. Spectacle here is not all-encompassing. The mundane and everyday exist, however uncomfortably and half-consciously, on the same plane as the spectacular.

Another important link between these sequences in "Once More, with Feeling" and The Dream Ballet of *Oklahoma!* comes in their intimations of the trance film. A key component of avant-garde cinema, the trance film is characterized by sustained presentation of an altered state experienced by a protagonist. P. Adams Sitney refers to trance films as featuring a "possessed questor."[12] This idea of possession appears in the avant-garde long before blockbuster horror films such as *The Exorcist* deal explicitly with demonic possession. The trance film occurs in a space of alterity. It is often unclear whether we are watching a protagonists' dream, nightmare, or some other hallucinatory state. The image of Laurey holding her hand up and out to her double in order to initiate the Dream Ballet in *Oklahoma!* is remarkably similar, for example, to the gesture Maya Deren's protagonist performs in *Ritual in Transfigured Time* (Deren, 1946) or the one essayed by Stan Brakhage in *The Way to Shadow Garden* (1954), both important trance films, their protagonists wandering an oneiric landscape that announces an existential crisis. Whedon had experimented before with the aesthetics of the trance film in the early scenes of "The Body" (05.16), where Buffy moves like an automaton through the suddenly uncanny Summers home, a mute wanderer in a now-unfamiliar, dreamlike space haunted by death. "Once More, with Feeling" is a more extended engagement with trance, a waking dream/nightmare in which emotional secrets are laid bare through compulsive singing and dancing. Many musicals feature similar "dream ballets." *Singin' in the Rain, An American in Paris* and *The Band Wagon* (Minelli, 1953), for example, contain sequences that feature darker themes than the main narrative and often suggest a somnambulistic quality to the main characters appearing in them. Despite their presence in mainstream musical films, these protagonists fit the description of the trance film's possessed questor. "Once More, with Feeling" offers an equivalent to these dream sequences and their lost or searching characters.

If anything undercuts the nostalgic return to the musical in "Once More, with Feeling," it is the episode's pervasive melancholia. Sigmund Freud argues in "Mourning and Melancholia" that melancholia is "loss of a more ideal kind" than mourning.[13] Like dread, melancholia has lost sight of the object that has caused the emotional state of mourning; that object, no longer merely dead, but missing, results in longing and transference by the subject, who then identifies with that lost object. Buffy's grim realization that being resurrected by her friends is a punishment rather than a gift frames the entirety of season six. Her loss of the heaven-like state found in her mystical death haunts Buffy, making the Sunnydale reality of constant oncoming monsters all the more difficult to bear. While Buffy may be the most outwardly melancholic of the Scoobies, all of the supporting characters harbor secret pain and longing that parallel the Slayer's conflict. Willow's struggle to overcome a lifetime of bullying and shyness through magic becomes an increasing addiction, and Tara's suspicion of this development forces her away from Willow, one of the only people with whom she has managed to form a meaningful bond. Giles, too, realizes he must break from the group, feeling he is now more a hindrance than a helper to Buffy, his importance as a Watcher long past. Xander and Anya's marriage jitters are based on more than the stresses of planning and future commitment; their pasts haunt them both in the form of Xander's dreadful, curse-induced vision of a future where he has become his father, and in the form of Anya's constant reminder by vengeance-demon friend, Halfrek (Kali Rocha), that she is giving up her autonomy for a union that she spent years (centuries, even) fighting against. All of these creeping realizations that show the characters to be stranded in loss and longing occur through song in "Once More, with Feeling." For Freud, "[i]n mourning it is the world which has become poor and empty; in melancholia it is the ego itself."[14] "Once More, with Feeling" confronts this impoverished emptiness head-on in each musical number, with the characters offered—for themselves and eventually each other—a painful lucidity in being "cursed" to confront (and perform) a longing that would otherwise have remained denied, suppressed. Melancholia tied to unconscious emptiness is the disturbing undertone that haunts the otherwise geeky, nostalgic verve of musical numbers in "Once More, with Feeling."

The question of nostalgia—itself always attached to loss—haunts the episode. Furthermore, the lost or "abandoned object" in "Once More, with Feeling" also attends its framing of the musical genre itself. "Once More, with Feeling" oscillates between paying outright homage to specific beloved musicals and undercutting that reverence with avant-garde distancing devices. In its almost vaudevillian, performative display of a range of styles in the context of horror, the episode becomes a treatise on the living-death of the musical: it revives the musical in ways that suggest it is outmoded, a kind of uninvited ghost. Yet, at the same time, the return of the dead past in musical form is, in this episode, something temporarily to celebrate, just as the presence of a specter in a ghost story is both terrible, and thrillingly revelatory. It is in this reflexive pastiche of celebrated form and formula that "Once More, with Feeling" most exhibits an avant-garde self-consciousness around genre. The next section surveys the major ways in which Whedon's musical episode self-consciously explores the concept of a melancholy musical by collapsing the horror and musical genres together with the skeptical strategies of the avant-garde.

Alienation, Anxiety, and Existential Dread

"Once More, with Feeling" features a series of musical numbers associated with musical spectacle, but its cataloguing of such a variety of styles also foregrounds a self-reflexivity that borders on Brechtian alienation.[15] There are numerous examples of ruptures in tone and plot that call attention to style, construct, and genre, and suggest Whedon's cinephilic conversance with a genre that had its heyday in the 1930s and 1940s. During the opening number, Buffy kills her backup dancer/singers, two vampires and a demon. Here, action, horror, comedy, and musical function on the same plane, all staged as choreographed spectacle. There is a clear precedent for "killing" supporting players during numbers in the musical *Top Hat* (Mark Sandrich, 1935), where Fred Astaire uses his cane as a gun and "shoots" his backup dancers during the number "Top Hat, White Tie and Tails." When Buffy sings the final word of her song, "alive," she emerges from the dust of a vampire she has just dispatched, and the camera pulls up and back into a dramatic crane shot. Farther on in the episode, Spike pulls a sour face as he begins his rock-inspired song, "Rest in Peace." He and Buffy have just discussed the phenomena of people bursting into song and dance, and Spike's expression and eye-rolling signal his awareness that he is about to do just that. In a later scene, Dawn starts singing a song about no one noticing or caring about her. Earlier in the episode, and throughout the season, she steals things in a perverse attempt to be noticed, so this number might qualify as Dawn's "secret" confession. She manages to sing only one line, however, before she turns to see one of Sweet's henchmen, humanoid save for a large wooden puppet head, who pushes her into the waiting clasp of two other henchmen. Dawn's singing is quickly cut short by piercing screams so common to horror. The episode constantly undoes expectations in this and a variety of other manners. The clash, the surprise, of a song cut so short by a monster is a moment when horror usurps the musical in a clever play on what horror scholarship terms a "startle effect," that moment where a visual or aural jolt cuts through the tone of creeping dread.[16]

The opening number, "Going through the Motions," links Buffy to different characters played by Fred Astaire in several films made between 1933 and 1958. Buffy is alone in a graveyard on an evening of slaying—typical for the series, were it not for the singing. We see Buffy in a medium-long shot as the camera tracks back from her moving resignedly from left to right across the set. The scene has precedent in *The Band Wagon* (Vincente Minnelli, 1956), which opens with Tony Hunter (Fred Astaire) disembarking from a train. He is clearly expecting to be met, but no one appears to greet him. Astaire begins sauntering along the platform, singing the lament, "By Myself." The camera tracks back from him, then moves left to right, keeping Astaire in a medium-long shot as he walks and sings. Both shots showcase the effortless, jaunty elegance of the characters, and both highlight declarations from the main protagonists about feeling alone—Tony's about accepting and embracing solitude, and Buffy's about an existential crisis regarding merely "going through the motions" instead of really living. Neither character dances. They move purposefully from left to right. The fact that Tony is an isolated, self-aware character is remarkably similar to Buffy's status and her initial song in the episode. In a similar moment at the end of the episode, Buffy sings about her belief that the hell from which her friends rescued her was actually heaven. Her refrain, "I think I was in heaven," with the final word drawn out and wilting as it slides into a flat note, calls to mind one of the most famous songs in musical history, "Cheek to Cheek," written by Irving Berlin for *Top Hat* (Mark Sandrich, 1935). The song features the lyrics "Heaven, I'm in Heaven," and aligns "dancing cheek-to-cheek" with "find[ing] the happiness I seek." However, Buffy's bleak, lamenting refrain undercuts the usual tone of such mainstream fare. Once again, the private angst in such scenes is remarkably unsettling against the backdrop of the musical.

The positioning of two characters who share the same space but are otherwise isolated or distant from each other is repeated throughout the episode (see Figure 4.1). When, for example, Buffy's Watcher, Giles, sings "Standing," a ballad, to Buffy, he moves at regular speed while Buffy works out in slow motion. The use of two different speeds—Giles in real time,

Figure 4.1   Tara and Giles occupy separate emotional spaces during a musical number set in the Magic Box.

Buffy in an accentuated "other" time and space—suggest that the two characters are isolated in their own private worlds.[17] The moment is painful: Giles expressing his feeling of failing Buffy, yet Buffy does not hear him, because the song is an exploration of Giles's internal crisis—stay in Sunnydale and "fail" Buffy, or leave and allow her to thrive.

A later scene in the Magic Box featuring Buffy, Giles, Xander, Willow, Tara and Anya is a variation on this opening-up of emotional space within the musical *mise-en-scène*. Giles, Xander, Willow and Tara begin a communal song suggesting potential reasons for the curse on Sunnydale. The number has a Broadway feel, as characters come together to brainstorm. Anya suddenly interrupts their song with her own short number about her abiding fear of bunnies. Two spaces and two styles collide in this moment: on the one side, a Broadway-style chorus of singers trying to come up with solutions, on the other a solo singer whose singing and performance styles borrow heavily from the more anthemic songs of rock opera. Anya's performance is underscored by the creation of a separate performance space within the shop, effectively "removing" her from the others through dramatic spotlighting, sweeping camera movements, and canted angles. Anya's space suggests that she is in a music video or on stage. Augmenting the rock video quality of the piece, her "Bunnies" song ends with pyrotechnics. The design and editing recall

Kenneth Anger's *Inauguration of the Pleasure Dome* (1954) in which figures have separate spaces enhanced by colors, costumes, and props that effectively throw the moment into relief against the rest of the *mise-en-scène*. The scene's heightened artificiality, a strategy shared by avant-garde and horror, is key here, where an abrupt shift of style is meant to startle, to shock, even as it also encourages laughter. "Once More, with Feeling" normalizes this avant-garde practice, however, attaching different musical styles and films, with their own sets and lighting schemes and colors, to characters as cues that reflect their personalities and conflicts.

Despite conventionalizing some of the more avant-garde strategies it uses, "Once More With Feeling" most resembles darker, melancholic musicals such as *Carousel* (Henry King, 1956), its typically exuberant musical numbers undercut by the central conceit that its main character has been killed in a robbery. Billy Bigelow (Gordon MacRae) is not a particularly good man, but he is allowed to return to earth to see his daughter as a young woman. Ghost Billy hovers near his wife and daughter but cannot be seen or heard. Pathos is foregrounded in the finale, "You'll Never Walk Alone," where Billy remains a mournful, haunting presence. In "Once More, with Feeling" that presence is Buffy. While it features the humor characteristic of *Buffy*, the episode is, as I argue above, ultimately a melancholy musical. Buffy is no ingénue. Spike is not the boy next door. This is a fractured, frayed version of the musical that parallels the rifts between main characters. Another link to *Carousel* is that Buffy feels alone *throughout* the episode, separated from her friends by her secret belief that they have wrenched her from "heaven." Again, the episode turns upon horror's disunity, rather than the musical's conventional emphasis on ultimate unity. The song and dance numbers reveal strife between characters. Giles does not know how to protect Buffy. Buffy can only connect through violence with Spike, a vampire. Tara and Willow's number, "I'm Under Your Spell," is, as discussed elsewhere, an ode to cunnilingus, that also points to Willow's overuse and potential abuse of magic.[18] Willow and Tara wear dresses suggestive of medieval princesses, and the song features Disney-style animation. Stars emanate from both Tara and Willow's fingers when they point and make circles and when Tara dances, two women appear in the background, all suggesting that this number is an idyll, a total fantasy. However, Tara seems to be under two spells: Willow's and Sweet's, subtly linking Willow's influence over Tara to something more sinister, even monstrous. This song is the most overt, clear declaration of love and desire in the episode, and it happens between two women, a clever subversion of the heteronormativity privileged by musicals. As we think Tara will continue to sing "You make me complete," the drawn-out cadence is on the syllable, "come," or "cum," and a cut occurs on the phrase, "You make me . . . ." In these and other insistent ruptures of tone that cut off songs in the episode, unease surfaces. The discomfort with alternative sexualities, lesbianism, and abject fluids spill over into the next shot, with Xander commenting on Willow and Tara's "get a roominess." Songs in classic musicals are "complete" in a way that satisfies viewer expectations of resolution. In "Once More, with Feeling," we instead experience disruption, disjunction, and a comment on the potentially sexualized nature of the song from another character.

Beyond self-reflexivity, there is something else operating in "Once More, with Feeling." Most of the songs do not simply convey one concept or plot point but have concurrent narrative strands, such as "I'll Never Tell," sung by Xander and Anya. Their song is both an ode to love and a declaration of anxieties about their future together. They sing *to* each other *about* each other, but oddly—in keeping with the episode's focus on emotional isolation and alienation—they do not "hear" each other. Their number most resembles a Hollywood musical, but their duet is one in form only. The love duet is usually a declaration that unifies two people. In a way, "I'll Never Tell" is not unlike "People Will Say We're in Love" from *Oklahoma!* because the singers are denying their feelings even as their expression of said feelings is very clear to viewers. The Xander and Anya duet is most reminiscent of an Astaire/Rita Hayworth pairing, but it references *Singin' in the Rain* as the two characters finish their song laughing, echoing the end of "Good Morning," sung and danced by Gene Kelly, Debbie Reynolds and Donald O'Connor in the 1951 musical. As previously mentioned, the shot following the "I'll Never Tell" number features Anya, Giles and Xander walking on a street left-to-right. Xander and Anya are describing their song. She says "It was like we were being watched, like there were only three walls but not a fourth wall," uncannily reminding the audience of its own position vis-à-vis the entire series. Anya also self-consciously bemoans the fact that their number is a "retro-pastiche." It is rare for a performer in a classic musical to comment on their song and find it lacking, a mere copy. It is also rare for background players to have their own songs, as the "mustard" man and the "parking ticket" woman do; both are incidental characters whose mundane moments are humorously, audaciously, turned into massive performances. Such moments serve to make private pain into public spectacle, an uncanny conceit that *Buffy* explored in earlier episodes such as "Nightmares" (1.10) and "Restless" (4.22), where characters experience their secret fears projected into reality in excessive ways.

The Quotidian Made Strange

The focus on the uncanny strangeness of mundanity in "Once More, with Feeling" is also an avant-garde strategy that often informs horror's effects. But it is an effect not without precedent in the musical. In *Les parapluies de Cherbourg* (1964), Jacques Demy notably has his characters sing continuously, so even the simple request to fill a tank with gas is sung. Again, this is mirrored in the episode's two shortest songs, "The Mustard" and "The Parking Ticket." In the latter, the camera begins as a close up of one man singing "They got the mustard out!" as he enthusiastically holds up a clean shirt. The camera moves back and cranes up to reveal a dancing chorus of other satisfied customers. The background performers, typically extras, become foregrounded as the woman with a parking ticket and the man celebrating a dry-cleaning miracle take center stage briefly. The moment is uncanny because its excess undoes the usual order of things, in which supporting performers react/engage in choreography but are not the focus, and in which satisfied customers express their pleasure typically with a quiet smile, and not an elaborately staged musical moment. "The Mustard" is a brief song—a kind of punctuation, even—but it is an important indicator of the stylistic strategy of rupture that informs "Once More, with Feeling." An impressive chorus of singers and dancers backs up the man. The colors and choreography are grand. The subject alone is mundane, even boring. The crane shot, though brief, aligns the choreography with Busby Berkley's incredible abstractions of female dancers' bodies from above. As in the example later in the episode, when a woman sings a plaintive melody about the unfairness of her parking ticket, bit players have moments where "their" musical is the main attraction. Much like the way Buffy confers power on all the potential slayers in the final season, everybody here is a star in their own musical. The inherent surrealism of musicals is echoed here, too, as characters engage in songs that comment on the strangeness of singing anything at all, a strategy highlighting the uncanny atmosphere of an "all-singing, all-dancing" Sunnydale cursed by the demon Sweet.

The Death (and Resurrection?) of Genre

During the showdown with Sweet, Buffy spouts a string of clichéd musical lines as she beats up his henchmen. Some—"whistle while you work," "where there's life there's hope," and "every day's a gift"—are optimistic lines fitting the musical's absurd reality, but they belie the emotional pain that Buffy has suffered following her resurrection by the Scooby Gang, a pain that is expressed across her songs in the episode. Buffy, sings "Don't give me songs / Give me something to sing about," another rejection of the musical's naïve optimism. Buffy may find herself in a musical, but she cannot embrace the optimistic essence of the genre. In this sense, Buffy, the closest thing the episode has to a Fred Astaire figure, *rejects* the traditional musical. Buffy's asking for content and meaning befitting her lament moves this episode closer to avant-garde strategies such as distanciation and rupture. Buffy calls upon everyone to reject the "spell" of the musical. This key moment in the finale begs the question: does the episode celebrate or reject the power of the musical genre? In language more befitting the episode's horror elements, does "Once More, with Feeling" announce the death of the musical, or is it an attempt to resurrect it? Whedon would later attempt to resurrect the western, a genre that many see as "dead" with *Firely*, and he and Drew Goddard would make similar genre death-and-resurrection allusions in the script and imagery of *The Cabin in the Woods*, which essentially suggests the horror genre must apocalyptically degenerate into cliché and stereotype before it can be revived anew.[19] If the primary strategy of "Once More, with Feeling" is self-conscious pastiche, and the definition of pastiche presumes that the model for the mock-up is "dead" already—a style that haunts us with nostalgic longing because it is lost—then another uncanny element of Whedon's melancholy musical is its nostalgia for a "dead" genre that brings it to life in unexpected and startling ways. Sweet is defeated but not killed. "Now that was a show-stopping number," he says, applauding after Buffy nearly dances herself to death before Spike intervenes. The spirit of the musical, albeit a twisted one, will go on it seems.

The simultaneous strategy of un/making a musical is a complex process of homage, pastiche, and parody. If the creation of many classical musicals aims for the suggestion of effortless unconscious expression of emotion by performers, "Once More, with Feeling" offers self-conscious figures in the throes of a kind of horrific possession. Musicals are a nearly-extinct style but "Once More, with Feeling" equivocates. It resurrects the musical in some ways, only to announce its death in others—another element that may go unnoticed, and that signals horror.

Notes

1. Clive Hirschhorn, *The Hollywood Musical* (London: Octopus Books, 1981).
2. Tom Gunning, "The Cinema of Attractions: Early Film, Its Spectator and the Avant-Garde," *Wide Angle* (8.3–4, Fall, 1986), 63.
3. Jane Feuer, "The Self-Reflexive Musical and the Myth of Entertainment," *Film Genre Reader II*, Ed. Barry Keith Grant (Austin: University of Texas Press, 1995), 441–455.
4. Ibid., 452.
5. Tom Gunning, "The Cinema of Attractions: Early Film, Its Spectator and the Avant-Garde," *Wide Angle* (8.3–4, Fall, 1986).
6. Diana Sandars and Rhonda V. Wilcox, "Not 'The Same Arrangement': Breaking Utopian Promises in the *Buffy* Musical," *Music, Sound, and Silence in Buffy the Vampire Slayer*, Ed. Paul Attinello, Janet K. Halfyard, and Vanessa Knights (London and New York: Routledge, 2010), 190.
7. Robin Wood, "The American Family Comedy: From Meet Me in St. Louis to The Texas Chainsaw Massacre," *Wide Angle: a film quarterly of theory, criticism and practice* 1979, 5–11.
8. Sandars and Wilcox, 190.
9. The other is "Conversations with Dead People" (7.7).
10. Sandars and Wilcox, 194, 196.
11. Amy Bauer, "'Give Me Something to Sing About': Intertextuality and the Audience in 'Once More, with Feeling'," *Music, Sound, and Silence in* Buffy the Vampire Slayer, Ed. Paul Attinello, Janet K. Halfyard, and Vanessa Knights (London and New York: Routledge, 2010), 210.
12. P. Adams Sitney, *Visionary Film: The American Avant-Garde 1943–1978* (New York: Oxford University Press, 1979), 20–36.
13. Sigmund Freud, "Mourning and Melancholia," *The Standard Edition of the Complete Psychological Works of Sigmund Freud*, Translated by James Strachey, Anna Freud, Volume XIV (London: The Hogarth Press, 1974), 245.
14. Ibid., 245–6.

15. Brechtian "alienation effect," "estrangement effect," "distancing effect," or "distanciation" strategies ("verfremdungseffekt") remind spectators of the nature of the entertainment before them *as* entertainment—as construct—highlighting reflexively form, style, narrative, and performance elements, as well as the audience's position as active spectator. See Paul Willeman, "Distanciation and Douglas Sirk," *Screen*, 12.2, 1971, 63–67, and John Willett, Ed. and Trans., *Brecht on Theatre* (New York: Hill and Wang, 1964), 91.

16. See, for example, Robert Baird's "Startle Effect: Implications for Spectator Cognition and Media Theory, *Film Quarterly*, 53.3, Spring 2000, 12–24.

17. The moment suggests a reference to *Easter Parade* (Charles Walters, 1948) where, in the foreground, Fred Astaire dances in slow motion on a stage while the supporting players in the background are at regular speed.

18. Rhonda Wilcox, "Song: Singing and Dancing and Burning and Dying: Once More, with Textual Feeling," *Why Buffy Matters* (London: I.B.Tauris, 2005), 191–205.

19. See Kristopher Karl Woofter, "Watchers in the Woods: Meta-Horror, Genre Hybridity and Reality TV Critique in *The Cabin in the Woods*," in *Reading Joss Whedon*, Ed. by Rhonda V. Wilcox, Tanya R. Cochran, Cynthea Masson, and David Lavery (Syracuse, NY: Syracuse University Press, 2014).

5

Angel's Dreams, Our Nightmares: Oneiric Horror in *Angel* and *Buffy the Vampire Slayer*

Cynthia Burkhead

"[H]orror films [...] are our collective nightmares."
— Robin Wood[1]

"I'm only saying that once you see true evil, it can have some serious after burn, and then you can't unsee what you saw. Ever."
— (Sunnydale High Principal) Robin Wood[2]

Scholars have written extensively about the cultural and political metaphors made uncomfortably visible by the horror film. That the audience may be only half-conscious of these realities is an intimation of the audience-as-dreamer notions of early film theorists such as Hugo Munsterberg (1916).[3] Bringing filmmakers into the equation, Robin Wood offers that "popular films [...] respond to interpretation as at once the personal dreams of their makers and the collective dreams of their audiences, the fusion made possible by the shared structures of common ideology."[4] For both filmmaker and audience, those things repressed in the full consciousness of wakefulness are loosened in sleep and play out "as fantasies" in our dreams—or nightmares. From this Wood arrives at a deceptively "simple definition of horror films; they are our collective nightmares."[5] In Wood's Marxist-psychoanalytical framework, these nightmares derive from oppressive ideological forces that cause "surplus repression," or that repression which is built upon a constant state of paranoid self-surveillance (conscious or otherwise).[6] Wood identifies certain essential elements of the horror film that draw out the anxieties caused by surplus repression in the form of the monster, which in this context becomes "normality's shadow."[7] First, is the basic formula: "normality is threatened by the Monster."[8] Normality here is anything, good or bad, that stands in tension with a monstrous "other," or that which stands outside the circle of capitalist, patriarchal, monogamous, heterosexual, bourgeois normativity.[9] Second, there is an uncanny "re-emergence" of "all that our civilization represses or oppresses," the very substance of that which surfaces in the "nightmare" process.[10] Third, horror encourages a productive ambivalence—about good and evil, and about normativity its monsters.[11] *Angel* (1999–2004) is a series built upon the metaphorical possibilities of dreams, nightmares, and prophetic visions that dredge up the repressed/oppressed, yet the series' literal nightmares—in the form of the bad dreams characters are actually having—are not given solely as extensions of Whedon's universal humanistic concerns, those things we collectively fear. While Whedon's nightmares can and do function as nightmares for the audience, ones revealing the ideological tensions that are at the heart of horror film, they also constitute individual fears produced by a long-developed narrative familiarity and sympathy for Whedon's characters. There is a tension here. At one level, we respond as part of Wood's collective, horrified about the general possibilities offered by the character's dreams/nightmares; at another, we experience very personal fears for the characters themselves on the level of narrative and form.

This tension features prominently in episodes from the first two seasons of *Angel*. In season one's "Somnambulist" (1.11). Angel dreams that his soulless self, Angelus, is killing a woman who, in the waking world, is actually killed by another vampire. The vampire Angelus is one of the Whedonverse's most horrific characters, one of its worst nightmares: ruthless, sadistic, and gleefully engaged in staging the elaborate suffering of others. This resurgence of horror is felt by Angel as well as viewers who have seen the death and destruction he wrought in Sunnydale and through flashbacks of his history across the first three seasons of *Buffy the Vampire Slayer* (1997–2003). Witnessing Angelus kill the woman in Los Angeles in his dream is meant to be experienced as a nightmare for viewers who have acquired understanding of Angelus' potential and might respond with the fear and anxiety characteristic of horror. This response is magnified when Angel, awake, tells Cordelia and Wesley he has been having "killing dreams," and then corrects Cordelia when she calls them nightmares; Angel counters that they can't be nightmares because "I've enjoyed them."[12] The frisson produced by Angel's unexpected reaction of pleasure to this dream is thus a nightmare more directed towards the space of reception. Angelus on the loose is horrible enough, not only because of his potential for evil, but also because we know the guilt Angel carries for Angelus' actions. The suggestion that this, our nightmare of Angel, actually offers him the enjoyment more akin to fantasy—a break from his characteristic brooding guilt—is disturbing. Whedon and his writers have constructed our sympathy for Angel through three seasons of *Buffy* and the episodes of *Angel* leading to "Somnambulist," and our dread of what this might mean for Angel is as great as what it might mean for innocents. Add to this Angel's confession of enjoyment in a series that characterizes him as penitent and seeking atonement, and this nostalgic nightmare of violent pleasure takes on deeply unsettling associations for an audience who has empathized with his plight. The reactions of the character and viewers are both similar and distinct. We, along with Angel, feel relief at the awakening of his repressed desires; we, too, welcome the emergence of the id, controlled as it is through the horror of Angel's story. As Wood might tell us, Angel's enjoyment of violence is, at least temporarily, our own; we wish to break free from repression even when it is in our best interest not to. And horror delights in offering us the opportunity to find some pleasure in the forbidden. But viewers also have a discrete reaction to the nightmare born of a cultivated sympathy for Angel. We are both afraid *with* and afraid *for* the ensouled vampire.

We eventually learn what is going on in Angel's original dream in "Somnambulist" through another sleeping reveal. In the past, Angel turned a vampire named Penn, and because he was Penn's sire, Angel is supernaturally tied to him such that in his sleep he witnesses Penn's killing—as though he had access to a mystical drone equipped with a Go-Pro camera. It is Angel's ceaseless guilt over past actions that causes him to see himself rather than Penn doing the killing. And it is this unconscious, guilt-fueled role-playing that causes a "collective nightmare" for viewers. Because our sympathies lie with Angel, our distress over fears of the "other" are moderated by guilty complicity as viewers in the act of dream-killing. In catching the audience up in a sensation that equivocates between desire for, and repulsion regarding violence, the scenario here conjures the "struggle for recognition of all that our civilization represses or oppresses" which, according to Robin Wood, forms the "true subject of the horror genre."[13]

With Angel's "Somnambulist" dream and others in the analysis to follow here, we are provided with both the "emotional resonance" and "rocket launchers" that Joss Whedon claims are most important to him.[14] The dreams in *Angel's* second-season, three-episode reintroduction of his own vampire sire, Darla, seem meant to evoke an anxious response in viewers similar to that of "Somnambulist." "First Impressions" (2.3) opens with Angel finishing a karaoke number at demon-friend Lorne's karaoke bar, Caritas, followed by receiving some advice on music and romance from Lorne. The karaoke bar is a clever variation on the *Buffy the Vampire Slayer* episode, "Once More, with Feeling," which also equates singing with baring its characters' repressed fears and desires.[15] After leaving the stage, Angel finds Darla, and they begin dancing and making out. This is the point where viewers read the scene as a dream. We saw Darla die in season one of *Buffy*.[16] Angel is disturbed when he wakes, but doesn't share this with the Angel Investigations team, which goes after the demon problem of the week. Midway through the episode, Angel has another dream of Darla, in which she both seduces him and attempts to separate him from his friends. After the demon problem is solved, the episode ends with Angel having yet another very romantic dream of Darla—except viewers see that Darla is really in the bed *with* Angel, manipulating his subconscious while he sleeps.

The episode's title thus refers both to the mistaken first impressions over the informant, Jameel, who is really the demon Deevak, and to the initial impression shared by Angel and the viewer that Darla is only the stuff of dreams. In both cases, Angel's first impressions are false impressions that initially controvert reality. Darla has disguised herself in dream, and Deevak has disguised himself as Jameel. For both, the disguise is fortified by probability. Jameel's disguising of his identity as Daveek is convincing because of his successfully feigned fear. And Angel staked Darla in Sunnydale, so there is no reason to believe that she could return in reality. While Angel's enjoyment of Darla's sexual play in the dreams can be rationalized by a romantic history with his sire, or even his extreme loneliness in the City of Angels, the pleasure he receives from it parallels the disturbing fantasy of the killing-dream in "Somnambulist." The scene is thus set up so that viewers have a much more radical response to the implications around Darla's presence in dream and reality, reading the scenarios as nightmare rather than dream. Darla's presence can never be good, even if it is only in Angel's sleeping visions. Darla in the flesh adds a new level of horror. And Angel *unaware* of Darla in the flesh, potentially manipulating his dream sleep, tinkering in his unconscious like a puppet-master, is horror most magnified.

The elements of this dream are clearly intended to subvert horror conventions that the audience would normally use to navigate reality-versus-dreamscape. There is none of the iconography of horror—no storms, shadows, cemeteries, forests, or laboratories, not even *Angel*'s typical dark alleys or murky hotel hallways. There is a friendly monster nightclub with a karaoke stage and Angel's well-lit bedroom. Even when Angel later dreams of romantically enjoying some moon rays with Darla beside the pool, the scene does not evoke associations with iconic swimming pool scenes in films such as *Cat People* (Jacques Tourneur, 1943), where an unwitting swimmer is stalked by a shadowy panther; *A Nightmare on Elm Street 2: Freddy's Revenge* (Jack Sholder, 1985), where Freddy goes on a killing spree at a pool party; or *Let the Right One In* (Tomas Alfredson, 2008), where Eli dismembers her friend Oskar's bullies. First, the *mise-en-scène* in which Angel is placed uncharacteristically includes colorful beach towels, tropical flowers, Angel wearing swim trunks in Sunnydale High colors, and both of the dream lovers wearing sunglasses, all of which create a non-horrific absurdity that works against us reading this as a horror moment. Second, there can be no sense of a monster hiding in the water waiting to spring on the helpless victim because the only likely monster is in full view sporting a blue bikini and looking more like a character from *Beach Blanket Bingo* (William Asher, 1965) or *Boogie Nights* (Paul Thomas Anderson, 1997) than *Piranha* (Joe Dante, 1978).

"Untouched," (2.4) the second episode in Darla's reintroduction arc, clears up the mystery of what she is up to. In a meeting with Lilah Morgan at Wolfram & Hart, who have performed a raising ritual to resurrect Darla specifically to torture Angel, Darla tells Lilah she has been using Calynthia powder, a mystical drug, to manipulate his dreams. The viewer's position now fully shifts from a sympathetic experiencing of Angel's dreams as nightmares to mere observation of Angel's dreams, the reality of which are nightmarish. In other words, Darla as puppet-master of Angel through his unconscious promises both a dream world and a reality not under Angel's control. This shift may be an even worse position for viewers, who are privy to harmful secrets the other characters cannot know, and who are now in the impossible position of wanting to wake the sleeping vampire from his dreams.

"Dear Boy" (2.5) is the final episode in the restoration of Darla to Angel's life. While Angel is still meeting Darla in his dreams, in this episode he finally has a waking encounter with her. Having not gotten much sleep because of Darla's herbal manipulation, Angel becomes agitated after the team kills a thrall demon, and when he goes to walk it off, he sees Darla, who quickly disappears. Wesley and Cordelia suggest that his dreams and spotting of Darla are manifestations of his guilt for killing her three years earlier, a guilt for killing his sire, as Wesley notes, or a general guilt because, as Cordelia says, "Who loves guilt like you love guilt?"[17] Angel's broader guilt connects back to Darla as it is rooted in the evil he accomplished as Angelus, a legacy she bestowed upon him. The fault in their explanation is that if Angel's guilt for his deeds is nothing new, then all of his dreams should be a veritable plague of nightmares from his past. What Angel sees in his "Somnambulist" dream may be influenced by guilt over his history as Angelus, but it is still Penn's actions, not his own, that he is witnessing. And since the Darla dreams are unique to Angel's experience, another solution must be found. Viewers' understanding of this difference from the more generalized, allegorical use of dreams in horror is primarily responsible for the sympathy driving the horror created by Angel's dreams. His friends don't share this reaction because, ironically, they are looking for psychological answers to explain away what Angel has reported rather than considering supernatural or mystical possibilities. Only the audience knows that Darla is alive and how that came to be. Here, viewers' collective and individual anxieties, their fears *with* and *for* Angel coalesce, and they are situated alongside the horror audience who know the monster is "behind the door," but are helpless to warn the victim getting ready to open it. On top of this, viewers are wrapped up in the equivocal pleasure and dread that horror conventionally encourages in such situations.

Not only do we know Darla is behind that door and that Wolfram & Hart put her there, we soon learn their motives for doing so. Angel Investigations is putting a crimp in the activities of the even-more-evil-than-usual law firm, and Angelus would be a good addition to the Wolfram & Hart team, so they resurrect Darla to make this happen. Hearing this reinforces our fears that Angel will be drawn back into a life that he has worked so hard to atone for, but it is Angel himself who puts our fears to rest. Darla and Wolfram & Hart have laid a trap for him in which she poses as DeEtta Kramer, who accuses Angel of stalking her. He goes to the address for Mrs. Kramer, where domestic violence is staged for Angel's benefit. Angel rushes in to rescue her, and in this heroic action he nearly succumbs to the trap. Later, Darla attempts to seduce Angel to bring out the "moment of happiness" that will break the curse that restored his soul and thus cause him to transform back to Angelus. Angel does engage physically with Darla; it is clear from his dreams that relating sexually to her does not revolt Angel, but he does reject yielding to her intentions of turning him through "one little moment of happiness."[18] In this horror story, the monster Darla is overcome by an admission from Angel that also settles the fears of many viewers: "'You took me places, showed me things, huh? You blew the top off my head. But you never made me happy'."[19] Darla doesn't have what it takes to bring Angel perfect happiness, but when she says "There is nothing so lovely as dreams. Everything is in them, everything hidden," she serves as a reminder that Angel's dreams, our nightmares, are important.[20] Yet, these dreams are dramatically different from those most frequently seen in *Buffy the Vampire Slayer*. From the first episode of that show, when Giles challenges Buffy by saying, "The signs could be wrong. It's not as though you're having the nightmares ...",[21] we are given to understand that Buffy's dreams are at least a quality or symptom of her Slayer nature. However nightmarish, the dreams are prophetic, and once we know this, they diminish the horror reaction. Much like Cordelia's visions in Angel, Buffy's dreams are horrific to watch, but viewers are consciously interpreting what we know to be clues for future action, while for the characters the dreams/visions are an unconscious experience. In these cases, we are horrified *for* the dreamers, but less horrified *with* them. Since Angel does not have this power of prophecy, his dreams remain doubly horrifying. While this is also true for Wesley's dream in the season-three episode "Loyalty" (3.15), a specific prophecy is the cause of the dream that is horrifying for both the audience and the demon-hunting detective.

The prophecy in question is actually a bit of edited divination. An original prophecy from the Nyazian Scrolls foretold that Angel's son Connor would destroy the demon Sahjihan, but the demon managed to revise the prophecy to read, "The father will kill the son."[22] Only Wesley knows about this prophecy, and between secretly holding the information and trying to find a loophole, he is exhausted. And he dreams. But because of some cinematic dream trickery, we don't know we're witnessing a dream when "Loyalty" opens and Gunn and Fred walk in on Wesley sleeping. Gunn comments, "You got to admire the loyalty. All night here, hitting the books. Logging serious alone-time, delving into the secret mysteries of . . . Man, Wesley needs a life." Wesley wakes, and Angel walks in holding baby Connor. Like a doting new father, Angel says, "Do you wanna see Connor do something cool?" He then changes into vampire face and says, "I'm teaching him how to die!"[23] Blood begins to rush from Wesley's books, and we catch on that he is still asleep. As with Angel's dream in "Somnambulist," the sight of a vampire feeding on an innocent is gruesome, but the true horror results from the connection we have formed with this vampire. Angel dreams himself feeding on a victim, and in a moment exemplary of ambivalence in horror as described by Wood, we are horrified *by* Angel and *with* him. Since it is Wesley's dream of Angel feeding on a victim, and since Wesley is another character for whom our compassion has been well developed, our horror is magnified by the sympathy we now feel for both men.

A necessary element for the collective nightmare is collective familiarity. If we are universally afraid, we must have a universal familiarity with that which frightens us. And this suggests that the horror response is relative not only to cultural and ideological similarities more generally, but also the viewer's familiarity with the narrative, with the world that it portrays diegetically. Uninitiated viewers will see these dreams and react to the violence and blood of the vampire's action; this is a culturally universal reaction to the undead and all they allegorically represent. It is also the standard response of the horror film viewer who is ironically "attracted in these movies to characters and creatures they would run from in real life."[24] For the "drop-in" viewer, then, the attraction is the thrill of facing down on the screen this vampire who would maul an infant, grossly transgressing the cultural taboos that Wood traces around children. But within the larger culture watching *Angel* is a subgroup whose familiarity is so great the horror is complicated and heightened by the torment the dreams cause to those we know so well as to almost call them family.

A full treatment of the dreams/nightmares in *Buffy the Vampire Slayer* is beyond the scope of this essay, but some analysis is necessary as useful counterpoint to the discussion of *Angel*. Generally, it is the nature of the dreams and not the degree to which viewers are familiar with *Buffy the Vampire Slayer* that accounts for the lesser degree of horror experienced through that program's oneiric moments. This distinction is the rationale for beginning this analysis with and giving greater focus to the dreams from *Angel*. As already noted, the dreams in *Buffy* are often prophetic; this includes both the Slayer's dreams and those that come to other members of Buffy's circle. Once we know that, we attune our reaction to the dreams, rather than being simply horrified, our conscious understanding of the dreams' function adds the processes of interpretation and anticipation to our response. Even the *Buffy* episode "Nightmares" (1.10), obviously inspired by Wes Craven's late slasher film, *A Nightmare on Elm Street* (1984), fails to shift us fully out of the conscious interpretive mode and into the horror mode most of *Angel*'s dreams produce. While this episode allows us to witness the deepest fears of the program's main characters through their supernaturally induced dreams and be horrified with them—as indeed performance anxiety and clowns are almost universally feared—our supplementary and mindful inclination to read and interpret the dreams tempers the horror effect. In this way, the conscious interpretive mode of reception is something akin to the cognitive processes that theorist Noël Carroll (1990) attributes to spectatorial (and readerly) pleasure when confronting horror. Carroll's "thought theory" of horror holds that audiences come to horror because of the cognitive challenges and pleasures encouraged by a narrative revolving around curiosity and disclosure of monstrous objects or entities. Working within philosophical traditions tracing notions of spectatorial sublimity, Carroll summarizes the theory's potential potency for pleasurable reception of "art-horror" in saying that the thought theory "offers an operational construction of what authors grope at with notions like 'aesthetic distance'."[25]

By season three our relationship with Buffy Summers has developed to the point at which we both empathize with her pain and more fully experience her horror. When we see her at one of her lowest points in the series at the beginning of this season, living in self-inflicted isolation in Los Angeles suffering the loss of Angel and the guilt of having been the hand that killed him, we are positioned for the same sympathetic reaction to her nightmares as we feel in response to Angel's dreams. And like the most anxiety-producing of Angel's dreams, Buffy's come in a series of three episodes, "Anne" (3.1), "Dead Man's Party" (3.2) and "Faith, Hope, and Trick" (3.3). Aside from the three mini-arcs both series use to fully develop introductions to their seasons' primary conflicts, we find the title characters in both *Angel* and *Buffy the Vampire Slayer* suffering in isolation, real or figurative, unwilling or unable to fully reveal to their friends the depth of their anguish. In Angel's case, it is the torture of having Darla back in his life. For Buffy, it is the agony of having killed and lost the man she loved.

We know Buffy is dreaming in the opening scene of "Anne" even before we know she's living in LA under an assumed name. She must be dreaming because she is on a beach and approached by Angel, whom she killed in the last episode of season two. The exchange between the two is short.

> Buffy: "Stay with me."
> Angel: "That's the point. I'll never leave. Not even if you kill me."[26]

Buffy wakes from the dream horrified. She has already experienced the waking nightmare of having to kill her lover after he turns evil. This, more than any action we've thus far seen the Slayer take, shows just how great is the burden of being the chosen one. The dream and the guilt we know it implies for Buffy makes seeing her sleepwalk through life as Anne even more appalling, more horrifying. We are happy to see Buffy return to Sunnydale in "Dead Man's Party," but it is clear she hasn't shaken the weight of Angel's loss, because in that episode's dream she sees him again as she walks around an empty Sunnydale High campus. Her return to Sunnydale has not alleviated her loneliness; indeed, it seems to have intensified as her mother and her friends are still angry at her for running away after killing Angel. She is lonely and vulnerable in the same way Angel is lonely and vulnerable when he dreams of Darla. Both characters are isolated in the realm of dream with lovers who isolate (or, in the case of Darla, *would* isolate) them in reality. The final dream in this three-episode introduction to season three again features Angel, but this time, the Scooby Gang are there as well, standing on the edges of the dance floor at the Bronze as observers. When the ring Angel gave her in "Surprise" (2.13) drops from her finger to the dance floor, seeming to signify a break between them—and Buffy tells Angel, "I had to," and he replies with "Go to Hell. I did"[27]—our initial horror over Buffy's pain and Angel's cruelty quickly subsides. Buffy goes finally to tell Giles why she had to kill Angel, and with that, her waking and sleeping nightmare seems to find its end: "I've been holding on to that for so long—felt good to get it out."

There are many dreams in *Buffy the Vampire Slayer* and *Angel* not covered in this essay. Most of those dreams provide what Jason Mittell calls "narrative pyrotechnics,"[28] but because they are so deeply tied to the stories being written, our job as viewers is to try to follow as the narrative is built. Dreams in these series create emotional responses, but that effect is shared with the narrative responsibility of interpretation. While the dreams discussed here are also important to their respective narratives, the horror we feel on behalf of the characters and (because of our sympathy for them) ourselves is the primary and initial reaction we experience. J.P. Telotte notes that, "every horror film becomes something of a reflexive text, referring back not only to its own generic workings, but also to its audience which, through its visual participation in the events unfolded, contributes to their impact and affirms man's [sic] capacity to bear with such traumatic encounters."[29] In their treatment of horror conventions through dreams and nightmares, *Buffy the Vampire Slayer* and *Angel* ask us not only to participate in the "events unfolding," but also to suffer their effects.

Notes

1. Robin Wood, *Hollywood from Vietnam to Reagan . . . and Beyond* (New York: Columbia University Press, 2003), 70.
2. *Buffy the Vampire Slayer,* "Bring on the Night." Directed by David Grossman. Written by Marti Noxon and Douglas Petrie. UPN. December 17, 2002. [Editors' note: There is no evidence that Whedon or season seven co-show-runner Marti Noxon intended Principal Robin Wood's name as an allusion to

the famous theorist. The name was selected for its gender-neutral qualities, as the character had not yet been cast.]

3. See Hugo Munsterberg, *The Film: A Psychological Study* (1916) (New York: Dover, 2012).
4. Robin Wood, ibid., 70.
5. Ibid., 70.
6. Robin Wood, "An Introduction to the American Horror Film," *Planks of Reason: Essays on the Horror Film*, edited by Barry Keith Grant, and Christopher Sharrett, (Lanham, MD: Scarecrow Press, 2004), 108.
7. Ibid., 119.
8. Robin Wood, "An Introduction to the American Horror Film," in *American Nightmare: Essays on the Horror Film*, edited by Andrew Britton, Richard Lippe, Tony Williams, and Robin Wood (Toronto: Festival of Festivals, 1979), 14.
9. Robin Wood, "An Introduction to the American Horror Film," *Planks of Reason: Essays on the Horror Film*," 108.
10. Robin Wood, "An Introduction to the American Horror Film," in *American Nightmare: Essays on the Horror Film*, 10.
11. Ibid., 14.
12. Angel. "Somnambulist." Directed by Winrich Kolbe. Written by Tim Minear. WB. January 18, 2000.
13. Robin Wood, "An Introduction to the American Horror Film," in *American Nightmare: Essays on the Horror Film*, 28.
14. Joss Whedon. Audio Commentary for "Innocence." *Buffy the Vampire Slayer: The Complete Second Season* on DVD. Fox, 2002. DVD.
15. See Anne Golden's chapter in this collection for an extended discussion of song in "Once More, with Feeling" as the return of the repressed. [Ed.]
16. Angel kills Darla in the *Buffy the Vampire Slayer* episode "Angel" (1.6), also the episode in which we learn that she was Angel's sire.
17. *Angel*. "Dear Boy." Directed by David Greenwalt. Written by David Greenwalt. WB. October 24, 2000.
18. *Buffy the Vampire Slayer*. "Innocence." Directed by Joss Whedon. Written by Joss Whedon. WB. January 20, 1998.
19. *Angel*. "Dear Boy." Directed by David Greenwalt. Written by David Greenwalt. WB. October 24, 2000.
20. *Angel*. "Untouched." Directed by Joss Whedon. Written by Mere Smith. WB. October 17, 2000.
21. *Buffy the Vampire Slayer*. "Welcome to the Hellmouth." Directed by Charles Martin Smith. Written by Joss Whedon. March 10, 1997.
22. *Angel*. "Couplet." Directed by Tim Minear. Written by Tim Minear and Jeffrey Bell. WB. February 18, 2002.
23. *Angel*. "Loyalty." Directed by James A. Contner. Written by Mere Smith. WB February 25, 2002.

24. Lester Friedman, et al., *An Introduction to Film Genres* (New York: W.W. Norton and Company, 2013), 369.

25. Noël Carroll, *The Philosophy of Horror, or Paradoxes of the Heart* (London and New York: Routledge, 1990), 10–11.

26. *Buffy the Vampire Slayer.* "Anne." Directed by Joss Whedon. Written by Joss Whedon. WB. September 29, 1998.

27. *Buffy the Vampire Slayer.* "Faith, Hope & Trick." Directed by James Contner. Written by David Greenwalt. WB. October 13, 1998.

28. Jason Mittell. "Narrative Complexity in Contemporary American Television," *The Velvet Light Trap* 58 (2006), 32.

29. J.P. Telotte. "Through a Pumpkin's Eye: The Reflexive Nature of Horror," *Literature/Film Quarterly* 10, no. 3 (1982). 139–49.

6

Dollhouse's Terrible Places: Hauntings, Abjection, and the Repressed

Bronwen Calvert

Joss Whedon's *Dollhouse* (2009 – 10), though it ran for only two seasons, is a text that continues to attract critical attention. Its complex narrative and rich thematic structures encourage critical engagement in a variety of ways. For example, the collection *Joss Whedon's Dollhouse* (2014) includes chapters on abuse and transgression, romance, viewing pleasure, posthumanism, intertexts, race and representation, among others.[1] Much close analysis of the series has focused on its controversial content which includes exploitation, sex work, human trafficking, commodification of bodies and identities, and the enforced breakdown of identity.[2] Indeed, the creative team's treatment of these themes has led to accusations that the series reinforces the troubling attitudes it purports to expose[3] and it is certainly possible to argue that the show exploits the audience-as-voyeur positioning for dramatic purposes.[4] It should not be surprising that audiences find *Dollhouse* problematic and disturbing: the premise of the series, that technology can remove an individual's personality and imprint it with a new one, is immediately frightening. As the overarching narrative presents increasingly manipulative and destructive uses for that imprinting technology, it points clearly to themes and tropes of horror. These include aspects of possession (of bodies and of identities), the representation of empty bodies that stand as ghost or as zombie figures, and the ominous encounters of nightmares or dreamscapes.

The series' storylines focus on the Los Angeles Dollhouse, one of several centers operating throughout the world, controlled by the Rossum Corporation.[5] The central character, code-named Echo, has signed herself over to the Dollhouse for a five-year period, during which her own personality as Caroline Farrell is removed, and she is imprinted with a series of constructed, artificial personalities. While imprinted, Echo and others are called "Actives"; this reflects the way in which they are activated or programmed with these artificial personalities in order to fulfil the wishes of Rossum's clients. Echo turns out to have special capabilities and, by the second season, retains and alternates imprinted personalities at will. We see other characters shifting between 'tabula rasa' Doll state and a variety of Active identities. As indicated by Echo's name and role particularly, the series builds aspects of horror into its themes relating to the "uncanny" and "abject" bodies of the Doll/Active characters and the dystopian possibilities of the imprinting technology that overwrites personalities.[6] Such elements of horror are foregrounded in performance aspects that see these uncanny bodies in a range of troubling situations, including the dramatization of coercion, rape, and murder. Horror in this series is also produced through its setting, though this aspect tends to be underplayed in reviews or analysis. My focus here is on those aspects of *Dollhouse*'s setting, such as its interior spaces and *mise-en-scène*, that work to produce a variety of horror-related effects, and reinforce readings of horror tropes in relation to the series narrative as a whole. Throughout the series, the House's spaces connect thematically with spaces of horror, such as the haunted house, the asylum, or the prison, and these spaces function both as part of the everyday world and as locations for monstrous reversals of norms and expectations.

The Dollhouse and Spaces of Horror

As Kristopher Woofter suggests, there are parallels between *Dollhouse* and the overt horror of *Cabin in the Woods* (Drew Goddard, 2012) in terms of series' and film's emphasis on "the ethics of visual and virtual technologies" with "chilly creator types observ[ing] their made-to-order fantasy constructs out in the field".[7] There are parallels, too, in the horror tropes of place that appear in both narratives. This is excessively so in *Cabin*, where in one much-discussed scene characters descend the stairs to the horror-cliché basement to find a mass of visual cues to other horror tropes or clichés. Such tropes are dealt with more mutedly in *Dollhouse*, where visual and narrative elements of horror sit among other elements that are more closely associated with science fiction, and that blend into the overall series' aesthetic and narrative arc(s). However subtle they may be, *Dollhouse*'s horror elements serve to expose the fearful foundations of its premise and to highlight particular aspects of the series' narrative strategies and thematic preoccupations.

In Whedon's works in general, certain key settings recur through a narrative. Settings like the Summers house and the school library in *Buffy the Vampire Slayer* (1997–2003), the Hyperion hotel in *Angel* (1999–2004), and the ship *Serenity* in *Firefly* (2002–3) fulfil important functions in the integration and bonding of character groups within the narratives, and often serve additionally as actual or substitute domestic spaces. In contrast, *Dollhouse*'s key setting, the Los Angeles House, is a location for the *dis*integration of identity and morality, and thus a significant aspect of the series' use of horror of place. The L.A. House assumes the (Freudian) status of uncanny, "unhomely" haunted house, incorporating aspects of the Gothic such as themes of imprisonment, confinement, and "interiority".[8] As Robin Wood notes, the family, and its disintegration, has an "overwhelmingly consistent" connection to thematic developments around the notion of home and of monstrosity in the (American) horror film.[9] Horror monsters "are [...] shown as products of the family" and their supposedly safe and secure houses become the location of dreadful and monstrous acts.[10] The L.A. Dollhouse follows this pattern. The House resists the status of "home" partly through the corporate/institutional/technological functions of its spaces, and partly through how these spaces affect those who inhabit them. The House is a location where traditional notions of "family" are not permitted; presumably, this prohibition is replicated across all Rossum Dollhouses. When, for example, some of the Dolls are seen consistently to seek each other's company, they are described as "grouping [...] flocking [...]" and likened to "the herd" and to "bison."[11] Their behavior is analyzed and treated as a problem.[12] And in contrast to other Whedon narratives, the House's regular employees fail to form any sort of "chosen family"; instead we can observe uneasy and shifting connections and loyalties (e.g., between Adelle De Witt and Topher, Topher and Boyd, Boyd and Claire Saunders), which are always on the verge of falling apart.[13]

In line with Wood's analysis, the House becomes, in Carol Clover's terms, a "terrible place," a "not-home,"[14] the site of violence, abjection, and terror. Both the erased Dolls and the imprinted Actives can be viewed as ghosts, a point that is emphasized when Dolls are imprinted as individuals who have died.[15] Such thematic connections are brought to an extreme in "Epitaph One" (1.13),[16] in which the episode's plot and *mise-en-scène* underline the House's status as "haunted" and its propensity for ghostly visitations. This episode explicitly frames the location of the House and its spaces as a haunted house whose inhabitants are stalked and killed. At the same time, the House becomes a "terrible place" of secrets, complete with resident ghost in the form of Whiskey/Claire Saunders. Place and its relation to horror are also examined in "The Attic,"[17] where repressed terrors erupt in nightmare sequences within a series of virtual locations. Examining *Dollhouse* in this way underlines the ways it follows horror narratives in being "very much about ambiance, place, surroundings and environment."[18]

Uncanny locations, such as the haunted house, or the institution (the asylum, the prison, the boarding school) are established settings for explorations of "returning history and constrictive geography"[19] in horror/Gothic narratives on the page, in the cinema, or on the television screen. As Rebecca Williams notes, "television horror is linked to the spatial"[20] through such features as the historical sense of place in television narratives, and specific filming locations in television production. *Dollhouse*—possibly deliberately, since the underlying premise of the series is the erasure of an individual's past—avoids much sense of history as it relates to place, but maintains a marked focus on the narrative setting and filming location of the Los Angeles House.[21] The action of the series takes place in, and certainly centres around, the physical and architectural space of this particular Dollhouse. The rooms of the main House set were designed very deliberately to reflect a "minimalist Japanese," spa-like aesthetic,[22] with spaces associated with therapy (yoga, tai chi, massage), technology (the programming suite, the imprint chair), and the corporate (shiny lobbies, elevators, and offices). These form an uneasy combination of asylum, prison, office, hotel, and spa; additionally, the entire House is hidden underground, beneath a high-rise office building, a feature that once again calls attention to the untypical, uneasy positioning of these spaces.[23] The institutional overtones of the House's physical space, in particular, mark an extreme version of the therapeutic establishment, where efforts are made "to impose order on the chaos indicated by disruption of [the self]. Order is achieved through structuring therapeutic settings, in both their architectural layout and the permissible use of space."[24] The institution itself is a regular setting for horror-inflected narratives in cinema and television with its "regulated spaces," its boundaries and borders that are constantly "prone to rupture,"[25]

A typical *Dollhouse* episode narrative begins and ends in the House's spaces, while different storylines may follow an Active on a particular client engagement, and so depart the House itself. Dolls not on engagement are located in other rooms in the House, carrying out various simple, repetitive tasks such as painting, exercizing, having massages or medical examinations, showering, eating, and sleeping. The House contains places for its employees, too, such as Adelle DeWitt's or Topher Brink's office spaces, or Dr Claire Saunders' examination room. The House's uncanny status derives in part from this strange combination of everyday, ordinary space (an employee's workplace) and different, separated or segregated space (the imprint room, the Dolls' sleeping pods), as well as from the repetition of the activities carried out in the spaces (activities like the yoga and tai chi, as well as the persistent wiping and imprinting of the Dolls). The civilized and spa-like veneer of the L.A. House is the locus for dreadful violations and horrific possibilities. Thus, as Catherine Pugh argues, the space fosters a sense of "unease"; the House, simultaneously "retreat" and "asylum," incorporates "institution and horror discourse."[26] The status of the Dollhouse as a whole is hidden, secretive, and repressed. While the television audience is able to see inside the House and follow its activities, this place and its activities are kept hidden—literally buried beneath the ground level—from the rest of the world.

Houses, as well as institutions, have a particular status in the uncanny representations of horror texts. As Peter Hutchings explains, "we can understand the uncanny as a process by which the return of secrets from the past, which are often but not always psychological secrets, is dramatised via the representation of the house."[27] In the horror text it is the (Gothic, haunted) house itself that contains and reveals dreadful secrets in, for example, hidden rooms, passageways, secrets in attics and basements. This is certainly the case for the L.A. House, which contains, masks, and hides all manner of horrifying secrets in its office and living/ institutional spaces. The House is the site of the officially sanctioned recruitment of new Dolls and of the wiping/imprinting process that is depicted as painful and distressing. It is likewise the site of hidden crimes, such as the rape of the Doll Sierra by her "handler" Hearn, the individual she is programmed to trust.[28] That example, horrifying in itself, also highlights the horror and abjection inherent in all the Dollhouse's transactions involving the Doll/Actives. Any storyline that follows an Active on engagement will feature the imprinting room, where the Doll receives the Active personality imprint and has that imprint removed; this is a repeated enactment of coercion and abjection. There is, additionally, a strong element of sexual violation bound up in the imprinting process and its aims and function. Because so many of the Dolls' "Active engagements" are sexual in nature (coded "romantic" in House terminology), the imprinting process becomes a tool in that cycle of coercion and abjection. After an engagement, when an Active is "wiped" and returned to Doll state, Doll and programmer repeat a standard script: "Did I fall asleep?" "For a little while." This situates the Doll/Active's coercion, abjection, and violation within the realm of sleep and dream; this realm is invaded and made monstrous through the imprinting process and the activities of the Dollhouse.[29]

The House locations are sometimes employed as ironic counterpoint to the disturbing and transgressive activities carried out there. This is especially apparent in the scene in which Rossum executive Ambrose turns up in the kitchens, in the body of the Doll Victor, to announce to Adelle DeWitt that the Dollhouse now offers its clients "complete anatomy upgrades."[30] Ambrose/Victor's matter-of-fact delivery, and his unusual choice of location for this meeting with De Witt, contrasts disturbingly with the dreadful implications of the process he is outlining (a proposal to sell the Dolls themselves to clients wishing to pay for the "upgrade" service).[31] In other examples, the House is the location for enactments of the "ruptured" institutional order. It becomes a murderous "terrible place" when infiltrated (more than once) by the dangerously unstable Doll Alpha, who maims and kills.[32] Similar "rupture" occurs when Alpha's modifications cause Dolls to attack their handlers and other staff, in a situation that includes aspects of the horror narrative's attacks by zombies or other possessed bodies.[33] In each of these examples, "rupture" is the appropriate description, since the deadly attacks come from people occupying space within the House's institutional location.

"Epitaph One": Memory in the House of Horror

For most of its two seasons, *Dollhouse* maintains its representation of the House as a coded space of horror, a space that encompasses aspects of haunted house and bizarre institution, and oscillates between elements of the everyday and the extraordinary. In certain episodes, however, the House moves from being a symbolic "haunted" place to serve as a literal, tangible location in which hauntings and horrible occurrences take place. Through visual, aural, and narrative techniques, the House is represented as a horror-film haunted house in the season 1 finale "Epitaph One"; in season 2's "The Attic," virtual spaces become similarly haunted places of horror. In both these episodes, horror features become overt, and the technique offers a way for the series writers and the regular audience to uncover aspects of horror that were always part of the Dollhouse and its activities. In such instances, the space of the House, and its representation in the narrative, connect with another facet of horror narrative, "one of spaces, and of doors opening [. . .] to other spaces";[34] in the context of the haunted house, of "the opening of doors or basements from the realm of the domestic into the abject spaces of hell and the underworld."[35] Such narratives reveal "two zones," the second of which is "sublime, terrifying, chaotic" and replete with "Otherness."[36] For *Dollhouse*, the overt representation of the House as a haunted place overlays this chaotic second zone onto the space of the House itself.

In "Epitaph One," the combination of flashforward and flashback techniques highlights the narrative transformation of the L.A. House into an overt representation of haunted house/terrible place. The episode disorients the regular viewer by moving the series narrative forward a number of years, to a time period in which a technological apocalypse has wiped or forcibly re-imprinted the minds of most of the population. A group of people who retain their own identities—"actuals" in their terminology—stumble upon the L.A. House while searching for an underground hideout where the destructive technology cannot reach them. Their one-syllable names—Mag, Zone, Lynn, Griff—echo the Doll call signs.[37] The majority of the action in "Epitaph One" takes place in the Dollhouse location, the same space that regular viewers of the series are used to, even though the timeline, the characters, and the episode storyline are completely unfamiliar, and the usual sets (the programming suite, the shower room) are made unfamiliar or uncanny. In this way the episode "both ruptures the world of the show and denies viewers their familiarity with that world."[38]

Accentuating the connection with horror *mise-en-scène* in this episode, the spaces of the House are shown in very different ways from the other twelve episodes in the season; indeed, since "the main story is filmed on video" there are immediately "clear aesthetic distinctions" between the present and future narratives.[39] In contrast to the lighter, open spaces of the present-day narrative, the "actuals" in the future narrative move through spaces that are dark, confusing, and threatening. Sound is cacophonic, and lighting creates extremes of contrast, with flares or torch beams illuminating only parts of the Dollhouse spaces—references to the sound and lighting effects of screen horror. The characters have trouble describing or classifying the spaces they find; for example, the programming suite can only be explained as "some kind of romper room? Must have been a daycare." Other spaces come to have radically different functions in this new and appalling future narrative where, for example, the shower room and kitchen become murder scenes. Horror *mise-en-scène* is accentuated in the scene in which the character Lynn discovers hot water in the shower room, takes off her clothes to bathe, and is killed by an unseen assailant. The peril of Lynn's naked vulnerability, the dim and obscuring lighting (the only light source in this scene is a small flashlight), and the ominous musical score (pulsing beats that signify suspense) all encourage the viewer to make connections with such classic horror works as *Psycho* (Alfred Hitchcock, 1960). The addition of an unseen killer preying on the group is a similar link to a familiar horror trope, which reinforces the positioning of the House as a literal house of horror, Clover's "terrible place."[40]

In horror narratives, especially Gothic horror, memory, secrets, and the past have significance. The House in "Epitaph One" becomes a place of memory in a number of ways, representing the uncovering of secrets in the form of a series of "ghostly" visitations through memory imprints and the return of a Doll character to the narrative. These aspects of the episode reinforce the Gothic horror trope of "the return of secrets from the past [. . .] dramatised via the representation of the house."[41] However, in the case of *Dollhouse*, the repression and uncovering of secrets works a little differently. The secrets in question are memories that have been "repressed" in the sense that they have been removed from an individual's personality. Memory and personality still exist on a form of hard drive, and can be accessed and restored. If memory is "repressed" in a way that is consistent with tropes of horror, then it is a specifically *technological* repression. However, this process is still signalled as a form of the Gothic/horror trope in which a character's discovery of a house's hidden rooms is linked to the recovery of whatever horrific memory that character has repressed.[42] The imprinting room takes the status of "hidden room," and the imprinting chair is the means by which (repressed) memory is retrieved.[43] Since the "actuals" have rejected technology, and fear it as the means by which they could be forcibly wiped and imprinted, both room and chair take on frightening and ominous connotations. Fear and horror are also evoked in the repeated imprinting of "Mr Miller," a man whose identity has been "wiped" and who is now a passive "dumbshow" reminiscent of the Dolls. This character becomes a disturbing focus as the abject, empty body that is overwritten time and again with a different personality. His is a body and an identity that has been abused before the timescale of the episode, but rather than react with pity, the "actual" characters appear repulsed by his presence among them; Zone, for example, objects to "dragging that dumbshow around [. . .] we don't go near those freaks of nature" and he suggests that Mr Miller should be "put out of his misery." Mr Miller's abject, empty, and violated body is a reminder of the catastrophic effects of the imprinting war, and of the possibility that any of the "actuals" could be similarly "printed" or "wiped." And, despite their distaste, when the "actuals" hope that they can gain information about a potential place of refuge, they are only too willing to use Mr Miller's empty body as a temporary location for the variety of memories stored in the imprinting room.[44] Once again, the evident horror inflection of these activities draw connections with other episodes when Dolls are imprinted as different Active identities.

The House's haunting through memory and the past is realized literally through the character Whiskey, who appears mid-way through the episode, terrifying the group of "actuals," "like a ghost in the ruins of the Dollhouse".[45] She is even costumed appropriately in a long, flowing white dress with Goth-inspired smudgy eyeliner (see Figure 6.1). Her repetitive speech and behavior is ghostlike, and Zone gives an accurate summary of her abject status when he refers to her as "empty" and as a "wind-up doll." Indeed she was a Doll, though this piece of information is withheld from the regular viewer until the penultimate episode of season 1. In a sense, Whiskey figures as the Dollhouse's repressed history, the past that now exists as a series of memory imprints. We might see in Whiskey a form of representation in which this one character evokes all Dolls. Whiskey also evokes her former imprinted identity as the person known as Dr Claire Saunders. However, even that identity bears aspects of the ghostly, since "Claire Saunders" was never an authentic, "actual" personality—although she appeared, and was treated by others working in the Dollhouse, as such—but a constructed personality based on the (male, deceased) Dr Saunders. In this sense, "Claire" is a resurrected, undead identity, while "Whiskey" is a blank, Doll self, and both abject identities are present in Whiskey's representation in "Epitaph One." This Doll character's appearance as Whiskey, together with the memory of her history as Claire, strongly emphasizes the horror that is inherent in all the appearances of Dolls and created Active personalities in the series.

Figure 6.1   Whiskey as ghost.

Throughout "Epitaph One," memories and the past are as Echo described the Dolls' original personalities, "lost [...] not gone."[46] Paradoxically, it is through engagement with the dreaded "tech," the imprinting chair and its archives of memory imprints and original personalities, that the "actuals" are able to uncover the past, connect present and future through the original imprint of Echo/Caroline, and begin to move beyond the haunted House. The *mise-en-scène* of the final sequences in this episode reflects this, from the climb through the elevator shaft into the brightly sunlit space of De Witt's former office, to the focus on a wall of photographs headed by the lettering "To Remember" (both memorial and command), and finally to the disappearance of the characters as they continue to climb upwards, towards the future and "Safe Haven" in an enactment of "utopic desire"[47] that overlays the preceding dark, haunted, and horror-filled sequences.

"The Attic": Virtuality and Nightmare

The horror trope of the hidden room is present once again in the virtual space known as "the Attic," which features as the equivalent of a prison in the Dollhouse. We might consider the Attic in terms of the hidden room that "features [...] as an expression of something that has been repressed psychologically by the characters associated with the house."[48] If the Attic is a space that marks such repression, it is perhaps more obviously associated with secrets that the Rossum Corporation *want* to keep repressed or hidden. As DeWitt deduces, "the Attic is where Rossum is keeping some of its darkest secrets";[49] further, she describes it as "whatever hell you imagine," clearly signalling its virtual-nightmare aspect. Before the episode that uncovers the virtual world and its workings, the Attic exists in the narrative as a hidden space, specifically one that is disavowed by the House's employees, who rarely refer to it. The Attic as concept features dramatically at the end of "A Spy in the House of Love" (1.9) when Dominic is sent to the Attic as punishment for betraying Rossum. From visual and other cues in the scene in which he is prepared for his fate by having his personality wiped, it is evident that he is being dispatched to a terrifying, horrific place, though its literal space is not yet revealed. Dominic is not merely seated in, but is tied to the imprinting chair; the room is darkened, lit only with blue lights and flashes from the electrical impulses that erase Dominic's identity. The soundtrack combines Dominic's screams with a drum-heavy musical score, further contributing to the horror cues. By season 2, when Echo, Sierra/Priya and Victor/Tony are all sent to the Attic on the apparently vindictive wishes of DeWitt, the audience is primed to think of this place as a hidden room of horror.

Further, the Attic's status as horror "hidden room" is doubled: it is a hidden virtual and physical space. It must have a location in the physical world, somewhere within the Dollhouse itself, firstly because the living bodies whose minds are incarcerated in the Attic must be kept somewhere, and secondly because Rossum is using the energy generated by these bodies to power its computer mainframe. There are aspects of horror once again in the visual presentation of these inert bodies, wrapped in transparent plastic on fluid-filled medical trolleys that "simultaneously evoke coffin and womb,"[50] with metal skewers stuck into their heads. The visual cues combine abject body horror and features of the institution (the prison, the hospital), with their horror-trope connotations. The visual impact of the bodies of Echo, Sierra, and Victor encased in plastic, as we see in Figure 6.2, encourage connections with aspects of science fiction cinema's body horror, such as the alien pods of *Invasion of the Body Snatchers* (Philip Kaufman, 1978) or *Alien* (Ridley Scott, 1979), or the technological pods of *The Matrix* (The Wachowskis, 1999). The latter narrative is also evoked in the Attic's existence as a form of

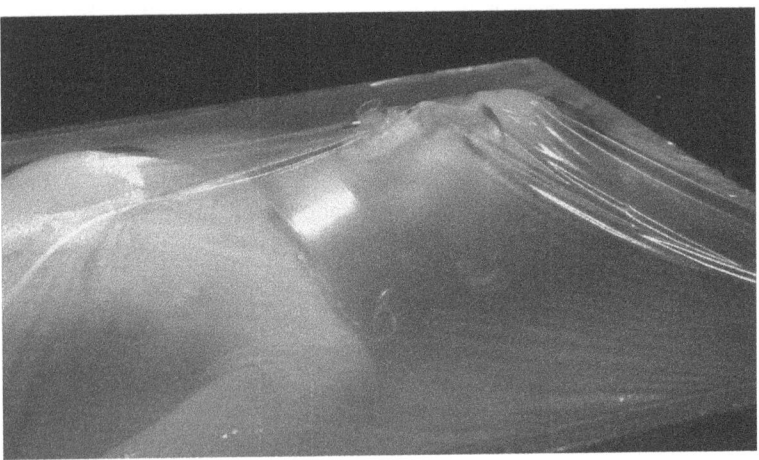

Figure 6.2 Echo, wrapped in plastic.

116

human-powered computer mainframe, in which the minds of those inside its virtual spaces generate energy to power Rossum's physical ones. Energy is generated through feedback loops that repeat and enact individuals' greatest fears: Echo's failure to save her friends and fellow Dolls; Sierra/ Priya's murder of her Rossum-approved rapist, Nolan Kinnard;[51] Victor/ Tony's military experiences;[52] a Japanese employee's realization that he has become a weak link in Rossum's mainframe.

The virtual space of the Attic is thus a dream/nightmare space of repressed terrors, located within the mind of each individual who is connected to the mainframe. However, as in other narratives of virtual reality, occurrences in dream space are represented as embodied experiences that have effects on the physical body. All these characters' nightmare scenarios are presented through confusing fast cutting and partial viewpoints, in environments with extremes of light (Tony's desert battlefield, the Japanese employee's sushi restaurant) or dark (Priya's room, Echo's jumbled assortment of memories).[53] Specific horror tropes are located very clearly in the content and presentation of Sierra/Priya and the Japanese employee's nightmares. Sierra/Priya's takes the form of a zombie attack in which Kinnard's corpse is reanimated. The Japanese employee is literally consumed by the Rossum Corporation, as Echo discovers that the man's severed legs are the source of the delicious sushi he is eating. And this episode, like "Epitaph One," includes the trope of the menacing, mysterious and faceless killer who preys on the group, picking them off one by one. Here, the trope is both utilized, with the killer "Arcane" attacking various characters inside the virtual space, and undercut, when he is revealed to be the alter ego of nerdy Clyde, Rossum founder and inventor of the imprint technology. At this point, the episode narrative circles back to the end of the previous season, as the future world that was explored in "Epitaph One" appears in "The Attic" as Clyde's nightmare place. The connection of these specific places of shock and terror with established horror tropes and themes thus serves to underline the horror that is inherent in *Dollhouse*'s developing storyline about the impending apocalypse, and serves additionally to underline the horror inherent in *Dollhouse*'s conceit as a whole.

The use of horror themes in *Dollhouse* contributes strongly to the effect of this television text on the viewer. That the unease identified by successive viewers has its source in the series' unsettling imagery of horror is, I would argue, significant. The places of horror within *Dollhouse*'s two seasons reflect established tropes: the institution, the haunted house, the nightmare, degeneration, apocalypse. Inside these places, fearful, abject, and disturbing narratives play out. In the developing analysis of television horror, it is perhaps especially useful to examine those narratives that do not overtly position themselves as horror texts, but that nevertheless make effective (implicit and explicit) use of horror tropes. The fact that *Dollhouse* comes to present these tropes more directly at the end of each season suggests that, at these key points, the narrative trajectory moves towards a more overtly realized representation of horror. In this way, horror tropes and themes work with, and within, the narrative, accentuating and emphasizing aspects of its overall trajectory.

Notes

1. Sherry Ginn, Alyson R. Buckman, and Heather M. Porter (eds), *Joss Whedon's Dollhouse* (Lanham, MD: Rowman & Littlefield, 2014).
2. Eve Bennett, "Deconstructing the Dream Factory: Personal Fantasy and Corporate Manipulation in Joss Whedon's *Dollhouse*," *Slayage: The Journal of Whedon Studies* 9, no. 1 (2011): n.p.; Samira Nadkarni, "'In My House and Therefore in My Care': Transgressive Mothering, Abuse and Embodiment," in *Joss Whedon's Dollhouse: Confounding Purpose, Confusing Identity*, ed. Sherry Ginn, Alyson R. Buckman, and Heather M. Porter (Lanham MD: Rowman & Littlefield, 2014), 81–95; Sharon Sutherland and Susan Swan, "'There's No Me; I'm Just a Container': Law and the Loss of Personhood in *Dollhouse*," in *Reading Joss Whedon*, ed. Rhonda V. Wilcox et al. (Syracuse NY: Syracuse University Press, 2014); Ananya Mukherjea, "Somebody's Asian on TV: Sierra/Priya and the Politics of Representation," in *Joss Whedon's Dollhouse*, ed. Ginn, Buckman, and Porter, 65–80.
3. Meloukhia, "Much Ado about *Dollhouse* [Television Tuesday]," Deeply Problematic, 1 September 2009, www.deeplyproblematic.com/2009/09/much-ado-about-dollhouse-television.html; Maureen Ryan, "Sex, Secrets and Dollhouse: Interview with Joss Whedon," *Chicago Tribune*, 3 December 2009, http://featuresblogs.chicagotribune.com/entertainment_tv/2009/12/dollhouse-fox-joss-whedon.html.
4. Bennett, "Deconstructing"; Don Tresca, "'Fantasy Is Their Business, But It Is Not Their Purpose': The Metaphor of *Dollhouse*," in *Joss Whedon: The Complete Companion*, ed. Mary Alice Money (London: Titan Books/Popmatters, 2012), 411–25; Bronwen Calvert, "'Who Did They Make Me This Time?': Viewing Pleasure and Horror," in *Joss Whedon's Dollhouse*, ed. Ginn, Buckman, and Porter, 113–26.

5. K. Dale Koontz, "Czech Mate: Whedon, Čapek, and the Foundations of *Dollhouse*," *Slayage: The Journal of Whedon Studies* 8, no. 2–3 (2010): n. p. As Koontz notes, the naming of the corporation deliberately invokes aspects of Čapekapek's drama R.U.R. [Rossum's Universal Robots] (1920). Čapekapek's use of the word "roboti' (robot), derived from the Czech "robota" (forced labour) and "rab" (slave), was adopted in English, specifically in science fiction writing.

6. Calvert, "Who Did They Make Me," 114–15; Madeline Muntersbjorn, "Disgust, Difference, and Displacement in the Dollhouse," *Slayage: The Journal of Whedon Studies* 8, no. 2–3 (2010): para. 4; Tom Connelly and Shelley Rees, "Alienation and the Dialectics of History in Joss Whedon's *Dollhouse*," *Slayage: The Journal of Whedon Studies* 8, no. 2–3 (2010): para. 18.

7. Kristopher Karl Woofter, "Watchers in the Woods: Meta-Horror, Genre Hybridity, and Reality TV Critique in The Cabin in the Woods," in *Reading Joss Whedon*, ed. Wilcox et al., 275.

8. Lorna Jowett and Stacey Abbott, *TV Horror: Investigating the Darker Side of the Small Screen* (London; New York: I.B.Tauris, 2013), 107; Helen Wheatley, Gothic Television (Manchester: Manchester University Press, 2013), 92.

9. Robin Wood, "An Introduction to the American Horror Film," in *Movies and Methods*, vol. 2, ed. Bill Nichols (Berkeley: University of California Press, 1985), 208.

10. Ibid.

11. "Gray Hour," *Dollhouse*, written by Sarah Fain and Elizabeth Craft (2009; Los Angeles: 20th Century Fox Home Entertainment, 2009), DVD.

12. In some contrast, Topher's programming counterpart in the D.C. House, Bennett Halverson, remarks, "You let them [the Dolls] roam. They roam like free-range chickens. We keep ours more like veal." This suggests that the L.A. House does afford its Doll inhabitants some small measure of freedom. "Getting Closer," *Dollhouse*, written by Tim Minear (2010; Los Angeles: 20th Century Fox Home Entertainment, 2010), DVD.

13. As Michael Starr notes, it is Boyd (secretly Rossum's director), the villain of the narrative, who describes the people of the House as "family"; Echo vehemently rejects this definition. "'I've Watched You Build Yourself From Scratch': The Assemblage of Echo," in *Joss Whedon's Dollhouse*, ed. Ginn, Buckman, and Porter, 3–19. The nearest examples of "family group" in this series emerge after the technological apocalypse: the community of Safe Haven; and Priya, Tony and their son T, who seek refuge as a family within the House. "Epitaph Two: Return," *Dollhouse*, written by Maurissa Tancharoen, Jed Whedon, and Andrew Chambliss (2010; Los Angeles: 20th Century Fox Home Entertainment, 2010), DVD.

14. Carol J. Clover, *Men, Women and Chainsaws: Gender in the Modern Horror Film* (London: BFI Publishing, 1992), 25.

15. Calvert, "Who Did They Make Me," 121.

16. "Epitaph One," *Dollhouse*, written by Maurissa Tancharoen, Jed Whedon, and Joss Whedon (2009; Los Angeles: 20th Century Fox Home Entertainment, 2009), DVD.

17. "The Attic," *Dollhouse*, written by Maurissa Tancharoen and Jed Whedon (2010; Los Angeles: 20th Century Fox Home Entertainment, 2010), DVD.

18. Brad Tabas, "Dark Places?: Ecology, Place, and the Metaphysics of Horror Fiction," *Miranda. Revue Pluridisciplinaire Du Monde Anglophone/ Multidisciplinary Peer-Reviewed Journal on the English-Speaking World*, no. 11 (7 June 2015): 1, doi:10.4000/miranda.7012.

19. Catherine Spooner, in Rebecca Williams, "'The Past Isn"t Dead . . . It's Deadly': Horror, History and Locale in Whitechapel," *Journal of British Cinema and Television* 11, no. 1 (2014): 70, https://doi.org/10.3366/jbctv.2014.0192.

20. Williams, 71.

21. Further, the narrative suggests that attempts to erase an individual's past, memory, or self cannot be wholly successful; this is signalled in the first episode, when De Witt offers Caroline (not yet Echo) the chance for a "clean slate." Caroline replies, "You ever try and clean an actual slate? You can always see what was on it before." "Ghost," *Dollhouse*, written by Joss Whedon (2009; Los Angeles: 20th Century Fox Home Entertainment, 2009), DVD. De Witt's mention of "clean slate" is reminiscent of the description of the Dolls as "blank slates," apparently unaware of anything that happens to them during their assigned term in the House, an assumption undercut by the actions of Sierra and Victor, who remember and return to each other while in Doll state.

22. *Dollhouse*'s production designer, Stuart Blatt, also worked on *Angel*; similarities between the L.A. House and the Wolfram & Hart offices can be seen in elements such as the central staircase and the minimalist furnishings. With thanks to Stacey Abbott for helpful discussion of this topic. Maria Elena Fernandez, "For *Dollhouse* on Fox, the set is one of the stars," *L.A. Times*, 1 February 2009, www.latimes.com/entertainment/la-ca-dollhouse1-2009feb01-story.html; *Angel*, created by David Greenwalt and Joss Whedon (1999; Los Angeles: 20th Century Fox Home Entertainment, 2006), DVD.

23. See Alanna Thain's chapter in this collection for discussion of the space of *Dollhouse* with respect to complacent, passive bodies.

24. Annie E.A. Bartlett, "Spatial Order and Psychiatric Disorder," in *Architecture and Order: Approaches To Social Space*, ed. Michael Parker Pearson and Colin Richards (London: Routledge, 1997), 192.

25. F. E. Pheasant-Kelly, "Institutions, Identity and Insanity: Abject Spaces in Shutter Island," *New Review of Film and Television Studies* 10, no. 2 (1 June 2012): 218, 215, doi:10.1080/17400309.2012.658677. Pheasant-Kelly examines one film's representation of repressed horror erupting into the "regulated" space of the asylum. On television, *Kingdom* (*Riget*) (von Trier, 1994–97) offers an example of the way "liminal" institutional setting and horror narrative can combine (Jowett and Abbott 167).

26. Catherine Pugh, "Broken But Home: Institutions, Control and the Non-Place in *Dollhouse*," in *At Home in the Whedonverse: Essays on Domestic Place, Space and Life*, ed. Juliette C. Kitchens (McFarland, 2017), 50.

27. Peter Hutchings, *The Horror Film* (Harlow: Pearson Educational, 2004), 73.

28. "A Spy in the House of Love," *Dollhouse*, written by Andrew Chambliss (2009; Los Angeles: 20th Century Fox Home Entertainment, 2009), DVD.

29. The connection with sleep/dream and violation is referenced, too, in the episode "Briar Rose" in which the Sleeping Beauty story is invoked as Paul Ballard makes his way into the House, planning to rescue Echo/Caroline. With thanks to Kristopher Woofter who reminded me of the sleep/dream/violation parallels here. "Briar Rose," *Dollhouse*, written by Jane Espenson (2009; Los Angeles: 20th Century Fox Home Entertainment, 2009), DVD.

30. "Epitaph One," 1.13.

31. Ambrose is in the kitchen so that he can eat a plate of seafood, something his allergies will not allow him to consume in his own body.

32. "Briar Rose," 1.11.

33. "A Love Supreme," *Dollhouse*, written by Jenny DeArmitt (2010; Los Angeles: 20th Century Fox Home Entertainment, 2010), DVD.

34. Manuel Aguirre, "Geometries of Terror: Numinous Spaces in Gothic, Horror and Science," *Gothic Studies* 10, no. 2 (November 2008): 2.

35. Barry Curtis, *Dark Places: The Haunted House in Film* (London: Reaktion, 2008), 110.

36. Aguirre, 3, 4.

37. In "Epitaph Two: Return," 2.13, these names merge with the call signs that the former Doll "tech-heads" still use: Kilo, Yankee, Victor.

38. Lorna Jowett, "Stuffing a Rabbit in It: Character, Narrative, and Time in the Whedonverses," in *Reading Joss Whedon*, ed. Wilcox et al., 309.

39. Ibid., 310.

40. Clover, *Men, Women*, 25. The discovery that the killer is an imprinted identity occupying the body of the child Iris adds further to the horror theme, recalling the many creepy children of classic horror film—as discussed by Wood, "An Introduction," 208—as well as evoking themes of possession and coercion, in line with the overall thematic trajectories of *Dollhouse*.

41. Hutchings, *The Horror Film*, 73.

42. Ibid.

43. We can also view this episode as a repressed memory in the series as a whole, at least at the time of broadcast when it was not shown on US network television. "Epitaph One" was broadcast to an international audience (e.g., on the UK's Sci Fi Channel, 11 August 2009), and then included on the season 1 DVD. It is conceivable that a North American viewer following the original broadcast of *Dollhouse* might have reached the end of season 2 unaware of the impending apocalypse outlined in this episode.

44. The abject effect is somewhat muted for the viewers, however. After Mr Miller speaks as an imprinted identity on the first occasion (the scene cuts to a

flashback with Adelle DeWitt, so the audience can infer that he is imprinted with her memory), he does not do so again. Instead, the cut to flashback occurs immediately after each of his successive imprints, so that it is possible to forget that these flashback memories are only retrieved because they are forcibly imprinted onto Mr Miller. In this way, the "actuals" replicate the actions of those in the Dollhouse who precipitated the apocalypse.

45. Jowett, "Stuffing a Rabbit in It," 309.
46. "Vows," *Dollhouse*, written by Joss Whedon (2010; Los Angeles: 20th Century Fox Home Entertainment, 2010), DVD.
47. Derrick King, "'We're Lost. We Are Not Gone': Critical Dystopia and the Politics of Radical Hope," in *Joss Whedon's Dollhouse*, ed. Ginn, Buckman, and Porter, 171.
48. Hutchings, *The Horror Film*, 56.
49. "The Attic," 2.10.
50. Ian G. Klein, "Ritual, Rebirth and the Rising Tide: Water and the Transcendent Self," in *Joss Whedon's Dollhouse*, ed. Ginn, Buckman, and Porter, 205.
51. "Needs," *Dollhouse*, written by Tracy Bellomo (2009; Los Angeles: 20th Century Fox Home Entertainment, 2009), DVD; "Belonging," *Dollhouse*, written by Maurissa Tancharoen and Jed Whedon (2010; Los Angeles: 20th Century Fox Home Entertainment, 2010), DVD.
52. "Stop-Loss," *Dollhouse*, written by Andrew Chambliss (2010; Los Angeles: 20th Century Fox Home Entertainment, 2010), DVD.
53. Some of these memories are her own; others appear to derive from her imprints. For example, Echo sees "the tree from one of [her] childhood homes," but the women she describes as "my hateful relatives" look like the female relatives of killer Terry Karrens, whose personality was accidentally imprinted on Echo in the episode "Belle Chose," *Dollhouse*, written by Tim Minear (2010; Los Angeles: 20th Century Fox Home Entertainment, 2010), DVD.

7

Inscription and Subversion: *The Cabin in the Woods* and the Postmodern Horror Tradition

Stephanie Graves

Fueled by the compulsion to both look and not look and conflating fear and repulsion with curiosity and attraction, horror thrives in creating spaces that are liminal and entropic. Often at play with its own tightly circumscribed generic structures, much of contemporary horror relies on the savvy exploitation of formulaic constructions and tropes. *The Cabin in the Woods* (2012) incorporates these categorical concerns rather directly. Written by longtime collaborators Joss Whedon and Drew Goddard and directed by Goddard, the film was ready for release in 2010 but was delayed for two years by the bankruptcy of MGM Studios, finally getting a theatrical release in 2012.[1] Goddard, a staff writer on Whedon's TV shows *Buffy the Vampire Slayer* and *Angel*, had also written the screenplay for the 2008 horror film *Cloverfield*, a cleverly staged found-footage monster film that was both a critical and box office hit. Within Whedon's oeuvre, *The Cabin in the Woods* (hereafter *Cabin*) acts as a bridge between early work like *Buffy* and companion *Angel* and the later cynicism of *Firefly* and *Dollhouse*.[2] As Erin Giannini argues in "'Charybdis Tested Well with Teens': *The Cabin in the Woods* as Metafictional Critique of Corporate

Media Producers and Audiences," the film "fits fairly easily between the 'supernatural' threats of early Whedon and the latter Whedon focus on man-made dangers."[3]

Upon the release of *Cabin*, many critics hailed it as a "reinvention" or "correction" to the horror genre. *Cabin* was well-received by film critics, and often lauded as groundbreaking in some essential way; Peter Debruge's *Variety* review declares that "not since *Scream* has a horror movie subverted the expectations that accompany the genre to such wicked effect as *The Cabin in the Woods*."[4] Like Debruge, many reviewers draw a direct line from horror auteur Wes Craven's 1996 *Scream* to *Cabin*, ignoring the wealth of self-referential horror that came between (not to mention before) the two. *Rolling Stone's* Peter Travers claims that "horror honchos Joss Whedon and Drew Goddard have taken an ax to slasher cinema in *The Cabin in the Woods* and chopped it up for kindling."[5] Yet such a declaration is not merely hyperbolic—it also does a disservice to both *Cabin* and to the horror genre at large. And perhaps it *is* the genre with which critics have a problem; Travers goes on to claim that *Cabin* turns "splatter formula on its empty head,"[6] while *Slate's* Dana Stevens gives *Cabin* faint praise while dismissing the genre: "I thoroughly enjoyed this movie's gory silliness, but I have the feeling it may be overpraised for infusing a modicum of wit *into a genre that usually demonstrates so little*."[7] For critics who are so clearly disdainful of horror, it may be simpler to laud Whedon (already a critical darling, in many ways) for being clever and breathing life into a flagging genre, but this completely dismisses a rich horror tradition in which *Cabin* takes part. Postmodern horror has long taken pleasure in establishing and then subverting the classic horror formula; in *Recreational Terror: Women and the Pleasures of Horror Film Viewing*, Isabel Cristina Pinedo identifies the "central lesson of the postmodern horror film, namely that cloaked in a mantle of normalcy, chaos lies just beneath the surface ready to erupt at any moment."[8] In Pinedo's construction, the postmodern horror film: 1) features a constant and relentless threat of violence (and argues that violence is a constitutive element of everyday life), 2) creates an ambiguity regarding traditional conceptions of good and evil as well as "normal" and "abnormal," and 3) includes the subversion of both causal logic and authority figures.[9] *Cabin* is but one entry into an established tradition of postmodern horror concerned with these elements, and, like its progenitors, it participates in this tradition through self-referentiality, intertextuality, and an appeal to audience knowledge of generic tropes.

Carol Clover's landmark text, *Men, Women, and Chainsaws: Gender in the Modern Horror Film* (1992) argues that horror audiences are often more off-put by overt modulation of the formula rather than the adherence to it.[10] The formula is in fact so inviolable that it has been made narratively explicit in films such as horror auteur Wes Craven's highly influential *Scream* (1996), a self-reflexive and intertextual postmodern masterpiece that grossed upwards of $100 million in the US alone. Andrew Syder, a horror scholar at Florida State University's film school, contextualizes *Scream* and the other postmodern horror films that followed in its wake as reinvigorating the flagging genre in the mid-1990s, due in large part to their "extremes of self-reflexivity with copious intertextual references to earlier horror landmarks." In particular, Syder notes, *Scream* is a slasher film in which the characters explicitly acknowledge and are fluent in the formulaic construction of horror movies, especially earlier slasher films.[11] In many ways, what *Scream* does is to acknowledge horror fandom's savvy and interest in seeing horror formula both earnestly performed and wickedly subverted—something horror always already does. In Craven's film, argues Dean Lockwood of the University of Lincoln, "the intertextuality in effect constitutes the text," and its "concomitant sophistication and media literacy" and "proclivity for reflexive genre-bending" are significant markers of the postmodern in horror.[12] Philip Brophy identifies this reflexivity as a trait of contemporary horror as early as his 1985 essay "Horrality—The Textuality of Contemporary Horror Films," arguing that the "contemporary horror film *knows* you've seen it before; it *knows* that you know what is about to happen; and it knows that you know it knows you know."[13] As evidenced by Brophy's article, the self-aware horror film is not a twenty-first-century construct—postmodern intertextuality has long populated the genre, and *Cabin* is a participant in this established tradition rather than "the start of something new: a smarter, more self-aware kind of chiller," to quote Debruge's *Variety* review.[14] Such conscious generic awareness and acknowledgement of a film's own historical and cultural lineage relates to cultural theorist Ihab Hassan's construction of the postmodern as engaging a double view, as containing both "sameness and difference [. . .], filiation and revolt."[15] Pinedo argues, similarly, "the postmodern horror film transgresses the rules of the classically oriented horror film, but it also retains features of the latter, which form the backdrop against which violations of the rules are intelligible as such."[16] In this postmodern iteration, the contemporary horror film acknowledges its generic lineage before subverting the formula thereof.

Influenced by the widespread success of *Scream*, other reflexive horror films soon followed—films that both emphasized sameness by reveling in the established generic tropes while also crafting disjunctive, ironic narratives that acknowledged and played with those very same generic conventions. These films were centered on a parodic distancing from the wider horror genre; though they reference other horror films and play extensively with horror tropes, following in *Scream's* highly successful footsteps, there is an ironic detachment from the wider genre at work in these films. Entries such as *I Know What You Did Last Summer* (Jim Gillespie, 1997), *Urban Legend* (Jamie Blanks, 2000), *Final Destination* (James Wong, 2000), remakes/ reimaginings of legendary horror director William Castle's *House on Haunted Hill* (William Malone, 1999) and *Thir13en Ghosts* (Steve Beck, 2000), the wildly successful *The Blair Witch Project* (Daniel Myrick and Eduardo Sanchez, 1999), *The Strangers* (Bryan Bertino, 2008), and reboots of both the long-standing *Friday the 13th* and *Nightmare on Elm Street* franchises all exhibit this parodic postmodern tendency toward self-awareness, intertextuality, and hybridity. These films reflect sociologist and cultural commentator Todd Gitlin's conception of postmodern anxiety and the loose collection of attributes with which he demarcates the notoriously slippery category:

> "Postmodernism" usually refers to a certain constellation of styles and tones in cultural works: pastiche; blankness; a sense of exhaustion; a mixture of levels, forms, styles; a relish for copies and repetition; a knowingness that dissolves commitment into irony; acute self-consciousness about the formal, constructed nature of the work; pleasure in the play of surfaces; a rejection of history.[17]

Just as postmodernism can be viewed as a crisis of systems of regulation, the postmodern horror film reflects anxieties about the horror genre's vitality and longevity. The commonplaces of generic tropes and conventions are concomitantly a source of both restrictive apprehension and creativity. And the postmodern horror audience responds in kind, enjoying the reiteration of The Rules while simultaneously celebrating the subversion of them. Here occurs what Syder contextualizes as a postmodern "rhetorical deconstruction,"[18] the move from strict sets of rules governing rhetorical creatures such as vampires, werewolves, and other classic horror monsters to a postmodern demystification of the "rhetorical nature of representations of the unknown"[19] by tacit acknowledgement of the fictionality of the monster as narrative device. Essentially, the postmodern orientation reframes traditional horror narrative and aesthetics, rupturing the unity exhibited in classic horror films and instead, as Hassan argues, inviting participation in the signification of the conventions rather than a distanced remove from them.[20] The post-1996 emergence of films such as those cited above embraced postmodernism as a mode, but also took a parodic stance toward the genre wherein tropic inclusions became the punchline of jokes and visual gags, carving out a subgenre that might best be categorized as postmodern horror parody. These films, as Kristopher Karl Woofter argues in his essay "Watchers in the Woods: Meta-Horror, Genre Hybridity, and Reality TV Critique in *The Cabin in the Woods*," can be characterized as part of a "baroque aestheticism" wherein filmmakers "make straightforward use of as many conventions as they ridicule (because they know that horror fans love the genre's function *as* ritual)."[21] In this manner, these films were able to both have their horror cake and eat it too; they capitalized on the rich traditions and conventions of the horror genre while simultaneously distancing themselves from it through humor.

Following this well-established tradition of the parodic self-aware horror film, Whedon and Goddard's *The Cabin in the Woods* also tidily fits these definitions of the postmodern as multilayered, ironically detached, and simultaneously traditional and subversive while similarly distancing itself from the genre by satirizing it. *Cabin* is a textbook example of what postmodern scholar Linda Hutcheon terms "postmodern parody."[22] Using a framing similar to cultural theorist Fredric Jameson's concept of *pastiche*, Hutcheon distances the term in her usage from the more traditional, narrower concept of parody as a tool of ridicule and wit, and rather takes an expansive, inclusive definition to incorporate "ironic quotation, pastiche, appropriation, [and] intertextuality."[23] Crucial to Hutcheon's postmodern parody is a sense of historicity, a refiguring of the past rather than a denial or departure from it. "For artists," she argues, "the postmodern is said to involve rummaging through the image reserves of the past in such a way as to show the history of the representations their parody calls to our attention."[24] Brophy identifies post-1979 horror as "a genre which mimics itself mercilessly—because its statement is coded within its very mimicry";[25] there is a clearly established precedent of self-awareness and generic referentiality. In this tradition, *Cabin* not only exhibits this sense of historicity through its thick intertextuality but also by its appropriation and subversion of genre conventions and horror tropes. Whedon and Goddard rely on intertextual references to these tropes as a means of establishing a cultural continuity and as an appeal to an audience familiar with the trappings of the genre. Paul Maltby contextualizes the postmodern as a means of foregrounding the mechanics of meaning: "postmodernist writers," he notes, "have developed an aesthetics of 'self-reflexiveness,' that is, a mode of fiction which investigates the very process of signification or meaning production."[26] In horror, then, the tropes themselves act as a cultural signifier, and the rather shameless and flagrant deployment of tropes in *The Cabin in the Woods* becomes a stylistic method to investigate and deliberately call into question the signification encoded within said tropes.

Tropes such as storms, old dark houses, forests, full moons, knife-wielding hands, plangent musical cues, wide-eyed close-ups and screams, to name a few, act as a shorthand, an appeal to cultural memory, easily recognizable and familiar. Most horror films make repeated use of tropes as a tool of storytelling, but the tropic references in *Cabin* are practically legion. *TVTropes.org*, a wiki site dedicated to cataloging tropes not only in television but also in film, videogames, and other media, maintains an extensive collection of user-inventoried tropic content. Based on this aggregated taxonomy, Whedon and Goddard include, to name only a portion: "The Abandoned Cabin," "Ancient Evil," the "Creepy Basement," "Creepy Children," "Dangerous Windows," "Death by Sex," "Dropping the Weapon," "Dumb Blondes," "Dumb Jocks," a "Final Girl," the "Jump Scare," "Let's Split Up, Gang," an "Ominous Music Box Tune," "Summoning Artifacts," a "Surprisingly Sudden Death," "Taxidermy Terror," and the "Torture Cellar."[27] Many of these tropes (some of them endemic to horror, some of them more the product of a kind of mythic view of horror) are easily identifiable in Whedon and Goddard's other collaborations as well—they are classic horror conventions that are often

128

evident in both *Buffy the Vampire Slayer* and *Angel*. In *Cabin*, however, they are used so self-consciously that they risk being emptied out of inherent significance to form another, meta-significance relating to the genre's mechanics; they are all immediately recognizable conventions that border on horror film clichés, but the manner in which the tropes are utilized is a self-conscious reinscription and evaluation of the signification of the tropes themselves. As the film plays out, we learn that the rural, abandoned cabin that belongs to a cousin of Curt (Chris Hemsworth) exists solely for the purpose of hosting the five sacrifices who gather there, and, later on, that Curt does not actually have a cousin who owns a cabin— the trope here has been employed as a believable fiction, and a virtual reality, by the mysterious and shadowy organization who manipulates the environment. The creepy gas station attendant acts as the prophet of doom, warning the group away from their path. This prophet character who serves as a warning to the main characters is seldom given an actual name—but in *Cabin*'s reflexive mechanics, he is *explicitly* referred to as The Harbinger (Tim De Zarn). Maltby argues that, in postmodern texts "in particular, literary-narrative conventions like plotting, use of metaphor, and omniscient narrator are parodied so as to expose their role in the fabrication of meaning; so as to present the text as a fiction-making apparatus."[28] The generic device of the grotesque figure warning the protagonists away from their path is here parodied as a way to foreground the archetypal/fictional construct of The Harbinger within *Cabin*'s narrative.

Likewise, the Creepy Basement is *deliberately* and absurdly "creepy" in service of the sacrifice, complete with a mechanically actuated cellar door that flies open at a narratively opportune moment (that moment arguably readable as an allusion to Sam Raimi's highly self-aware *The Evil Dead* [1981] and *Evil Dead 2* [1987]). The deliberateness of this self-conscious set design, as well as the plethora of items that horror filmgoers will recognize as "Summoning Artifacts," both appeals to and satirizes horror historicity while, in terms of the framing narrative, it emphasizes the "free will" of the characters to make the choices that lead to them becoming sacrifices. Another classic hazard of horror films, the danger of standing in front of a window, exists in *Cabin* as well; the film toys with viewer expectation by having Marty (Whedon regular Fran Krantz), alone in his room, linger in front of the dark void of the bedroom window, silent for a beat before zombie killer Judah Buckner (Matt Drake) smashes through and pulls Marty outside. Anyone versed in horror parlance knows that something is going to burst through the window, and the trope plays out, but the traditional outcome of that trope is subverted when we discover later that Marty has been the victor in the encounter, dismembering Judah with a trowel.[29] Despite cognitive tampering via her hair dye, the "Dumb Blonde" in the film, Jules (Anna Hutchison), retains enough intelligence to be aware that it is a culturally acknowledged bad idea to have sex in the woods (thereby echoing the audience's knowledge of the generic motif), but the combination of a temperature-controlled environment, moonlight produced on cue, and aerosol pheromone mists nevertheless lulls her into the act, manipulating her into the perfect sacrificial "Whore" (as she is referred to in the script) in order to fulfill the narrative requirements.[30]

Yet Whedon and Goddard are playing with the wider cultural stereotype of the "Dumb Blonde"; it is established early in the film that Jules has *just* dyed her hair blonde, and Dana (Kristen Connolly) indicates that Jules is pre-med, but the Chemistry Department's Lin (played by another Whedon favorite, Amy Acker) explains that they have slowed cognition through the hair dye, literally shoehorning Jules into the so-called Dumb Blonde trope. Similarly, Dana is first introduced as having just ended an affair with her professor, but ostensibly through more chemical interference she assumes the role of the virginal girl, even confusing herself when she indicates such to Holden (Jesse Williams) while they are kissing. This both situates her as the sacrificial Virgin within the framing narrative *and* positions her as the textbook Final Girl, a term coined by Carol Clover that refers to the last girl standing in a slasher film who is usually virginal, demure, and often has a unisex name.[31] Later, confronting the Director (Sigourney Weaver), Dana scoffs at being typecast as the Virgin, to which the Director admits, "We work with what we have,"[32] acknowledging that the pressing of each character into these stereotypes is frustrated at best, and foregrounding the particular way that *Cabin* and other postmodern horror parodies often rely on oversimplifying these tropes in order to satirize them. In *Cabin*, these stereotypes become what theorist Jean Baudrillard constructs as *simulacra*—objects or ideas that reference an empty concept, a blank; the Virgin, the Whore, the Fool, the Athlete, and the Scholar are all mythotypes, but the essential, specific nature of them is not "real" and for the means of the ritual, the characters

130

in *Cabin* act only as a *trompe l'oeil*.[33] This mythotypical remove acts as a way of recognizing while also ironizing the use of stereotypical characters so prevalent in the horror genre; as each character is forced into the stereotype in order to fit the demands of the sacrifice, *Cabin* both takes advantage of the prevalence of these stock characters while also parodying their ostensible recurrence within the horror genre. But *Cabin* is not alone in doing this; the *Scream* franchise did the same, containing metacommentary on the attributes of horror film characters, so by acknowledging horror's reliance on stereotypes *Cabin* again participates in an established postmodern horror parody tradition.

The use of other tropes reemphasizes the "fiction-making apparatus" so crucial to *The Cabin in the Woods* and how it participates in the postmodern inversion of horror formula. When Dana drops the knife with which she stabs Matthew Buckner, we see Sitterson (Richard Jenkins) in the control room operating a joystick that sends an electrical shock to the knife, *causing* her to drop it,[34] at last providing the audience with an explanation for what Whedon and Goddard seem to see as a disturbing tendency in horror films for the protagonist to mindlessly discard her weapon—or, rather, making a self-reflexive comment upon the proliferation of the trope. Hutcheon terms this "postmodern denaturalizing—the simultaneous inscribing and subverting of the conventions of narrative."[35] The generic tendency of characters to discard their weapons is repeated, yet is here reinterpreted by offering an explanation for the behavior. This tiny moment in *Cabin* illustrates exactly this parodic postmodern tendency—the paradoxical reiteration and subsequent subversion and satirization of horror tropes.

Similarly, the Ominous Music Box Tune that emanates from the jewelry box Holden plays with in the basement is not merely an object that justifies some diegetic, dissonant music in a minor key for atmospheric benefit—we later discover through musical refrain in the film score that the object would have summoned the delightfully Whedonian "Ballerina Dentata" monster: a young girl in a ballet costume who, as she turns, reveals a gaping circle of teeth where her face should be.[36] In fact, it is not a singular "Summoning Artifact" in the basement, but rather an entire collection of them linked to different monsters and different means of death. These artifacts recall the fetishization of signifying objects in other films, from Freddy's knife-gloves in *A*

Nightmare on Elm Street (Wes Craven, 1984) to Jason Voorhees' hockey mask in the *Friday the 13th* series, as well as the puzzle box in *Hellraiser* (Clive Barker, 1987) and the Ghostface Killer mask in *Scream*. The objects in the basement mesmerize the five students as arcane items in horror films do, and when Dana and Marty discover these objects were a means with which to decide their fate,[37] the audience's previous experience of horror films informs the imaginative possibilities of what nightmare each object would have summoned. They call attention to what Gitlin terms the "constructedness" of the postmodern— "a cultivation of surfaces endlessly referring to, ricocheting from, reverberating onto other surfaces."[38] The objects are a literal catalogue of nightmares, and the trope of the inescapable allure of the "Summoning Artifact" is included because the film diegetically acknowledges—and simultaneously mocks—the inescapability of this fascination with arcane items for characters in horror films.

Further asserting *Cabin*'s claim to self-referential postmodern parody, even the advertising campaign leading up to the film's release acknowledged these horror tropes and lampooned them by making them explicit; the pre-release movie posters included phrases such as, "If you hear a sound outside... have sex" and "If something is chasing you ... split up." These horror chestnuts are indeed employed in the film; while the cabin is being attacked by the Buckner family of "redneck torture zombies," Curt suggests they all stay together—until Sitterson flips a switch and releases some aerosolized drug that makes Curt pause, sway, and then decide the group should instead split up. It is the audience's immediate familiarity with these tropes and the explicit acknowledgement of them within the diegesis that both establishes *Cabin* as part of a postmodern tradition and pushes this ironic treatment into the realm of postmodern parody. Hutcheon argues that the explicit acknowledgement of tropes brings into focus the complex politics of representation: "Irony makes these intertextual references more than simply academic play or some infinite regress into textuality: what is called to our attention is the entire representational process [...] and the impossibility of finding any totalizing model to resolve the resulting postmodern contradictions."[39] The film unnaturally foregrounds these tropic narrative devices and then subverts their essence, establishing a "paradoxical installing as well as subverting of conventions."[40] It is this textual nod that *Cabin* makes toward the collective method of representation in horror that establishes it not as a "reinvention" or "reimagining" of the horror genre but rather as part of a longstanding parodic postmodern horror tradition.[41]

Playing on—and with—this common cultural experience of horror films, Whedon and Goddard encode myriad filmic references in *The Cabin in the Woods*, trading on the audience's presumed comprehensive knowledge of the genre. This fundamental intertextual nature of horror is something Brophy identifies: "It is not so much that the modern Horror film refutes or ignores the conventions of a genre, but it is involved in a violent awareness of itself as a saturated genre."[42] Rather than bounded by only its own narrative space, *Cabin* overemphasizes horror's conventional intertextuality, which, historically speaking, both grounds the film as part of a tradition of horror films and argues for its own inclusion in the spectrum of the horror genre. The essential plot, the setting, and often even the *mise-en-scène* borrow heavily from Sam Raimi's classic *The Evil Dead* (1981); in Raimi's film, five friends visit a remote cabin for a weekend of fun, but they unwittingly unleash a demonic evil by reading from a mysterious book in the cellar, after which they are picked off one by one.[43] *Cabin*, like *The Evil Dead*, is set in a ramshackle, remote cabin, accessible only by an easily destroyed means of access—the dilapidated bridge in *The Evil Dead* and the mountain tunnel in *Cabin*—both of which become impassable once the protagonists are on the other side. Even the camera shots create direct visual references to *The Evil Dead:* the low-slung tracking shot of initial approach toward the cabin, a cellar door that slams open seemingly of its own accord, and the lantern-lit descent down the cellar stairs by both Ash (Bruce Campbell) and Marty are all direct, clear moments of visual intertext. Additionally, the manner in which scenes are lit becomes intertextual—the same non-diegetic cool-blue diagonal back-lighting highlights both Curt and Ash after the initial descent into the cellar, and the two shots are nearly visually identical (see Figure 7.1). Indeed, *The Evil Dead*'s taxonomy of monsters also gets preferential treatment on the framing narrative's monster whiteboard[44] (see Figure 7.2), where both DEADITES and ANGRY MOLESTING TREE appear—the latter of which makes a brief yet memorable appearance in the first round of elevator purges.

Other immediately recognizable intertextual references to postmodern horror include parallels in both the countenance and physical mannerisms

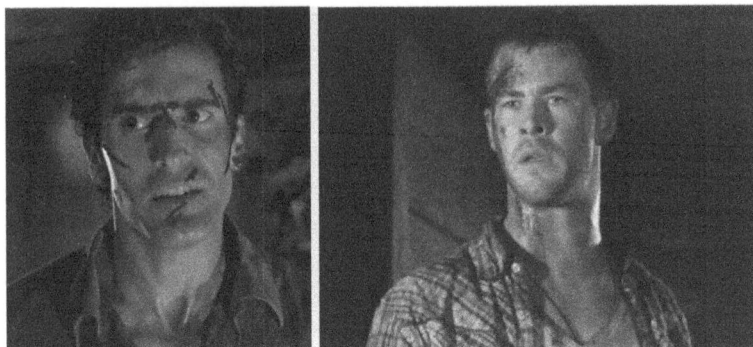

Figure 7.1 Left: Ash in *The Evil Dead* (1981, dir. Sam Raimi); Right: Curt in *The Cabin in the Woods* (2012, dir. Drew Goddard). Despite the reversal of angle, note how the lighting and framing in *Cabin* echo that from *The Evil Dead*—in both instances, the central figure in the scene is lit by a non-diegetic blue-black diagonal that highlights the jaw and neck, and Curt's facial abrasions allude to Ash's similar cuts.

between Matthew Buckner (Dan Payne) and Michael Myers (Tony Moran) from John Carpenter's *Halloween* (1978), particularly the echoing of Myers' trademark silent head tilt.[45] When Matthew appears rising slowly out of the water after his fight at the dock with Dana, it is a direct visual reference to the *Friday the 13th* series and Jason Voorhees rising out of

Figure 7.2 The Monster Whiteboard in the "downstairs" portion of the narrative features both generic and specific referents to the horror genre.

Crystal Lake. Also taken from the *Friday the 13th* series playbook is Jules's death during the sex act; while death during and/or associated with sex is a common horror trope, the mid-coitus murder is a particular affinity of Jason's. The scenic design of *Cabin's* Black Room (the basement torture chamber into which Dana and Holden flee to escape Mother Buckner)[46] calls to mind *Hellraiser's* (Clive Barker, 1987) alternate hell-dimension torture chamber with its excess of dangling fetishistic chains and hooks.[47] The Harbinger's gas station recalls both the *Texas Chainsaw Massacre* (Tobe Hooper, 1974)[48] as well as that of *The Hills Have Eyes* (Wes Craven, 1977),[49] both films that suggest *Cabin's* designation of the Buckners as not just zombies, but a "zombie *redneck* torture *family*." These intertextual references—and their immediate recognizability to anyone passingly familiar with the horror genre—remark upon the mass production of narrative; these filmic references point to a cultural hybridity that, in the postmodern horror tradition, *Cabin* both catalogues and criticizes.

Foregrounding what Syder refers to as the postmodern turn toward the "film medium itself becoming more expressly implicated in how we perceive and make sense of the world,"[50] the intertextuality only increases once Dana and Marty descend into the "downstairs" portion of the film and a ceaseless onslaught of intertextual references and outright pastiche begins. The enigmatic Hell Lord (or, as he is listed in the credits, Fornicus, Lord of Bondage and Pain) is a markedly clear reference to the Cenobite Pinhead from the *Hellraiser* films. So quickly you might miss them, Goddard and Whedon include references to the elevator of blood and the Twin Girls from *The Shining* (1980), the doll-masked murderers from *The Strangers* (2008), the mutants from *The Hills Have Eyes* (1977, remake 2006), Evil Surgeons from the remake of *House on Haunted Hill* (1999), a flaming-headed Jack 'o Lantern from *Pumpkinhead* (1988), a *Nosferatu*-style vampire (1922), and a bevy of others, including references to television, fairy tales, popular literature, and video games. These inclusions create a rich, visually allusive framework that links *The Cabin in the Woods* to the postmodern horror genre and yet simultaneously distances it from the classic horror film—it is Hutcheon's concept of postmodern parody's use and abuse, installation and subversion at work. *Cabin* catalogues these monsters in a self-conscious, rapid-fire visual onslaught, and in doing so, moves toward actively lampooning the genre while still claiming to participate in it.[51] Horror has long been intertextual and generically

135

self-referential, but *Cabin* exhibits a reflexive self-awareness that transcends mere generic reference and instead makes text from its intertext. Critics, quick to laud the film, treat it as a postmodern exegesis on contemporary horror, but by and large fail to recognize the attendant ironic distance that establishes *Cabin* as parody.

Cabin is not alone in this tendency. In Craven's *Scream*, Lockwood argues, there is an evident intertextuality that "in effect constitutes the text."[52] Even *Scream* is part of a long tradition of self-aware horror films meant to parody (and capitalize upon) familiar monsters; such films include, among many others, *The Old Dark House* (James Whale, 1935), *Abbott and Costello Meet Frankenstein* (Charles Barton, 1948), *The Fearless Vampire Killers* (Roman Polanski, 1967), and *Piranha* (Joe Dante, 1978). Similarly, *Cabin* uses its self-referential intertextuality as a constitutive element of its narrative. The multivalent narrative and references create a space in the interior story (that of the five protagonists on a nightmare vacation to a cabin) which participates in tropic generic convention, while the framing narration (that of Sitterson and Hadley and the ambiguous entity for which they become architects of the sacrifice) acts as a means of criticizing a perceived overreliance on these conventions by horror artists. In doing so, *Cabin* both participates in and yet hypocritically derides this generic characteristic. It takes part in inscribing a larger cultural meaning onto these conventions, suggesting that the horror genre acts as a means of catharsis for our voyeuristic desires, yet it also castigates the audience for this desire by critically depicting Sitterson and Hadley as voyeuristic, opportunistic letches. As such, *Cabin's* narrative turn functions as both an argument that, though implicitly acknowledged as overly familiar, horror tropes approach a mythic importance, while it simultaneously criticizes this importance by situating these tropic references as repeated punchlines.

The elements of postmodern parody in *The Cabin in the Woods* arise out of this generic pastiche and appropriation of catalogued and subverted tropes and allusions. However, the postmodern horror parody does not revisit its own generic history out of sentimentality or from an urge to ground itself in the past. Hutcheon argues, "this parodic reprise of the past is not nostalgic; it is always critical. It is also not ahistorical or de-historicizing; it does not wrest past art from its original context and reassemble it into some sort of presentist spectacle."[53] Instead, she argues, this reprisal acts as a denaturalization, a double process of "installing and ironizing" past representations in order to foreground ideological departures between past and present.[54] This hearkens back to Hassan's definition of the postmodern as that which exhibits both sameness and difference; in *Cabin*, we have a horror film that literally catalogues the genre, emphasizing sameness, yet, as other parodic postmodern horror films before it, ironically distances itself from its referents. This distancing might be due to a fundamental disagreement with genre conventions, and there is certainly encoded in *Cabin* a criticism of "torture porn" and of the influence of reality television and a removed scopophilia.[55] Yet there is an argument to be made that this distance functions as an indication of superiority, and that this critical generic recursivity is not a love letter to horror, as Goddard has suggested in interviews,[56] but is instead a means of expressing what he and Whedon consider the opprobrium of contemporary horror. The postmodern is always defined in relation to— or against—that which came before; *Cabin* tends more towards the latter tactic, sometimes establishing its genealogical heritage by setting up generic traditions like convenient targets. Again, as Brophy states, "the contemporary horror film knows you've seen it."[57] In a film like *Scream*, knowing and reciting the rules of the genre may possibly help a character survive the film, a phenomenon Giannini refers to as "narrative redundancy";[58] likewise, *Cabin* crafts a world in which those rules are reiterated and then parodied. There is a generic ambivalence at work in these films; they both function entirely as a reaction to the horror genre, yet they obsessively reinscribe genre conventions as if they expect the audience to *not* be familiar with these conventions. This hesitation between arrogant superiority over, and honest engagement with, horror convention is the fulcrum on which postmodern horror parody pivots; its horror is made palatable to the horror interloper or dilettante, so that what for the horror fan reads as reflexive redundancy can function as a primer for the uninformed audience. These contemporary horror films hedge their bets, anticipating that maybe the audience *has not* seen this film before—and perhaps is also disdainful of the genre.

"Postmodern parody is both deconstructively critical and constructively creative,"[59] Hutcheon reminds us, and this is the force we see at work in *Cabin in the Woods*. By utilizing classic horror tropes and including a thick intertext, Whedon and Goddard—like other parodic horror filmmakers before them—have used the narrowly circumscribed formula as both a means of creative storytelling and of criticizing their targeted generic conventions and viewing practices. Although *Cabin* is implicitly critical of a tendency toward using rote characterizations in place of more complex, individualized characters of agency, as Hutcheon points out, complicity always attends postmodern parody's critique.[60] By criticizing the genre in which it participates, *Cabin* ultimately illuminates its own hypocrisy. In its attempt to simultaneously reinscribe and subvert generic conventions, *Cabin* concurrently utilizes and criticizes tropes that it holds up as "tired," embodying a disjunction that distances it from other postmodern horror that is still intertextual and self-reflexive but eschews the ironic distancing affected by the parodic approach. *The Cabin in the Woods* participates in a longer horror genre tradition by deliberately evoking classic horror films and tropes and foregrounding the way the cultural shorthand of a trope functions, but by examining and evaluating the thick intertextuality, it becomes clear that *The Cabin in the Woods* is firmly situated within a wider parodic postmodern horror tradition rather than any imagined "reinvention" thereof.

Notes

1. Peter Debruge, "Review: *The Cabin in the Woods*," *Variety* (2012): http://variety.com/2012/film/markets-festivals/the-cabin-in-the-woods-1117947213/.
2. See Kristopher Karl Woofter's discussion of parallels between *Cabin* and *Dollhouse* in "Watchers in the Woods: Meta-Horror, Genre Hybridity, and Reality TV Critique in *The Cabin in the Woods*," *Reading Joss Whedon*, eds Rhonda V. Wilcox, Tanya R. Cochran, Cynthea Masson, and David Lavery (Syracuse: Syracuse University Press, 2014): 268–79.
3. Erin Giannini, "'Charybdis Tested Well with Teens': *The Cabin in the Woods* as Metafictional Critique of Corporate Media Producers and Audiences," *Slayage: The Journal of the Whedon Studies Association* 10.2/ 11.1 (Fall 2013/ Winter 2014): par. 7, www.whedonstudies.tv/uploads/2/6/2/8/26288593/giannini_slayage_10.2-11.1.pdf.
4. Debruge, "Review: *The Cabin in the Woods*."
5. Peter Travers, "*The Cabin in the Woods*," *Rolling Stone* (2012): www.rollingstone.com/movies/reviews/the-cabin-in-the-woods-20120412.
6. Ibid.
7. Dana Stevens, "Cabin in the Woods," *Slate* (2012): www.slate.com/articles/arts/movies/2012/04/cabin_in_the_woods_reviewed_with_no_spoilers_.html; Emphasis mine.

8. Isabel Cristina Pinedo, *Recreational Terror: Women and the Pleasures of Horror Film Viewing* (Albany, NY: SUNY Press, 1997), 6–7.
9. Ibid., 5.
10. Carol Clover, *Men, Women, and Chainsaws: Gender in the Modern Horror Film* (Princeton, NJ: Princeton University Press, 1992), 10.
11. Andrew Syder, "Knowing the Rules: Postmodernism and the Horror Film," *Axes to Grind: Re-Imagining the Horrific in Visual Media and Culture:* special issue of *Spectator* 22:2 (Fall 2002), 78.
12. Dean Lockwood, "Webs of Simulation: Horror in the Postmodern," *Zen Films* (2008): www.zenfilms.com/blog/Horror_in_the_postmodern.pdf.
13. Philip Brophy, "Horrality—The Textuality of Contemporary Horror Films," *Screen UK* 27, no. 1 (1986), 5.
14. Debruge, "Review: *The Cabin in the Woods.*"
15. Ihab Hassan, "Toward a Concept of Postmodernism," *A Postmodern Reader* (Albany, NY: SUNY Press, 1983): 277.
16. Isabel Cristina Pinedo, "Recreational Terror: Postmodern Elements of the Contemporary Horror Film," *Journal of Film and Video* 48 (1996): 19.
17. Todd Gitlin, "The Postmodern Predicament," *Wilson Quarterly* June 1989: 67.
18. Syder, "Knowing the Rules," 84.
19. Ibid., 85.
20. Hassan, "Toward a Concept of Postmodernism," 280.
21. Woofter, "Watchers in the Woods," 271.
22. Linda Hutcheon, *The Politics of Postmodernism* (New York: Routledge, 1999): 93.
23. Ibid.
24. Ibid.
25. Brophy, "Horrality," 3.
26. Paul Maltby, "Excerpts from *Dissident Postmodernists,*" *A Postmodern Reader* (Albany, NY: SUNY Press, 1993), 520.
27. "Horror Tropes," *TV Tropes,* accessed June 1, 2017, http://tvtropes.org/pmwiki/pmwiki.php/Main/HorrorTropes.
28. Maltby, "Excerpts from *Dissident Postmodernists,*" 520.
29. Despite the humor of this reversal, the trowel recalls the most disturbing death in George A. Romero's *Night of the Living Dead* (1968).
30. Joss Whedon and Drew Goddard, "Screenplay," *The Cabin in the Woods: The Official Visual Companion* (London: Titan, 2012): 44–151.
31. Clover, *Men, Women, and Chainsaws,* 35–40.
32. *The Cabin in the Woods,* 01:24:04.
33. Jean Baudrillard, "Simulacra and Simulations," *Jean Baudrillard: Selected Writings* (Stanford: Stanford University Press, 1988), 167.
34. *The Cabin in the Woods,* 00:54:02.
35. Hutcheon, *The Politics of Postmodernism,* 49.
36. *The Cabin in the Woods,* 01:10:43.
37. Ibid., 01:11:06.
38. Gitlin, "The Postmodern Predicament," 69.

39. Hutcheon, *The Politics of Postmodernism*, 95.
40. Ibid., 13–14.
41. Arguably, horror's longevity as a genre more generally is the result of a similar combination of replication and subversion of tropes and formula. What postmodern horror does, it seems, is to turn this reality into a self-awareness meant to induce laughter more than screams.
42. Brophy, "Horrality," 5.
43. *The Evil Dead*, directed by Sam Raimi (1981; Michigan: Anchor Bay, 2010), DVD.
44. *The Cabin in the Woods*, 00:33:24.
45. *Halloween*, directed by John Carpenter (1978; Michigan: Anchor Bay, 1997), DVD.
46. *The Cabin in the Woods*, 00:52:38.
47. *Hellraiser*, directed by Clive Barker (1987; Hollywood: Image Entertainment, 2011), Blu-Ray.
48. *The Texas Chainsaw Massacre*, directed by Tobe Hooper (1974; Orland, IL: Dark Sky Films, 2014), Blu-Ray.
49. *The Hills Have Eyes*, directed by Wes Craven (1977; Hollywood: Image Entertainment, 2014), DVD.
50. Syder, "Knowing the Rules," 86.
51. Perhaps problematically so, considering this parading of monsters renders them as serving one function, stripping them of their individual, more complex meanings within narrative and historical contexts.
52. Lockwood, "Webs of Simulation."
53. Hutcheon, *The Politics of Postmodernism*, 93.
54. Ibid.
55. For a longer discussion of this criticism, see Woofter's "Watchers in the Woods."
56. Robert Levin, "'Cabin' Director Drew Goddard Creates Love Letter to Horror Films," *Newsday* (2012): www.newsday.com/news/new-york/cabin-director-drew-goddard-creates-love-letter-to-horror-films-1.3653633.
57. Brophy, "Horrality," 5.
58. Giannini, "Charybdis Tested Well with Teens," par. 10.
59. Hutcheon, *The Politics of Postmodernism*, 98.
60. Ibid., 99.

PART II

Mutant Enemies: TV Horror,
Industry, and Influence

8

"For All I Know, It Could be Really Hilarious or It Could Suck": Situating the Film *Buffy the Vampire Slayer* (1992) in Period Vampire Comedy

Jerry D. Metz Jr.

The vampire has been a constant in Western horror and horror-associated cultural production for well over a century and is what author Stephen King calls one of three "archetypes" of "modern horror fiction, both in print and on celluloid," along with Frankenstein, and the werewolf/shape-shifter.[1] King's comment "*Frankenstein* has probably been the subject of more films than any other literary work in history"[2] frankly underestimates the situation; a keyword search on imbd.com for "vampire" returns 2,372 film and television titles, while "Frankenstein" yields 207. Joss Whedon was only twelve years old when Anne Rice's influential novel *Interview with the Vampire* (1976) was published, and thirteen, when David Cronenberg released his controversial, vampire-themed *Rabid*. Two years later in 1979, when Whedon might have been learning to drive, at least eight full-length vampire pictures were released,[3] ranging from Stan Dragoti's comedic *Love at First Bite*, to John Badham's psycho-erotic *Dracula*, to Warner Herzog's brooding, melancholic *Nosferatu the*

Vampyre, and Tobe Hooper's made-for-television adaptation of King's *Salem's Lot* (arguably the most successful of all King adaptations). In the midst of such profuse diversity, Nina Auerbach's oft-quoted phrase "each generation creates and embraces its own"[4] vampire becomes problematic. Did one of those vampire films represent "1979" better than the others? By what metric is that measured? Or are the iterations assessed together as one composite vampire? And how are the generations to be defined?[5]

1992 was a banner year for screen vampires, with *Innocent Blood* (John Landis), *Sleepwalkers* (Mick Garris), and *Bram Stoker's Dracula* (Francis Ford Coppola) all released around the same time as the subject of this chapter: *Buffy the Vampire Slayer,* directed by Fran Rubel Kuzui, from a script written by Whedon. (Although it is routinely reported that Whedon disavowed the film, nonetheless he maintains having "major involvement"[6] with it.) Its lukewarm reception suggests this film fell short of resonating with its generation, and when seeking positive reviews one benefits from patience and a robust search engine. Valerie Frankel labors to find merit, recruiting Joseph Campbell and Heroic tropes to suggest that Buffy is a sort of female Luke Skywalker, but even she nonetheless concludes the "movie is about a superficial teen kickboxing people in monster suits."[7] Still, the *Wall Street Journal* called *Buffy* "entertaining" and "surprisingly sweet,"[8] while *Maclean's* deemed it "fun" and "more charming than *Death Becomes Her.*"[9] *Screen International* suggested: "Although *Buffy* runs out of steam as it reaches its conclusion, it has by that time established enough goodwill to be forgiven its shortcomings."[10] Generally, reviews were overwhelmingly negative. Even stalwart David Lavery (1949–2016), who long defended the House of Whedon, wrote bluntly that the movie "flopped."[11] Describing Buffy as a "Cheerleader turned dewy feminist avenger," *The Village Voice* jibed that "*someone* had to follow Catwoman and Sharon Stone, and Buffy got the job."[12] *Variety* called it "bloodless" and "bargain basement stuff," but noted, with some insight, that the film was "more effective as a sendup of Valley Girls than as a clever take on bloodsuckers."[13] Similarly, *Sight & Sound* observed that the film, part of a "wave of vampire movies ... is hurt by a basic indecision about its tone. Oddly, the most effective element of the film is its parody of the California life style."[14]

This chapter aims at a broad filmic excavation, situating *Buffy* in contexts of its production and of cinema leading up to and neighboring it that most resembles it: live-action vampire comedies and horror spoofs featuring vampires. I screened every English-language vampire comedy made between 1979 and 1992 that was identified and obtainable (see Table 8.1).

I chose 1979 as a starting date because *Love at First Bite* was the first successful modern feature-length vampire-based comedy in US theaters since 1948's *Abbott and Costello Meet Frankenstein*.[15] Its success inspired filmmakers to experiment with vampires and their hunters. Ensuing production could be creative—Anthony Hickox's modern-day-vampire-comedy-Western, *Sundown: The Vampire in Retreat*, depicts a civil war

Table 8.1 Vampire Horror/Comedy Films, 1979–1992

Title	Rating	Release Date	Teen/Adolescent Protagonist?
Love at First Bite	PG	April 1979	No
Saturday the 14th	PG	October 1981	Yes
Fright Night	R	August 1985	Yes
Transylvania 6–5000*	PG	November 1985	No
Once Bitten	PG-13	November 1985	Yes
Vamp	R	July 1986	Yes
The Lost Boys	R	May 1987	Yes
The Monster Squad	PG-13	August 1987	Yes
Teen Vamp	R	January 1988	Yes
Fright Night 2	R	May 1988	Yes
My Best Friend's a Vampire	PG	May 1988	Yes
Saturday the 14th Strikes Back	PG	August 1988	Yes
Vampire's Kiss*	R	June 1989	No
Transylvania Twist	PG	October 1989	No
Beverly Hills Vamp	R	November 1989	No
Sundown: The Vampire in Retreat	R	January 1990	No
Rockula	PG-13	February 1990	No
My Grandpa is a Vampire	PG	June 1992	Yes
Buffy the Vampire Slayer	PG-13	July 1992	Yes
Innocent Blood	R	September 1992	No

* = See Endnote 16.

Source for release dates: imdb.com.

between two vampire groups fought with firearms shooting wooden bullets—or cynical—Landis's *Innocent Blood* is a vampire-mobster mash-up capitalizing on the success of 1990's *Goodfellas*. All but one (*Teen Vamp*) of the twenty vampire-comedy films released through 1992[16] used *Bite*'s modern American settings, rather than historical European ones.[17] The legacy and enduring popularity of *Love at First Bite* loom large; the editors of a recent volume on horror-comedy film dismiss *Buffy* as the "most promising" of a "string of largely unsuccessful imitations" of *Bite*,[18] while their contributors ignore it outright.

This chapter focuses on three overlapping aspects of *Buffy*. First, its production is briefly explored to show how the filmmakers imagined and engaged the project; and to demonstrate that, at this early stage in his career, Whedon's work was susceptible to outside revision and alteration. Second, as Table 8.1 indicates, the modern vampire comedy was becoming an established subgenre by 1992, so *Buffy* is examined in the context of major themes and notable variations (including the feminist sensibility *Buffy* seems to court). Third, I consider how *Buffy* recycles aesthetic and textual elements from other successful teen horror films while fitting the lucrative PG-13 teen market. Whatever its vampire trappings, *Buffy* has all the characteristics of a "teen movie" as defined by Catherine Driscoll: "youthfulness of central characters; content usually centered on young heterosexuality, frequently with a romance plot; intense age-based peer relationships and conflict either within those relationships or with an older generation; the management of adolescence by families, schools, and other institutions; and coming-of-age plots focused on motifs like virginity, graduation, and the makeover."[19]

Making *Buffy*

Buffy's plot has been discussed elsewhere in detail.[20] Briefly, vampires have infiltrated the Southern California suburbs to feed on youthful prey and plan a takeover. High-school cheerleader Buffy (Kristy Swanson) is informed by stranger Merrick the Watcher (Donald Sutherland) that she is uniquely qualified to fight the vampires. He directs her training, assisting her transformation from Valley Girl to mature young woman, but is killed by the vampires. Buffy blames herself for his death and retreats, focusing on "childish things" such as the senior dance. Finally when vampires invade the dance looking for her, Buffy vanquishes them and their leader Lothos (Rutger Hauer), the world is saved, and she gains acceptance and a new boyfriend, polite rebel-without-a-cause/outsider Pike (Luke Perry).

Buffy got underway at Fox on February 20, 1992, backed partly by a Los Angeles-based production house owned by Dolly Parton and her manager.[21] The budget is reported by various sources as $7–9 million. Kuzui, with permission, had intervened in Whedon's script, yet even so a degree of tension surfaces when both sides reminisce. Whedon notes, "My original script for the movie was kind of dark and scary and it was comedic, but the final project was more a broad comedy [...],"[22] and "It didn't turn out to be the movie I had written."[23] To Kuzui, the script was a gem that needed substantial polishing:

> [It had] been rejected by almost every studio in the United States. [...] I saw an enormous potential in it. I optioned it, and then paid Joss to rewrite it according to my concept and ideas. Joss's screenplay had Buffy just roaming around sticking stakes through vampires' hearts. There was no humor. [...] I [...] suggested we use [John Woo's] elements of martial arts and humor.
>
> [He] had written the character of Buffy as being so stupid and empty, she was totally unbelievable. I said to Joss, 'It simply isn't going to hold up for an entire movie.'
>
> [Buffy's] a girl who eventually takes personal responsibility for her power. I saw the whole concept of Buffy as very much about girls in high school who don't want to acknowledge that they are different. They don't realize that their difference is also their power.[24]

Kuzui's public statements claiming to be the author of the film's Buffy character and her coming-of-age transition are striking, as these qualities are widely seen as the film's contribution to the subgenre and pop culture generally. (Notably, Whedon, who benefited considerably from the film's perceived feminism, continued to work with Kuzui on projects, and I find no record of his refuting her claims.) Merrick has a curious place in this formulation: he is critical to Buffy's transformation but still part of the modern horror film's brotherhood of men who show up to explain but not to resolve scary things—one that includes the doctor "diagnosing" Norman

Bates at the end of *Psycho* (1960), and the hapless Dr Loomis in *Halloween* (1978).

Buffy was not the only vampire comedy in 1992 to have a female lead. *Innocent Blood* starred Anne Parillaud as Marie, a conscientious vampire who feeds on New York City's villains, neutralizing their corpses (and hiding her trail) with shotgun blasts to their heads. When one gets away—a mob boss, who wants to create an invincible vampire mafia—Marie goes after him with help from a cop, Joe, a love interest, once he gets over his aversion to her being a vampire. Both Marie and Buffy are physically stronger than their male partners: "Don't make me hurt you," Marie half-pleads, half-warns Joe, while Buffy tells Pike, "Don't piss me off." Marie is tough, smart, and ethical, but she admits she "take[s] lives"—a sympathetic female monster feminists might have found wanting.

Fox had already turned down Whedon's script, and Whedon suspected that *Beverly Hills, 90210* star Luke Perry's joining the cast reversed his fortunes.[25] Sutherland and Hauer were added because Perry was thought to be unknown internationally, although Kuzui was frank about wanting "to capture the same audience that *90210* had."[26] Producer Howard Rosenman gushed, "What we have here is a hip, inexpensive movie on which the studio could make a killing. It's like *Wayne's World* meets *Heathers* meets *Beverly Hills, 90210* meets *The Lost Boy*s meets a Bruce Lee movie." The project reportedly cut numerous corners (ditching pages of script and celebrity vampire cameos) to save money and make the vital summer release, leading Swanson to observe, "It could be really hilarious or it could really suck."[27]

The indecisive tone, noted by sensitive reviewers, likely stems from the hybrid script fashioned by two strong-willed people. Tension during filming arose over ad hoc departures from that script; Whedon grew so angry over Sutherland's changes to Merrick's lines, which Kuzui permitted, that he once stormed off set.[28] Only Swanson embraced her unusual role: Sutherland's Merrick has the flat, stony affect of a 6'4" garden gnome; Hauer winces through many of his lines (some, especially his dying words, are awful howlers); Perry looks throughout as though he'd rather be anywhere else. During the climax, when vampires invade the school dance, one pauses to mug and shimmy to the loud rock music in a semi-comic but jarring way. It is a strange, incomplete moment, neither horrific nor hilarious.

Buffy, Vampire Comedy, and a Changing Slayer

Kuzui's remark about *Buffy* being about what people think of vampires is significant given the way the subgenre at the time operated. A running gag in *Love at First Bite* is that no one in New York City except Van Helsing's grandson—and the secretary of Dracula's love interest—recognizes the Count, who complains he is all washed up,[29] and who is pursued in bat form by a hungry family thinking he is a chicken. Characters needing to learn about vampires in these films often resort to reading Stoker's *Dracula* (1897). *Teen Vamp*'s Reverend, confronted by a young vampire, admits "I don't know anything about vampires, just what I've seen in the movies." The boy's mother replies, "I remember something about crosses and garlic," supposing that onions should work just as well. (They don't, and the Reverend heads off to read Stoker.) That *Buffy* lampoons popular ideas about vampires, depicting them as physically threatening but ridiculous— Paul Reubens as Amilyn, Lothos's second in command, overacts throughout, and sports neon lipstick under his moustache—seems to reinforce, not challenge, convention. Scholars like Philip Brophy and Rick Worland maintain that horror-comedies work best when each genre's material is allowed to operate at the extremes of its registers,[30] something unlikely in the "teen-pic" milieu of *Buffy* and its vampires, which instead dance a campy conga down the middle.

Buffy echoes *Lost Boys* and *Sundown* in its emphasis on a head vampire, uncommon in the majority of vampire-comedy films in this period. In *Sundown* the head vampire turns out to be Dracula reformed, spared the fatal effects of an improvised cross because he has received divine forgiveness for leading the effort to stop killing humans and instead drink synthetic blood. In some films killing the head vampire cures vampires it created (e.g., *Fright Night* 1 and 2), while in others its death cures all the vampires it is responsible for, potentially a far greater number. *Beverly Hills Vamp* (1989), an erotic vampire comedy, ends on a scarier note. Here the conventional wisdom that killing the head vampire will restore the others, conveyed to the hunters by a Hollywood-script-writing priest, proves false: after she and her preexisting vampires are dispatched, the film's first victim, Brock, is not only still a vampire but has created another—and they fully intend to feast on the "victorious" hunter. In *Buffy* killing Lothos has global significance, because he is the ultimate head vampire, the uber-Dracula (and the Slayer is reborn precisely to defeat him), allowing *Buffy* a thoroughly happy, if arrogant, ending: Buffy and *Buffy* render the vampire extinct.

Buffy's novel conceit, a teen girl represents humanity's best chance against vampires, loses some inspirational potential given that she is class elite—her wealthy parents appear to be on permanent vacation, and she is a habitual mall shopper—and, as a pretty, white, blonde cheerleader, high-school elite. A female vampire hunter is fully conceivable as part of a trend in vampire comedies where the Van Helsing role is democratized; the mystic "Slayer" architecture that raises one pretty person in the world as uniquely competent to fight the monsters breaks that mold. The quasi-religious "Birthright" concept emphasizes destiny rather than historically contingent forces. Merrick, reborn "for a hundred lives" to repeatedly find and train slayers, always "Chosen" teen girls. Additionally, *Buffy* proposes a cyclical battle between the Slayer and Lothos, taking place for centuries until this Valley Girl Slayer wins.[31] This asks a lot of audiences accustomed to seeing average people rise to the occasion and fight against the monster—and that *becoming* the monster: situations played for winces and laughs in *Saturday the 14th, Once Bitten, Vamp, My Best Friend is a Vampire, Teen Vamp, Sundown*, and *Innocent Blood*, but more grimly in *Fright Night* 1–2, and *The Lost Boys*. Several of these films show how this frightening transition actually boosts teen power, self-esteem and confidence. But being bitten and becoming a proto-vampire cannot happen to Buffy, as this would signal vulnerability and the likelihood of needing help to save her—a scenario the film's nascent feminism logically militates against. In addition, from *Vamp, Teen Vamp* and *Beverly Hills Vamp* to *Fright Night* 1 and 2, female vampires are depicted conventionally as innately monstrous. Only *Innocent Blood* attempted, however imperfectly, to create a morally complex feminist vampire universe.

The devolution of an elite male vampire killer to more popular, everyday characters is clear in these films. There is no Van Helsing figure in *Abbott and Costello Meet Frankenstein*, even though Dracula drives the plot.[32] The Van Helsing family legacy is invoked in four period teen-vampire-comedies, although none of these new Van Helsing figures is anything like the classic agent of patriarchal establishment, competence and authority. In *Love at First Bite* he is a psychiatrist, degreed and professional, but inept as a slayer (he pulls a revolver with silver bullets and a Star of David on the smirking Count), and loses "his" girl to George Hamilton's suave vampire because of his reluctance to marry her. In *Transylvania Twist* the younger Van Helsing initially appears effective, but ultimately lack of instinct leads him to be bitten and turned into a vampire himself. Similarly in *Sundown*, Van Helsing's great grandson is driven by family grudge to kill vampires, but he bumbles, gets bitten and eventually fights for peaceful coexistence with humans (and is ultimately "rewarded" by the comely vampire who bit him). In *Saturday the 14th*, the Van Helsing character brought in to solve a bat infestation turns out to be a villain, pursuing the "Book of Evil" in order unleash world chaos. However, Jeffrey Tambor's vampire (possibly actually Dracula) destroys him with the aid of a precocious ten-year-old boy.

What characterizes the majority of films surveyed in this chapter is the real, if limited, demographic diversity of their slayers: there are more young people and females than adult males, though all played by white actors. It is common to feature duos or groups rather than individuals, and in *Beverly Hills Vamp* the larger adult male of two slayers is ineffective and easily seduced by a nubile vampire, while the younger, coded as an inept geek, kills them with ardor (squealing "Have some Pope soda!" as he douses the head vampire with holy water). Of the core duo in *Fright Night* 1 and 2 and its sequel, the older man has access to anti-vampire information and equipment by virtue of playing a movie Vampire Hunter, but teen Charley can effectively wield a cross because he actually "believes." Vanquishers of a Dracula-led monster troupe in *Monster Squad* range from a senior-age man (who translates Van Helsing's diary) to a clutch of schoolboys and a five-year-old girl, while it takes both Grandpa and teen Michael to dispatch the head vampire of *The Lost Boys*. Girls sometimes fight vampires and provide real help in films that were ostensibly "about" the boys, such as *Once Bitten* and *Fright Night* 2. And in *Innocent Blood*, Marie becomes a formidable vampire hunter herself, suggesting that vampires can seek atonement, a trope continued in TV shows *Forever Knight* (1992–1996)[33] and Whedon's co-created spinoff from the *Buffy* TV series, *Angel* (1999–2004).

The demotion of the traditional, patriarchal Van Helsing to "helper" or sidekick has as much to do with a capitalistic film industry seeking new angles as with social factors like the rise of feminism and distrust of establishment authority following Vietnam and Watergate.[34] Whedon's oft-repeated-with-variations line that *Buffy* was inspired by his exhaustion with seeing pretty blonde girls go down the alley and get killed by the monster suggests he was seeing the wrong movies. Content analysis in three studies of 1980s Slasher films shows that eighty-three top-ranking movies had no significant difference in the number of male and female victims.[35] Before Buffy, girls fighting back effectively might have been the exception, but they existed, particularly in the Slasher subgenre that Whedon's comment seems to reference: Laurie in *Halloween*, Amy in *The Funhouse* (1981), Nancy in the initial three *A Nightmare on Elm Street* films (1984, 1985, 1987), Stretch in *The Texas Chain Saw Massacre* 2 (1986), Kirsty in *Hellraiser* (1987), and even Veronica from *Heathers*, who successfully fights J.D. and his plan to blow up the high school full of students.

Ripley in *Alien* (1979) was the character held up by *Buffy*'s producer as a "strong, seminal, idiosyncratic female heroine, something you don't see much of in horror movies."[36] As should be clear, that view was myopic. For example, 1984's PG-13 zombie-comedy *Night of the Comet* has two mall-loving teenage sisters (one a cheerleader, with a dog named Buffy!) battle zombies and psychotic scientists in post-apocalypse L.A., rescuing two children, with as much help from male survivor Hector as Buffy later receives from Pike. At the film's conclusion, eighteen-year-old Regina in particular has matured, her early ditzier preoccupations with shopping, videogames, and casual sex traded for the obligatory convention of recreating a family structure and being a good, civilized role model for the kids. By the 1990s a strong female lead in a vampire comedy was just a matter of time, though with neither *Buffy* nor *Innocent Blood* gaining popular success further progress likely slowed.

Buffy, PG-13, and the Recuperation of Teen Horror

The PG-13 rating, born out of concerns with horror and violence, was almost certainly desired by *Buffy*'s makers. Given the demographics of Perry's and Swanson's fan bases, it was the best option. A delineated space between PG and R had been discussed since the 1970s; momentum increased in 1982 after Tobe Hooper / Steven Spielberg's *Poltergeist* risked an R for "terror." The R rating would have limited exposure in theaters to viewers over seventeen, a massive blow when the "sweet spot" for box office returns was PG. Millions of dollars hung in the balance[37] and Spielberg's team successfully appealed for the lower rating. Public outcry in 1984 over the PG given to Spielberg projects *Gremlins* and *Indiana Jones and the Temple of Doom* forced a change, and PG-13 debuted on 1 July of that year[38] (first applied to *Red Dawn*). For James Kendrick, the new rating was "really about three things: 1) attempting to resolve the complexities of screen violence, 2) fully embracing the teenage marketplace [and] 3) avoiding conflict while still protecting the industry's profit potential."[39] The new PG-13 rating was especially attractive since it was advisory, meaning no gatekeepers at theaters would ask kids' ages. Fox executives likely knew that in 1991 PG-13 films were responsible for 35% of all box office receipts while R-rated films took 31%.[40] Specifically, industrial trends indicated a decline in production and consumption of R-rated teen horror films after 1988.[41] An R rating would thus have excluded much of *Buffy*'s young target audience, while in the wake of PG-13, the PG label was less enticing to older adolescents and teenagers.

The first PG-13 horror smash hit was 1999's *The Sixth Sense*. This provoked a wave of toned-down PG-13 horror films aimed at the broadest possible audience. Some proved successful, such as *The Others* (Alejandro Amenábar, 2001) and *Drag Me to Hell* (Sam Raimi, 2009), but Kendrick (writing elsewhere) suggests that the genre's tendency was always towards the core audience wanting more explicit violence, not less, and PG-13 seemed a better direction for "supernatural" films (e.g., 2010's *Insidious*) rather than "monster" movies.[42] So, working against broader, longstanding genre trends, *Buffy* retreats from modern horror's specularity, metatextuality, and postmodern tendencies—all of which deeply intensified in the 1990s and later—to deploy a more reassuring, inspirational, teen-friendly narrative of a pretty girl growing into her destiny to fight vampires and restore order. Often-cartoonish vampires and the middlebrow PG-13 rating were ways to appear edgy yet safe—hip but not transgressive. In Kuzui's own words, it was a "kid's movie" intended to appeal to the teen population "on the crest of interest in screen vampires."[43]

Producer Rosenman's remarks at the time show that *he* had the R-rated *The Lost Boys* (1987) and *Heathers* (1988) in mind as cinematic pillars of reference for *Buffy*. It is plausible that these films were discussed during script development (Buffy stating that she wanted eventually to marry Christian Slater is a giveaway). I suspect Moss is correct that *Buffy* channels *Lost Boys* in its glam vampire/rock-band aesthetic.[44] With his heavy eye shadow, teased hair, high-end black jacket and dangly earrings, Paul Reubens' vampire resembles an extra from a Guns'n'Roses video shoot. Shared musical set-pieces that pause the narrative in a sort of surprise channel-change to MTV connect the two: musical cheerleading and training interludes in *Buffy* suggest the beach party in *Lost Boys* featuring the oddly paired Aerosmith-Run D.M.C. hit "Walk This Way" (its forced hybridity a perfect song for half-vampire Michael). 1990's *Rockula* is important here, because it more directly anticipates *Buffy*'s diegetic presentation of characters in performance (the "show within a show"). Numerous live musical set-pieces in *Rockula* showcase the cast, most at the "Club Hell," with one turning out literally, through clever editing, to be a televised music video that characters are watching along with us.

Buffy, *The Lost Boys*, and *Rockula* all share a California setting: the apex and limit of the American frontier. Despite the comedic turns these films deploy, vampires infesting and likely reproducing in California suggests the shuttering of the frontier dream. Manifest destiny ends in corruption, future possibilities are foreclosed, and there is nowhere left to go. This sense of wholesale foreclosure remains even if *Buffy*'s happy ending tries to mitigate *The Lost Boys'* ambivalent conclusion, that the vampires might not have been taken out completely.[45]

There are indications an earlier *Buffy* script might not have been located in a high-school: a Whedon interview refers to a draft title "Martha the Immortal Waitress."[46] However, Whedon and Kuzui borrow freely from surface elements of *Heathers*, though eschewing its nihilistic humor and the cruelty and alienation of high-school culture. Here are the backstabbing Valley-type girls with their distinct phraseology ("How very"); the opulent but vapid and non-empathetic parents; the loopy New-Age school staff member (teacher Pauline Fleming in *Heathers* is obviously translated into the cliché-shouting basketball coach in *Buffy*); and the unlikely outsider boyfriend (the sociopathic, cycle-riding Jason Dean, or J.D.). The climax at a whole-school pep rally in *Heathers* becomes a senior dance in *Buffy*; and most notably, the film's protagonist is a teen girl hero who makes a journey and matures, discovering her values. Roz Kaveney highlights *Heathers'* importance to *Buffy*:

> The perception that, in a high school context, being popular is a
> social role that transcends any personal relationships, that it is a way

of being a celebrity whom everyone wants 'as a fuck or a friend' as Heather Chandler puts it, is one of the film's major contributions to the genre [of teen film] [... It] is a key issue in *Buffy the Vampire Slayer* [which] positioned its heroine as part of a clique somewhere between the social aggression of the Heathers and the fluffy likability of the central group in *Clueless*. It is only gradually that Buffy accepts that she cannot be the Chosen saviour of humanity from vampires and socially acceptable to flutter-brained teenagers at the same time. The ally and eventual boyfriend that Buffy finds in the film, Pike, is in a very mild way from the same stable as J.D. in *Heathers*—he is mildly alienated and slightly sardonic.[47]

It is perhaps not ironic in this globalized age that *Buffy* derives much of its representation of Valley Girls and the vacuous adults around them from a film set in Ohio. *Buffy* deploys a familiar screen world through its perceptibly neutered specific teen and teen-horror cinematic evocations. Exaggerating the pre-Slayer Buffy's airheaded traits should make her transition into mature Buffy more plausible. The comic model of social satire provided by *Heathers* is particularly strategic to making the new feel normal, which may be why it resonated more with reviewers than *Buffy*'s haphazard leveraging of the vampire trend and its camp sensibility. In "Humor in Vampire Films," Mary Y. Hallab observes: "Whereas horror purveys gloom or hopelessness and maintains dogmatic and inflexible positions (rigid opposition between good and evil, or us and them, for example), true humor is tolerant and open-minded toward new ideas, new people, new creatures—angels, giant spiders, superheroes—or toothy villains."[48]

Buffy is far from the first film to translate elements from sterner preexisting cultural material into a "safer" version for younger audiences. The PG-rated *Labyrinth* (Jim Henson, 1986), for example, features sixteen-year-old Sarah, yet another strong girl who survives a maze, monster attacks, and poisoned fruit to save her brother from the Goblin King. This fantasy film quietly resets the opening of *Halloween*—parents leave the older sister in charge of her small brother but rather than having sex and ignoring her brother (paying a heavy price) as in *Halloween*, Sarah journeys to rescue the helpless tot, overcomes obstacles and succeeds—a frequent stylistic gesture in family-friendly horror comedies. *Saturday the 14th* includes scenes referencing *Jaws* (Steven Spielberg, 1975), *Shivers*

(David Cronenberg, 1975), and *The Texas Chain Saw Massacre* (Tobe Hooper, 1974), but will not follow those films into explicit scares. *Buffy* takes a similar approach more comprehensively to Brian De Palma's R-rated *Carrie* (1976) and tries to redeem a controversial protagonist into something positive, kid-friendly and free from ambiguities.

Many elements in *Buffy* suggest that it is recuperating *Carrie*'s dark terrain: the centrality of the school dance as massacre site (nearly half *Carrie*'s running time is at the dance), where both girls, wearing white dresses, use their unique powers. The smiling pig mascot iconography on Buffy's gym walls recalls both the pig blood in the rafters and the painted pigs adorning the farm where John Travolta's Billy obtains the blood; and the fact that in *Buffy* all the students are "Hogs" rescues Carrie from loneliness and mockery. The menstruation and cramps that terrified and embarrassed Carrie are, in Buffy's case (derisively termed "PMS power, magic cramps"[49] by Frankel), something helpful, welcomed as a vampire "alert system." Just as rich, popular Buffy is the anti-Carrie, who is poor, humble, and bullied, their mothers are opposites: Carrie's hyper-religious mother clutches at her and stifles her with negative attentions, even trying to kill her, while Buffy's is (more typically of horror) barely around—diffident but not actually dangerous, leaving adult space to grow into. A classmate arranges for her boyfriend to take Carrie to the dance, while Buffy replaces her controlling, macho ex with a boy who respects her, and who shows up on his own to be with her. *Carrie* provided a template of unpleasant, starkly represented aspects of horrific teen-girl experience that *Buffy* could both exploit and remedy in order to bolster its PG-13 rating for the younger teen audience by way of presenting a more positive and empowering portrait of a girl with special powers: a girl who is different in a definitively good way.

For a teen-vampire film, *Buffy* is surprisingly empty of sex. Within the films discussed in this chapter, the long association of vampires and illicit sex is deflected into illegal prostitution in three, and sex is a constant theme in many. *Once Bitten* has teen Mark search for another woman after his girlfriend won't oblige his hormonal desires. He finds a vampire (Lauren Hutton), who needs to feed from a male virgin three nights in a row—after which he will become a full vampire. He has no memory of their relations but his proactive girlfriend Karen learns that the feedings are platonic. On the third evening she saves Mark from the undead

Countess by sleeping with him so he is no longer a virgin. *Buffy* is light years distant from any of that. Perry and Swanson had reputations as wholesome, mainstream actors. Perry, still starring in *Beverly Hills, 90210* at the time, even compared himself deprecatingly to milquetoast teen-idol singer and *Beach Party* star Frankie Avalon.[50] Girl-next-door Swanson's Buffy is supposed to be pretty, but not in an overtly objectifying way, hence the full coverage of her body offered by the thick, electric-blue bodysuits she wears under her cheerleading uniform (compare the visual treatment of cheerleaders in *Heathers*). Better to exploit the young stars' pre-existing, more innocent sex appeal[51] than risk losing the PG-13 rating. And it is no coincidence that in this "progressive" film, the two teen male dopes who make unwanted sexual comments or advances on Buffy—Andy and Benny—both wind up as vampires: a traditional moral code paralleling most Slashers and vampire films where guys who visit prostitutes (or "strange women") will get bit. One apparent exception here, although still in keeping with the Slasher's moral code, is Eddie Deezen's Kyle in *Beverly Hills Vamp* who follows his buddies to a brothel but quickly runs away because he wants to stay faithful to his girlfriend.

Against this backdrop, I believe Moss actually reads *too much* sex into the scene where Buffy and Lothos finally meet and he appears to hypnotize her. For Moss, Buffy's "lack of ownership of her own sexuality, displayed when she is reduced to a trance state during her pseudo-seduction at the hands of vampire Lothos, results in the death of her Watcher."[52] Perhaps there is a sexual undercurrent here, given Buffy's dreams, but it's frankly incidental to the visual presentation of the scene, obviously a tribute to the famed "battle of the wills" in *Dracula* (1931), when Van Helsing first perceives that the aristocratic Count is really a vampire (see Figure 8.1). The two face off, each knowing the other's identity (and knowing that the other knows). Dracula places Van Helsing in a trance and summons him closer. The doctor obeys at first, then fights the spell to engage Dracula as his equal. Buffy is unable to do this— Merrick tells Lothos that "she's not ready" and in the vein of *Star Wars*'s Obi-Wan Kenobi, Merrick has to die so that his young protégé will learn discipline and fight harder against evil.[53]

The prototypical scene from *Dracula* (1931) is replicated frequently in our group of films, starting with *Love at First Bite* when the younger Van

Figure 8.1 Pike attempts to break the psychic hold Lothos has on Buffy during the "battle of the wills," a scene revealing *Buffy*'s partial adherence to the lineage of Tod Browning's *Dracula* (1931).

Helsing confronts Dracula in a restaurant, they sit down and each immediately starts trying to put the other to sleep, succeeding only in causing a nearby waiter to pass out. The scene is conveyed with more fidelity to *Dracula* in *Fright Night*, while in *Saturday the 14th* the battle involves supernatural physical power—electric beams, ugly faces and loud noises. In *Innocent Blood* Joe does not hunt Marie, so the stakes are lowered (ahem) and a table lamp becomes their battleground (on or off?), while *Transylvania Twist* gender-swaps the original. Sexuality, as lesbianism, is potently invoked here as vampire Patricia (erotic actress Monique Gabrielle, well-known to mainstream audiences after 1984's *Bachelor Party*) tells Marissa lustily "I want to give you a big kiss." This was merely an enticement to lure Marissa to a spot where she might be killed by a falling chandelier.

Vampire comedies tailor their scripts to pay homage to Tod Browning's iconic scene while still exploring its potential for silliness[54]—*Buffy* stages it within whimsical parade floats in suburban Pasadena, and that scene is a microcosm of the film itself. Whatever tension is generated here (sexual, horrific or some combination of the two) quickly deflates to absurdity when the camera reveals the confrontation being solemnly witnessed by a seedy Pegasus and an enormous bucktoothed squirrel, implying that if *they* are taking it seriously, the "real" audience should feel ridiculous for doing so. Audiences seem to have gotten the message.

Conclusion

Whedon and Kuzui's *Buffy the Vampire Slayer* does not stand out from the diverse glut of vampire comedies produced in the 1980s and early 1990s. It means well with its message of (again, elite) female empowerment, but the scale of its achievement is problematized by a male Watcher explaining it all to her, and by the film's uncertainty about how scary its vampires should be. The film remains an intriguing if troubled historical document of the tension between pursuing two distinct ends: the first, an honest effort at creating a powerful, teen-female-centered monster movie, and the second, all the concessions, adaptations and strategies necessary to make a movie that will entertain as many people as possible—and make money doing it. Fans and scholars of the *Buffy* TV show often skip over this film, perhaps given Whedon's problematic history with it. Yet it merits study as a very rare opportunity to be a rough draft for a later work for the writer-*cum*-director of a celebrated show.

Notes

1. Stephen King, *Danse Macabre* (New York: Berkley Books, 1986), p. 77.
2. Ibid., p. 51.
3. https://mubi.com/lists/vampire-films-a-chronology. I also examined 'The Cold, Hard Stats of Vampire Comedies,' https://thedissolve.com/features/by-the-numbers/929-the-cold-hard-stats-of-vampire-comedies-1948-2012/.
4. Nina Auerbach, *Our Vampires, Ourselves* (University of Chicago Press, 1995), p. vii.
5. Kendall Phillips attempts to answer this in *Projected Fears: Horror Films and American Culture* (Westport, CT: Praeger, 2005), which periodizes nine classic horror films from *Dracula* (1931) to *The Sixth Sense* (1999). Many of his arguments are compelling, but this sort of historical reconstructionism tends to create and reify "eras" that have of necessity been defined rhetorically as distinct from each other, while fostering a sense of inevitability. There is a lurking post-hoc determinism.
6. Robinson, "Joss Whedon: Interview."
7. Valerie Frankel, *Buffy and the Heroine's Journey: Vampire Slayer as Feminine Chosen One* (Jefferson, NC: MacFarland & Co., Inc), 18.

8. "Film: The Roommate from Hell," *Wall Street Journal*, August 13, 1992, p. A12.

9. Victor Dwyer, "Death Springs Eternal," *Maclean's* 105 no. 32, August 10, 1992 p. 45.

10. Leonard Klady, "*Buffy The Vampire Slayer*," *Screen International* Issue 871, August 21, 1992, p. 12.

11. David Lavery, *Joss Whedon: A Creative Portrait* (London: I.B.Tauris, 2013), p. 5.

12. "Reel to Reel: *Buffy the Vampire Slayer*," *The Village Voice*, August 11, 1992, p. 64.

13. Todd McCarthy, "Reviews: *Buffy the Vampire Slayer*," *Variety* 348 no. 2, August 3, 1992, p. 40.

14. Kim Newman, "*Buffy the Vampire Slayer*," *Sight and Sound* 2 no. 7, November 1992, p. 39.

15. The "blaxpoitation" films *Blacula* (1972) and *Scream Blacula Scream* (1973) had limited impact.

16. Viewed but not commented on are two "vampire" comedies without real vampires. *Transylvania 6-5000* and *Vampire's Kiss* depict human characters who think they are vampires, although such an interpretation is more conceivable in the latter.

17. '*Salem's Lot* had done this as well, following King's 1975 novel, although *Teen Vamp* locates its story back in the 1950s. The geographical outlier, *My Grandpa is a Vampire* (a gentle vehicle for *Munsters* alum Al Lewis to develop his vampire act into a deeper, full-feature character) was filmed in New Zealand.

18. Cynthia J. Miller and A. Bowdoin Van Riper, "Introduction," in Miller and Van Riper, eds, *The Laughing Dead: The Horror-Comedy Film from Bride of Frankenstein to Zombieland* (Lanham, MD: Rowman & Littlefield, 2016), p. xvii.

19. Catherine Driscoll, *Teen Film: A Critical Introduction* (Oxford: Berg, 2011), 2.

20. Valerie Estelle Frankel, *Buffy and the Heroine's Journey* (Jefferson, NC: McFarland & Co., Inc.), 2012; Gabrielle Moss, "From the Valley to the Hellmouth: *Buffy*'s Transition from Film to Television," *Slayage* 2 March 2001 [1.2].

21. "'Buffy, The Vampire Slayer' Began Filming Feb. 20," *PR Newswire*, 4 March 1992.

22. Erin McCarthy, "33 Fun Facts About *Buffy the Vampire Slayer*," *Mental Floss*, March 10, 2016. http://mentalfloss.com/article/56496/33-fun-facts-about-buffy-vampire-slayer.

23. Tasha Robinson, "Joss Whedon: Interview," September 5, 2001. www.avclub.com/article/joss-whedon-13730.

24. Mitch Persons, "Movie Director Fran Rubel Kuzui: The Architect of the Franchise Formula Plans Another Film," *Cinefantastique* 29(11), March 1998, p. 44.

25. "Vampire Pop," *Movieline*, August 1, 1992. http://movieline.com/1992/08/01/vampire-pop/.
26. Persons, "Movie Director Fran Rubel Kuzui," 45.
27. "Vampire Pop."
28. See Robinson, "Joss Whedon: Interview" and Mitch Persons, "Prime Mover Joss Whedon," *Cinefantastique* 29 no. 11, March 1998, p. 37.
29. *Transylvania Twist* riffs on this in the opening sequence when a "helpless" woman beats up likenesses of Leatherface, Jason, and Freddy Krueger, calling them "amateurs" and revealing her vampire fangs.
30. Philip Brophy, "Horrorality," *Art & Text* 3 (Melbourne), 1983, www.philipbrophy.com/projects/rstff/Horrality_C.html; Rick Worland, Chapter 11, "*Re-Animator* and Slapstick Horror," in *The Horror Film: An Introduction* (Malden, MA: Blackwell Publishing, 2007).
31. *Rockula* competes with *Buffy* in its premise of destiny and rebirth. This film, with Thomas Dolby as villain, became an unlikely cult favorite.
32. Jeremy S. Miller, *The Horror Spoofs of Abbott and Costello: A Critical Assessment of the Comedy Team's Monster Films* (Jefferson, NC: MacFarland & Co., 2000), pp. 39–41.
33. See Erin Giannini's chapter in this collection for a discussion of *Forever Knight*.
34. Stephen King has described how secrecy and uncertainty enveloping Watergate and the political system influenced his writing of *Salem's Lot* (Auerbach, 157).
35. Barry S. Sapolsky & Fred Molitor, "Content Trends in Contemporary Horror Films," in *Horror Films: Current Research on Audience Preferences and Reactions*, ed. James B. Weaver, III & Ron Tamborini (Mahwah, NJ: Lawrence Erlbaum Associates, 1996), p. 40.
36. "Vampire Pop."
37. Steven Vaughn, *Freedom and Entertainment: Rating the Movies in an Age of New Media* (Cambridge: Cambridge University Press, 2006), pp. 114, 55.
38. "New Language Rules Set Forth by CARA for PG-13 Films," *Variety* 29 August 1984, p. 13.
39. James Kendrick, *Hollywood Bloodshed: Violence in 1980s American Cinema* (Carbondale, IL: Southern Illinois University Press, 2009), 199.
40. Kia Afra, "PG-13, Ratings Creep, and the Legacy of Screen Violence: The MPAA Responds to the FC's 'Marketing Violent Entertainment to Children (2000-2009)'," *Cinema Journal* 55 no. 3, Spring 2016, p. 47.
41. Timothy Shary, *Generation Multiplex: The Image of Youth in Contemporary American Cinema* (Austin, TX: University of Texas Press, 2002), pp. 138–46.
42. James Kendrick, "A Return to the Graveyard: Notes on the Spiritual Horror Film," in *American Horror Film: The Genre at the Turn of the Millennium*, ed. Steffen Hantke (Jackson, MI: The University Press of Mississippi, 2010), p. 143.
43. "Vampire Pop."
44. Moss, "From the Valley to the Hellmouth."

45. See Chapter 10 of Stacey Abbott's excellent *Celluloid Vampires: Life After Death in the Modern World* (Austin, TX: University of Texas Press, 2007).
46. Hibberd, "Joss Whedon: The Definitive EW Interview."
47. Roz Kaveney, *Teen Dreams: Reading Teen Film from Heathers to Veronica Mars* (London: I.B.Tauris, 2006), pp. 61, 80.
48. Mary Y. Hallab, "Humor in Vampire Films: The Vampire as Joker," in Miller and Van Riper, eds, *The Laughing Dead*, 139.
49. Frankel, *Buffy and the Heroine's Journey*, 21.
50. "Vampire Pop."
51. *Variety* noted: "Swanson has a robust, athletic sexiness that will keep boy viewers happy, while the amiable Perry ... will make this a must-see for many adolescent girls." Todd McCarty, "*Reviews.*"
52. Moss, "From the Valley to the Hellmouth."
53. The *Star Wars* cycle directly inspired *Saturday the 14th Strikes Back*.
54. Mel Brooks's 1995 *Dracula, Dead and Loving It* is beyond the purview of this essay: here the "battle of the wills" is rendered hilariously as a competition between Van Helsing and Dracula to always get the last word during conversation. It continues until the final scenes.

9

Monstrous Puppet Masters:
Negotiating Violence and Horror
in the Whedon Tele-verse

Stacey Abbott

While Joss Whedon's work is indelibly associated with the horror genre through his television series *Buffy the Vampire Slayer* (WB/UPN 1997–2003) and *Angel* (WB 1999–2004), *Cabin in the Woods* (2012), arguably, remains to date the only horror *film* within Whedon's body of work as writer, director, or producer.[1] Co-written by Whedon and *Buffy/Angel* writer Drew Goddard, the film was directed by Goddard, with Whedon directing second-unit material and operating on set as Producer. This was a highly collaborative process. In "We Are Not Who We Are," the behind the scenes special feature on the *Cabin in the Woods* DVD/Bluray, both creators display their passion for the horror genre, with Goddard in particular presented as an enthusiastic director, not only paying tribute to the history of the genre that has influenced him, but immersing himself in its aesthetic excesses. Throughout the feature, both Goddard and Whedon comment on Goddard's commitment to getting the genre right by, for instance, lighting the cellar scene very carefully "to get it really dark ... get really rich blacks"; ensuring, where possible, that special effects were achieved practically through special make-up, prosthetics, and

163

animatronics; and dousing the sets in gallons of blood and guts.[2] Goddard's zeal for the excesses of the genre are reiterated by other members of the crew interviewed on set, such as Special Make Up Effects artist David Leroy Anderson, standing in front of a lobby in which the walls and floors are streaming with blood, who describes Goddard's approach to shooting a zombie attack:

> What you are witnessing here is our first zombie attack. Drew, our fearless leader out there, is directing the four stunt zombies who are actively tearing a guy apart . . . feeding on this body over here. Drew has very enthusiastically explained what he wants so they are fighting over intestines, tearing the bits to pieces. As you can see there is just a little bit of blood . . . As long as you bring the zombies and provide Drew with what he wants, which is nasty horrible looking zombies doing bad things, you can't go wrong.[3]

Similarly, Production Designer Martin Whist and Special Effects Coordinator Joel Whist explain that they have used between 120–220 gallons of blood in this scene, and Goddard is shown excitedly spraying the walls with blood and requesting a "big bag of guts" to help dress the set.[4] The emphasis in this portion of the feature is not only on the gore but Goddard's relish in wallowing in the cinematic carnage.

As many fans and scholars have noted, Goddard's visible pleasure and excitement in the genre seems, however, at odds with the film's explicit critique of the pleasures of watching horror.[5] The film tells the story of a ritual sacrifice in which a group of college students are manoeuvred by a group of, primarily, white middle-class bureaucrats, technicians, and scientists into enacting the conventions of a teen horror film for the perverse pleasure of the "Old Ones," Gods who require not only a blood sacrifice but also to see the young people terrorized in the process. While both creators acknowledge that the film is asking the question "what is it about watching kids get killed that we as a people enjoy?'",[6] Gerry Canavan points out that their various commentaries on the film suggest

> that Goddard and Whedon may have made different films: Goddard, still at the start of his career as a director, tends to promote *Cabin* primarily as a great horror film, while Whedon, having already established himself, tends to suggest it alternatively

as the *last* horror film—the ultimate one, the very last one you will ever need to watch.[7]

So while Whedon emphasizes the film's thematic connection with *Buffy*, by asking "why do these things keep happening to the blond girl?" Goddard states: "I don't think you can set out to subvert a genre. I think you have to set out to embrace the genre and just try to do something new."[8] While I agree with Canavan's reading of the film's seeming ambivalence to horror through these diverging agendas, I also think the discourses surrounding Goddard's—and Whedon's—enthusiasm for the genre betray an excitement about the ability to make a horror *film*, perhaps in opposition to the restrictions upon them when they were making horror television. Both creators seem extremely excited about the aesthetic possibilities in making this film, whether it be in planning and staging the torture room or the moment when all of the monsters are released and pounce upon a team of paramilitary soldiers in an orgy of blood and gore. Whedon explains that "Drew definitely has a higher tolerance for blood than I do. A lot of the time, I said, 'I don't think there's this much blood in the world,' and then I'd look at the footage and go, 'This is pretty. Drew was right. This is pretty'."[9] While Goddard and Whedon do not overtly set up an opposition between film and TV, the paratexts that surround the film, including the behind the scenes feature, the DVD/Bluray audio-commentary, and the publication *The Cabin in the Woods: Official Visual Companion* devote extensive discussion to the graphic elements of the film, including detailed discussions of special effects and the construction of gore. In contrast, the more subtle engagement with horror in *Buffy the Vampire Slayer* enables the creators to celebrate the genre while also offering a social critique without generating the same level of dissonance. The seemingly restrained televisual approach, fuelled by network restrictions rather than creative choices, fostered a cerebral engagement with genre over the visceral, and thus avoids the tension between wallowing in the conventions of genre while simultaneously critiquing them.

The aim of this chapter, accordingly, will be to examine how the creators working within Whedon's longest-running television series, *Buffy* and *Angel*, negotiated the restrictions of television in order to explore and develop the potential for horror, utilizing it for social/cultural critique and critical allegory without eschewing entirely the genre's more excessive elements. In particular, I will focus upon the direction of the episodes to explore how the conventions of horror are aestheticized and how televisual restrictions offered opportunity to creatively redefine the genre rather than cause an affective dissonance due to the distancing effects of self-conscious restraint. As a result, these series exist alongside an established tradition of horror cinema, similarly and creatively influenced by production and censorship restrictions.

TV Context

At the time of writing, the horror genre has become one of the most visible and, with the phenomenal success of *The Walking Dead* (AMC 2010–present), one of the most popular genres on twenty-first-century television. There is a wealth of programs produced for mainstream networks, cable channels and pay-to-view streaming services that openly present themselves as horror through distinct visual and aural styles, from expressionist *mise-en-scène* to unsettling aural soundscapes to graphic special effects. While debates still occur about what is acceptable of the genre on television, series such as *American Horror Story* (FX 2011–present), *Ash vs. Evil Dead* (Starz 2015–2018), and *Santa Clarita Diet* (Netflix 2017–present) overtly showcase the excesses of the genre, contributing to the gradual erasure of certain distinctions between film and television horror. This has, however, not always been the case. Until recent years, the genre was traditionally rendered acceptable for television through its association with the Gothic[10] or integrated within a veil of genre hybridity.[11] While *Buffy* and *Angel* openly address and engage with the tropes of horror, they seemingly must contain their genre credentials through hybridity, with *Buffy* functioning as a teen horror series and *Angel* merging horror with the conventions of film noir.

Despite their hybridity, horror underpins *Buffy* and *Angel* and they stand as pivotal moments within the evolution of the genre on television in the twenty-first century, highlighting an intense fascination with the genre that prefigures the development of the television-horror boom in the late 2000s and early 2010s. Significantly, they share many of the same narrative and thematic concerns as *Cabin* in terms of challenging or calling attention to genre conventions as well as raising questions common to the genre around gender, voyeurism, and institutional evil.

The manner in which they are directed, however, render them seemingly less contradictory through their emphasis upon suggestion over graphic content. This is not to fall back on a false hierarchy between implicit and graphic horror, as there are long-established traditions of horror filmmaking that utilize violence, splatter, and gore to offer an intellectual and allegorical commentary (see, for example, the work of Wes Craven, David Cronenberg, and George A. Romero). Rather, it is my aim to highlight how the televisual context supported the construction of a particular allegorical approach to horror that suited the Whedon brand in ways that became unsettled by *Cabin*'s more overt (albeit fraught) celebration of the genre.

The Monster as Metaphor

It is well-established that in approaching *Buffy the Vampire Slayer*, Whedon's interest in horror was to undermine the woman-as-victim trope, particularly in the slasher film, but also to galvanize the genre as a metaphor for the horrors of adolescence.[12] The first season makes this transparent with its narratives surrounding bullying ("The Pack" [1.6]), online predators ("I Robot, You Jane" [1.8]) and social exclusion ("Out of Mind Out of Sight" [1.11]). This is particularly embodied in "Nightmares" (1.10), where the power of the Hellmouth and the traumatized soul of a child who was beaten into a coma by his little league coach causes everyone's worst nightmares to emerge within their waking state, forcing Buffy and her friends to confront their worst fears. While *Buffy*'s storylines contain many references to dreams, particularly through the slayer's possession of often-prophetic visions, this is a unique example of the dream state blurring with, and emerging into, the waking state.[13] With a story by Whedon, teleplay by co-executive producer David Greenwalt, and directed by established television director Bruce Seth Green, who was the only director to direct more than one episode of season one ("Teacher's Pet" [1.4], "The Pack," and "Nightmares") and then returned to direct five episodes in season two as well as three episodes of *Angel*, this episode brings together key creative forces behind the show's first season. The contribution of practitioners such as Greenwalt and Green, particularly in season one, should not be underestimated given their previous experience and the fact that Whedon was largely untested in terms of direction.[14]

As such, this episode offers an insightful illustration of how horror is carefully constructed on the show and in the service of the metaphor.

The episode begins firmly in horror territory, as the camera cranes up and over rubble within the sewers, covered in hundreds of lit candles, with Buffy appearing first as a shadow wielding her stake, and then emerging from a large tunnel. The lair into which she enters is cavernous and filled with shadows, and as she moves through the space toward the camera, the Master—Buffy's primary vampire-nemesis in season one—is glimpsed in the foreground of the frame, hiding behind columns. As she walks toward the crumbled remains of an old church altar, the Master approaches her from behind. When she turns to face him, she is held firmly within his gaze and drops her stake, unable to resist. As he leans in to bite her, she calls out and then the sequence cuts to her waking up from her nightmare. The scene is shot in a claustrophobic and expressionist style, featuring restricted close-ups, chiaroscuro and exaggerated shadows, Gothic architecture, and distorted sound effects, which overtly present it as nightmarish. The self-consciously baroque-Gothic design of the sequence uses the aesthetic conventions of horror to signal that this is a dream. As the episode continues, however, the emergence of nightmares in the real world is presented initially in a very "realistic" way without early indicators that these are dreams made real. They, largely, take place in the bright light of day and are couched within scenes that are not nightmares but rather represent the mundane everyday actions within the school, such as Xander, Buffy, and Willow discussing the homework before the teacher enters and calls upon one of the students, Wendell, to read from the text book. When he opens the book, dozens of spiders emerge and begin to crawl all over him as he screams. Other examples happen so naturalistically, and in the style of high school dramas, that no-one realizes that they are nightmares, such as Willow and Xander witnessing the embarrassment of a fellow student when his mother turns up in school and begins to mollycoddle him in front of his friends. Similarly, Cordelia appears suddenly to tell Buffy that there is a history exam. In the exam room, Buffy finds herself unable to answer any of the questions and notes that time is passing in the blink of an eye, experiencing a classic high school anxiety, while Cordelia later is confronted by her worst nightmare, which is to have bad hair and be dragged off to join the chess club. These scenes are presented in a naturalistic and mundane fashion, lacking the tropes of horror and thus reinforcing the message that the true horror of adolescence emerges from the everyday and not the fantastic.

As the episode continues, however, the nightmares become increasingly surreal and horrific, not only in their content, but in their stylistic atmosphere and in this manner the episode increasingly looks like, and evokes, horror. For instance, when looking for Buffy, Xander finds himself in an abandoned part of the school under construction, covered in plastic sheeting and with swastikas painted on the wall. From off screen, maniacal laughter is heard and suddenly a knife-wielding clown, reminiscent of Stephen King's Pennywise from *IT* (ABC 1990), bursts through the sheeting. Elsewhere in the school, Buffy attempts to escape a monster, "the Ugly Man," by crawling through a hedge to find herself suddenly in the cemetery at night, undermining real-word geography and temporality in the tradition of both nightmares and horror films such as *A Nightmare on Elm Street* (Wes Craven, 1984). At this point, the direction of the episode repeatedly evokes familiar horror imagery and iconic film moments such as Buffy being buried alive, shot in claustrophobic style from within the coffin. Later Giles finds Buffy's grave and, mourning her loss, gently lays his hand on the earth only to have a hand suddenly emerge to grab him, reminiscent of the conclusion of *Carrie* (Brian De Palma, 1976). As Giles falls back in horror, he pulls Buffy out of the earth, and she rigidly sits up, *Nosferatu*-style (F.W. Murnau, 1922), revealing that she is a vampire. Later when they return to the hospital to wake Billy from his coma, they find the corridors filled with hysterical staff and patients including one patient lumbering down the hallway in zombie fashion and a doctor staring in shock at his now-shrivelled hands. The horror is increasingly constructed not simply through the narrative events and cinematic allusions but through the claustrophobic and horror-filled *mise-en-scène* as reality becomes unhinged. Importantly, these overtly expressionistic scenes are designed to force each of the characters to confront their fears, beginning with Xander who stands up to the clown who terrorized him as a child, followed by Buffy who accepts her strength as a vampire to defeat the Ugly Man, and finally Billy who must unmask the Ugly Man in order to wake up from his coma and confront his attacker. The aesthetic conventions of horror are utilized to evoke the generic tradition that the genre is a space through which the audience, like the characters, confront fears. This technique is characteristic of how *Buffy* builds upon an established tradition within horror cinema to turn subtext into text, as discussed by Clayton Dillard in chapter 1 of this collection, "The Slasher Template: *Buffy the Vampire Slayer* vs. John Carpenter's *Halloween*."

One scene in this episode stands out as a significant corollary to *Cabin* through its deliberate stylistic evocation of the slasher film. Before nightmarish chaos ensues in the school, a young girl, Laura, decides to sneak into the basement to have a cigarette. While in the dark basement, the scene utilizes the I-camera, a slasher film convention in which Laura is filmed from the point of view of an attacker, the Ugly Man, as he skulks within the shadows, deliberately calling to mind iconic horror films such as *Black Christmas* (Bob Clark, 1974) and *Halloween* (John Carpenter, 1978).[15] As she lights up the cigarette, he approaches her and begins to beat her with what appears to be a club—later revealed to be his monstrous arm. The scene is an exemplary illustration of deliberately suggestive shooting and editing in which no actual contact or blood is shown but which still conveys extreme violence. The scene begins in long shot as he lunges at her, swinging his club-arm to hit her and hitting the overhead lamp in the process, causing it to swing, pendulum-like, creating pools of light and shadow. The scene then intercuts between a close-up of the light, a low-angle shot of the Ugly Man swinging down on Laura (toward the camera) and a medium close-up of her on the floor, screaming and turning away from each blow. The sound of the club's loud thudding links the shots together and suggests violent impact. The swinging lamp, an overt nod to the conclusion of *Psycho* (Alfred Hitchcock, 1960), provides glimpses of Laura and the monster, but carefully conceals the violence while the sharp cutting sound of the music, again evoking *Psycho* and Bernard Hermann's violin score for the infamous shower scene, reinforces the conveyance of violence. The final shot of the scene, a close-up of a sign which reads "Smoking Kills," strengthens the allusion to the often morally driven imperative of slasher films in which young people, usually women, are seemingly punished for their transgressive behaviour. Although Laura never overtly links this attack with a nightmare, the scene seems to represent her fear of being punished for smoking, her guilt conveyed by her desire to sneak into the basement and her embarrassment when she explains her actions to Buffy. The scene as it stands seems to contradict Whedon's desire to overturn presumed horror film conventions of young women being punished for their behavior, but its presence in the episode also calls attention to a culture of victim blaming, as both the girl and Billy blame themselves for the attack, the former because she was smoking and the latter because he lost the baseball game. Green's carefully constructed aesthetic design for the sequence, channelling the proto-slasher film *Psycho* as well as *Halloween*, enables the scene to evoke graphic visceral horror, emphasizing the brutality of the attack, while operating within network restrictions by not overtly showing violence.[16] The subsequent scene in which Buffy visits Laura in the hospital, where she is clearly physically and emotionally traumatized by her attack, humanizes her in a way that is not usually possible or desirable for minor characters within the slasher film, who are allegorical in nature, serving the genre's horror set pieces and thus are not granted sufficient screen time for character development. The monster as metaphor is explicit in "Nightmares" as well as its reflection on the tropes of horror. The references to iconic horror films like *Psycho, Halloween, A Nightmare on Elm Street,* and *Carrie* stand in for the genre's more explicit components and serve the thematic continuity of the episode.

Zombie as Metaphor in the Whedonverse

"You know what? It's always a great time for zombies. What I've learned about zombies, it's never a bad time for them" (Drew Goddard).[17]

Zombies remain one of the most popular cinematic and televisual sub-genres of horror, which has become ubiquitous across twenty-first-century popular culture. They have a long history, "shuffl[ing] out of the margins of empire, from Haiti and the French Antilles, making the leap from folklore to film in Victor Halperin's *White Zombie* (1932)," and, as Roger Luckhurst points out, their nature is widely known: "the zombie is that species of the undead that returns by some supernatural or pseudo-scientific sleight of hand. Zombies are speechless, gormless, without memory of prior life or attachments, sinking into an indifferent mass and growing exponentially."[18] While their initial foray into cinema grew out of Haitian folklore, and focused upon the zombie as an undead figure controlled by the voodoo witchdoctor who brought it back from the grave, since George A. Romero's *Night of the Living Dead* (1968) and *Dawn of the*

Dead (1978), they have largely been associated thematically with both apocalyptic visions of Vietnam-era social breakdown and anti-capitalism, and more practically with spectacular special make-up effects, blood splatter, body mutilation, and graphic depictions of cannibalism. Post-Romero zombies, as evidenced in contemporary television series such as *The Walking Dead, Z Nation* (Syfy 2014–present) and *Santa Clarita Diet*, not only stalk the living but graphically feed on them. In contrast to the similar carnage that could be visualized in the R-rated *Cabin in the Woods*, Whedon's TV shows were made in a broadcast context in which these elements were generally prohibited on screen. Despite such restrictions, however, zombies are surprisingly prevalent within the Whedonverse, appearing in a multitude of fashions and drawing upon both the zombie's Haitian legacy as well as the Romero tradition, sometimes simultaneously.[19] Within the Whedonverse, the zombie appears as monster-of-the-week in *Buffy* and *Angel* ("Dead Man's Party" *Buffy* 3.2, "The Thin Dead Line" *Angel* 2.14); Glory and Hive's mind-controlled slaves/inhumans in *Buffy* season five and *Agents of S.H.I.E.L.D* season three; ravenous cannibals in space in *Firefly* (Fox 2002) and *Serenity*'s (2005) Reavers; the placid and pliable Dolls, slaves to corporate programming, and the mindless and violent Butchers, who attack the living indiscriminately in *Dollhouse* (Fox 2009–10); and even Buffy's Mom returns as a zombie in "Forever" (5.17).

In most cases, working within the restrictions of network television meant that any forays into the zombie genre had to be handled with care and metaphor. For instance, in "Forever," when Buffy's sister Dawn performs a black magic spell to bring their mother Joyce Summers back from the dead, Joyce is shown only in two shots: a close-up of her feet moving slowly toward their house and her recognizable shadow on the living room curtains as she approaches their front door. Images of a zombiefied Joyce are withheld in favor of repeated close-ups of the photo of her used in the spell. The emphasis in this scene, written and directed by Marti Noxon and indebted to W.W. Jacobs' horror story "The Monkey's Paw" (1902) in which a mother's grief nearly revivifies the body of her son, is therefore not upon body horror or the decay of death but, like Jacobs' story, is upon the horror of grief as Buffy and Dawn face a world without their mother. In both texts the dead are not shown but instead emphasize absence over the corporeal presence of the zombie.[20] When there is a knock at the door, Buffy eagerly rushes to open it, prompting Dawn to break the spell by tearing up the photo. When Buffy opens the door her mother is gone—an apt metaphor for her death—encouraging the sisters to turn to each other to share their grief. The potential return of Buffy's Mom in the form of a zombie offers an opportunity to have her back but Noxon's stylistic presentation of this trope actually reinforces her absence and creates a space for mourning.

Similarly, the zombie metaphor is evoked when Buffy is brought back to life in season six. The metaphor is established from the start of the season when Buffy's body is revealed in her coffin in "Bargaining, Parts 1 & 2" (6.1/2), written by Noxon and David Fury respectively, with both episodes directed by David Grossman. In this sequence, Grossman presents Buffy's return by having the camera swoop below the surface of the grave and into the coffin to reveal her decomposing corpse before she revives, reconstitutes, and, finding herself buried alive in her coffin, claws her way, in true zombie fashion, through the earth (see Figure 9.1). In this sequence, the close-up of her skeletal face is kept brief before showing it re-form and re-animate. Despite its brevity, it is a graphic glimpse of Buffy's decomposing face, emphasizing the materiality and physicality of her death which stands in contrast to the fact that her friends talk about her death singularly along spiritual lines in terms of her soul being trapped in

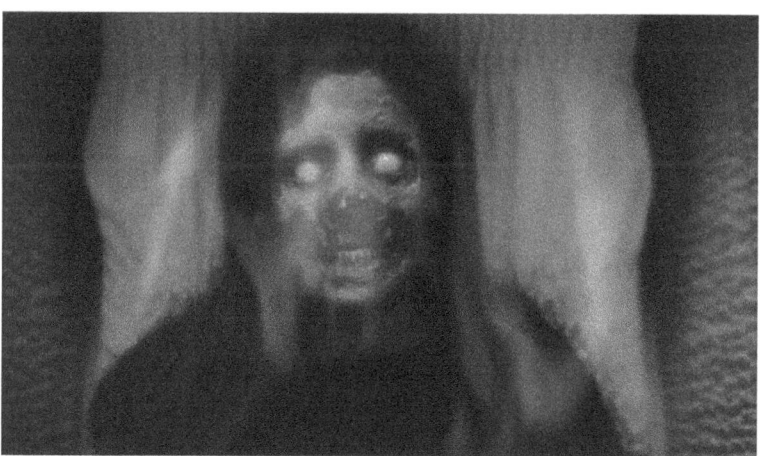

Figure 9.1 Buffy as a zombie in "Bargaining, Parts 1 & 2."

hell. In restoring her soul, they also revivify her body, leaving her trapped in her coffin. So where "Forever" is about loss, "Bargaining, Parts 1 & 2" is about death. The "glimpse" of gore is a technique that is used repeatedly in *Buffy* and *Angel* in order to provide the impression of graphic violence within the confines of broadcast television to support the series' thematic concerns, which in this case establishes Buffy as a zombie. This is later reaffirmed by her concerns that the spell that brought her back has brought her back "wrong," a possibility that was suggested in "Forever." Having aesthetically and narratively established her position as a zombie in these first two episodes, Buffy is presented throughout the season as oscillating between functioning as a zombie slave to external forces—the evil Trio who torment her as well as the friends for whom she performs normality—and mindlessly going through the motions of adult life, zombified by the trauma of being expelled from heaven on the one hand and the banality of adult existence, having to worry about employment, household maintenance, and paying bills. The carefully constructed image of horror regarding bodily frailty and decay established in these opening episodes lingers uncomfortably in subsequent episodes, overtly serving the adult themes of the season.

While broadcast on the same network as Buffy's first five seasons, The WB, and thus subject to the same broadcast restrictions, *Angel* was designed as a darker, more adult series than its parent-text, aimed at a twenty-something audience over *Buffy*'s target teenage viewers. As a result, a closer examination of the show reveals comparatively more liberal use of graphic violence than *Buffy*. The series frequently displays torture ("In the Dark" (1.3), "Origin" (5.18)), dismemberment ("Hellbound" (5.4)), physical beatings ("Billy" (3.6), "Power Play" (5.21)) and bodily penetration or breakdown ("Birthday" (3.11), "Underneath" (5.17)). Even so, as Matt Hills and Rebecca Williams argue, *Angel* is often marked "by its use of abject bodily fluids as stand-ins for images of actual bodily dismemberment and disintegration, as well as by its withholding, or symbolic translation, of full-blooded representations of abjection."[21] It walks a fine line between suggestion and display that marks a period of transition in television. This hybrid approach to horror also serves the series' thematic priorities. This is in evidence in how the show represents the zombie, in particular.

While *Buffy* uses the zombie to explore personal identity questions, on *Angel*, as in Romero, it is presented as part of a social critique. For instance, in "Habeas Corpses" (4.8) written by Jeffrey Bell and directed by Skip Schoolnik, the Beast, a demon from hell, murders all of the lawyers employed by evil law firm Wolfram & Hart, causing them to rise again, according to Angel, as "slow-moving, dim-witted things that crave human flesh" (see Figure 9.2). As a result of the attack, the building is locked down and when Angel and his team break in to retrieve Angel's son Connor trapped inside, they find it filled with corpses. These images are relatively graphic as the bodies are strewn across the floors and covered in blood, although the manner in which these scenes are lit by flashlight result in carnage flashing across the screen in glimpses. As the team walk through the building, stepping over corpses, they hear noises that suggest movement. Later the camera lingers on a close up of a woman's dead body as her eyes suddenly open in a moment that is highly reminiscent of similar scene in *Resident Evil* (Paul W.S. Anderson, 2002). In that film, a group of paramilitaries are sent in to investigate why the computer program, the Red Queen, that manages a scientific facility has poisoned its entire staff and locked the building down. As the team discover a flooded lab with glass windows through which they see bodies floating, the scene holds on a close-up of one of the bodies as her eyes open. This allusion to *Resident Evil* in "Habeas Corpses" builds up the reveal of the living dead in ways typical of the genre, which relies on intertext and reflexivity as part of a horror discourse.[22] Once they begin to rise, the undead first attack in small

Figure 9.2 Zombie as corporate evil in "Habeas Corpses."

numbers, with Angel and Connor pursued by a singular zombie who exhibits the standard lumbering movements of classic zombie films. Later the group become overrun, trapped in a room in *Night of the Living Dead* fashion, as the undead break through each of the doors. Stylistically, director Schoolnik favours close-ups and cramped compositions to convey the imposing presence of the zombies, reinforced by the extreme chiaroscuro of the lighting via flashlight. As Angel explains to Connor, zombies "are slow and stupid so we have a decent chance of beating them—unless of course there's hundreds of them." The montage of fragmented, claustrophobic close-ups of each of Angel's team fighting off zombies, gives the impression of large numbers swarming around our protagonists in keeping with genre convention.

This episode, however, holds back from having the zombies kill any of the humans and, while Gunn is bitten, the bite is not graphically presented, he does not become infected, nor is there any other visible evidence of cannibalism. The one bite to Gunn is sufficient to confirm that these monsters are flesh-eaters and thus a threat. Furthermore, the liberal use of blood is sufficiently graphic to clearly position the episode within the context of contemporary zombie texts without distracting from the episode's use of the undead as an allegory; not for a society tearing itself apart from within, as explored in Romero's *Night of the Living Dead*, or for consumerism as explored in his *Dawn of the Dead*, but rather for institutional and corporate evil. The lawyers for the firm have literally signed away their souls to the company, returning from the dead as a mindless workforce enslaved to the firm, and thus the episode emphasizes their numbers over the realities of their cannibalistic desires. While the zombies are visualized in Romero-fashion, with deathly pallor, blank expressions, and a seeming insatiable hunger for human flesh, this visualization is used to serve the show's evocation, in pre-Romero fashion, of the zombie as symbol for slavery in keeping with traditional folkloric zombie traditions from Haiti. As Gerry Canavan argues, the defining characteristic of the Haitian zombie mythology is "the submission of its will to the will of a master."[23] These lawyers have risen from the dead to remain in service as slaves to the corporate machine, continuing to pursue Angel and his team in their attempt to consume them (see Figure 9.2).

This theme is reiterated in "Home" (4.22), written and directed by Tim Minear. In the episode, former lawyer Lilah Morgan returns from the dead, having been murdered in the episode "Cavalry" (4.12), to present Angel and his team with an offer from Wolfram & Hart. Lilah explains her return by pointing out that her contract with the firm "extend[ed] beyond her death . . . standard perpetuity clause." That she is dead is confirmed by her revealing the 360-degree scar around her neck, where her head had been cut off. She is not a ghost or a vampire but rather a reanimated corpse, still bearing the scars of her death and working for the firm. The scar is presented as a clean and fine line around her neck, suggesting the sanitization of her reanimation—she is not a decaying corpse, but in true Lilah fashion is immaculately dressed in designer clothes and wearing an elegant scarf to conceal the scar (although she does later point out when Angel attacks her that the head comes off rather easily). More importantly—in a clever play on the slave origins of the zombie figure— the episode emphasizes the loss of Lilah's individual will to the will of her employers, explaining that once she's delivered this message, they will send her right back to hell. Even Wesley's attempt to burn her contract, and thus offer her release, proves useless. She remains a slave to the corporate machine. This theme is reiterated throughout season five, when the show's protagonists, Angel and his team, agree to take over the LA branch of Wolfram & Hart, in a bid to fight the monster from within the belly of the beast—a return to the zombie consumption theme. The team are repeatedly presented as puppets or slaves of the firm's Senior Partners, a metaphor that is literalized when Angel transforms into a puppet in "Smile Time" (5.14). In this manner, the series offers a humorous critique of the dehumanizing qualities of institutional manipulation and control, which is a significant theme of *Cabin in the Woods*. Wolfram & Hart's Senior Partners could as easily be replaced by *Cabin's* Ancient Ones, monstrous puppeteers manipulating humanity to do its perverse bidding and spearheading the apocalypse.[24] The manner in which the creators of *Angel*, both writers and directors, utilize the aesthetic conventions of horror with a liberal sprinkling of graphic gore to ground the show within the genre, allows this allegory to remain dominant.

Joss Whedon's two flagship horror series, *Buffy the Vampire Slayer* and *Angel*, predate the recent growth of television horror, the result of an increasingly liberal attitude to what can be shown on both network and cable television. As such, the series creators, from Joss Whedon as Executive Producer to staff writers and episode directors, had to carefully negotiate between genre convention and network restriction. Rather than impede the construction of horror, the stylistic approaches to the genre in these series wove a careful balance between suggestion and graphic display; genre hybridity, and overt shout-outs to specific horror films, subgenres and conventions, demonstrating a commitment to genre while also highlighting the construction of a Whedon brand of horror. The critical success of Whedon's brand has, in part, been linked to how these series carefully negotiated the representation of violence and horror, reinforcing, for many, established perceptions of suggested horror as more intellectually rigorous and revisionary than the perceived exploitation of graphic horror. This perception has been reinforced by Whedon, whose commentary as outlined above in relation to *Cabin*, has often distanced his brand from many popular traditions of horror. Yet this analysis of the production processes involved in *Buffy* and *Angel* highlights a desire to construct horror and push the boundaries of acceptability on television within a landscape of enforced restraint that fostered creativity, meaning that the Whedon brand of horror is in part the result of its TV production context. Significantly, these contexts facilitated *Buffy* and *Angel's* development of horror as allegory moving from the personal, focused around questions of gender and identity, to the institutional, exploring notions of corporate evil. These themes come together and underpin *Cabin in the Woods*, but are imbalanced by Whedon and, perhaps more so, Goddard's enthusiasm for aesthetic excess, no longer curtailed by the networks. As a result, the Whedon brand was ideally suited to television particularly at this pivotal moment in the development of horror for the small screen but rather than critically distancing Whedon's work from the excesses of the genre, the creative impact of these production restraints actually position *Buffy* and *Angel* as key moments within a long tradition of horror.

Notes

1. The 1992 film *Buffy the Vampire Slayer*, written by Whedon, is a hybrid of comedy and horror that leans more to the former than the latter.
2. Joss Whedon and Drew Goddard, qtd in "We Are Not Who We Are: Making the Cabin in the Woods," *The Cabin in the Woods* DVD/Bluray, Lions Gate Entertainment, 2012.

3. David Leroy Anderson, qtd in "We Are Not Who We Are: Making the Cabin in the Woods."

4. Martin Whist and Joel Whist, qtd in "We Are Not Who We Are: Making the Cabin in the Woods."

5. Joe Lipsett, "'One for the Horror Fans' vs 'An Insult to the Horror Genre': Negotiating Reading Strategies in IMDB Reviews of *The Cabin in the Woods*," *Slayage* 10.2/11.1 (Fall 2013/Winter 2014). Available at: www.whedon studies.tv/uploads/2/6/2/8/26288593/lipsett_slayage_10.2-11.1.pdf (accessed June 12, 2017); Kristopher Karl Woofter and Jasie Stokes, "Once More into the *Woods*: An Introduction and Provocation", *Slayage* 10.2/11.1 (Fall 2013/ Winter 2014). Available at: www.whedonstudies.tv/uploads/2/6/2/8/26288593/canavan_slayage_10.2-11.1.pdf (accessed June 12, 2017).

6. Drew Goddard, qtd in "We Are Not Who We Are: Making The Cabin in the Woods".

7. Gerry Canavan, "'Something Nightmares are From': Metacommentary in Joss Whedon's *Cabin in the Woods*", *Slayage* 10.2./11.1 (Fall 2013/Winter 2014). Available at: www.whedonstudies.tv/uploads/2/6/2/8/26288593/canavan_slayage_10.2-11.1.pdf (accessed June 12, 2017).

8. Joss Whedon and Drew Goddard, qtd in "We Are Not Who We Are: Making The Cabin in the Woods".

9. Joss Whedon, qtd in "Joss Whedon and Drew Goddard on the Making of the Film", *The Cabin in the Woods: The Official Visual Companion* (London: Titan Books, 2012), 9.

10. See Helen Wheatley, *Gothic Television* (Manchester: Manchester University Press, 2006); Matt Hills, *The Pleasure of Horror* (London: Continuum, 2005).

11. Stacey Abbott, *Angel* (Detroit: Wayne State University Press, 2009), 27–43; Lorna Jowett, "Plastic Fantastic? Genre and Science/Technology/Magic in *Angel*", in Lincoln Geraghty (ed.), *Channeling the Future: Essays on Science Fiction and Fantasy Television* (Lanham, MD: Scarecrow Press, 2009), 178.

12. Rhonda V. Wilcox, *Why Buffy Matters* (London and New York: I.B.Tauris, 2005), p. 18.

13. For more on the topic of horrific visions, dreams, and nightmares in Whedon's productions, see Cynthia Burkhead's Chapter in this collection: ""Everything is in them, everything hidden": The Prophecy of Horror in Dreams in *Buffy the Vampire Slayer* and *Angel*."

14. Prior to working on *Buffy*, David Greenwalt had worked as a writer and/or producer on series such as *The Wonder Years* (ABC 1988–1993), *Doogie Howser M.D.* (ABC 1989–1993), and *The X-Files* (Fox 1993–2002), while Bruce Seth Green was an established television director with past credits that include *Knight Rider* (NBC 1982–86), *T.J. Hooker* (ABC 1982–86), *Swamp Thing* (USA Network 1990–93), *Xena: Warrior Princess* (MCA Television 1985–2001), and *American Gothic* (CBS 1995–96).

15. See Clayton Dillard's chapter in this collection, "The Slasher Template: *Buffy the Vampire Slayer* vs. John Carpenter's *Halloween*".

16. It is worth noting that while *Psycho* is recognized as a classic of Hollywood cinema, often applauded for its restraint, its aesthetic design at the time of production was perceived by many as violent and salacious, particularly the brutal shower scene. Many critics thought it had gone too far in its graphic display of horror. While allusions to *Psycho* in this episode may seem to evoke high art comparisons that privilege suggested over graphic violence, the evocation of this scene is far more complicated.

17. Drew Goddard, qtd by Jordan Zakarin, "Drew Goddard on 'Cabin in the Woods', The Whedonverse, and Internet Geekery (Q&A)," *Hollywood Report* 13 April 2012. Available at: www.hollywoodreporter.com/heat-vision/drew-goddard-cabin-woods-joss-whedon-lost-star-wars-311683 (accessed January 1, 2017).

18. Roger Luckhurst, *Zombies: A Cultural History* (London: Reaktion Books, 2015), 7.

19. For a broader discussion of the history and evolution of the zombie, see the following key works on the zombie and horror cinema: Robin Wood, "An Introduction to the American Horror Film", in Barry Key Grant (ed.), *Planks of Reason: Essays on the Horror Film* (Lanham, MD & London: The Scarecross Press, Inc, 1996), 164–200; Kyle William Bishop, *American Zombie Gothic: The Rise and Fall (and Rise) of the Walking Dead in Popular Culture* (Jefferson, NC and London: McFarland & Company, Inc., 2010); Kim Paffenroth, *Gospel of the Living Dead: George Romero's Visions of Hell on Earth* (Waco, TX: Baylor University Press, 2006); Stacey Abbott, *Undead Apocalypse: Vampires and Zombies in the 21st Century* (Edinburgh: Edinburgh University Press, 2016).

20. Thank you to Kristopher Woofter for reminding me of the parallel between "Forever' and "The Monkey's Paw'.

21. Matt Hills and Rebecca Williams, "*Angel's* Monstrous Mothers and Vampires With Souls: Investigating the Abject in 'Television Horror'", Stacey Abbott (ed.), *Reading Angel: The TV Spin-off with a Soul* (London and New York: I.B.Tauris, 2005), 208.

22. A further allusion to *Resident Evil* is evoked by the Conduit to the Senior Partners, that takes the form of a small child in a red dress reminiscent of the visual and vocal interface for the Red Queen computer system which is also in the form of a small child.

23. Gerry Canavan, "Fighting a War You've Already Lost: Zombies and *zombis* in *Firefly/Serenity* and *Dollhouse*", *Science Fiction Film and Television* 4.2 (2011), 178.

24. The glimpse of a silhouette of multi-tentacled monster buried beneath the offices of Wolfram & Hart in "You're Welcome" (5.12) is reminiscent of the Ancient Ones, the Gods kept below the organizational facility for the ritual sacrifice in *Cabin*.

10

Forever Knight, Angel, and *Supernatural*: A Genealogy of Television Horror/Crime Hybrids

Erin Giannini

A vampire, haunted by centuries of misdeeds, decides to dedicate his (un)life to helping the helpless in a major city, hoping that someday his actions will help him become human again. He is aided by human friends, including one with whom he has slow-burning potential romance, and his dark past continually comes back to haunt him. In broad terms, this is the over-arching plot of five seasons of the US television series *Angel* (1999–2004). It also fairly accurately describes the early-1990s Canadian[1] series *Forever Knight* (1992–1996). Similar to earlier series such as the simultaneous airing of the "gothic sitcoms"[2] *The Addams Family* (1964–1966) and *The Munsters* (1964–1966), which both "satirized and venerated the American family"[3] portrayed in earlier sitcoms such as *Leave It To Beaver* (1957–1963), both *Forever Knight* and *Angel* share similar televisual DNA with the TV horror tradition, stretching back to the daytime soap opera *Dark Shadows* (1966–1971) and forward to the long-running horror series *Supernatural* (2005–present).

Developed by James D. Parriott from his television movie *Nick Knight* (August 20, 1989), *Forever Knight* initially aired as part of CBS Television's

181

"Crimetime After Primetime" syndication block.[4] The protagonist, Nick Knight (Geraint Wyn Davies), is an 800-year-old vampire trying to atone for his sins by working as a police detective in Toronto, while being tormented by either his own blood lust, or the machinations of his vampire mentor, LaCroix (Nigel Bennett). The genre of the series itself is primarily a procedural, but with enough gothic and horror touches to qualify the series as a gothic-horror/procedural hybrid.

Angel was a spin-off of *Buffy the Vampire Slayer* (1997–2003); 240-year-old vampire Angel (David Boreanaz) attempts to atone for past (and more recent) evils by "helping the helpless" of Los Angeles, often directed by visions funneled through friend and coworker Cordelia Chase (Charisma Carpenter) from the "Powers-That-Be," a mystical force that operates as the good counterpoint to the equally mystical "Senior Partners" of law firm Wolfram & Hart as a force for evil. The series is a generic hybrid of horror and neo-noir in a way that ties it to its direct predecessor (*Forever Knight*) and progeny (*Supernatural*), as well as the wider range of "gothic television,"[5] complete with dead mothers in *Angel* and *Supernatural*, and in all three intimations or instances of incest, and violent pasts/secret lives that impinge upon their protagonists' present.[6] As Stacey Abbott argues, however, *Angel* not only offered "complex and ambitious narrative arcs and an exciting interplay of genre conventions," but also "broke the conventions of television drama,"[7] something *Supernatural*, a series about two brothers who fight supernatural threats, would embrace across multiple seasons and episodes that were defiantly metatextual, tying these series to their historical antecedents in gothic/horror television.[8]

In this article, I examine both the narrative and production correspondences between *Forever Knight* and *Angel*, extending into *Supernatural*, building on both Jeffrey Bussolini's and Alyson Buckman's examinations of television intertextuality, particularly their work around what Bussolini terms "intertextuality of casting" and Buckman's "intra-auterial"[9] casting in the Whedonverse, and Bussolini's analysis of "constitutive intertextuality"; that is, "the practice in which major structural elements or images of one show [...] are built into the dramatic world or discourse of another."[10] The connections between these three series are part of a larger pattern in what Helen Wheatley has termed "gothic television": "a domestic form of the genre [...] deeply concerned with [...] stories of unspeakable family secrets and homely trauma."[11] Particularly important are the ways in which these gothic series both reference and are influenced by their televisual forebears, a project also taken up by Lorna Jowett and Stacey Abbott in their analysis of the television horror genre in both US and UK broadcast contexts.[12] While these three series do not require knowledge of the others to understand their narratives, the diegetic (narrative) and non-diegetic (production/ casting) similarities between the three provide the opportunity to examine both their narrative and extratextual correspondences and resonances as part of the wider corpus of North American horror television.

Not Blood, Cocktail Sauce: Seen and Unseen Horror, From *Forever Knight* to *Supernatural*

The third episode of *Forever Knight*, "For I Have Sinned," features a serial killer targeting Catholic parishioners he feels are hypocrites. While the episode description included with the region 1 DVD refers to these murders as "gruesome," the viewer is not privy to the sight of said murders; the horror is confined to the expressions of Nick and his human partner Schanke (John Kapelos). Debuting three years after *Forever Knight* ended, *Angel* also frequently used this strategy, as Matt Hills and Rebecca Williams elucidate, conveying horror through the absence of gore.[13] They cite the episode "Expecting" (1.12)—in which Wesley (Alexis Denisof) and Angel fight a demon about to give birth—as one such example; the killing of the demon is portrayed in shadows and slime, rather than explicitly seen. In previous decades, broadcast standards restricted both language and image, which made television horror difficult to categorize as such. As a result, Hills points out, the horror genre on television has previously been marginalized or dismissed as "inauthentic"[14] within television and television genre studies,[15] partly due to its inability to show graphic images on broadcast television.[16] By the time *Supernatural* debuted in 2005, these restrictions had eased, allowing that series to offer far more graphic images than its predecessors, including episodes featuring a man transforming into a cannibalistic monster (his eating habits are depicted in detail ("Metamorphosis" (4.4)); a man killed by razor blades in Halloween candy and a young woman scratching herself to death ("I Believe the Children Are Our Future" (5.6)); or a couple literally devouring one another during sex ("My Bloody Valentine" (5.14)).

Angel, as Abbott notes, aired during a period of transition in terms of what broadcast television horror could show. The horrific is often implied through language,[17] as Abbott cites lawyer Lilah Morgan's (Stephanie Romanov) threat to skin an employee and have it "stapled back on inside out" ("Quickening" (3.8)), or off-screen, as in several demon-killing scenes in "That Old Gang of Mine" (3.3).[18] As Stephen King points out, suggestion is an effective strategy, citing William F. Nolan's contention that the most frightening thing is that "behind a closed door"; once that door is opened, the tension is released: "'A bug ten feet tall is pretty horrible [...], but I can deal with a ten-foot-tall bug. I was afraid it might be a *hundred* feet tall.'"[19] Abbott points out while *Angel* did show some graphic depictions, even within its first season,[20] the camera does not linger on these images, making the "'glimpse' [...] all the more disturbing."[21]

Hills suggests one reason horror had been marginalized within television studies is due to the earlier acceptance of John Ellis' "glance theory," which holds that television as medium does not offer compelling visual or narrative work that rewards audience investment; also, because of a domestic sphere full of other distractions, they merely "glance" at television as they would any other domestic appliance.[22] My goal here is not to argue against Ellis' contention, which is already well-canvassed territory (John Thornton Caldwell's *Televisuality* is a book-length repudiation of Ellis' theory[23]; Wheatley uses this to examine neo-Gothic series such as *Twin Peaks*[24]), but rather to marry Abbott's contention that series such as *Angel* use the "glimpse" as a stylistic choice to convey horror within the boundaries of television's censoring of such images, to Hill's citing of Ellis' theory as one reason scholars had not focused on horror television, while also undermining Ellis' concept that television narratives do not command audience attention. In their examination of the *Frankenstein*-inspired *Buffy* episode "Some Assembly Required," Jowett and Abbott suggest that the "glance" of horror, as in Cordelia's reaction to a pieced-together female body or the use of science to resurrect a beloved brother, positions that particular episode's narrative as "foreground[ing]... emotional realism" rather than "graphic horror," thereby working around the broadcast standards by focusing on reactions and consequences rather than overt display.[25] *Angel*, a transitional text between the relatively bloodless *Forever Knight* and the more graphic displays in *Supernatural*, uses this strategy to convey horror or gore within broadcast standards, something that *Supernatural*'s visual display of horrific or graphic content did not have to consider.

Indeed, the increased targeting of niche (or fan) audiences in light of the proliferation of cable and satellite original programming competing for viewer time,[26] Hills argues, is one particular shift that can be cited as a reason for a re-evaluation of the quality of television horror; this targeting also allows a certain amount of visual (that is, graphic) latitude.[27] While Jowett and Abbott point out that premium-cable horror series such as *True Blood* (2008–2014) and *Dexter* (2006–2013) are able to show excessive displays of graphic violence, they take issue with the idea that such graphic displays represent the definitive definition of TV horror. Series such as comedy/drama *Pushing Daisies* (2007–2009) employ "spectacle"; that is, "visual and aural excess" that easily "encompass[es] both terror and horror."[28] In this respect, both their niche positioning— *Forever Knight* as a Canadian-produced-and-filmed[29] program that aired in a late-night slot on US broadcast (and later, cable), *Angel* and *Supernatural* airing on the netlet the WB[30]—and varying degrees of suggestive visual or aural display of terror or horror, allow all three series to fit comfortably within the scope of television horror whether or not they offer overt displays of gore.[31]

"In hell you tend to know a lot of the people": Where *Angel* meets *Supernatural*

Not only do these three series represent the shifts in television horror, from the gothic (*Forever Knight*) to the hybrid (*Angel*) to the graphic (*Supernatural*), they also share narrative- and production-level similarities and intertextual play that underscore their relations. The final two points I consider—the shared casts between *Angel* and *Supernatural*, and the ways in which all three series employ metafictional strategies—illuminate the context in which they are produced. To that end, I examine two episodes from each series: *Forever Knight*'s "Stranger Than Fiction" (2.3) and "Curiouser and Curiouser" (2.22); *Angel*'s "Awakening" (4.10) and "Smile Time" (5.14), and *Supernatural*'s "The Monster At the End of This Book" (4.18) and "The French Mistake" (6.15). As with the aforementioned evolving visual representations of horror, the use of metafiction also grows more obvious, with nearly every season of *Supernatural* featuring a fourth-wall-breaking episode.[32]

Building on both Bussolini's analysis of casting choices and "constitutive intertextuality,"[33] and Buckman's examination of what she terms "intra-auterial casting"—the reuse of actors in multiple Whedon-verse series in roles that recall their previous Whedonverse characters[34]—I would add another term: inter-auterial casting. That is, *Supernatural*'s heavy re-use of notable (if often secondary) Whedonverse actors in roles strikingly similar to the roles they played within the Whedon series.

This "intertextuality does not relativize or sweep away artistic practice in an open-ended play of references and associations. Rather [...] awareness of it multiplies possibilities for artistic practice by dramatically expanding the 'palette' available to cultural creators and emphasizing the inherently social and relational aspects of artistic production," under-mining the concept of the "individual genius and solitary creation."[35] It is the "palette" Bussolini suggests that is the most appropriate description of the visual, production, and narrative correspondences between these three series.

In addition to the character correspondences between Nick and Angel, the *mise-en-scène* of both series is remarkably similar. Both series rely on night shots as well as panning aerial shots; however, these shots offer different connotations in both series. With *Angel*, the city of Los Angeles functions as a character in its own right; as Benjamin Jacob writes, Los Angeles is the home of Hollywood and the setting for much film noir (a category *Angel* functions comfortably within), sits on a fault, and has a history of inequality, violence, and riots. Los Angeles thus provides an excellent setting for the (unreal) vampire with a history of violence, who too sits on a fault (between Angel and his alter-ego Angelus).[36] Episodes often position Angel on rooftops following panning shots of the city itself; this underscores his role as protector and is visually reminiscent of both the multiple iterations of Batman and the angels in Wim Wender's *Wings of Desire* (1987).[37] In *Forever Knight*, however, the precise location in which Nick and Schanke police (Toronto) is never made clear; therefore, the city functions less as a separate character in the way Los Angeles does on *Angel* and more as allegory. Further, the panning aerial shots in *Forever Knight* are diegetically linked to one of Nick's abilities (he can fly), and serve as between-scene transition shots.

In *Supernatural*, the road serves as both transition and character, moving the Winchesters from town to town and episode to episode; until the eighth season, their most permanent home was a 1967 Chevy Impala, suggesting the ship *Serenity* in Whedon's series *Firefly* (that is, a vehicle that is both home and workspace) rather than the more permanent precinct/loft and hotel of *Forever Knight* and *Angel*, respectively. Road-tripping is such a feature of *Supernatural* that each season finale episode begins with a pre-episode recap titled "The Road So Far." As Sam and Dean are human, *Supernatural* never employs the aforementioned aerial shots, which position Angel and Nick as either above or separate from humanity. That being said, their knowledge of and interaction with the supernatural, itinerant lifestyles frequently maintained through criminal activity, and lack of community, position them as outside the mainstream.[38] The brothers' liminal states, the violence of their work, and a dark *mise-en-scène* tie *Supernatural* to the previous two series in the kind of constitutive intertextuality described by Bussolini. Further, the way both *Angel* and *Supernatural* structure their narratives, particularly in *Supernatural*'s first five seasons, also fall under this rubric. While *Forever Knight* gestured toward ongoing storylines—Nick's relationship with Janette and Natalie and LaCroix, hiding the existence of vampires from those closest to him—both *Angel* and *Supernatural* relied heavily on story arcs that bridged multiple seasons and terminated with the close of their fifth seasons, in which the respective teams faced a life-or-death apocalypse scenario that they may or may not survive ("Not Fade Away" (5.22) and "Swan Song" (5.22), respectively). Finally, both often find greater strength and support in families of choice rather than those of blood; the staff of Angel Investigations, although not related by blood, often operate as a family structure, and characters such as older hunter Bobby Singer (Jim Beaver) or hacker Charlie Bradbury (Felicia Day) stand in as father and sister figures, respectively, to the Winchester brothers. While Sam and Dean's bond as brothers is a key element of the series' narrative, the idea that "family don't end with blood" ("No Rest for the Wicked" (3.16)) also serves as a vital element within *Supernatural*.

This extends to the intertextual casting between both *Angel* and *Supernatural*. At least thirty actors who originally appeared within the Whedonverse (if not always *Angel* specifically) have also appeared on *Supernatural* in both major and minor roles. With the high volume of crossover,[39] I am electing to focus specifically on those who first appeared within the Whedonverse in a role significant enough to provide some level of characterization, and were developed within *Supernatural*. This intersection has different resonances depending on the series in which the actor/actresses had the most significant role. That is, *Supernatural's* casting of Amber Benson ("Bloodlust" (2.3)), Mercedes McNab ("Fresh Blood" (3.7)), Jewel Staite ("The Girl Next Door" (7.3)), and Charisma Carpenter and James Marsters ("Shut Up, Dr. Phil" (7.4)), all call upon the actors' previous roles as a point of reference in their characterization: McNab plays a vampire in both series; Benson's vampire gives up human blood and recalls the gentleness of Tara Maclay in *Buffy*; Staite's Amy Pond,[40] protective of friends and family and loathe to do violence, is similar to her earlier portrayal of mechanic Kaylee Frye on *Firefly*; and Carpenter and Marsters' characterizations as a married couple in *Supernatural*, with Carpenter's wealthy and entitled Maggie Stark and Marsters' Don Stark a romantic with a contentious relationship with the woman he loves suggest both Cordelia and Spike. Much like mainstream genres such as hospital dramas and police procedurals have "co-opted" horror signifiers in the service of their particular "realistic" narratives (healing people, solving crimes),[41] the (re)use of these actors in roles so structurally similar to their previous roles relies on the viewers' understanding of the greater corpus of the TV horror landscape; the previous character is thus "co-opted" by *Supernatural* as both a draw to viewers and a short-hand characterization of a minor role.

There is, however, another casting category in which one could place Mark Sheppard, Felicia Day, and Jeffrey Dean Morgan—three individuals whose original portrayal within the Whedonverse was deepened within *Supernatural* due to their greater prominence within the latter. Sheppard is probably the most significant case: a recurring then main cast member from season five's "Abandon All Hope ..." (5.10) to season twelve's "All Along the Watchtower" (12.23), Sheppard's Crowley, the King of Hell, shared many features with criminal opportunist Badger, the petty crime lord in *Firefly*. Day, who first appeared on *Buffy* as potential Slayer Vi, was initially characterized as shy and scared, yet in the final episode, after all the potential Slayers become actual Slayers, is decisive and strong ("Chosen" (7.22)). This is mirrored in the seasons-long trajectory of Day's Charlie, once a shy and scared child ("Pac-Man Fever" (8.20)), and later a hacker convinced by the Winchesters to help take down an evil corporation through the invocation of her favorite female heroines ("The Girl With the Dungeons and Dragons Tattoo" (7.20)), and then continuing to fight demons. Finally, Morgan may be the most interesting case; on *Angel*, he played a man whose partner has been killed by vampires. His desire for revenge causes him to lose his job and engage in borderline criminal activity in order to avenge the man he loved ("Provider" (3.12)).[42] This is a close analog to his later role as John Winchester, whose wife's death via demon ("Pilot" (1.1)) spurs him onto a decades-long, country-wide revenge spree with his sons in tow. In that respect, what is suggested in his portrayal on *Angel* is brought to fruition within *Supernatural*'s narrative.[43]

Given that these constitutive and casting intertexts are so prevalent across these series, it is not surprising all three have also employed metafictional strategies that comment directly on their constructed narratives.[44] In this final section, I examine six episodes across the three series that both figuratively and literally operate as "fictions about fiction,"[45] as well as "bubble episodes," which differ from the usual episodes either narratively or structurally to "capitalize on the audiences' taste for innovation."[46] Yet this difference allows each of the episodes examined below to comment on ongoing series' elements, such as the story arc, the characters, or the context in which they are produced and consumed.

Nowhere is the metafictional impulse as strong and as frequently used as in *Supernatural*; however, *Forever Knight* made tentative steps in its second season, with two episodes that directly reference literary work (both fictional and real) as the central part of the narrative. "Stranger Than Fiction" involves a novelist, Emily Weiss, who has written a series of bestselling novels about vampires that so adequately capture the experience, the vampire community is literally out for her blood—a plot that deliberately echoes Anne Rice's *Vampire Chronicles*, in which the protagonists of both *Interview With the Vampire* (1976) and *The Vampire Lestat* (1985) are outcasts for revealing vampire secrets. It is, however, the various sequences throughout the episode, in which the author herself, as well as most of the major characters—Nick, Schanke, and Natalie—take on the roles of the novel's characters that suggests the later fourth-wall-breaking of *Angel* and *Supernatural*. While it is not surprising that Nick and Natalie, albeit in separate sequences, imagine themselves as the fictional vampire Christian and his mortal love Sophie, respectively, it is Schanke's casting of himself as Christian's controlling vampire mentor that offers the most insight into a character frequently portrayed as bumbling and powerless compared to his partner.

The characterization of Schanke as powerful and in control is continued in the other metafictional episode of the series, "Curiouser and Curiouser" (2.22), which both directly and indirectly references Lewis Carroll's *Alice in Wonderland*. Overwhelmed by a shooting Nick feels he could have prevented, Nick's guilt creates an alternate reality in which he is no longer a vampire; instead, he is a beleaguered husband to Janette, and has previously experienced a breakdown that included delusions he is a vampire. The Carroll connection is not only emphasized by the appearance of a stuffed caterpillar throughout the episode, but also the fact that Nick's internal affairs investigation is headed by a woman named Carol Lewis (Judith Scott). While it is possible to dismiss the events of the episode as a dream sequence, the ways in which the narrative progresses, the oft-repeated ties to Carroll's work, and the off-kilter and surreal visuals that the episode engages in, pushes it into the territory of metafiction. That is, as will be examined below with regard to the *Angel* episode "Awakening" (1.10), Nick's alternate reality operates as a type of wish fulfillment—he is human, which is his avowed desire throughout the series—and none of those within this reality are acting entirely out of character; rather, different aspects of said characters are highlighted due to the different context in which they operate. Schanke is the dominant partner to Nick's troubled detective, Nick and Janette's centuries-old connection is manifested in a failing marriage, and his affair with Natalie speaks to his desire for her that his vampirism prevents him from enacting.

While neither "Awakening" (1.10) nor "Smile Time" (5.14) directly references either invented or real books, both reference filmic or televisual texts. In "Awakening," Angel's soul is removed through magic that creates "perfect happiness"; the requirement for his soul to exit his body. Unlike the earlier "Spin the Bottle" (4.7), which uses a framing device that speaks directly to the constructed narrative,[47] there is little initial indication that what the viewer sees is itself a fantasy. The metafictional conceit is more subtle here, and ties into *Forever Knight*'s "Curiouser and Curiouser," both in that the events of the episode are occurring in the mind of one individual (Nick or Angel) and that the actions of those within the fantasy subtly (or not-so-subtlety, as the narrative progresses) shade into the vampire-in-question's wish fulfillment. The story itself, in which Angel's soul must be removed to gain information on one of the season's antagonists, gradually accrues details that point to fantasy over reality: the weapon to defeat said antagonist is (relatively) easily obtained, the deep divisions between the group are resolved one by one, and the characterizations of certain individuals, particularly teammates Gunn and Wesley, recall their pasts rather than their subsequent growth and development.

The pop-culture genesis of Angel's perfect-day fantasy is referenced directly in the next episode, when his alter-ego Angelus asks Wesley: "What's the deal with Angel and the *Raiders of the Lost Ark* ... caves, booby traps, the requisite phallic sword?" ("Soulless" (4.11)). Commenting on the filmic genesis of Angel's fantasy adds another dimension to the episode; namely, its position as a fiction about fiction within the additional fictive context of the series itself. "Smile Time," however, shares more in common with *Supernatural*'s "The French Mistake" (both episodes written by Ben Edlund, the only Whedonverse writer to date that crossed over to *Supernatural*[48]); rather than only engaging the narrative context of the series, this episode's metafiction also speaks to the series' production context.[49] *Smile Time* is a children's program whose creator, Gregor Framkin (David Fury) made a deal with demons in order to boost the show's ratings and keep in on the air. The deal's adverse effect is that not only do the demonic puppets use the series to drain the life force out of its audience, but Framkin is turned into a puppet subjected only to their whims. When Angel goes to investigate, he too is turned into a puppet; a fate that articulates his own feelings of being controlled and manipulated by the corporation within which he works (see Figure 10.1).[50] While the entire fifth season was an examination of how the corporate environment changes those who work within it,[51] "Smile Time" brought both character and production issues to the surface. If Framkin is viewed as a stand-in for Whedon (Fury is one of Whedon's regular stable of writers), the episode makes manifest the idea of being controlled by his characters/producers. That Framkin's puppet-ness is not apparent until we see the hand of one of the puppets in Framkin's back underscores the somewhat invisible control exerted on showrunners and writers by network executives, something Whedon's later film *The Cabin in the Woods* addresses more directly.[52]

Figure 10.1 Puppet Angel is not happy about who is pulling the strings in "Smile Time."

This lack of agency is mirrored in *Supernatural*'s "The Monster at the End of This Book" and "The French Mistake," two episodes that resonate with both the popular culture genesis of *Angel*'s metafictional episodes and *Forever Knight*'s focus on real and imagined novels. "The Monster at the End of This Book" focuses on the brothers' discovery of a series of books that accurately chronicle their hunting adventures. They confront the author, who is shocked to discover that both they and their adventures are real, and tells them that the book he is working on in the series features himself as author being confronted by his characters, referencing Vonnegut's *Breakfast of Champions*. (Although Luigi Pirandello's *Six Characters in Search of an Author* is arguably a closer analog.) The angel Castiel (Misha Collins) reveals Chuck (Rob Benedict) is a prophet and what he writes cannot be changed; the brothers are doomed to follow the script as written, just as the actors themselves do. That they manage to subvert what Chuck writes[53] allows them a narrative agency that sets up the next season's arc: the brothers are fated to act as vessels for archangels Michael and Lucifer and engage in an apocalyptic battle, an endgame they also manage to undermine by embracing their own free will to choose. As Hugh Davis writes in his analysis of the series *Dollhouse* through Pirandello's work, Pirandello's "takes on reality center around a belief that his characters, as people, embody roles that outside forces make them play,"[54] a concept that the Winchester brothers—embracing free will—manage to subvert in "The Monster at the End of This Book," but nonetheless find themselves struggling with in season six's "The French Mistake."

K.T. Torrey analyzes how in season six Castiel's battle to defeat angels that wish to restart the apocalypse instead robs the brothers of this hard-won narrative agency. Like "Curiouser and Curiouser," the brothers are thrust into an alternate reality with no demons and monsters; they are instead the stars of a series known as Supernatural (an adaptation of a fake series of books about fictional characters), in which Sam and Dean are actors known as Jared Padalecki and Jensen Ackles. "Reduced to mere characters in TV's Supernatural, Sam and Dean have become the empty vessels the archangels so desperately desired; they say other people's lines, stand where they are told, and keep their mouths shut."[55] This sense of emptiness, in which they are merely the playthings of more powerful forces, was also a significant feature of *Angel*'s narrative trajectory, particularly in the ways it became difficult for the protagonist(s) to discern what constituted both moral action and free will.

Much as the representation of horror on television can be traced from the relatively bloodless *Forever Knight* to the standards-pushing gore on *Supernatural*, so too can the trajectory of metafictional commentary on television horror genre itself be traced in an arc through these three series. It is arguable that *Supernatural*'s frequent recourse to metafictional episodes signals genre exhaustion. This does not account for the use of this conceit in older series such as *Route 66* or *The Munsters*[56]; indeed, Jowett and Abbott argue, building on Jeffrey Sconce's concept of "haunted media,"[57] that the technology of television itself can be a site for horror, particularly the ways in all of the episodes examined above reference or build upon media texts (print, film, and television). They write:

> The notion of TV as a conduit to other worlds grows out of, and reverses, the mundanity of television, defamiliarizing TV as a communication medium that is not only able to link the natural with the supernatural but also to network this uncanny communication. Networking ups the horror, shifting from a one-to-one confrontation, a personal threat, to something on a viral scale, an apocalyptic potential made possible by the very ubiquity of TV.[58]

The increased generic hybridity and the metatextual touches from *Forever Knight* to *Supernatural* do not necessarily have to indicate a genre in decline, but rather a creative awareness of the multiple (and continually changing) contexts in which these series operated.[59] Further, the strangeness of the media in question impinging upon or directing the lives of the characters, as well as the ways in which these "fictions about fictions," become more ubiquitous and obvious (shifting from imagining oneself as a character in a novel ("Stranger Than Fiction") to being reduced to one ("The Monster at the End of This Book")) can itself be considered a site for horror.

Conclusion

While these series are narratively unrelated, viewing them together allows the viewer to trace particular facets of the evolution of television horror on visual, narrative, and production levels. As a noir/horror series, *Angel* was a strange fit for the WB Network, with its dark themes, noir-ish *mise-en-scène*, and the moral relativism of its characters. Yet taken with both *Forever Knight* and *Supernatural*, the series represent what *TV Tropes* has dubbed "Spiritual Successors": "a type of sequel that is not part of the same world or story as its predecessor, but is nonetheless considered to be a successor because it's made by the same creators; shares common themes, styles, or elements."[60] The thematic, casting, and production correspondences between these series offer a window into the shifts within the television horror genre over the past two decades, including greater genre prominence on broadcast, cable, and streaming services, and the co-option of TV horror techniques into mainstream genres.[61] This mainstreaming indicates that "rather than being incompatible with horror, television is, and has always been, a significant location for horror."[62]

In writing about *Supernatural*, Jowett and Abbott argue that, despite its reliance on decades of horror tropes, "the series' 'newness' lies in merging conventions drawn from various places" and "without the complex weaving together of soap-style relationship arcs that involves the viewer in the intimate emotional lives of its protagonists, its horror monsters would have little resonance."[63] As I've striven to show through this article, such techniques are part of a longer history of complex characters, visual interest, and evolving story arcs within the larger trajectory of television horror, as well as the more intimate trajectory of *Forever Knight, Angel,* and *Supernatural.*

Notes

1. The series was a co-production between two Canadian production companies (Glen Warren Productions and Paragon Entertainment Corporation), two US companies (TriStar Television and USA Network [owned by NBC Universal]), and the Germany-based Tele München.
2. Helen Wheatley, *Gothic Television* (Manchester: Manchester University Press, 2006), 1.
3. Ibid., 145.
4. This syndication block was a mix of American- and Canadian-produced content; the series imported from Canada were initially created to meet the Canadian Broadcasting Company's requirement for Canadian-produced content ("Broadcasting Act" 1991). This blend presaged, to some extent, the later move of series such as *The X-Files* (1993–2006, 2016–present) and *Supernatural* to Vancouver, lured by its lower production costs. Like the later *Angel,* its broadcast history was fraught; after being cancelled by CBS, seasons two and three were picked up and aired on the US cable network USA before being abruptly cancelled.
5. Wheatley, *Gothic Television*, 1.
6. Indeed, the "gothic-ness" of *Supernatural* is present nearly immediately; of the series' first six episodes, three involve deadly family secrets ("Pilot" (1.1), "Dead in the Water" (1.3), and "Bloody Mary" (1.5)).
7. Stacey Abbott, *Angel* (Detroit: Wayne State University Press, 2009), 83.
8. Wheatley, *Gothic Television*, 131–133.
9. Alyson Buckman, *Cleaning a Blank Slate: Joss Whedon, Intra-Auterial Casting, and the Whedonverse* (Jefferson, NC: McFarland), forthcoming.
10. Jeffrey Bussolini, "Television Intertextuality after Buffy: Intertexuality of Casting and Constitutive Identity," *Slayage: The Journal of Whedon Studies* 10.1, no. 35 (2009): para 6, accessed February 12, 2017. www.whedonstudies.tv/uploads/2/6/2/8/26288593/bussolini_slayage_10.1.pdf.
11. Wheatley, *Gothic Television*, 1.
12. Jowett, Lorna, and Stacey Abbott, *TV Horror: Investigating the Dark Side of the Small Screen* (London: I.B.Tauris, 2013).
13. Matt Hills and Rebecca Williams, "*Angel*'s Monstrous Mothers and Vampires With Souls: Investigating the Abject in 'Television Horror'," in *Reading* Angel: *The TV Spin-Off With a Soul,* ed. Stacey Abbott (London, I.B.Tauris, 2005), 205.
14. Ibid., 114.
15. Matthew Hills. *The Pleasures of Horror* (London: Bloomsbury Academic, 2005), 111.

16. Ibid., 115.

17. Abbott, *Angel*, 53.

18. Ibid., 49–51.

19. Stephen King. *Danse Macabre* (London: Hodder, 1991), 132–133.

20. Abbott, *Angel*, 50–1.

21. Ibid., 54.

22. John Ellis, *Visible Fictions: Cinema, Television, Video* (London: Routledge, 1982), 164.

23. John Thornton Caldwell, *Televisuality: Style, Crisis, and Authority in American Television* (New Brunswick: Rutgers University Press, 2005).

24. Wheatley, *Gothic Television*, 162–199.

25. Jowett and Abbott, *TV Horror*, 67; see also Abbott, Stacey. "Monstrous Puppet Masters: Negotiating Violence and Horror in the Whedon Tele-verse," in *Joss Whedon vs. the Horror Tradition*, eds Kristopher Woofter and Lorna Jowett (London: I.B.Tauris, 2018).

26. Written in 2005, Hills' analysis does not take into account the rise of streaming services' production of original programming, such as Netflix's *Stranger Things* (2016–present), long before Netflix, Amazon, and Hulu existed as sites for production. Not restricted by the same censorship rules that govern broadcast, horror series on streaming services can employ a much more graphic visual style as well as harsher language.

27. Hills, *The Pleasures of Horror*, 124–128.

28. Jowett and Abbott, *TV Horror*, 132.

29. It should be noted that the original pilot film of *Forever Knight* was both filmed and set in Los Angeles, thereby making *Forever Knight*, rather than *Angel*, the first series to feature an LA-based vampire detective.

30. *Supernatural* debuted the final year that the WB existed as a network; the WB was merged with the network UPN to form a new network, the CW, as one of a handful of dramas transitioned from the WB to the CW.

31. While I'm speaking particular of horror/procedural hybrids, it should be noted that *American Gothic*, a series that aired contemporaneously with *Forever Knight* (and on the same network), was closer in its graphic displays of violence to the later series *Supernatural* than either *Forever Knight* or *Angel*.

32. Such narratives span much of the series run from "Hollywood Babylon" (2.18) to "Scoobynatural" (13.16).

33. Bussolini, "Television Intertextuality after *Buffy*, para 3.

34. Buckman, *Cleaning a Blank Slate*, forthcoming.

35. Bussolini, "Television Intertextuality after *Buffy*," para 57. Also, see Mary Ellen Iatropoulos "Of Whedonverse Canon and 'Someone Else's Sandbox': Marvel, *Much Ado*, and the Great Auteur Debate," in *After the Avengers: From Joss Whedon's Hottest, Newest Franchises to the Future of the Whedonverse*, ed. Valerie Frankel (Chicago: PopMatters Media, 2015), and her take on the application of auteur/authorship in Whedon's *Much Ado* and Marvel works.

36. Benjamin Jacob, "Los Angelus: The City of Angel," in *Reading* Angel: *The TV Spin-Off With a Soul,* ed. Stacey Abbott (London: I.B.Tauris, 2005), 78 – 80.

37. As Bussolini points out, this type of shot and its associated meaning was also used in the later CBS series *Moonlight,* about a vampire private detective attempting to atone for his sins. Given the short duration of the series, I have elected not to include an in-depth analysis of it within this article, despite the striking similarities between *Angel* and *Moonlight,* not limited to both being set in Los Angeles, a blonde love interest, a brief return to mortality given up to save the woman he loves ("Fated to Pretend" (1.13)), and *Angel* co-creator David Greenwalt (briefly) serving as showrunner. It also aired on the same network as *Forever Knight.*

38. See: Aaron C. Burnell. "Rebels, Rogues, and Sworn Brothers: *Supernatural* and the Shift in 'White Trash' from Monster to Hero," in *TV Goes to Hell: An Unofficial Roadmap of* Supernatural, eds Stacey Abbott and David Lavery (Toronto: ECW Press, 2011), 47 – 59.

39. A short list includes Jeff Kober, Amy Acker, Julie Benz, Rob Benedict, Chad Lindberg (who played a computer geek on *Buffy* and a computer genius on *Supernatural*), John Rubinstein, Frederic Lehne, Adrianne Palicki, Harry Groener, and Keith Szarabajka. It should be noted that John Kapelos, who played Schanke on *Forever Knight,* also had a significant role in the *Angel* episode "Are You Now Or Have You Ever Been" (2.2).

40. While not germane to this analysis, it is interesting to note that naming Staite's character Amy Pond was a clear nod to the then-companion Amy Pond (Karen Gillan) on the BBC series *Doctor Who* (1963 – present).

41. Jowett and Abbott, *TV Horror,* 18 – 22.

42. That Morgan's character is named Sam offers is an amusing sidenote, much as Padalecki (Sam on *Supernatural*) played a character named Dean on the WB's *Gilmore Girls* (2000 – 2007, 2016) immediately prior to his role on *Supernatural.*

43. Morgan's later casting as the evil Negan, with his signature weapon—a bat wrapped in barbed wire he has named Lucille—in AMC's *The Walking Dead* (2010 – present), is referenced in the twelfth season of *Supernatural,* in which Dean returns from a job with a baseball bat wrapped in barbed wire; as he puts it away, he says, "Dad loved this thing" ("Somewhere Between Heaven and Hell" (12.15)).

44. Alberto N Garcia, "Breaking the Mirror: Metafictional Strategies in *Supernatural,*" in *TV Goes to Hell: An Unofficial Roadmap of* Supernatural, eds. Stacey Abbott and David Lavery (Toronto: ECW Press, 2011), 146 – 160.

45. William Gass, "Philosophy and the Future of Fiction," *Syracuse Scholar* 1, no. 2 (1980): 11.

46. Stacey Abbott, "Innovative TV," in *The Cult TV Book,* ed. Stacey Abbott (London: I.B.Tauris, 2010), 91 – 99.

47. Abbott, *Angel,* 90 – 95.

48. On the directing side, Canadian-based television director Allan Kroeker has directed episodes of *Forever Knight*, Whedonverse series *Firefly* and *Dollhouse*, and *Supernatural*, making him the only individual to have worked with Parriott, Whedon, and Kripke.
49. Adding to its connection with the later *Supernatural*, the young boy, Tommy (Ridge Canipe), whose life energy is drained at the start of the episode, plays a younger version of Dean Winchester in "Something Wicked" (1.18) and "A Very Supernatural Christmas" (3.8).
50. See Cynthea Masson, "'Break Out the Champagne, Pinocchio': *Angel* and the Puppet Paradox," *Studies in Popular Culture* 35, no. 2 (2013), 43–67.
51. See Harrison, Janine R., "Gender Politics in Angel: Traditional vs. Nontraditional Corporate Climates," in *Reading* Angel: *The TV Spin-Off With a Soul*, ed. Stacey Abbott (London: I.B.Tauris, 2005), 117–131, and Erin Giannini, *Joss Whedon vs. the Corporation: Big Business Critiqued in the Films and Television Programs* (Jefferson, NC: McFarland, 2017), 22–37.
52. Erin Giannini, "'Charybdis Tested Well With Teens': *The Cabin in the Woods* as Metafictional Critique of Corporate Media Producers and Audiences," *Slayage: The Journal of Whedon Studies* 10.2–11.1, no. 36–37 (2013/2014), accessed January 31, 2018. www.whedonstudies.tv/uploads/2/6/2/8/26288593/giannini_slayage_10.2-11.1.pdf.
53. It should be noted that the eleventh season of the series reveals that Chuck is actually God ("Don't Call Me Shurley" (11.20)), making Sam and Dean's subversion of his words more impressive.
54. Hugh H. Davis. "'The Drama Is In Us': Pirandellian Echoes in *Dollhouse*," *Slayage: The Journal of Whedon Studies* 8.2-3, no. 30–31 (2010), accessed January 31, 2018, www.whedonstudies.tv/uploads/2/6/2/8/26288593/davis_slayage_8.2-3.pdf.
55. Torrey, "'We're Just Food. . .and Perverse Entertainment'," 62.
56. Wheatley, *Gothic Television*, 133–132.
57. Jeffrey Sconce, *Haunted Media: Electronic Presence From Telegraphy to Television* (Durham, NC: Duke University Press, 2000).
58. Jowett and Abbott, *TV Horror*, 182. Indeed, *Supernatural* uses the concept of viral networking as a site of horror in its first season ("Hell House" (1.17)).
59. Ibid., 272.
60. "Spiritual Successor," TV Tropes.
61. Jowett and Abbott, *TV Horror*, 17–30.
62. Ibid., xiv.
63. Ibid., 54.

PART III

"It's About Power": Revisiting Whedon's "Revisionist" Horror

11

Whedon, Feminism, and the Possibility of Feminist Horror on Television

Lorna Jowett

With increasing numbers of women entering the horror genre behind the cameras, increasingly vocal audiences commenting on the genre's representations, and an ongoing boom in TV horror production, it seems timely to examine the increasing possibilities for feminist horror. Academic study of horror has long focused on issues of identity, power, and gender, with debates highlighting the abject, body horror, castration and phallic symbolism, the male gaze, voyeurism, female passivity, female victimhood, women in jeopardy, and heteronormativity, yet are we any closer to seeing feminist horror? In order to think through some of the possibilities, this chapter takes Joss Whedon as a starting point. Whedon identifies as a feminist, and his fans have tended to see his work as critiquing, deconstructing, and even revising the genres it draws on, particularly where gender identity and representation are concerned. Horror directly informs both the film (1992) and the subsequent television series *Buffy the Vampire Slayer* (1997–2003), as well as the 2012 film *The Cabin in the Woods*, while contributing to many screen productions "by" Whedon. *Buffy* may have been innovative in 1997, yet such representations are now more commonplace. The tide of approbation for

Whedon's feminism seems to have turned, despite—or possibly because of—increased awareness of representation and (lack of) diversity in popular media.[1]

Thinking about Whedon and horror in 2017 therefore raises several questions. Is Whedon's work in the horror genre really feminist? Has Whedon's work, particularly *Buffy*, inspired a new generation of female-centred horror? If there has been such a shift, why is a white cis-gendered heterosexual middle-class male taking the credit for it? Is such horror now seen as "not really horror" and how do such re-categorizations function to close down the possibility of feminist horror? In this chapter, I explore (rather than present) answers to such questions in relation to Whedon's work, to his often ambivalent attitudes to the genre that made his name, and to contemporary examples of TV horror.

I anticipate debating rather than answering these questions because the categories they depend on have no clear definitions: what is considered to be "Whedon" is as shifting as what is considered to be "feminist" and as nebulous as what might be considered "horror." Different definitions of each term might be used by different individuals or groups with different investments in each category. I have my own such investments, of course. My first academic monograph was on gender and *Buffy the Vampire Slayer*, and at the time of writing I am vice-president of the Whedon Studies Association. Feminism has been both a scholarly interest and a personal passion of mine for decades. Likewise, the horror genre has been a lifelong interest, personal and professional, and as a scholar I am particularly engaged in analyzing horror on television, where it is often neglected.[2]

Horror has conventions, tropes, and structures that may well lead to gender (and other) stereotypes, but these are neither as typical nor as deep-rooted as might be assumed. My argument proceeds from two characteristics essential to the genre.

1. Horror oscillates between the everyday/mundane and the fantastic/supernatural. In this respect, while horror need not be realistic, it includes enough of the familiar to tie its fantasy to the operation of our "real" world. Horror is not about the ghosts, monsters, indestructible killers, haunted houses, and supernatural events that form its main conventions—it is about us and things that concern us: society, power,

relationships (personal, social, cultural, national), boundaries, and limits.

2. Horror aims for a visceral effect that is not only physical but emotional. Horror reaches its audience through the body and intellect in ways that can be progressive and critical. In other words, horror aims to make us feel and, consequently, to think through the body and the sensations evoked within it.

Horror endures as a genre because it tells stories about us, and it makes us *feel* these stories as well as see or hear them. I contend that it is possible to glimpse feminist horror on television, and that some contemporary TV horror, including Whedon television series, seems designed to attract viewers who describe themselves as feminists.

Whedon vs. Horror

When discussing the inspiration for *Buffy*, Whedon often recollects how he was tired of horror movies where "bubblehead blonds wandered into dark alleys and got murdered by some creature."[3] This signals his desire to challenge the "usual" dynamics of the horror film by making the blonde girl the slayer of monsters, not their victim. Holly G. Barbaccia, however, notes that while "his description suggests his awareness of the pervasive, archetypal quality of the traditional, mainstream horror film," it simultaneously "rather coyly fails to account for the more marginal genre of the 'slasher film,' in which the pretty girl often does kill the monster in the alleyway."[4]

Whedon is certainly not the first horror writer or director to bend or break the "rules" of the genre. In at least two cinematic subgenres—the rape-revenge film and, as Barbaccia notes above, the slasher movie— women are integral to conventions and narratives. The rape-revenge film, generally considered part of 1970s exploitation cinema, includes both rape and revenge; the central rape motivating an act of revenge on its perpetrator/s. The term, Alexandra Heller-Nicholas observes, "evoke[s] associations between serious physical acts of violence [and] weighty moral and emotional responses,"[5] and she argues that films in this category tend to embody the way "contradictory and often hypocritical attitudes [about gender and sexual violence] can co-exist."[6] The slasher subgenre gave us a

Figure 11.1   The controversial ad for *Captivity* (2007).

female protagonist whose keen observation, ingenuity, and agency enable her to survive while her friends are killed, a character Carol Clover dubbed "the Final Girl."[7]

The Final Girl—along with female action heroes of the late 1970s and 1980s—undoubtedly paved the way for a plethora of female heroes on screens big and small, including Buffy. Catriona Miller argues that Clover's book, *Men, Women, and Chainsaws: Gender in the Modern Horror Film* (1992), "was an important critical intervention in the understanding of the slasher genre, reexamining [sic] some assumptions about the supposed masculine essence of horror."[8] More recently a project by the Geena Davis Institute on Gender in Media developed software to measure gender imbalances on screen. It found that horror is the only genre where women are seen on-screen more than men (53%), and also the genre with the highest speaking time for female characters (47%).[9] Of course, women having greater screen time doesn't mean they are represented positively in horror movies; however, it is equally presumptuous to conclude that women feature in horror only to be exploited, considering the number of horror films that make women and women's experiences central to their narratives.

Whedon's fairly negative views about horror and how it represents women are indicated by comments he has made about the so-called torture porn subgenre. The US billboard advertising campaign for *Captivity* (2007 Lionsgate/After Dark Films) provoked complaints about its depiction of a female character. The ad (see Figure 11.1) featured three images of a woman's face in extreme close-up, and one of her constrained body in a polyptych series, labelled with the tags, "Abduction," "Confinement," "Torture," "Termination." Jill Soloway, writing in the *Huffington Post*, castigated the campaign for presenting "adult" material on public billboards seen by children and adults alike, and called for action to "stop all horror/ torture filmmakers from advertising their vile fantasies in front of the rest of us."[10] Soloway includes Whedon's "awesome" letter to the Motion Picture Association of America (MPAA) in her article, lauding his support for the campaign to remove the "R" rating from *Captivity* (and therefore prevent it from making money in US cinemas). In his letter Whedon states:

> I've watched plenty of horror—in fact I've made my share. But the advent of torture-porn and the total dehumanizing not just of women (though they always come first) but of all human beings has made horror a largely unpalatable genre. This ad campaign is part of something dangerous and repulsive, and that act of aggression has to be answered.[11]

Such responses assume that horror films depicting violence against women are endorsing said violence, and imply that the primary audience for such films will be men. Yet, the research of scholars such as Isabel Cristina Pinedo (1997) and Brigid Cherry (2002, 2008) with female audiences of horror challenges this notion.[12] The focus here on horror *film* also inflects these arguments about its misogyny, or otherwise.

Cinema vs. Television

Whedon and Drew Goddard's film *The Cabin in the Woods* attracted a fair amount of attention, in part because of Whedon's involvement, and in part because it seemed to both revive and critique the slasher subgenre. Andrew Patrick Nelson argues that *Cabin* displays "the disparagement of trends in horror cinema; the valorisation of horror of the 1970s and 1980s; and the desire to reclaim the qualities that made films of this era classics."[13] For years—decades, even—critics have been saying that US horror film production is variably in crisis, failing, or lacking originality. The rise of "torture porn," derided by Whedon in his protest against the *Captivity* billboard campaign, as well as in many interviews about *Cabin*, is often seen as symptomatic of this so-called decline.[14] Yet horror still has the potential to offer new stories, attract new audiences, and create new paradigms, and it is, as per Whedon's first big success with *Buffy the Vampire Slayer*, doing this primarily on TV.

Despite an ongoing boom in television horror that includes female-issue-centred series such as *Black Mirror* (2011–present), *The Fall* (2013–2016)[15], and *Penny Dreadful* (2014–2016), while researching this chapter I found that online search engines generate results for "feminist horror" that almost exclusively deal with horror cinema. Assumptions about cinema, TV, horror, and their audiences continue to permeate debates about feminism, representation, and genre. Barbaccia comments that "Buffy becomes a hero with whom her predominately [sic] female audience can identify in a way not accounted for by most feminist criticism about horror"[16] and I would suggest this is because horror scholarship has tended to be about cinema—though it also overlooks some important published work on TV horror, as noted above. Moreover, while *Buffy* did demonstrably attract female viewers, given its hybridizing of several genres (horror, action adventure, melodrama, comedy, teen drama) it may not always be seen as real or authentic horror by fans of more "extreme" or traditional horror cinema. Fan cultures, subcultural capital, "authenticity," mainstreaming, journalistic responses, and the different associations that come with the terms "fangirl" and "fanboy" all play their part in valuing—and creating/categorizing—types of horror. Milly Williamson notes that mainstream horror has historically been denigrated as feminized mass culture.[17] The success of the *Twilight* novel (2005–2008) and film series (2008–2012) is a prime example, with virulent anti-fandom directed at *Twilight*'s audience of girls and "moms." "[C]riticism of the [*Twilight*] saga and surrounding franchise," Natalie Wilson observes, "often relies on the same sort of gendered lens that not only constructs females as rabid hysterical consumers, but also as silly fangirls."[18] Fans themselves lambasted *Twilight* for perpetuating outdated models of gender, while holding up *Buffy* as "feminist" or progressive in its representations.[19] though both could be termed "horror lite." Yet horror tales "have always responded to changing cultural conditions," as Sue Short argues, and *Twilight*'s version of gender is as much part of its cultural zeitgeist as *Buffy*.[20] Short highlights "concerns voiced about male violence and the brutalities of life" in horror, as well as a "championing [of] female characteristics."[21] Both *Buffy* and *Twilight* contain these elements, since horror with female protagonists foregrounds female concerns and experience, whether created by feminists or not.

Times have changed since *Buffy* first aired on March 10, 1997. Female protagonists in both film and television have become more frequent in action genres, and studies show that films with female leads actually perform better at the box office.[22] Of course, the shift to fourth-wave feminism with its call-out culture and challenges to "men's rights activists" (aka misogynists) may simply mean that debates about diversity have become more public and thus impact the industry, however slowly. Whedon, and *Buffy*, have not so much inspired a new wave of female-centred horror and female heroes, as been part of it. Several post-*Buffy* female-centred horror films, as Short outlines, adopt strategies also identifiable in *Buffy* to engage female viewers while going "some way to avoid alienating male viewers entirely,"[23] offering ambivalent representations so "we are seemingly invited to celebrate female transgressions while also shrinking from their excesses."[24] Casey Ryan Kelly, however, argues that a film like *Teeth* (2007) operates as a "subversive iteration of rape-revenge cinema" which "intervenes in the gendered politics of spectatorship by cultivating identification with a violent heroine who refuses to abide by the stable binary between masculine violence/feminized victimhood."[25] In the context of these two views, "Whedon" characters such as Buffy, Faith, Veruca, Drusilla, Darla, and Illyria, tend to follow the former trend, though subsequently Echo in *Dollhouse* seems designed to elicit less "shrinking," again I would argue, as part of a continuing trend for both sympathetic "monster" heroes and celebration of female power.[26]

Male vs. Female Creators

So why is Whedon given credit for this shift towards "feminism"? This too is perhaps more perception than actuality, given that *Buffy* has several TV forebears, including *The Hardy Boys/Nancy Drew Mysteries* (1977–1979), *Wonder Woman* (1975–1979), and *The Bionic Woman* (1976–1978). Whedon has been lauded for his feminism and for actively using it in his creations. Christine Jarvis notes that "directors and creative teams have, to varying degrees, ideological and political perspectives which they seek to explore and demonstrate through their art" and "filmmakers have tremendous resources at their disposal and their creations have a global reach."[27] Whedon, she argues, is one such "radical educator" in that "he enables his audiences to experience ways of looking at the world that challenge aspects of neo-liberal hegemony, and also encourages them to become critical thinkers."[28] Certainly, the Whedon "brand" positions itself in this way, flattering viewers by assuming that they are intelligent enough to engage with "critical thinking" about television. When Whedon won an award from Equality Now in 2006, his acceptance speech described constantly being asked in press interviews why he creates such strong female characters: "because you're still asking me that question."[29] This speech is often used to establish Whedon's feminism along the lines described by Jarvis. Lauren Schultz argues that Whedon's feminism develops to become more complex, so that *Buffy* appears more obviously "feminist" than *Dollhouse* in its negotiation of identity. *Buffy* thus established Whedon's reputation as a feminist auteur and heightened expectations for his future work"[30] that have, more recently, been challenged.

Of course, there are well-regarded female-centred horror movies created by men that might also be dubbed "feminist": *Teeth, Martyrs* (Pascal Laugier, 2008), *The Woman* (Lucky McKee, 2011), as well as female-helmed horror films, among them *American Psycho* (Mary Harron, 2000), *Jennifer's Body* (Karyn Kusama, 2009), *American Mary* (the Soska sisters, 2012), *The Babadook* (Jennifer Kent, 2014), *A Girl Walks Home Alone at Night* (Ana Lily Armipour, 2015), and *Prevenge* (Alice Lowe, 2016). Female directors and writers, however, battle against what Brigid Conor calls the "implicitly gendered understandings of heroic, individual creativity."[31] They also work within the limitations and restrictions of film industries: in the UK a film is six times more likely to be directed by a man than a woman, and women "directors are also disproportionately under-represented within certain genres, such as action, crime, horror and sci-fi."[32] Clearly, this has knock-on effects for career development, and as Conor observes, "studies of creative labor have only just begun to interrogate the exclusionary dynamics of particular creative sectors, the ways in which inequalities are reinforced, even deepened, and often denied."[33] Press coverage of anthology film *XX* (2017), for example, focused on the "novelty" of its five female directors. One of these directors, Jovanka Vuckovic, states that the film was "created in direct response to the lack of opportunities for women in film, particularly in the horror genre," which, she argues, was "badly in need of new perspectives."[34]

Arguably, the very nature of television horror encourages such new perspectives, or more female-friendly horror. The long-form narrative development now typical of TV drama allows for more complex and nuanced representations than a ninety-minute horror movie, and almost requires TV creators to move beyond standard tropes and genre conventions to retain audiences. Complexity of representation need not follow complexity of narrative, yet story in serial television drama is generally character-driven, rather than characters servicing the story. In addition, longer-form narrative (i.e., television soap opera and serial melodrama) has been seen by scholars as foregrounding female-centred narratives: the US daytime Gothic soap opera, *Dark Shadows* (1966–1971) is just one example. Owing to the limitations and inequalities of the industry outlined above, acclaimed horror TV series of recent years have most often been "created" or initially helmed by men: Alan Ball / *True Blood* (HBO 2008–2014) and Ryan Murphy / *American Horror Story* (FX 2011–present), Rob Thomas and Diane Ruggerio-Wright / *iZombie* (2015–present), and John Logan / *Penny Dreadful*. However, these, like all of Whedon's TV series, employed female writers (including big names with impressive credits such as Jane Espenson) and directors, who then become showrunners (Espenson, Marti Noxon, Maurissa Tanchareon). Moreover, diversification of TV markets via on-demand, streaming, alternative and niche platforms, and "original programming" encourages increased risk-taking to attract "new" demographics or to market "distinctive" productions.

Certainly, creators and audiences alike bring their lived experience to their work or their choice of viewing. This line of enquiry can appear essentialist (write what you know) but studies (Conor's and others) indicate that it does carry weight. In an article pointedly titled "When a Man Writes a Woman" Lara Stache describes the way respondents to her research into Whedon's *Avengers* seemed to discount male privilege: "quite a few of the respondents did not think [men writing women] was an issue ... Others voiced the fact that the male perspective is perhaps even more perceptive since men are outsiders to the female perspective."[35] Some of the best-known female-friendly TV horror series in recent years, *True Blood*, *American Horror Story*, and *Penny Dreadful*, all have white male creators (Alan Ball, Ryan Murphy, and John Logan, respectively, though Murphy is co-credited with Brad Falchuk as "creator" of *AHS*). Yet it is notable that all three men are openly gay and have an "outsider" as well as an "insider" perspective on patriarchy and male privilege.[36]

Creation vs. Reception?

So what effect might an experience lacking the unfair advantages of a privileged white straight cis-gendered male have on horror? Returning to the characteristics of horror identified in the introduction—that horror blends the fantastic with the mundane and everyday, and that horror aims for affect as well as effect—I propose the following corollaries.

1. The everyday for many women is horrific. (Men are afraid that women will laugh at them. Women are afraid that men will kill them.)[37]
2. Horror allows women to experience emotions that in the everyday might be repressed—fear, horror, disgust, violent rage, or violent glee. Sara Ahmed debates how feminism becomes "sensational," as feminists experience or *feel* the effects of it on personal and social/cultural levels. "[T]he sensations that lead us to feminism are often the very same sensations that follow being a feminist," she says, acknowledging the negative responses being a "feminist killjoy" can elicit.[38] Yet Ahmed also identifies "the political labor necessary of having to insist that what we are describing is not *just* what we are feeling or thinking" [my emphasis].[39]

Examples where I glimpse feminist horror—outlined below—demonstrate these principles, suggesting that horror can move away from women as seen/told by men occupying positions of privilege and dominance (the female as castrating, monstrous, abject, sexualized) and towards presenting women seen by those who aren't white straight cis-gendered men, maybe as women might see themselves.

Director Karyn Kusama (of 2009's *Jennifer's Body* and 2015's *The Invitation*), for example, explains her response to Jennifer Kent's female-centred horror film *The Babadook*: "I've been that woman in some way or another—I know how body-shaking fear can morph into a no-holds-barred kind of rage. I know how shaken, and then how strong, we have to be to get there. I understand Amelia, and clearly, so does the director."[40] As Kusama's comments indicate, horror's perceived excesses are in large part a kind of spectacularization of everyday pain and struggle, particularly of disenfranchised groups, and thus it encourages a kind of communality. Projects like Everyday Sexism[41] collect evidence of routine verbal, physical, and sexual harassment experienced by women. Horror's violence against women and the rage driving its female protagonists could well, therefore, be seen by feminist viewers as not fantasy but as a recognizable, visceral, if exaggerated, part of women's "everyday" lives.

Allison S. Henward and Laurie Macgillivray's (2014) investigation of how young children, particularly girls, respond to and co-opt horror indicates that viewers of all ages and backgrounds can tune in to the subversive potential of horror as feminist. They recount how one respondent, Jakaysha, tells a horror story made up from various TV representations and thereby "creates a space for local concerns and knowledge beyond the scope of many media texts."[42] Seeing this as a form of what Henry Jenkins dubs "textual poaching," Henward and Macgillivray note that although "horror is often deemed 'inappropriate' for children," poaching it "brings an element of power to the tale which would not be possible in more docile storylines."[43] Thus the sensational violence of horror adds to its power, and enables discussion of everyday life experiences: "[c]oncerns of violence that may be too real in everyday life can be more safely articulated within the confines of a fictional narrative."[44] For girls as well as women, then, horror can function as sensational feminism, raising consciousness of everyday problems.

As the attempted rape scene in *Buffy*'s "Seeing Red" (6.19) demonstrates, sexualized and gendered violence can be presented as distinctly uncomfortable for any viewer, potentially moving such horror from exploitation to sensational feminism.[45] "Thus," as Miller argues of slasher films, "it may be looking at the phenomenon from the wrong perspective to insist that" such horror productions "depict a repressive violence against women; rather, they may be a particularly stark representation of what it feels like to be female within a patriarchal society."[46] Likewise, female characters in contemporary horror television allow viewers—male, female, or otherwise—to see, and possibly empathize with or relate to, situations experienced by many women every day. On television, horror tropes, characters, and situations have the potential to be nuanced and slowly developed via long-form structures, and are often inflected by traditionally female genres from teen drama to romance to family sitcom, frequently refracted or remade by a perspective that feminizes or queers conventional horror narratives, tropes, and forms.

With this kind of queering in mind, I glimpse feminist horror in the following moments.

A teenage vampire slayer fights a soulless vampire who, only weeks ago, was her lover. He appears to have won, points a sword at her and taunts, "No weapons ... No friends ... No hope. Take all that away and what's left?" He thrusts at her with the sword but she catches it between the palms of her hands and answers, "Me."[47] A few years later, the slayer is "tested" by an organization formed largely of men. She fails the tests but recognizes that traditional, patriarchal structures can be resisted. "Power, I have it. They don't. This bothers them."[48] Finally the Slayer realizes that she can further subvert the patriarchal structures that dominate her life. Rather than "one girl in all the world" having the power of the slayer, she and her friends give the power to all of the potential slayers. "Every girl who could have the power, will have the power."[49]

These glimpses are refracted in HBO's gory, sexual, and chaotic *True Blood*, where outsider identities become central, where masculinity, romance, and sex are reimagined and played with, where femininity is something to be performed by a former brothel mistress-turned-vampire, where relationships of all kinds can be negotiated and renegotiated by the child of an alcoholic mother struggling to find self-worth, and where a gay black man can confront a table of homophobic rednecks and be applauded by other customers.

American Horror Story likewise develops such glimpses and exploits its premium cable position by exploring—again and again—ageing female identity, the embodiment of women as mature adults not teenagers. Each season changes the setting, story, and characters but each offers meditations on femininities, sexualities, race and ethnicities, and female power. So much so that the series' representations of women and the complex relationships between female characters in any given season attract talented actors like Angela Bassett, Kathy Bates, Jessica Lange, and Gabourey Sibide as well as celebrities like Stevie Nicks and Lady Gaga.[50]

More recently, *iZombie* infiltrates network television with a mash-up of zombie apocalypse and police procedural/forensic crime drama, developing its own perspective on the female experience. Its female protagonist is a zombie who has to eat brains to survive. Luckily she works in a police morgue. Consuming brains forces her to experience personality traits and memories of their previous owners, leading to an uncanny ability to solve crimes as well as a constant performance of femininity, appropriate or inappropriate (and this also showcases Rose McIver's acting skill). The series has McIver's zombie receive support from a staunch female friend, and from a male friend and colleague with no suggestion of romance or sexual interest—both unusual relationships for female characters in the genre. The underlying suggestion in the series is that she tries on identity after identity because her actual identity is too horrible to face, seeming to preclude being happy or having loving relationships.

Netflix original comedy series *Santa Clarita Diet* (2017–present) combines elements from all of the above, in addition to being a clever inversion of the tepid sitcom format. A female realtor somehow becomes a zombie, sending her professional and family life into chaos. Like *True Blood*, the series relishes the gory should-be-abject unruly female behavior, while asserting relationship bonds. That is, like *Buffy*, *Santa Clarita Diet* subverts its happy suburban Californian setting, yet emphasizes the new, stronger bonds between its protagonist, her husband and daughter. And like *American Horror Story*, it dwells on the ageing female body without abjectifying it or negating the joy our zombie takes in her zombification (which includes the occasional gleeful killing of a number of hyper-masculine types).

The webseries *Carmilla* (2014–2016) reimagines Sheridan LeFanu's 1872 female vampire novella of the same title, consciously sidestepping the tropes accreted around the many, conventionally patriarchal, versions of Bram Stoker's novel *Dracula* (1897), and populating its vlog-format, campus-set retelling with a cast of regular characters with non-conforming gender and sexual identities. Its female creators emphasize multiple, female voices who collectively tell the story, centring female agency and decentring binaries in a world dominated by male power and invaded by horrors.

The televisual medium and the horror genre both rely on balancing familiarity and novelty, bringing a sense of the strange or unusual into the everyday reality of the domestic sphere. Indeed, as Jeffrey Sconce argues, television in its early days was a logical medium for uncanny entertainment, as it brought phantom flickers into the comfortable spaces of home.[51] Thus, the combination of TV and horror encourages, even necessitates, innovation and evolution. TV horror must provide new attractions and new pleasures for its audiences. Some of these attractions come from experimentation with serial narrative; some come from the concerns addressed by such narratives and how the stories are told. Whedon is attracted to television "because [...] we get to examine the question we're interested in over and over from all these different angles"[52] and the series affording the most—and most exciting—glimpses of feminist horror continue to develop and refine this strategy.

Change vs. Stasis

David Greenwalt aptly summarized the difference between *Buffy* and its spin-off series *Angel* by saying, "*Buffy* is about how hard it is to be a woman and *Angel* is about how hard it is to be a man."[53] *Buffy* is one example of TV horror that examines how hard it is to be a woman over and over from all these different angles—but it is by no means the only one.

"The whole purpose of genre is to offer rules and tropes that both define and redefine it," states Nia Edwards-Behi, "No genre is a fixed, unchanging entity."[54] Responding to a (male) critic's view of contemporary horror, Edwards-Behi concludes, "The only thing that is too rigid about horror is the persistent and false belief from some that it is not good enough and not profound enough; and, somehow, not broad enough to encompass all that it does."[55] I have argued here that one of the things horror now encompasses, especially on TV, is sensational feminism in both senses of "sensational." Female horror fans are becoming more visible and demanding more from horror creators, particularly because of the radical glimpses of feminism horror has already shown them. As Kristina Busse points out, "The story of media fandom is one steeped in economic and gender concerns, from the beginning, when women began creating the narratives commercial media wouldn't offer—dominated as it is by male producers."[56] Changes in how media, particularly television, relates to fans and audiences, and how media negotiates changes to society and to feminism, mean that the (female) narratives commercial horror media previously wouldn't offer, or only hinted at, are starting to be seen, and felt. *Buffy* and other Whedon series have undeniably been part of this movement, but giving credit to Whedon personally diminishes the contribution of Whedon's many collaborators, male and female, as well as ignoring their place in TV history. *Buffy* may seem dated in comparison with contemporary TV horror, in form and structure as well as in its gender representations, yet this is how genre evolves—building on precursors and leaving a legacy for successors. I am hopeful that more horror will be written, directed, and created by feminist killjoys who aim not simply to rewrite the genre but to reform the industry.

Notes

1. See comments about the "sexist" *Wonder Woman* film script written by Whedon, e.g., Jack Shepherd, "Joss Whedon's leaked Wonder Woman script labelled 'sexist' by DC fans," *Independent*, June 21, 2017, www.independent.co.uk/arts-entertainment/films/news/joss-whedon-leak-wonder-woman-script-sexist-a7800571.html.
2. See Lorna Jowett and Stacey Abbott, *TV Horror: Investigating the Dark Side of the Small Screen* (London: I.B.Tauris, 2012).
3. Whedon quoted in Ginia Bellafante, "Bewitching Teen Heroines," *Time* 149.18 (1997): 82.
4. Holly G. Barabccia, "Buffy in the 'Terrible House'," *Slayage: The Journal of Whedon Studies* 1, no. 4 (2001): 1.
5. Alexandra Heller-Nicholas, *Rape-Revenge Films: A Critical Study* (Jefferson, NC: McFarland, 2011), 3.
6. Heller-Nichols, 1.
7. Carol Clover, *Men, Women and Chainsaws: Gender in the Modern Horror Film* (London: BFI, 1992). Arguably, the Final Girl derives from a tradition of Gothic narratives featuring curious women who encounter adversity and respond resourcefully, such as Anne Radcliffe's *The Mysteries of Udolpho* (1794), Jane Austen's *Northanger Abbey* (1817), and Charlotte Brontë's *Jane Eyre* (1847). This Gothic tradition establishes female-centred popular stories that eventually find their way to television.
8. Catriona Miller, "You can't escape: inside and outside the 'slasher' movie," *International Journal of Jungian Studies*, 6, no. 2 (2014): 112.
9. "The women missing from the silver screen and the technology used to find them," *Google*, accessed July 14, 2017, www.google.com/about/main/gender-equality-films/.
10. Jill Soloway, "Remove the Rating for Captivity," *Huffington Post*. November 17, 2011. www.huffingtonpost.com/jill-soloway/remove-the-rating-for-cap_b_44404.html.
11. Whedon quoted in Soloway. See also Holly Derr for a female perspective on torture porn and TV horror.
12. See Isabella Cristina Pinedo, *Recreational Terror: Women and the Pleasures of Horror Viewing* (Albany , NY: State University of New York Press, 1997); and Brigid Cherry's articles, "Refusing To Refuse To Look: Female Viewers of the Horror Film," *Horror: The Film Reader*, ed. Mark Jancovich (New York:

Routledge, 2002), 169–178; and "Gothics and Grand Guignols: Violence and the Gendered Aesthetics of Cinematic Horror," *Particip@tions*. 5.1 (2008) Online. Available: www.participations.org/Volume%205/Issue%201%20-%20special/5_01_cherry.htm.

13. Andrew Patrick Nelson, "*Trick "r Treat, The Cabin in the Woods* and the Defense of Horror's Subcultural Capital: A Genre in Crisis?" *Slayage* 10.2/11.1 [36-37], 2013/2014: 9.

14. The term "torture porn" has spawned much debate among horror scholars, particularly around intensified violence and spectacle that, to some, has always has been integral to horror. See Adam Lowenstein, 'Spectacle Horror and *Hostel*: Why "Torture Porn" Does Not Exist' *Critical Quarterly*, vol. 53, no. 1: 42–60.

15. *The Fall* positions itself within the crime genre, yet it draws on a range of tropes associated with horror and offers an intense, visceral exploration of violence and trauma.

16. Ibid., 2.

17. Milly Williamson, *The Lure of the Vampire: Gender, Fiction and Fandom from Bram Stoker to Buffy* (London: Wallflower Press, 2005), 56.

18. Natalie Wilson, "Foreword," in *Screening Twilight: Critical Approaches to a Cinematic Phenomenon*, ed. Wickham Clayton and Sarah Harman (London: I.B.Tauris, 2014), x.

19. As the many fan videos called Buffy vs Twilight, Buffy vs. Edward, or Buffy vs Bella demonstrate.

20. Sue Short, *Misfit Sisters: Screen Horror as Female Rites of Passage* (Houndmills: Palgrave Macmillan, 2006), 8.

21. Short, 9.

22. See, for example, www.forbes.com/forbes/welcome/?toURL=https://www.forbes.com/sites/ellenkilloran/2016/06/29/female-led-movies-show-strong-box-office-performance-lack-of-opportunity-persists-study/&refURL= https://www.google.co.uk/&referrer=https://www.google.co.uk/.

23. Short, 3.

24. Short, 106.

25. Casey Ryan Kelly, "Camp Horror and the Gendered Politics of Screen Violence: Subverting the Monstrous-Feminine in *Teeth* (2007)," *Women's Studies in Communication*, 39, no. 1 (2016): 88.

26. For a discussion that reads Buffy Summers and Willow Rosenberg as "monster" heroes, see Kristopher K. Woofter's chapter in this collection, "Weird Whedon: Cosmic Dread and Sublime Alterity in the Whedonverse."

27. Christine Jarvis, "Battle of the Blockbusters: Joss Whedon as Public Pedagogue," *Slayage: The Journal of Whedon Studies* 14, no. 1 (2016): 40.

28. Jarvis, 40.

29. Joss Whedon, Equality Now speech, *YouTube*, June 19, 2006 www.youtube.com/watch?v=cYaczoJMRhs.

30. Lauren Schultz, "Hot Chicks with Superpowers: The contested feminism of Joss Whedon," in *Reading Joss Whedon*, ed. Rhonda V. Wilcox, Tanya R. Cochran, Cynthea Masson, and David Lavery (Syracuse, NY: Syracuse University Press, 2014), 357.
31. Brigid Conor, *Screenwriting: Creative Labor and Professional Practice* (Abingdon: Routledge, 2014), 121.
32. Stephen Follows and Alexis Kreager, with Eleanor Gomes, *Cut Out of the Picture: A study of gender inequality amongst film directors in the UK film industry*. Commissioned by Directors UK. May 2016.
33. Conor, 6.
34. Quoted in Imogen Carter et al., "The Female Directors Bringing New Blood to Horror Film," *Observer*, March 19, 2017. www.theguardian.com/film/2017/mar/19/the-female-directors-bringing-new-blood-horror-films-babadook-raw-prevenge.
35. Lara Stache, "When a Man Writes a Woman," in *Fan Girls and the Media: Creating Characters, Consuming Culture*, ed. Adrienne Trier-Bieniek (Lanham, MD: Rowman & Littlefield, 2015), 79.
36. See, for example, John Logan discussing his interest in the issues of alienated perspectives: www.slate.com/blogs/outward/2014/05/09/penny_dreadful_s_john_logan_why_a_gay_writer_feels_a_kinship_with_frankenstein.html.
37. This circulates on the internet and is often ascribed to novelist Margaret Atwood, though it seems to be a simplification of an anecdote told about her.
38. Sara Ahmed, *Living a Feminist Life* (Durham, NC: Duke University Press, 2017), 38.
39. Ahmed, 6.
40. Quoted in Laura Prudom, "Unforgettable Horror: The Female Directors of XX reveal their female horror inspirations," *Mashable*, March 4, 2017. http://mashable.com/2017/03/04/xx-directors-roxanne-benjamin-karyn-kusama-jovanka-vuckovic/#VZ_qIbuNTqqJ.
41. The Everyday Sexism Project, https://everydaysexism.com/.
42. Allison S. Henward and Laurie Macgillivray, "Bricoleurs in preschool: girls poaching horror media and gendered discourses," *Gender and Education*, 26. No. 7 (2014): 735.
43. Henward and Mcgillivray, 735.
44. Ibid., 738.
45. *Buffy the Vampire Slayer*. Season 6, Episode 19. Directed by Michael Gershman. Written by Steven S. DeKnight. 2002.
46. Miller, 116.
47. "Becoming, Part Two," *Buffy the Vampire Slayer*. Season 2, Episode 22. Directed and written by Joss Whedon. 1998.
48. "Checkpoint," *Buffy the Vampire Slayer*. Season 5, Episode 12. Directed by Nick Marck. Written by Jane Espenson and Douglas Petrie. 2001.
49. "Chosen," *Buffy the Vampire Slayer*. Season 7, Episode 22. Directed and written by Joss Whedon. 2003.

50. See Lorna Jowett, "American Horror Stories, Repertory Horror and Intertexuality of Casting" for more on this.

51. Sconce writes: "The first "ghosts" of television, [...] did not speak *through* the technology [...], but seemed to actually reside *within* the technology itself," *Haunted Media: Electronic Presence from Telegraphy to Television* (Raleigh, NC: Duke University Press, 2000), 127.

52. Quoted in Schultz, 357.

53. David Greenwalt in Joe Nazzaro, *Writing Science Fiction and Fantasy Television* (London: Titan Books, 2002), 158. This comment suggests that *Angel* is basically a film noir, with a "hysterical male" protagonist, equivalent to the female Gothic heroine.

54. Nia Edwards-Behi, "A Brief response to 'Post-Horror'," *Warped Perspective*, July 6, 2017. http://warped-perspective.com/index.php/2017/07/06/a-brief-response-to-post-horror/.

55. Ibid.

56. Kristina Busse, "In focus: fandom and feminism: gender and the politics of fan production," *Cinema Journal* 48, no. 4 (2009): 105.

12

Weird Whedon: Cosmic Dread and Sublime Alterity in the Whedonverse

Kristopher Karl Woofter

"Weird does not so much articulate the crisis as [announce] that the crisis cannot be articulated."

—China Miéville[1]

Just past the halfway point of "Serenity" (1.0), the original pilot episode of the Joss Whedon- and Tim Minear-produced TV series *Firefly* (2002–3), is a moment of quiet terror. In a remote area of space, captain Malcolm (Mal) Reynolds (Nathan Fillion), and the crew of the *Serenity*, approach a shady, silent ship operated by a "raiding party" of Reavers.[2] At this point, Whedon's script has laid the groundwork for the moment's essential dread. *Serenity*'s typically wise-cracking pilot, Wash (Alan Tudyk), reports with gravitas on the Reaver ship's emanating excess radiation, evidence of their "operating with no core containment," something he remarks is akin to "suicide."[3] Ship's doctor Simon Tam (Sean Maher) comments that his only knowledge of Reavers is "campfire stories" about "men gone savage on the edge of space," to which first mate Zoë (Gina Torres) replies (in an oft-quoted line) that Reavers are quite real, and that if "they take the ship, they will rape us to death, eat our flesh, and sew our skins into their clothing. And, if we're very, very lucky, they'll do it in that order."[4] In such moments (as in all Whedon collaborations) *Firefly* alternates between clever banter among its characters, and showing their stunned silence. Here, it sets up an ambiguous, entropic monster—random in its abject acts, and sublime in its resistance to hermeneutic capture.

The two ships silently dance with each other, the *Serenity* trying to drift unnoticed past the sinister, deliberately paced Reaver ship. *Serenity*'s crew falls mute, and everything stops. Silence takes over—the dread silence of space outside, and the uncanny silence of Mal's crew inside. Whedon cross-cuts to crew members in different parts of the ship, eyes turned upward in paranoid anticipation, faces and bodies frozen in dread of monstrous possibility. The Reaver ship, steady and determined, comes nearer, bands of sizzling, blinding electric bolts shooting from what look like steel pincers at its nose. It ultimately slips by without heeding the *Serenity*, and the scene ends with a flurry of sighs from her crew. This powerful three-minute scene of sound and silence, movement and stasis, is characteristic of the way *Firefly* in its televisual incarnation leaves its audience to ponder and reflect upon the Reavers' terrible nature.[5] The moment, however brief, is arguably one of the most sublime in Whedon's work, a blend of wonder and terror confronting the beyond and the radically "other." Westerns, science fiction, and horror all revolve around the beyond in the form of frontiers, borders, and boundaries, and all three are melded in *Firefly*'s cauldron of genre hybridity.[6] Reavers may represent the traditional western's colonial figuration of the "savage" native, science-fiction's speculations on the (post)human subject of late (and eventually post-)capitalism, and horror's binary-collapsing hybrid bodies. Though the film *Serenity* (2005) later reveals that Reavers are a degenerate form of humanity—pure, rampaging Id force—*Firefly* maintains ambiguity regarding their origins and nature. *Firefly*'s Reavers mark Whedon's aesthetic as exemplary of the Weird tradition, a mode—or "expressive code"[7]—of horror attempting to push past the (proto-)psychoanalytical thrust of the Gothic to issues more cosmic.[8]

This chapter dwells in the realm of the Weird as manifest in *Firefly* and its follow-up film, *Serenity*, and, perhaps less obviously, in another of Whedon's most enduring works, *Buffy the Vampire Slayer* (1997–2003). I argue that tensions between the American Gothic and the Weird traditions in these works are productive in identifying how far Whedon as a series creator, and a writer, producer, and director of TV and film, works within and against horror traditions. Weird reality pricks the conscious-ness, not with the Gothic's uncanny resurfacing of things long repressed, but with the oncoming sense of a radical undoing of consciousness. I argue that the radical otherness of monsters like the Reavers also extends to characters like Buffy Summers and Willow Rosenberg, whose desire for extreme physical and mental experience reveals a yearning to mystically transcend a reality they feel cannot contain them. Their desire to experience radical alterity marks both characters' journeys as Weird. That is, these desires are not evidence of psychological trauma and resurfacing of repression, but part of a quest for confrontation with the radically unknown.

The Gothic vs. the Weird in *Firefly* and *Serenity*

The Weird is most often associated with the works of author and epistolarian H.P. Lovecraft (1890–1937), who coined and theorized the term.[9] While borrowing some trappings of the Gothic—particularly its gloomy atmosphere and battles of the will against seemingly predestined conditions—Weird works evince a conscious move away from the character-based psychological concerns of the Gothic. They shift focus and perspective from Gothic subjects haunted by repression, to subjects confronting a radically altered awareness of reality. To achieve a sense of the Weird, Lovecraft explains,

> A certain atmosphere of breathless and unexplainable dread of outer, unknown forces must be present; and there must be a hint, expressed with a seriousness and portentousness becoming its subject, of that most terrible conception of the human brain—a malign and particular suspension or defeat of those fixed laws of Nature which are our only safeguard against the assaults of chaos and the daemons of unplumbed space.[10]

Both traditions, then, are interested to varying degrees in the psychological and physical/sensational after-effects of confrontations with terrifying truths. Both also are essentially epistemologically driven, their narratives fueled by the desire of characters (and readers) to acquire knowledge of their unsettled worlds, as Susan Stewart (1980) and Noël Carroll (1990) suggest of horror narratives more generally.[11] Yet, where the Gothic tradition tends towards the hauntological—that is, a logic that sees subjectivity as always-already haunted by repressed personal and collective histories—the Weird tends towards confrontations with the radically other, the shockingly new, the unknown or indefinable.[12] Though an atheist, Lovecraft—and more recent authors such as Caitlin Kiernan and Thomas Ligotti, whose work admits his influence—often frames Weird desire as an attempt to recover sacred transcendence in a secular world. They seek what Rudolf Otto terms the "numinous," a sublime state akin to staring into the face of God.[13] The Gothic's dredging-up of past demons may inspire a combination of terror and wonder, but the Weird tradition (perhaps ironically, considering its authors' typical atheism/agnosticism) seeks to confront subjects with a sublimity marked by awareness of their absolute diminishment before the infinite.[14]

In Gothic's hauntological logic, existence in the present becomes a liminal, spectral state, a neither-here-nor-there-ness in the wake of something once known, now lost; the subject potentially freezes in an act of "back-looking," as William Faulkner puts it, a fugue state of post-traumatic anxiety, paranoia, melancholia, longing, and/or nostalgia.[15] In Derridian terms, the ghost is a tear in the fabric of history, an opening-up that destabilizes the present in potentially productive ways, forcing acknowledgment of overlooked or forgotten realities. It is thus, essentially, uncanny.[16] While Weird works do not entirely eschew this sense of a resurfacing past, they tend more towards the anticipatory or the speculative, threatening the knowledge-seeking subject with potential annihilation. In Weird works, audiences witness (perhaps experience) a mingled desire for, and dread of, contact with sublimely confounding new experience. In China Miéville's terms, "The Weird is the assertion of that [which] we did not know, never knew, could not know, that has always been and will always be unknowable."[17] Through what Miéville calls its "logic of confrontations," the Weird focuses on obsessive curiosity in the quest for "radical otherness, a counterposing alterity."[18] Confronting shocking unknowns is "sublime" because it mingles pleasure and pain, transcendent awe and terror in the "humbling failure of the imagination before reason" that occurs when confronting immensities beyond human scope.[19]

Perhaps the most important trope of the Weird tradition in confronting radical alterity is its anti-anthropocentrism, its decentering of the human. This is the key difference between the Weird's mysticism and that of monotheism, which, despite diminishing the human in light of a god always greater-than-human, positions humans as uniquely built to seek and experience transcendence. In Weird works humanity is an insignificant, ephemeral blot on a confounding spatial and temporal scale. The implications extend beyond morality and into the very mysteries and significance (or lack thereof) of human existence against infinite space and deep history, deep time. A central pessimism here is often balanced by enduring curiosity regarding discoveries of a greater reality, and by Weird works' keen interest in wresting understanding from near-insoluble mysteries, or artistically conjuring the "unpresentable."[20] The Weird thus operates somewhere between a *mode* combining horror, dark fantasy, and science fiction, and a *worldview* deriving from a negativistic (i.e., anti-positivistic) and productively nihilistic philosophical take on Nietzschean anti-moral reality.[21]

The conceptual variations in the Reavers of *Firefly* and *Serenity* are a good place to begin an assessment of Whedon's forays into Weird territory. The Gothic's past-oriented logic of haunting, trauma, and repression is evidenced in *Serenity*'s revelation that the Reavers are humanity's dark double, and the Weird's future-leaning logic of speculative, cosmically oriented existential dread shows in *Firefly*'s framing of the Reavers as categorically perplexing. Of course, in the series and the film, Reavers often occupy both positions. In "Bushwhacked" (*Firefly* 1.3), Mal remarks, "Reavers ain't men, or they forgot how to be. They're just nothin'. They got out to the edge of the galaxy, to that place of nothin', ... and that's what they became."[22] Gregory Erickson argues that "nothing" is key to investigating the (a)morality of the *Firefly* universe.[23] He indirectly identifies a primary concern of the Weird mode when he writes, "To be human is to insist on ontological existence—we are the opposite of nothing—and it is our own awareness of nothing that allows us to create and imagine ourselves as a unified body. In such a system, nothing then becomes a threat, a non-existence that by its very existence threatens being."[24] Mal's comments in "Bushwhacked" affirm this opposition between humanity as embodied "something" against a cosmos of "nothing" by which the Reavers have been irreversibly marked. Because little else is known of the Reavers having, in Mal's terms, melded with the chaotic infinite, their monstrosity in *Firefly* is consistent with the Weird's speculative interest in (and dread of) the effect on the human mind and body of contact with knowledge far beyond the ken of humanity. *Firefly*'s Reavers are radically other; they manifest insanity, having essentially stared into the infinite. Now they are "lurkers at the threshold," to borrow a phrase from Weird author August Derleth.[25] That is, they inhabit the outer rim of the galaxy, the lip of the void, the limits of consciousness—victims *and* guardians of knowledge that forever alienates them from humanity.

Firefly is negativistic in consistently framing the Reavers as inscrutable, resistant to capture within physical or hermeneutic nets. Reavers are, in *Firefly*, always "out there," never really present, appearing at random, their menacing ships and destroyed victims the only evidence of their monstrous existence. Are they human or cosmic monsters? *Firefly*'s fourteen episodes do not say. Therefore, I partly disagree with Erickson's reading of Mal's use of "nothing" in "Bushwhacked." Erickson writes, "Although *nothing*, in this case, is coded as evil, a void for humans to resist, historically the concept of nothingness has been used to represent dark *and* light, the abyss *and* possibility," and goes on to discuss the more transcendent religious linkages of "nothing" to God and the soul in the series.[26] Rather than "evil," however, "nothing" in Mal's comment seems to be less an indication that the Reavers' nature results from moral transgression or degeneration, and more that they have become, as Erickson implies, sublimely liminal, an *anti-moral* force of chaos. Reavers are creatures of terrifying wonder, evidence of something beyond human *because* they have come into contact with nothingness.

In the TV series, Reavers *inhabit* the boundaries between known and unknown. It is less clear whether they have, in Mal's words, "got *out to*" such a place from a point of normalcy, marked severely by exposure to the unknown, or whether they are simply a product *of* that unknown space. Even were they labeled as once-human, *Firefly*'s Reavers are still very much like Lovecraft's archaeologists in *At the Mountains of Madness* (1936), and the seekers of many other Weird works, who discover terrible unknowns and are marked by these discoveries to the point of paralyzing obsession or mind-scrambling madness. *Firefly*'s Reavers are configured, then, along Weird lines. Rather than an uncanny version of humanity—a possible reminder of our inherent violence, and the primitives we *once were*—*Firefly*'s Reavers instead represent either the sublime void itself, or a terrible *potentiality*, shocking evidence of what humans could *become* with knowledge that is beyond human capacity to cognize. The Reavers of the TV series are thus less a force of "evil" than they are an embodiment (or phantom suggestion) of how access to the unknown radically alters notions of reality. They have stared a new reality in the face.

The series' cinematic sequel, *Serenity*, however, wrests the Reavers from the Weird into the uncanny realm. The revelation that Reavers are the product of a past horror enacted upon human citizens by the governing Alliance, realigns them with the Gothic's focus on resurfacing trauma, repressed violence, and hidden histories. In the film's third act, the crew of the *Serenity*—their ship disguised with abject blood and bodies—slip past a threatening armada of Reaver ships to terra-formed planet Miranda. There, they learn of an experiment conducted by the Alliance to winnow out violence in the Mirandan settlers. Echoing Robert Louis Stevenson's *Strange Case of Dr. Jekyll and Mr. Hyde* (1886), this idealistic experiment to diminish violence with a drug called Pax fails, only isolating extreme states of being; the Mirandan citizens are split between being morbidly apathetic, or ferociously violent. A holographic message tells how the majority of the Mirandans essentially gave up their will to live, even to move, fading to inertia and death. Those remaining became Hyde-like Reavers, murderously active and utterly lacking respect for bodily integrity, or the laws of civilized society. This revelation renders the Reavers part of a past trauma, the result of horrible experiments—a tragic mistake made *by humans* against humanity. Rather than the ubiquitous and chaotic inhuman and/or non-human force of the TV series, *Serenity*'s Reavers become, definitively, entities that once were *us*.

In the film, gruff crewmember Jane comments that Reavers "show up like the boogeyman," associating them with monsters of the unconscious, particularly figures from childhood nightmares. Indeed, the childlike River Tam has nightmarish visions of them, affirming their link to already-known-but-secreted information she carries unconsciously.[27] The product of nightmares and repressed secrets, *Serenity*'s Reavers are uncanny doppelgängers. Thus they are simultaneously irrational and primal doubles of humanity (and the characters we love); evidence of a terrible Alliance secret relating to past trauma; and—because this is also a *Western*—"savages," indigenous inhabitants haunting the frontier demarcating the "civilized" world from uncharted territory. The Reavers' metaphorical significance as colonial other comes further into focus in the film, where their monstrosity demonstrates the inhumanity of the system (represented by the Alliance) and its tendency to objectify (or abjectify) human subjects on the fringe.[28]

The explanation of the Reavers' origins in *Serenity*—while assigning them an abject and uncanny form of monstrosity that is disturbing and politically interesting—ultimately limits their potential monstrosity in relation to human psychology, physiology, and culture. As victims of the Alliance, Reavers are culture's monsters. Jeffrey Weinstock notes a tendency in the Lovecraftian Weird to move away from anthropocentric framing: "Weird fiction along the Lovecraftian model is," he writes, "not about recognizing ourselves in the other, but rather the undoing of egocentrism."[29] In contrast to *Serenity*'s Reavers, *Firefly* sustains the notion that Reavers are a force—an *idea*, even—that troubles reality itself, evidence of something outside of what we (think we) know. Erickson's comment, "we are all potential Reavers on the edge of nothing," encapsulates how *Firefly* and *Serenity* vacillate in configuring the Reavers as Weird and/or Gothic monsters.[30] The Reavers are both corrupted human doubles, and *beyond* human. The latter is a Weird reminder of the potential for a total collapse of humanity and morality in contemplation of a cosmic void. *Firefly*'s Reavers are Weird because they resist definitive meaning; they are *potentially* abject or uncanny versions of humanity (as *Serenity* later confirms), but also, in their association with something entirely unknown, indicators of the fabricated, feeble nature of categories, and of an entropic, ultimately chaotic universe. American Gothic and Weird traditions intermingle and compete in *Firefly* and *Serenity* in strikingly upfront ways, yet they subtly undergird Whedon's first series, *Buffy the Vampire Slayer* (hereafter, *Buffy*).

"From Beneath You, It Devours": Radical Alterity, Weird Knowledge, and Retreats from Reality in *Buffy*

While tensions between the Weird and Gothic traditions weave through all of Whedon's work, their intermingling in *Buffy* is most prototypical of the tensions traced above in *Firefly* and *Serenity*'s Reavers.[31] I show, however, that *Buffy* is more radically Weird in terms of framing the monstrous—and contact with it—than any of Whedon's work, including *Firefly*. Topographically, *Buffy* is Gothic through-and-through. From the title's allusion to conventional monsters, to narratives and themes centered on strong female characters, the series fits into a long line of Gothic horror, as Milly Williamson (2005), Leigh Harbin (2005), Renée T. Coulombe (2007), Ananya Mukerjhee (2008), and others have noted.[32] But despite obvious Gothic trappings—the heavy metaphor, the emphasis on setting as psyche, the character-driven and enigma-centered narrative arcs, and the melodramatic intensity associated with those arcs—the entire run of *Buffy* follows a Weird logic. As Gregory Erickson and Jennifer Lemberg note, "the arc of the entire series can [...] be seen as a move from coherence to incoherence, order to chaos," a pattern more characteristic of the progressive revelations and fractured realities of Weird works than of classic Gothic.[33] What makes the series most Weird—beyond its aversion of continual reality-shattering apocalypses (always simultaneously global and personal)—is, I would argue, twofold: first, the significant time it devotes to computer whiz and magic-user Willow Rosenberg's series-long quest for greater knowledge and expanded consciousness (or, in terms related to *Firefly*'s Reavers, a desire to touch and be touched by "nothing"); and second, its establishment of uncomfortably coexisting alternative realities for both characters and audience, manifested most powerfully in "Normal Again" (6.17). Willow and Buffy embody the Weird trope of characters driven to escape to, or to create, realities alternative to the one they (and we) know, which they see as either a realm of hellish torment, or stultifying mundanity, or both.

Extreme Knowledge, Expanded Consciousness

Buffy takes on two interesting Weird character tropes: 1) the obsessive quest for extreme knowledge, power, and expanded awareness as yielding cosmic dread and severe torment; and 2) a need to retreat from the superficial reality of deluded normalcy represented by Sunnydale at large. Seasons six and seven, in particular, push these notions to extremes, with the Scoobies alienated from the superficial Sunnydale reality by their constant battle with darker forces, and retreating further into a psychological and supernatural darkness of their own that threatens to consume them. This rather bleak effect of the Scoobies' long-running fight against the supernatural causes several of them to seek experience and sensation beyond what traditional contact with others can offer. The search for real feeling and connection in *Buffy* is a series-long conceit, as Anthony Curtis Adler suggests,[34] and sees *Buffy* playing with classic Weird tropes, such as obsessive curiosity, dangerous crossings of frontiers, and morbid ruminations on death and the beyond. This trope is most concentrated in two less-conspicuous "monsters": Willow and Buffy. Willow's pursuit of (initially) knowledge and (eventually) extreme experience through magic is set up as attached to feelings of inferiority and "mousy"-ness.[35] It eventually brings her into contact with powerful forces that touch her (and through her, others) with cosmic horror. Forces beyond human ken endow Willow with the potential to remove herself from human reality by destroying it entirely in a combined act of suicide and global destruction— a Weird elaboration of the more microcosmic Gothic conceit, where a character's individual, psychological struggle is writ large, over a canvas that threatens to consume others. Buffy's journey into darkness is different, since her superpowers already connect her to shadowy, non-human forces that alienate her from others. The effect of this alienation, however, causes Buffy the same kind of "pain" that Willow wants to stop wholesale by creating an apocalypse at the end of season six.[36] Still, Buffy's arc also includes monstrous (and no-less-apocalyptic) moments; in season six the sense that she has come back "wrong" leads her to the near-destruction of her friends, and an (almost-totalizing) retreat from the Sunnydale reality we have come to know in the disturbing, "Normal Again" (6.17), discussed below. The factors that mark Willow and Buffy as Weird monsters can be traced in *Buffy*'s extension of radical alterity to both characters as they interact with forces beyond the human.

Girl power in *Buffy* is continually configured as monstrous; Buffy's inherent ties to primeval forces, and Willow's acquiring of dark (later goddess-like) powers mark the two as irretrievably alienated from friends, family, and the human reality represented by Sunnydale.[37] The idea of a "monstrous-feminine"[38] in *Buffy* calls up additional tensions in the series between Weird/cosmic and psychoanalytical/hauntological frameworks. Barbara Creed frames the monstrous feminine as a hauntological force linked to anxieties associating birth (individual, but also primordial, on a human scale) with a traumatic event (a primal scene) that carries echoes of return to a state of pre-subjective annihilation that both disturbs and fascinates.[39] This Gothic-inflected haunting-by-origins is a compelling way to view the alterity that Buffy and Willow manifest, and is constantly in tension with readings of the two characters as more radically, more Weirdly, "other." In the context of the Weird, Buffy and Willow are monstrous in the sense that each character is, in the words of Jeffrey Jerome Cohen, "a form suspended between forms that threatens to smash distinctions."[40] Neither character needs to be categorically "other" (a formless blob, for example, or a multidimensional creature) to achieve this kind of liminal status. There is a wide spectrum of radical alterity at play in *Buffy*. The series' many monsters and demons exhibit variety and randomness (with demons such as Spike's friend Clem being downright charming—akin to the metal-head you don't mind asking to babysit). Buffy stands somewhere between the demonic and the human; her individuation over the course of the series is an awakening to her own darkness, and accompanying dark obsessions: violence, masochism, melancholia, and morbidity among them. Willow's series-long progression is driven by fascination with becoming other-than-human, with radically alternative realities and states of (dis)embodiment. Initially, Willow seeks these experiences in the pursuit of knowledge (she remains an appealing representative of academic pursuit in a genre that tends to mistrust all representatives of institutional authority),[41] but ultimately her intellectual curiosity becomes an obsession with more dangerous mind- and body-altering experience.

Willow's desire for increasingly forbidden knowledge and experience links her to longstanding horror tradition—what Andrew Tudor calls the "knowledge narrative"[42] with its mad scientists and magicians—and it also makes hers the series' most typically Weird character arc.[43] In the Weird tradition new knowledge is always an expander *and* a punisher, a wondrous draw to the potentially terrifying shock of the new. The realm of the unknown in horror encourages perverse curiosity that survives all reason and logic, that outweighs all practicality and intuition for physical and mental safety (one's own, and that of others). Much of Lovecraft's fiction, for example, conjures protagonists driven to quest into the unknown by "the natural physical instinct of *pure curiosity*."[44] These protagonists feel a "perpetual gnawing toward the ultimate illimitable void" that propels them into an unfathomable realm where new experiences confound the senses, disintegrate the body, fragment identity, and may even madden and destroy the explorer-observer.[45] Such protagonists feel "a sense of impatient rebellion against the rigid & ineluctable tyranny of time, space, a natural law," and "a burning curiosity concerning the vast reaches of unplumbed & unplumbable cosmic space which press down tantalizingly on all sides of our pitifully tiny sphere of the known."[46] The draw to the beyond, or to a state of beyond-ness, is primary in the Weird.

Willow is a thoroughly Lovecraftian seeker. Her relationship to the unknown moves from attraction to addiction across the series. Her initial forays into magic playfully extend her scholarly leanings, eventually becoming part of her expanded sexuality and later pulling her into the realms of addiction through her draw to the experiences provided by demon magic supplier/pusher, Rack. Willow's attraction to extreme bodily states and mind expansion through magic ultimately becomes a way of unlinking from a reality that no longer stimulates her, a way for her to "voyage into forbidden celestial deeps."[47] Fan response to Willow's dark turn was a combination of confusion and outrage, but Willow's journey into chaos makes sense viewed as the trajectory of a Weird antihero. In the Weird tradition following Lovecraft, the "deeps" themselves are monstrous, but so are characters who come into contact with them, many left either alienated from others by insanity, or erased completely by suicide. Willow effectively relinquishes her humanity to the forces of darkness, giving herself up to mingle with the cosmic, and telling Buffy, as she heals wounds on her own face with a flourish, "This . . . is nothing. It's all *nothing*."[48] It is difficult here not to be reminded of Mal's association of Reavers with the "nothing" beyond the limits of space, discussed earlier. Willow has confronted and *become nothing*, and that word provocatively links her monstrosity to the Reavers of *Firefly*.

In horror, confrontations with new knowledge are often disturbing and violent. Carroll argues that "the horror story is driven explicitly by curiosity,"[49] and Cohen notes how the monster demonstrates that "curiosity is more often punished than rewarded."[50] Once she has allowed herself to be consumed by dark magic—literally manifesting the text of dark magic books as she consumes them up her arms and across her face— Willow is both victim and victimizer, seeker and transgressor (see Figure 12.1). Willow's journey across the boundaries separating known from unknown, can be aptly described by Cohen: "To step outside this

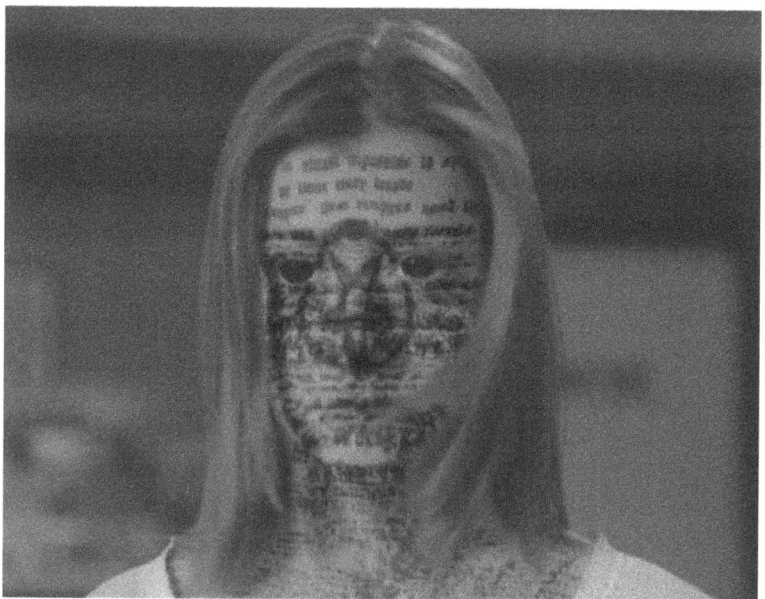

Figure 12.1 Willow's body literally manifests the dark magic knowledge she seeks.

official geography [of the known] is to risk attack by some monstrous border patrol or (worse) to become monstrous oneself."[51] Touching the unknown in any form marks one as an overreacher—one who morally transgresses in glimpsing the realm of the divine. This is true of much horror concerning a quest into unknown or unknowable territory, especially where science threatens to usurp divine power. Yet Willow's pursuits, despite association with addiction and transgression, are ultimately rewarded—and Weirded. That is, the show's mythology presents her magical powers as tied into a system of power originating in nature. "Everything's connected," she says ("Lessons" (7.1)).[52] Cross-legged and grinning faintly, seemingly resigned but with the calm restraint of a pacifist, Willow then pulls a flower from another part of the earth through the grassy lawn on which she sits. Her eventual goddess-like powers offer the opportunity to balance the scales after her atrocious acts in season six, averting another apocalypse at the end of season seven. By changing the rules to activate all potential Slayers producing a collective of empowered women, Willow's final act in the TV series ironically fulfills her original, grief-driven goal by *altering reality* forever.

David Kociemba and Mukherjea (both 2014) deftly trace Willow's later, darker developments to earlier insecurity and need to be noticed, and these readings hold, if in tension with Weirder ones.[53] I read Willow's quest for greater and greater knowledge through magic as part of a relentlessly future-oriented character trajectory that seeks out unknowns and newness. The tension here between Willow as either trauma-driven or curiosity-driven need not be mutually exclusive, however; her moral lapses (attempting to erase Tara's unpleasant memories in "Tabula Rasa" (6.8), for example, or her resurrection of Buffy at the beginning of season six) are part of a forward motion towards alterity. Matthew Pateman goes so far as to note "the sheer profusions of Willows, each related to the other but inassimilable into a neatly packaged, unifying entity."[54] Put another way, Willow's monstrous multiplicity, her ultimate resistance to being knowable, makes her the most liminal character in a show that features many—it Weirds her.

"You hate it here as much as I do": Turning Against Reality

Weird reality pricks the consciousness with the oncoming sense of a radical undoing of consciousness as we know it. Horror author Thomas Ligotti writes: "we can tolerate existence only if we believe—in accord with a complex of illusions, a legerdemain of deception—that we are not what we are: unreality on legs."[55] Ligotti's thoughts here are part of a larger treatise on what he calls "the ontological fraudulence of the human species"—the potential futility of all human endeavor against the creeping consciousness that we face annihilation, individually and as a race.[56] In this argument, our consciousness makes us unhappy. The only thing supporting a will to live in this context are the false structures we set up around the pursuit of happiness and the decrease of suffering. In Ligotti's fiction, protagonists continually seek an exit from this state of unconsciousness, this "puppeted" existence. Such false structures are the very things Willow (and Buffy, though less deliberately) seeks to escape.

This apparently deep hopelessness is also an attempt to think close to the "outer rim" of those illusions that separate most humans from real ontological knowledge about themselves—to see human logic, endeavor, history, and morality as perpetuating a state of harmful denial. Works in the Weird tradition follow this critical philosophy, creating characters who recognize conventional reality as a sham and crave expanded awareness of what lies beyond it, at whatever cost. Cohen's exploration of monsters as a response to cultural/ideological paradigms ties the monstrous to cultural illusions that create uncrossable artificial boundaries; monsters tear the fabric of the illusion, reveal its fragile, malleable, ephemeral nature. Willow resists such illusions, or seeks to transcend them, not only in service of what she sees as personal limitations, linked to her teen years, but also because she suspects that the world at large (ideologically and/or materially) is hiding greater awareness, greater sensations from her.

In certain ways, Buffy' trajectory, starting with "Welcome to the Hellmouth" (1.1), finds her increasingly struggling to *maintain* the illusion that there is something worth striving for. Dreading a prophecy that it will end her life, Buffy reluctantly prevents the Master's rise in season one; against all emotional instincts, she destroys her lover, Angel, to prevent a dimensional rift opening in season two; she organizes widely to stop the mayor's demonic Ascension in season three; she joins wills with her friends via Willow's magic to halt the Initiative's military techno-rule in season four, and finally welcomes the chance to "ascend," herself, accepting the "gift" of death, in season five (see Figure 12.2). Thus, Buffy's "monstrous" power progresses towards self-annihilation. In season six, she is wrested from a transcendent, inter-dimensional state—reanimated, left to feel as though she is in hell. And this terrible resurrection destabilizes her and the series' last two seasons. For most of season six, Buffy's energies are largely directed towards transporting herself away from that hell through violent sex with Spike and through nearly accepting an alternative reality in which Sunnydale is her own insane delusion. This near-apocalyptic turn towards an alternative reality in "Normal Again," highlights profound implications of Buffy's own trajectory and thus for Weird reality in the series. In this episode, Buffy retreats into a reality (the product of a spell cast by the villainous Trio) where her heroic Slayer self, and the familiar reality of Sunnydale, is the delusion of a mentally-scarred young woman. The world of Buffy's asylum is as totalizing and convincing as that of Sunnydale—we can't entirely be sure it isn't a viable parallel reality. The episode ends without definitively revealing which reality we should believe in. Buffy initially accepts the alternative reality, turning away from a world where

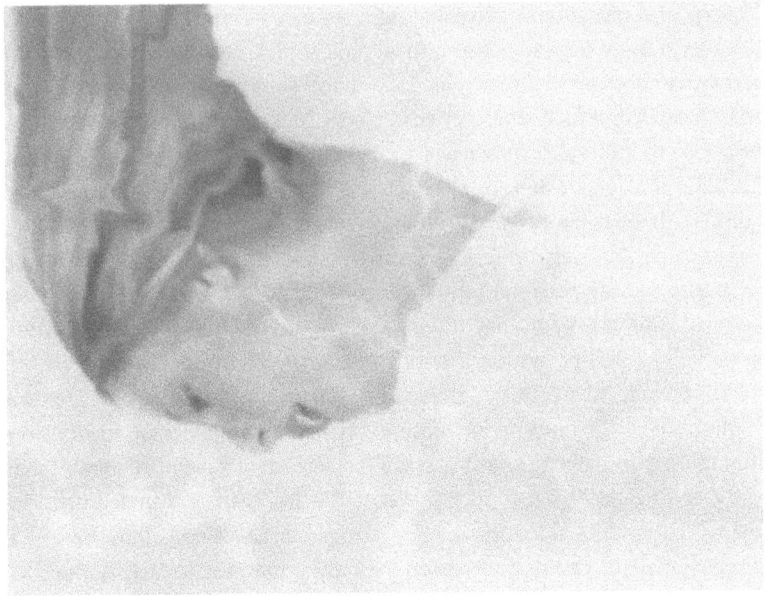

Figure 12.2 Buffy's sacrifice in "The Gift" is a willful acceptance of another reality and embodiment.

she is a superhero fighting evil to a more comfortable world where her mother is alive, her parents are still together, and her friends and sister are figments of a "delusion" she is being cured of. This act of accepting what the Scoobies (and the audience) see as another delusion, demonstrates the impulse to annihilate herself and the world that Willow manifests later in season six. More profound is the episode's—and the series'—equivocation on the two possible worlds: both of these realities remain viable, coexisting in the same universe.

Buffy's retreat from the series' reality as we know it in "Normal Again" is very different from the earlier episode, "The Weight of the World" (5.21), in which Buffy, traumatized by the loss of sister Dawn to villain Glory, lapses into a fugue state, dreaming herself into another, insulated reality. There are parallels; in her mental retreat, Buffy becomes a little girl constantly clinging to a doll. In response to Willow's urging to "come out," to "be with your friends," child-Buffy says, "I like it here."[57] "The Weight of the World" shows Buffy retreating into a protective delusion offered by her *psyche*; "Normal Again," however, offers her a viable escape because its reality is *real*, not a figment.[58] She might escape this terrifying reality, but the escape does not make it any less real. *Buffy* has already rewritten itself with the introduction of Dawn in season five, an act that Anthony Adler calls "a fantastic incursion on reality."[59] And in "Normal Again," Buffy might be said to attempt a retreat to the "unknowable, indescribable experience" she has between seasons five and six, when she believes she is in "heaven."[60] There are compelling parallels between Buffy reaching a heaven-like state of "nothingness," Willow's attraction to cosmic expansion of her mind and body, and the chaotic outer-rim-dwelling Reavers as they are incarnated in *Firefly*. Having touched different versions of the beyond, these characters—good, evil, sometimes both—return radically other, marked by things unfathomable.

In season seven of *Buffy*, the activation of all the potential Slayers is arguably another retreat in that Buffy essentially destroys reality to save it, changing the rules that make her the only active slayer. In an act mirroring Willow's eschatological goals, she, in essence, creates a new world (aided by Willow herself). Erickson and Lemberg's description of this act articulates the two characters' Weirding of reality: "Buffy and Willow's act can be seen as an act of anti-myth and as a dismissal of traditional metaphysical order, a releasing of chaos upon a cosmic order."[61] Arguably, Buffy's role in this reality-altering act shows her to have come to a new consciousness that puts her supernatural role, and all humanity, into stark perspective. One of the series' most *humanistic* Weird elements is that both Buffy and Willow progress from attempting to evade an unsatisfying reality to inventing a new reality that is marked by hope rather than despair.

Weird humanism is fraught because it arises out of the longings of a delusional humanity that plods along, maintaining an illusion they must stick to if they are to remain pleasantly ignorant of their insignificance in the cosmic scheme. Lovecraft's seekers risk death and madness to push past this illusion, and Ligotti's characters often even accept madness as the only viable alternative. The narrator of Ligotti's "The Mystics of Muelenberg" states:

> The worst fear of the race—yes, the world suddenly transformed into a senseless nightmare, horrible dissolution of things. Nothing compares, even oblivion is a sweet dream. You understand why, of

course. Why this peculiar threat. These brooding psyches, all the busy minds everywhere. I hear them buzzing like flies in the blackness. I see them as glow worms flitting in the blackness. They are struggling, straining every second to keep the sky above them, to keep the sun in the sky, to keep the dead in the earth—to keep all things, so to speak, *where they belong*. What an undertaking! What a crushing task! Is it any wonder that they are all tempted by a universal vice, that in some dark street of the mind a single voice whispers to one and all, softly hissing, and says: 'Lay down your burden'. Then thoughts begin to drift, a mystical magnetism pulls them this way and that, faces start to change, shadows speak ... sooner or later the sky comes down, melting like wax. But as you know, everything has not yet been lost: absolute terror has proved its security against this fate. Is it any wonder that these beings carry on the struggle at whatever cost?[62]

Ligotti's seekers, like *Buffy*'s, are searching for more than knowledge or truth; they seek connection and feeling, something transcendent rising up in a post-Christian world. They wish for the sky to "come down."

Conclusion

Miéville writes that, "The awe that Weird Fiction attempts to invoke is a function of *lack* of recognition, rather than any uncanny resurgence, guilt-function, the return of the repressed."[63] In this context, it might seem challenging to identify the Weird's place in a commercial television landscape. Prior to *Buffy*, a Weird tradition on television was as difficult to seek out as one of its many mysterious fictional grimoires. The most significant series to feature Weird tales (some of them derived from classic works of the tradition) were *Lights Out* (1946–1952, based upon the popular radio show of the same name); *One Step Beyond* (1959–1961), which blended fiction, documentary, pseudo-documentary, and even mock-documentary into its strange events; the dark sci-fi series, *The Outer Limits* (1963–1965); Rod Serling's *Night Gallery* (1969–1973); *Kolchak: The Night Stalker* (1974–1975), and its progeny, *The X-Files* (1993–2002; 2016-present); the Leonard Nimoy-hosted pseudo-documentary series, *In Search of . . .* (1977–1982); and *Twin Peaks* (1990–1991). The horror landscape on television at the time of *Buffy* was limited and limiting, as Stacey Abbott argues in her chapter in this collection.[64] *Buffy* is unique and challenging in its fusion of Gothic and Weird traditions, offering a space for a further exploration of the Weird's radical alterity that more recent television shows seem to have embraced. Indeed, the Weird mode seems to have taken a stronger foothold in series such as *True Detective* (2014 – present, inspired by and some claim plagiarized from Ligotti's *The Conspiracy Against the Human Race*, 2010);[65] David Lynch and Mark Frost's critically acclaimed 2017 revival of *Twin Peaks*, and the immensely popular, nostalgic pastiche, *Stranger Things* (2016 – present) with its sense of cosmic horror resistant to easy conclusions.

The Gothic-inflected possibility that the landscape of the entire *Buffy* series is a psychic extension of the trials, tribulations, and repressed trauma of the Slayer herself—a totalizing projection wherein her conflicts are played out on grand scale, and her community (close and at large) find themselves trapped—is compelling. In "Normal Again," both of the Slayer's possible worlds—one of super-strength and heroics in a fallen, supernatural world, or one of vulnerability and delusion in a world that institutionalizes her—are equally all-consuming, and equally possible. Such implications, as Erickson and Lemberg argue, reach out disturbingly to fans of the series, whom the episode asks suddenly to evaluate their relationship to a fictional reality they have believed in up to and beyond season six. Their argument about the show's final season is similar to Ligotti's conclusions about the futility of human struggle: "Throughout the season," they write, "it is stressed that although we may desire balance, order, a sense of self, and a definition of good and evil, these things are ultimately denied us."[66] The fact that both *Buffy* and *Firefly* risk going here at all, stranding viewers within such a possibility, suggests a willingness to accept the novelty, ambiguity, and terrible speculation upon annihilation characteristic of the Weird tradition.

Notes

1. China Miéville, "Weird Fiction," *The Routledge Companion to Science Fiction*, ed. Mark Bould, Andrew M. Butler, Adam Roberts, Sherryl Vint (New York and London: Routledge, 2009), 513.
2. "Serenity," *Firefly*, directed/written by Joss Whedon (2002; Burbank, CA: 20th Century Fox Home Entertainment, 2014), DVD. All subsequent references to *Firefly* are to this DVD collection.
3. "Serenity," ibid.

4. "Serenity," ibid.

5. I have more to say about the incarnation of the Reavers in the 2005 film *Serenity* below.

6. See Karen Herland's chapter in this collection for a discussion of Reavers in this context.

7. Thomas Elsaesser, "Tales of Sound and Fury: Observations on the Family Melodrama," *Film Genre Reader II*, edited by Barry Keith Grant, (Austin, TX: University of Texas Press, 1999), 359.

8. To speak of a Gothic or Weird "mode" is to highlight genre convention as an aesthetic orientation or attitude towards subject matter. Here, horror acts as a kind of language with conventions the vocabulary and phrasing. Haunting in the Gothic, for example, addresses an individual and collective framing of the past-present dynamic, making the Gothic a particularly useful mode for addressing forgotten or suppressed histories. The Weird's pervasive interest in sublime confrontations with the radically unknown, makes it suitable for addressing more speculative concerns.

9. For a helpful condensation of Lovecraft's theories on the Weird, see "Lovecraft on Weird Fiction," compiled by S.T. Joshi, in *The Annotated H.P. Lovecraft* (New York: Dell, 1997), 335–344; Lovecraft's novel, *At the Mountains of Madness* (pp. 179–331 in the same volume) and Lovecraft's extended treatment of horror and the Weird in his essay, *Supernatural Horror in Literature* (1927). See also, "Weird Story Plots," "[Notes on Weird Fiction]," "Notes on Writing Weird Fiction," and "Some Notes on Interplanetary Fiction" in *H.P. Lovecraft: Collected Essays, Volume 2: Literary Criticism* (Ed. S.T. Joshi, New York: Hippocampus Press, 2004), 153–181.

10. H.P. Lovecraft. (1927) *The Annotated Supernatural Horror in Literature*. Ed. S.T. Joshi. New York: Hippocampus Press, 2012.

11. Susan Stewart, "The Epistemology of the Horror Story. *The Journal of American Folklore*. (95.375 [Jan. – Mar. 1980]), 33–50; Noël Carroll, *The Philosophy of Horror, or Paradoxes of the Heart* (London and New York: Routledge, 1990).

12. The concept of "hauntology" is Jacques Derrida's, from his 1993 book, *Spectres de Marx* (*Spectres of Marx*, Trans. Peggy Kamuf (London: Routledge, 1994)). I zone in on the Gothic (and psychoanalytical) aspects of hauntology that suggest subjectivity as a state of hauntedness, where individual (natal), cultural and social pasts serve to strand a subject haunted by lack and loss in a place where moving forward is or seems impossible. For an extended look at how American horror cinema combines psychoanalytical and ideological schools in both critical and reactionary ways, see Robin Wood's "Intro to the American Horror Film," in *Planks of Reason*, ed. Barry Keith Grant and Christopher Sharrett (Lanham, MD: Scarecrow Press, 2004), 107–141.

13. Rudolf Otto, *The Idea of the Holy: An Inquiry into the Non-Rational Factor in the Idea of the Divine and Its Relation to the Rational*, (1917), translated by John W. Harvey (Oxford: Oxford University Press, [1950] 1980), 65–71.

Weird Whedon

14. Otto suggests the Gothic tries to replicate a sense of the numinous (ibid., 67). I argue here that the Weird goes further.
15. William Faulkner, *Absalom, Absalom!, Faulkner: Novels 1936–1940* (New York: Library of America, 1990), 7.
16. Derrida cites Freud's uncanny explicitly in *Spectres de Marx* (*Spectres of Marx* (1993), Trans. Peggy Kamuf (London: Routledge, 1994)), 168.
17. Ibid., 380.
18. Ibid., 380.
19. David B. Johnson, "The Postmodern Sublime: Presentation and Its Limits," *The Sublime: From Antiquity to the Present*. Ed. Timothy M. Costelloe (Cambridge and New York: Cambridge University Press, 2012), 120.
20. Ibid., 120.
21. See Eugene Thacker's *Cosmic Pessimism* (2015) for a discussion of the critical productiveness of Cosmic (Weird) pessimism. In *Cosmic Pessimism* (Minneapolis, MN: Univocal Publishing, 2015), 12–13.
22. "Bushwhacked," ibid.
23. Gregory Erickson, "Humanity in a 'Place of Nothin': Morality, Religion, Atheism, and Possibility in *Firefly*," *Investigating* Firefly *and* Serenity: *Science Fiction on the Frontier*, Ed. Rhonda V. Wilcox and Tanya R. Cochran (London: I.B.Tauris, 2008).
24. Ibid., 173.
25. *The Lurker at the Threshold* is a short novel, published in 1945 and written by Derleth using notes and fragments left behind by Lovecraft. Derleth is also responsible for bringing Lovecraft's works posthumously to a wider audience through the Arkham House imprint, founded in 1939 with fellow publisher Donald Wandrei.
26. Gregory Erickson, "From Old Heresies to Future Paradigms: Joss Whedon on Body and Soul," *Reading Joss Whedon*, ed. Rhonda Wilcox, Tanya R. Cochran, Cynthea Masson and David Lavery (Syracuse, NY: Syracuse University Press, 2014), 348, original emphases.
27. Erickson (2008) notes the similarity of the name "Reaver" to "River," who "has just like the Reavers reached a place of nothing." The association of the two as doubles is one that the film encourages. See Gregory Erickson, "'Humanity in a 'Place of Nothin': Morality, Religion, Atheism, and Possibility in *Firefly*," *Investigating* Firefly *and* Serenity: *Science Fiction on the Frontier* (London: I.B.Tauris, 2008), 179.
28. Thank you to Lorna Jowett for reminding me of this aspect of the Reavers' metaphorical configuration. For extensive debate on the topic, see also Agnes B. Curry in "B. Curry, We Don't Say 'Indian': On the Paradoxical Construction of the Reavers," *Slayage: The Journal of Whedon Studies*, 7.1 (1), versus J. Douglas Rabb and J. Michael Richardson, "Reavers and Redskins: Creating the Frontier Savage," in *Investigating Firefly and* Serenity: *Science Fiction on the Frontier* (London: I.B.Tauris, 2008).

29. Jeffrey Andrew Weinstock, "The New Weird," *New Directions in Popular Fiction: Genre, Distribution, Reproduction*, Ed. Ken Gelder (London: Palgrave Macmillan, 2016), 181.

30. Erickson, "From Old Heresies ...," 349.

31. See the Powers that Be in *Angel*, and the two "Epitaph" episodes of *Dollhouse*. Both are fascinating from a Weird perspective, and I hope this chapter will encourage further scholarship that explores them along Weird lines.

32. Milly Williamson, "The Predicament of the Vampire and the Slayer: Gothic Melodrama in Modern America," *The Lure Of The Vampire: Gender, Fiction And Fandom From Bram Stoker to* Buffy (New York: Wallflower Press, 2005), 76–96; Leigh Harbin, "'You Know You Wanna Dance': *Buffy the Vampire Slayer* as Contemporary Gothic Heroine" (*Studies in the Humanities* 32.1 (June 2005)), 22–37; Renée T. Coulombe, "'I Had It All Wrong': New Vampires, Grrrl Heroes and the Third Wave Body in *Buffy the Vampire Slayer*." *Nostalgia or Perversion?: Gothic Rewriting from the Eighteenth Century until the Present Day*, ed. Isabella van Elferen (Newcastle: Cambridge Scholars Publishing, 2007), 206–222; Ananya Mukherjea, "'When you kiss me, I want to die': Gothic Relationships and Identity *Buffy the Vampire Slayer*," *Slayage: The Online International Journal of Buffy Studies* (7.2 [26], Spring 2008). See "Appendix I: The Work of Joss Whedon and the Horror Tradition, A Selected Bibliography" in this collection for other works situating *Buffy* within Gothic conventions.

33. Gregory Erickson and Jennifer Lemberg, "Bodies and Narrative in Crisis: Figures of Rupture and Chaos in Seasons Six and Seven," *Buffy Goes Dark: Essays on the Final Two Seasons of* Buffy the Vampire Slayer *on Television*, ed. Lynne Y. Edwards, Elizabeth L. Rambo, and James B. South (Jefferson, NC: McFarland, 2009), 117.

34. Comparing the series to one of the "mourning plays" (*Trauerspiel*) discussed by Walter Benjamin in *The Origin of the German Mourning Play* (1928), Adler writes, "The object of this mourning," particularly in the latter seasons of the show, "is not the fallenness and transience of a creation abandoned by its creator, but the inability of a life that has outlived its own finitude to feel itself." In *The Afterlife of Genre: Remnants of the* Trauerspiel *in* Buffy the Vampire Slayer (Brooklyn, NY: Punctum Books, 2014), 45.

35. Season six's "Dark Willow" is the culmination of the character's insecurities, played out on an apocalyptic scale. In "Two To Go" (6.21), she remarks, "Let me tell you something about Willow. She's a loser. And she always has been. People picked on Willow in junior high school, high school, up until college. With her stupid mousy ways."

36. "Grave," *Buffy the Vampire Slayer*, ibid.

37. Highlighting Buffy and Willow's alterity, Xander, laments his role as all-too-normal, "guy who fixes the windows," in "Potential" (7.12).

38. Barbara Creed, *The Monstrous Feminine: Film, Feminism, Psychoanalysis* (London and New York: Routledge, 1993).

39. Barbara Creed, "Horror and the Monstrous-Feminine: An Imaginary Abjection," in *Feminist Film Theory: A Reader*, ed. Sue Thornham (New York: New York University Press, 1999).

40. Jeffrey Jerome Cohen, "Monster Culture (Seven Theses)," *Monster Theory: Reading Culture*, ed. Jeffrey Jerome Cohen (Minneapolis, MN: University of Minnesota Press, 1996), 6.

41. The exception might be the many incarnations of Abraham Van Helsing, beginning with Bram Stoker's *Dracula* (1897).

42. Andrew Tudor, *Monsters and Mad Scientists* (London, UK and Cambridge, MA: Wiley-Blackwell, 1989), 83.

43. This essay does not cover the show's comics incarnation of seasons eight and nine. Willow's relationship as student and sexual partner of trickster-demon-sorceress Aluwyn (also known as Saga Vasuki) constitutes another Weird arc within Willow's wider journey.

44. H.P. Lovecraft, *The Annotated H.P. Lovecraft*, ed. S.T. Joshi, (New York: Dell, 1997), 340, original emphasis.

45. Ibid., 341.

46. Ibid., 342.

47. Ibid., 343.

48. "Grave," *Buffy the Vampire Slayer*, ibid., emphasis added.

49. Noël Carroll, "Why Horror?" *Horror: The Film Reader*, ed. Mark Jancovich (London: Routledge, 2002), 35.

50. Cohen, ibid., 13.

51. Ibid., 12.

52. "Lessons," *Buffy the Vampire Slayer*, ibid.

53. See David Kociemba, "From Beneath You, It Foreshadows: Why *Buffy*'s First Season Matters" and Ananya Mukherjea, "'It's Like Some Primal, Some Animal Force ... That Use to Be Us': Animality, Humanity, and Moral Careers in the Buffyverse," both in *Reading Joss Whedon* (Syracuse, NY: Syracuse University Press, 2014), 22–39 and 53–69, respectively.

54. Pateman, ibid., 139.

55. Thomas Ligotti, "Thinking Horror," *Collapse: Philosophical Research and Development. Volume IV*, ed. Robin Mackay (Falmouth, UK: Urbanomic, 2009), 228.

56. Ibid., n209.

57. "The Weight of the World," *Buffy the Vampire Slayer*, ibid.

58. The possibility that multiple realities compete for supremacy seems an allusion to the "bizarro" world of *Star Trek*'s "Mirror, Mirror" (2.4) episode, where Kirk and the crew of the *Enterprise* learn of a darker version of their own reality that, despite their escape from it to a "better" version that the audience knows, remains intact and viable at the end of the episode.

59. Adler, ibid., 42.

60. Erickson and Lemberg, ibid., 119.

61. Erickson and Lemberg, ibid., 128.

62. Thomas Ligotti, "The Mystics of Muelenberg," in *Grimscribe: His Lives and Works* (New York: Carroll and Graf, 1991), 114.

63. China Miéville, "Weird Fiction," *The Routledge Companion to Science Fiction*, ed. Mark Bould, A.M. Butler, A. Roberts, and Sheryl Vint (London: Routledge, 2009), 512.

64. See also Lorna Jowett and Stacey Abbott, *TV Horror: Investigating the Dark Side of the Small Screen* (London and New York: I.B.Tauris, 2013).

65. Thomas Ligotti, *The Conspiracy Against the Human Race* (New York: Hippocampus Press, 2010).

66. Erickson and Lemberg, ibid., 126.

13

"All the Better to Know You": Investigating the Hybrid Monster and Allegories of Self/Other in *Buffy the Vampire Slayer*

K. Brenna Wardell

The *Buffy the Vampire Slayer* episode "Fear Itself" (4.4) pays homage to "Little Red Riding Hood" as Buffy, dressed as Red, and Xander walk to a Halloween party. Xander, who has long-harbored a crush, asks Buffy with a self-knowing, wolfish leer, "What's in your basket, little girl?" (see Figure 13.1). Buffy responds with a single word as she reveals her basket's contents, "Weapons." This interaction between the vampire slayer and her friend is, like the series and Joss Whedon's oeuvre, multi-referential and generically unstable, here gesturing to comedy, horror, and one of horror's significant antecedents— the fairy tale. A seeming throwaway, this moment—metaphoric and multifaceted; unexpected, and yet, particularly for long-time fans, completely in character with Buffy and her world—offers a précis of the multivalent nature of *Buffy*, fairy tales, and the horror genre.

Whedon and his collaborators' use of "Red" in *Buffy*, as in their use generally of fairy tale and horror tropes, is both literal, such as the dialogue and *mise-en-scène* in "Fear Itself," and figurative: drawing on the allegorical nature of fairy tale and horror texts with their mix of facile, surface meanings and complex, even interrogative, connotations. Thus the "little" girl

243

Figure 13.1 What's in your basket, little girl? Buffy as Red Riding Hood.

protagonist of "Red" is echoed by Buffy with her childlike name and petite frame, while the tale's Wolf becomes *Buffy*'s "monsters"—blending into Sunnydale's "woods." Red and Buffy's narrative arcs offer further parallels—moving from childhood naiveté to wisdom through trials of loss, death, and rebirth. The Slayer's fellow Scoobies, her chosen family, facilitate these trials, like figures in some versions of Red's tale, with further testing provided by the forces each girl faces—wolf, vampire, or human: the last including Buffy herself. In this chapter I use "Red" as a lens through which to examine the subversive play of Whedon and his collaborators with the comforting, familiar tropes of fairy tales and horror, collectively fairy tale horror, in *Buffy*'s content, form, and structure, a play facilitated by the figure of the monster—not necessarily a marker of evil but of difference.

Deep connections exist between fairy tales and horror: two forms whose liminality provides a space for imaginative investigations of gender, sexuality, class, and race.[1] Such fluidity is a central argument of Carol J. Clover's 1992 *Men, Women, and Chain Saws: Gender in the Modern Horror Film*, which addresses the sociocultural aspects of 1970s and 1980s horror. Clover argues that in horror texts, "We are both Red Riding Hood *and* the Wolf; the force of the experience, in horror, comes from 'knowing' both sides of the story."[2] Clover's observation foregrounds the expressive possibility of horror's "knowing" in investigating identity formation: often figured as innocent youngsters, such as Red, gaining experience through violence and confrontations with the nonhuman or monstrous.

As Clover indicates, horror texts, like fairy tales, contain a mutability and expansiveness that encourage viewers to read beyond facile Manichean identity binaries of self/other—that is, human or monster—and dig into the multifold nature of both individual characters and their pairings. To explore how Whedon and company play with the liminality of horror's "knowing" through their use of "Red," interrogating identity binaries of self/other through the tale's Red/Wolf dynamic, I focus on close readings of three *Buffy* pairings—Buffy/Angel, Buffy/Spike, and Buffy/Buffy. I argue that through the construction and conflict of these pairings the roles of self/other are reimagined, even collapsed. The key to this reimagining lies in the distinctly hybrid representation of the monster, whose liminality foregrounds the compound nature of *Buffy* itself. I begin with a short theoretical discussion of the nature of identity formation and its relation to the monster before sketching the history of "Red" and representations of the Red and Wolf figures in two seminal versions of the tale. Finally, I use close readings of those *Buffy* pairings to reflect on fairy tale horror's impact on the series and how the latter may, in turn, shape the horror genre.

In their characterization of individual characters and those characters' combinations, both fairy tales such as "Red" and *Buffy* present identity binaries of self/other that appear clear-cut but are, potentially, complex. First, a definition: discussing the process of identification in *Sex and the Slayer*, Lorna Jowett notes, "The usual construction is that of Self and Other, the Other being anything that is not Self."[3] Jowett stresses this division's sociocultural stakes, arguing, "Clearly such definitions of 'self' or 'norm' are constructed by dominant groups and work to exclude characteristics or identities that do not match those of the dominant group, and the 'default norm' is generally white, middle class, and often male and/ or heterosexual."[4] In this process, the monster is seemingly defined as other and separated from the self. However, as Clover indicates, fairy tale horror complicates this through a "knowing" that takes in both Red and Wolf, possible self and other, and mingles the two while, simultaneously, offering a more profound understanding of each one.

Joss Whedon vs. the Horror Tradition

The monster's disruptive potential is a central aspect of Jeffrey Jerome Cohen's "Monster Culture (Seven Theses)." Employing Marjorie Garber's concept of "category crisis," he argues, "Because of its ontological liminality, the monster notoriously appears in times of crisis as a kind of third term that problematizes the clash of extremes—as 'that which questions binary thinking and introduces a crisis.'"[5] It is thus the monster's difference, its otherness, that facilitates identify formation and, simultaneously, complicates it. Digging into the diverse effects of the monster's manifold representation in *The Horror Film: An Introduction*, Rick Worland contends, "the paradox of the monster is that it incites our fear, compels our attention, and quite often courts our empathy and fascination, even though it remains the most remote from any possible reality."[6] In sum the monster, whether in "Red" or *Buffy*, is a loaded figure offering a liminal space for viewers' fears and desires. To unpack the figure of the monster in "Red" and the tale's influence on *Buffy*'s content and form, I set up the tale's origins, the stakes of its portrayal of its liminal human and non-human characters, and its formal hybridity.

"Red's" origins lie in oral folklore, although contemporary readers and viewers usually connect with the tale's transgressive themes of fleshly appetite, multiple identities, and disobedience through written stories or contemporary film and television texts. Current iterations of the tale derive primarily from two written versions whose similar, yet distinct, treatment of their Red and Wolf figures significantly impact contemporary descendants. These texts are "Le Petit chaperon rouge" (1696/1697) or "Little Red Riding Hood" by Charles Perrault and "Rotkäppchen" (1812) or "Little Red Cap" by the Brothers Grimm, based on Perrault's work.[7] Both versions feature a young girl who ventures into the woods to visit her granny and encounters a Wolf who gets directions to Red's destination, devours granny, disguises himself as her, and then swallows Red; however, their endings differ. In Perrault's version, the women remain in the Wolf's belly; in the Grimm version a huntsman saves them, and they eliminate a second Wolf in the tale's conclusion.

Both versions offer a seemingly simple identity formation in their representation of Red, a human innocent who appears as a version—albeit female not male—of the self, opposed to the trickster Wolf, aligned with the monstrous other. The individual differences of Red and Wolf, highlighted through this pairing, enhance this sense of self/other.

Yet, closely reading Red, Wolf, and Red/Wolf complicates this binary, with the monster figure, anticipating Clover's complex "knowing," playing a particularly disruptive role. As a speaking, scheming beast who cross-dresses as granny, the Wolf mixes human and non-human, male, and female identities, his liminality echoing his folklore origins as a werewolf and providing a highly hybrid monster.[8] Red too is complex, a child who is, as her red garment—a hood in Perrault and a cap in the Grimm version—indicates, tied to bodily changes such as menstruation and budding sexuality. The association of both Red and Wolf with transgression is highlighted by Red's straying, figuratively and literally, from her path through the woods and her susceptibility to the Wolf's deception, so much so that in Perrault's version she agrees to get into bed with her supposed "granny," after first taking off her clothes.

Perrault's version is also notable for adding formal hybridity to the liminality of the characters by combining the sociosexual transgression of the tale with a moral epilogue. The latter warns readers to beware of "wolves" in the form of slick seducers, non-human or human, whose fair behavior conceals destructive purposes: "But alas for those who do not know that of all the wolves/the docile ones are those who are most dangerous"!"[9] In combining tale and epilogue, Perrault creates an ironic distance and tonal instability whose liminality creates the opportunity for diverse readings of the characters and tale—allowing its readers, like *Buffy*'s viewers, to read in their own way.[10]

This sense of multiple openings for varied, potentially interrogative, readings is why fairy tales such as "Red" and the horror texts Clover explores form ideal lenses to address the complexity of identity formation, including in regards to gender and sexuality. On the surface, fairy tale horror texts appear to foreground traditional gender roles and strict binaries regarding gender's relation to violence, like masculine power and feminine powerlessness; however, the situation is more complicated, as evident in descendant texts such as *Buffy*. Discussing the latter, Jowett notes, "The show attempts to destabilize binaries through ambivalence and ambiguity and through the multiple intersections of its generic hybridity. In reversing, subverting, or blurring boundaries between these binaries, *Buffy* potentially opens up an arena for alternative representations of gender and sexuality."[11] In the versions of "Red" discussed, Red and granny are initially presented as docile victims, their passivity highlighted by the active plotting and violence of the tale's male figures—the trickster Wolf and, in the Grimm version, the dynamic huntsman, a savior figure. Yet the characters' identities and relationships are not static but dynamic, evolving in each "Red" adaptation and citation. For instance, the Grimm Red does not remain a victim but, reborn from the Wolf's belly, transforms: helping the huntsman kill the Wolf and tricking and destroying a second Wolf.

This Red's metamorphosis from victim to participant, using her experience to outwit her assailant, anticipates the often-active roles performed by female protagonists in horror, a generic element played with in Buffy's character and narrative arc.[12] Setting up central aspects of 1970s and 1980s horror through a discussion of *Carrie* (De Palma, 1976) in *Chain Saws'* opening, Clover refers to horror protagonists of this kind as "the female victim-hero": the verbal combination stressing the figure's hybridity.[13] Clover argues that Carrie is both victimized (by her classmates' and mother's beastly acts) and a monstrous hero: a multivalent representation and binary blurring that anticipates Buffy's own hybridity and that of a handful of the monsters she faces.[14]

That *Buffy* is distinctly allegorical, like the fairy tale horror from which it stems, is an essential element of this blurring. The series is, as Whedon notes, built on the metaphor that high school and the passage to adulthood are hell, making the monsters that the Scoobies combat reflective of real-life demons, from self-doubt to toxic romances.[15] Lynne Y. Edwards, Elizabeth L. Rambo, and James B. South highlight this metaphor to address *Buffy*'s essential themes and structural elements while connecting these elements to its network move for seasons six and seven. They argue, "At the heart of *Buffy* from Season One has been the use of metaphor to explore the conflicts of growth, power, and transgression: characters have dual identities or shadow characters, the show's style, setting, and plots lend themselves to thematic dualities, and, at last, fortuitously, to the program's network duality."[16] The play of Whedon and his collaborators with such duality and its relation to the collapse of self/other is foregrounded from the first moments of the pilot with its nods to "Red" and fairy tale horror tropes.

The opening beats of "Welcome to the Hellmouth" (1.1) gesture to distinct stereotypes regarding fairy tale horror, such as the binary of victim/monster, and rework these: establishing the ironic, reflexive nature of the series. The episode begins as the camera moves through the darkened, empty Sunnydale High, lingering over uncanny objects in a biology classroom. A young man in a leather jacket, bent on seduction, breaks in, his companion a sweet-faced blonde in a Catholic schoolgirl outfit. A binary of experience and innocence, predator and victim, seems to be established, echoing "Red's" Wolf and Red figures, although knowledge of those figures' complexity leaves room for other readings. The combination of ominous music, a shadowy *mise-en-scène*, and a whiff of teen sexuality evoke horror, particularly slasher films' displays of endangered nubile couples.[17] Death arrives for the couple, dealt not by a monster, human or non-human, out of frame but by the young woman, Darla, who reveals her vampiric face and sinks her teeth into the man's throat. As their bodies drop out of frame, a cut transitions to the title sequence and images of another blonde—Buffy—in action. This sets up a link between the women as potential protagonist and antagonist and as similar to some degree, positioning Buffy, like Darla, as a hybrid, possibly monstrous, figure.

The play with binaries and viewer expectations here exists on multiple levels, echoing the complexity of Clover's "knowing." Viewers may read the human couple as self against the unknown other that might attack them; simultaneously, the drama of seeming experience versus innocence appears to set the man, a libertine in the model of Perrault's human "wolves," as other and the woman as self. The revelation of Darla's mixed nature—human and non-human, vulnerable girl and cunning beast—challenges easy divisions of self and other, destabilizing these readings and rearranging viewers' expectations. Darla's mingling of self/monstrous other anticipates that of her child/lover Angel, the ensouled vampire, and of Buffy, ordinary girl and supernatural slayer. The pairing of Buffy with Angel, variously her ally, lover, and enemy, sets up the first of the binary challenges of *Buffy*'s complex pairings. I first establish the intricacy of Angel's characterization and its heredity from horror texts, then explore the significance of the Buffy/Angel interplay in revealing hidden, liminal aspects of both characters through a focus on two episodes: "Innocence" (2.14), in which Angel becomes Angelus, and "Passion" (2.17), in which Angelus stalks Buffy and kills Scooby Jenny Calendar.

As Angel's backstory as the human Liam, the vampire Angelus, and the ensouled Angel unfolds over *Buffy*, viewers discover the multifold nature of each of his identities and the even greater complexity provided by these identities' combination, creating a truly hybrid monster. Taking these in order, Liam is, despite his humanity, flawed: a drunken philanderer who pursues women like Perrault's libertines; once turned, he becomes the bloodthirsty Angelus, and then, cursed, the guilt-ridden Angel. The latter personas are seemingly dichotomous, yet not necessarily so. As non-human figures, both Angel and Angelus are aligned with the other, the Wolf, although the ruthless Angelus seems most clearly othered; however, as the layers of Angel's nature are revealed over multiple episodes, this binary is unsettled. For instance, although Angel has eschewed drinking human blood, he uses violence and intimidation to support Buffy's mission, behavior that aligns him with Angelus; and while Angelus is predatory, unconstrained by Angel's empathy and guilt, he is also, albeit in a more limited way, complex: no simple beast but a cunning, self-reflective sadist.

That Angelus maintains a twisted version of his other self's romantic obsession with Buffy connects the two even as Angelus's torture of her highlights passion's dark side: the stalker inside the romantic. Disturbingly, it is increasingly clear that Angel/Angelus exist together, like Jekyll and Hyde in Robert Louis Stevenson's 1886 *Strange Case of Dr. Jekyll and Mr. Hyde*, each with the potential to become dominant.[18] That each persona is aware of the other and impersonates his opposite offers a further collapse of their distinction and echoes the Wolf's skill in performance and deception.[19] Along with Stevenson's Gothic novella, the figure of Angel and his relationship with Buffy also draws from and further develops the complexity of classic horror films based on novels, particularly *Frankenstein* (Whale, 1931) and *Dracula* (Browning, 1931). Elements of the diversity of Angel and other Wolf figures such as Spike in *Buffy* are anticipated by the creature in *Frankenstein*, whose child-like wonder and hurt, powerfully played by actor Boris Karloff, complicate readings of him by other characters and viewers as beastly.[20] This is particularly prominent in a censored scene in which the creature joyfully joins a young girl in a game and is then bewildered when he inadvertently causes her death.[21] To a lesser extent *Dracula*, released ten months prior to *Frankenstein*, also complicates the sense of its titular character as monstrous, largely through actor Bela Lugosi's performance of the Count as a suave mesmerist by whom the film's younger characters (men and women) are, initially, smitten. These diverse elements of Angel's hybrid monstrosity collide in the pivotal episode "Innocence," written and directed by Whedon.

"Innocence" illustrates the complicated emotional depths of *Buffy*'s Red/Wolf pairing of Buffy/Angel with a gravity lacking in the original prototypical "Red" narrative as developed by Perrault and the Brothers Grimm.[22] An early scene dramatically reveals Angel's transformation to Angelus and hints at this metamorphosis's devastating effects even as it subtly asserts that while this change seems disruptive, it also reveals the potential for violence and cruelty lurking in all the Angel personas. Following a focus on vampire lovers Spike and Dru and the Judge, the arc's putative Big Bad, the action moves to Angel leaving the bed he has shared with Buffy in their first lovemaking and going outside to an alleyway, where he falls to the ground and struggles in pain, watched by a weary-faced woman smoking in a doorway. A working girl who is several decades older than Buffy, her blonde hair echoes the Slayer—just as her red clothing parallels the red coverlet on Angel's bed. She approaches Angel and he rises, face hidden. When he turns he's in vamp face: a visual shock akin to the pilot's revelation of Darla's monstrousness. He feeds, drops her body, and exhales her smoke, clearly no longer Angel but Angelus: the hybrid monster at his most dangerous, seemingly fully othered.[23]

The serious repercussions of this collapsing of Angel's identities then build through the episode, particularly in the later scene in which he rejoins Buffy and pretends that he is Angel. In contrast to his killing of the blonde, this scene's destruction is psychological, its restraint and intimacy emphasizing its brutality. In its focus on physical and linguistic trickery, the scene returns us to the fairy tale and the manner in which the Wolf's disruptive quality lies not only in his devouring appetite but his mastering of the women's fates through manipulation: a position of experience poised against innocence that viewers share given that in *Buffy*, as in "Red," viewers/readers are aware of the Wolf's performance and potentially aligned with him even as they orient themselves to the texts' Red figures; the result is a disturbing "knowing."

While the episode's more overt transformation, physical and psychological, lies in Angel's shift to Angelus, Buffy also shifts, a turning point in the character's awareness of heroism's weight and of the darkness—of loss, of violence—she carries as both human girl and Slayer. Much of "Innocence" focuses on Buffy as a vulnerable girl in the mode of

Perrault's Red: her potential victimhood highlighted by her older doppelganger's death at Angelus's hands, and, later, Angelus's cruelty while performing Angel. However, Buffy's wounds do not, unlike the blonde's, destroy her—instead becoming the impetus for her destruction of the Judge and Angelus's plans. A Red who combines Perrault victim, Grimm survivor, and elements of the Wolf in her adoption of her opponents' strategic skills, she increasingly occupies multiple positions like Clover's "female victim-hero." Just as the presentation of Angel as predatory Angelus, flawed human Liam, and guilt-ridden Angel forms a distinctly hybrid monster, offering a nuanced "knowing" of the character and his relation to the series' complex meditation on inhumanity, literal and figurative, so Buffy too is an increasingly ambiguous figure.

Through Angel's and Buffy's individual transformations and increasingly combative interplay in "Innocence," Whedon and company not only create more multivalent characters and higher stakes, but also highlight the connection between the fantasy of fairy tale horror and real-life gender violence and the manner in which the former plays out aspects of the latter, as Whedon highlights in his DVD commentary for "Innocence."[24] The subsequent narrative arc, particularly in later episodes such as "Passion" with its destabilizing content and form, foregrounds the dark undertones of the couple's relationship and further highlights Angel's hybridity.

While "Innocence" disrupts viewers' expectations by defamiliarizing the nature of Buffy, Angel, and their romance, "Passion," directed by Michael Gershman and written by Ty King, further dislocates viewers through its use of narrative, visual, and aural elements rarely employed in the series, as Rhonda V. Wilcox notes in "The Darkness of 'Passion': Visuals and Voiceovers, Sound and Shadow." This dislocation begins with a shift in narrative perspective and camera position. *Buffy's* narrative normally focuses on Buffy and the Scoobies with the camera a third-person observer; however, in "Passion" Angelus's perspective directs the narrative and camera position: the Wolf taking over "Red." Formally, the camera stands in for the murderous gaze of the killer, echoing horror texts such as *Psycho* (Hitchcock, 1960) and *Peeping Tom* (Powell, 1960) and the '70s and '80s films Clover discusses, a shift that realigns viewers' reading of Buffy/Angel and creates additional layers of "knowing."[25]

"Passion" begins in the familiar space of the Bronze with the camera, positioned high overhead, moving over a series of red lights to show the

couples dancing beneath: an unusual perspective, literally and metaphorically, offering a fresh angle. This disorienting change sets up a new
perspective: Angelus's. The camera moves to the ground to focus on Buffy
and Xander dancing, then switches focus to a red-lit wall. A dancer
obscures the view, and then there is Angelus—staring at Buffy and Xander,
his gaze almost direct to camera. Adding to the visual disruption of his
dangerous presence is the aural uncanniness of his voice-over intoning a
word: "Passion."[26] As the scene continues, image and sound follow
Angelus's perspective, figuratively and, often, literally, as he moves around
the Bronze, the camera sometimes reproducing his gaze and encouraging
viewers to share it: an uncomfortable position given Angelus's brutality. If
"Innocence" moves to craft both Angel and Buffy as fully hybrid figures,
"Passion's" formal experimentation further reorients viewers' relationships
with both while setting up a further pairing: Buffy/Spike.

The opening of "Passion" echoes one of the most notable aspects of the
horror genre as discussed by theorists such as Clover: an inventive,
sometimes disruptive, use of the cinematic gaze to unsettle viewer
expectations and create tension.[27] Traditionally reserved from the teens on
for protagonists, perspective, literal and figurative, is rarely allowed
antagonists for more than a limited period. A shift occurs as early as the
1960s with films such as *Peeping Tom* and in the 1970s with revisionist
horror films including *Jaws* (Spielberg, 1975) and *Halloween* (Carpenter,
1978). In these films viewers often repeatedly, and for extended periods,
share the monster's gaze. Such closeness provides a degree of viewer
identification with the gazer although, as Clover notes, the nature and
effects of such sharing is complex.[28] Other horror films such as *An
American Werewolf in London* (Landis, 1981) develop an even more knotty
sharing of the killer's gaze, with *Werewolf* employing the gaze of a hybrid
protagonist/monster that anticipates Angelus's gaze in "Passion." In
Werewolf, viewers share the human protagonist's perspective both before
and after a werewolf's bite, inhabiting his transforming self's view as he
hunts in dreams and, eventually, reality. Viewers' awareness of the
protagonist as both sweet-natured everyman and vicious killer, like Angel/
Angelus and, to some degree, Buffy, makes this sharing fraught. While the
use of the killer's gaze to destabilize viewers is a well-worn practice by
Buffy's creation, it retains the potential to disturb. This may be particularly
the case here given that Angelus is no unfamiliar monster but a familiar,

once-beloved, figure, and Buffy, object of the gaze, is no disposable, anonymous victim.

These formal disruptions in the treatment of Angelus foreground his hybridity—monster and man—and create uncomfortable ambiguity. The calculation of his systematic stalking of Buffy and her friends—culminating in him staging a reunion between Giles and the dead Jenny as a site not of Eros but of death—emphasizes that he is no mindless predator, an argument evoked by his words in "Passion's" opening: "Passion . . . it lies in all of us. Sleeping, waiting, and though unwanted, unbidden, it will stir, open its jaws, and howl." Foregrounding passion's dangerous potential to awaken mankind's literal and figurative beast, Angelus gestures not only to his own predatory nature but all humankind's, including Buffy's, while highlighting their erotic link. "Passion" leads viewers to understand Angelus's focus on Buffy as not only the fascination of the predator tracking prey, but the shadowy twin to Angel's obsession, then love, for her, established in "Welcome to the Hellmouth." As Elisabeth Krimmer and Shilpa Raval note: "For Angelus, the desire to love merges with the desire to kill. He himself gives expression to this twisted conflation when he tells Spike that 'to kill this girl [Buffy], you have to love her.'"[29] This mingling of death and Eros echoes "Red," in which the Wolf's devouring of Red and granny stands in for sexual appetite. And while Angelus's violence marks him as monstrous, the character's darkness mirrors, to some extent, the ambivalence and moral grayness that Buffy and the Scoobies increasingly reveal over the season and in those to come.

Striking in its disruptions of form and narrative, "Passion's" opening scene is also twinned to an earlier scene, similarly overlaid with both threat and fascination, of Buffy being stalked. That scene, also set in the Bronze, from "School Hard" (2.3), directed by John T. Kretchmer and written by Whedon and David Greenwalt, marks the vampire Spike's first sighting of Buffy and the beginning of a complicated Red/Wolf pairing that both parallels and diverges from Buffy/Angel. In their matching narrative and visual elements, the scenes link these Wolf figures, reminding viewers of their blood ties (Angelus is Spike's grandsire) and decades together. This parallel with the lethal Spike highlights Angelus's distinctly predatory nature, moving him further from his Angel persona even as his resonant voiceover, an emotional element not included in "School Hard," complicates this. The voiceover foregrounds a desire, albeit twisted and dangerous, whose emotional strength, combined with the sharing of the gaze, may tempt viewers to identify with Angelus: a reception position that threatens to collapse another distinction of self/other—that of viewers/the monster—and implicate viewers in Angelus's monstrousness.[30]

In contrast to the complexity of this character and viewers' relations to him, Spike appears a more simple Wolf figure—his relationship with Buffy in "School Hard" clearly predator and prey. However, just as his grandsire evolves, so too Spike. As presented in "School Hard," Spike represents hard-bodied masculinity and violence: the opposite of the strong, yet tender, Angel of season one; however, his human backstory as the inept poet and caring son William, revealed in episodes such as "Fool for Love" (5.7), complicates this reading and the placement of him as monstrous other against Angel's self. For instance, while Angel's backstory reveals his selfish, libertine persona Liam, Spike's human past crafts him as a sympathetic figure, emotionally and physically vulnerable. And if Angelus's dialogue in "Passion" as he reproduces Spike's earlier gaze links the two, it also foreshadows Spike's shift to amorous, if thorny, desire for Buffy, inviting a retrospective rereading of the earlier Spike and of Buffy/Spike. Spike thus presents, as Jowett notes, a truly hybrid monster who, as she argues, "blurs boundaries between good and bad, 'masculine' and 'feminine,' hetero- and homosexual, man and monster, comic and tragic, villain and hero."[31] Further formal elements such as dress emphasize the vampires' complexity and binary blurring; for instance, their choice of black clothing unites them, while the presence of red differentiates Spike from Angel and foregrounds not only Spike's violence but his passionate relationships with his sire/lover Drusilla and, later, Buffy, who in her role as a Slayer and in her echo of Red and that character's association with bodily transformation is also associated with the color red.[32]

Not only are Angel and Spike represented as multilayered Wolf figures, their complexity inviting a similarly intricate "knowing," but their pairings with Buffy foreground surprising dimensions in the Slayer. As numerous commentators (Wilcox, 2002 and 2005; Helford, 2002; Dial-Driver, 2008) have noted, Buffy is multilayered, her liminality found in her own multiple identities and their evolution through her interactions with others. If season one presents a character torn between being a normal girl and a Slayer, further seasons complicate both positions and their seeming dichotomy, revealing Buffy in all her identities as both innocent and transgressive, like Red.[33] Numerous episodes display Buffy's imperfections and dark side, including the emotional cruelty she displays in "When She Was Bad" (2.1), her breaking of the law with Faith in "Bad Girls" (3.14), and her pursuit of a sadomasochistic relationship with Spike beginning in "Smashed" (6.9).[34] Her dynamic with Faith, her seeming opposite in background and behavior, offers a particularly interesting, gender-shifted version of Red, Wolf, and Red/Wolf, with both women assuming the hybridity of both Red and Wolf characters, a liminality enhanced through the interplay of their differences and similarities.[35] In Buffy's battles with Faith and Mayor Richard Wilkins III, season three's Big Bad, the Slayer reveals new levels of moral ambiguity, perhaps most clearly in her decision to kill Faith to save the poisoned Angel, even if she does not ultimately do so. In Buffy, viewers see a Red who grows beyond youthful self-involvement and naiveté to empathy and wisdom through traumatic trials that can only be survived by her acknowledgment of her own hybrid status as, echoing Clover, "a female victim-hero," one whose identity includes, like Carrie, an association with the monstrous and the other.

In considering the manner in which *Buffy* addresses horror's "knowing" by offering complex, ever shifting, Red/Wolf pairings, it is interesting not only to consider how *Buffy* draws from classic and revisionist horror films but to contemplate how it anticipates contemporary horror texts. A recent example is Showtime's *Penny Dreadful* (2014–2016), with its reflexive look at classic horror creatures, including Frankenstein's creature and Dracula, and a protagonist, Vanessa Ives, haunted, like Buffy, by her own dark side. *Get Out* (Peele, 2017), with its playful take on race and class, is another possible *Buffy* descendent—mixing horror and humor to destabilize viewers and encourage active viewing and critical consideration.

To close, I return to the exchange from "Fear Itself" with which I opened, and the manner in which it illustrates the multivalence in character, narrative, and form of *Buffy*—a liminality largely built through its citation of fairy tale horror and its use of the hybrid monster. For instance, Buffy, dressed as Red, is both battle-tested warrior, wielding the weapons in her basket, and still-naïve girl, not far removed from the tale's perhaps-not-so innocent girl who faces the Wolf's deceptions. Similarly, Xander is both fellow innocent and lusty Wolf, playing at being a libertine—or more. Even in this fleeting moment, the diegesis defies binaries, invites multiple readings, and helps viewers "know" the characters and, through them, themselves in unexpected, often delightful, sometimes horrific, ways.

Notes

1. Discussing central aspects of the horror film, Rick Worland notes that "another significant dimension of the horror tale is its affinity for the lesson, often metaphysical, implicitly social. Though we will never encounter such unnaturally powerful monsters in the material world, such stories serve as parables or convey a sharp message of warning." Worland, *The Horror Film: An Introduction* (Malden, MA: Blackwell Publishing, 2007), 8.
2. Carol Clover, *Men, Women, and Chainsaws: Gender in the Modern Horror Film* (Princeton, NJ: Princeton University Press, 1992), 12.
3. Lorna Jowett, *Sex and the Slayer: A Gender Studies Primer for the Buffy Fan* (Middletown, CT: Wesleyan University Press, 2005), 6.
4. Ibid., 6.
5. Jeffrey Jerome Cohen, "Monster Culture (Seven Theses)," *Monster Theory: Reading Culture* (Minneapolis, MN: University of Minnesota Press, 1996), 6.
6. Worland, *The Horror Film*, 9.
7. Discussing the tale's origin, Jack Zipes notes that it was "probably a tale told in a French or Italian dialect in the seventeenth century by women about a girl who must demonstrate her prowess when confronted by a werewolf or wolf so that she can be initiated into a sewing society." Zipes, *The Enchanted Screen*, (New York: Routledge, 2011), 11.
8. Ibid., 346–348.
9. Jack Zipes, *The Trials and Tribulations of Little Red Riding Hood: Versions of the Tale in Sociocultural Context* (South Hadley, MA: Bergin and Garvey Publishers, Inc., 1983), 71. Zipes includes the full text, which reads, "One sees here that young children,/Especially young girls,/Pretty, well brought-up, and gentle,/Should never listen to anyone who happens by,/And if this occurs, it is not so strange/When the wolf should eat them./I say the wolf, for all wolves/Are not of the same kind./There are some with winning ways,/Not loud, nor bitter, or angry,/Who are tame, good-natured, and pleasant/And follow young ladies/Right into their homes, right into their alcoves./But alas for those who do not know that of all the wolves/the docile ones are those who are most dangerous."
10. Perrault's cautions and the intended results of such regulation are not universal across "Red" texts, especially more recent interpretations. See Angela Carter, *The Bloody Chamber and Other Stories* (New York: Penguin Books, 1979).
11. Jowett, *Sex and the Slayer*, 12.

12. Discussing the origins of the series, David Lavery notes, "Whedon's long-time love of horror movies had led him to wonder what the result might be if the (usually) blonde-girl killed/terrorized by the monster in the alley were to kick his butt instead." Lavery, *Joss Whedon: A Creative Portrait* (London: I.B.Tauris, 2014), 88.

13. Clover, *Chainsaws*, 4.

14. Ibid, 3–4. Discussing *Carrie's* connection to feminism and social change in a response to Stephen King's discussion of the film in light of Women's Liberation, Clover notes of the character that "Throughout most of the movie she is the victim of monstrous schoolmates and a monstrous mother, but when, at the end, she turns the tables, she herself becomes a kind of monstrous hero ... She has become, in short, what I shall throughout this book call the female victim-hero (the hero part always understood as implying some degree of monstrosity, whose status in both roles has been indeed been enabled by 'women's liberation.'"

15. In an interview titled "Joss Whedon—About *Buffy*, *Alien*, and *Firefly*: The Shebytches.com Interview" with S.F. Said in 2006, Whedon discusses his approach to the show, noting, "And I thought, 'High school as horror movie.' And it really was." David Lavery and Cynthia Burkhead (eds), *Joss Whedon: Conversations* (Jackson, MS: University Press of Mississippi, 2011), 141.

16. Lynne Y. Edwards, Elizabeth L. Rambo, James B. South (eds), *Buffy Goes Dark: Essays on the Final Two Seasons of Buffy the Vampire Slayer on Television* (Jefferson, NC: McFarland, 2008), 6.

17. Clover notes that "In the slasher film, sexual transgressors of both sexes are scheduled for early destruction. The genre is studded with couples trying to find a place beyond purview of parents and employers where they can have sex, and immediately afterwards (or during the act) being killed." Clover, *Chainsaws*, 33.

18. Robert Louis Stevenson, *The Strange Case of Dr. Jekyll and Mr. Hyde* (Mineola, NY: Dover Thrift Edition, 1991).

19. Diane DeKelb-Rittenhouse notes that Angel and Spike are "in fact the logical evolution of the Vampire Lothario, a literary creature rooted in Eastern European folklore that has been fascinating the public eye ever since Lord Ruthven slunk into the pages of John Polidori's 'The Vampire' in 1819." DeKelb-Rittenhouse, "Sex and the Single Vampire: The Evolution of the Vampire Lothario and Its Representation in *Buffy*," *Fighting the Forces: What's at Stake in Buffy the Vampire Slayer* (Lanham, MA: Rowman & Littlefield, 2002), 143.

20. The association of the monster with childishness foregrounds Kristina Busse's argument regarding vampires' mixed identity. She notes, "The vampire is *both* a highly sexualized and a peculiarly infantlike figure, so that any relationship with and between vampires tends to collapse familial and sexual bonds." Thus Angel arguably also occupies the position of Red/self as well as Wolf/other, not only in his human past but also in his vampire selves. Busse, "Crossing the

Final Taboo," *Fighting the Forces: What's at Stake in Buffy the Vampire Slayer* (Lanham, MD: Rowman and Littlefield, 2002), 212.

21. This scene was censored in some US states on the film's release. See Worland, *The Horror Film*, 122–123.

22. Frequently discussed, this episode is reputedly Whedon's favorite. See Wilcox, *Why Buffy Matters: The Art of Buffy the Vampire Slayer* (London: I.B.Tauris, 2005), 111.

23. Regarding the scene, Wilcox discusses the erotic resonance of Angelus's smoking, noting that he first kills the blonde "and then, as if to emphasize the coital nature of the encounter, blows smoky air from his lips." Ibid., 123.

24. In the DVD commentary for the episode Whedon notes, "What we wanted to show was a horror movie version of the idea I sleep with my boyfriend, he doesn't call me and now he's killing hookers in alleyways."

25. Discussing the shift in identification in *Psycho* after the murder of Marion, the putative protagonist, Worland notes that we are then "uneasily stranded with Norman as the new protagonist. When he sinks Marion's car in the swamp with her body inside, we listen anxiously to the gurgling sounds as it begins to disappear, then catch our breaths when it won't go down. The second we fear Norman's exposure and sigh with relief when the gurgling resumes and the car disappears, the director has aligned our empathy, however unwittingly, with Marion's killer." Worland, *The Horror Film*, 86.

26. Wilcox examines the unusual, destabilizing nature of this point of view; focusing on the voiceover, she argues, "If not an omniscient 'voice of God,' a voiceover is usually given to the protagonist, recalling events or commenting as they proceed; normally, the voiceover gives the viewer a place to locate, often a character to identify with or at least pull for. How chilling is it, then, that the most dangerous antagonist gives the voiceover here?" Wilcox, "The Darkness of 'Passion'": Visuals and Voiceovers, Sound and Shadow," *Joss Whedon: The Complete Companion*, ed. Mary Alice Money (London: Titan Books, 2012), 104.

27. Clover notes of that gaze that "Predatory gazing through the agency of the first-person camera is part of the stock-in trade of horror" and argues, "The device is probably the most widely-imitated—and widely parodied—cliché of modern horror." Clover, *Chainsaws*, 183, 186.

28. Clover cites Steve Neale's complication of this construction of the gaze in *Halloween* with a sense of identification with both killer and victim, noting Neale's argument that "'the identifications of the spectator are thus split between the polarities of a sadistic, aggressive and controlling position and a masochistic, suffering, and controlled position.'" Ibid., 185.

29. Elisabeth Krimmer and Shilpa Raval, "Digging the Dead." *Fighting the Forces: What's at Stake in Buffy the Vampire Slayer*, eds. Rhonda V. Wilcox and David Lavery (Lanham, MD: Rowman & Littlefield Publishers, 2002), 155.

30. As Wilcox notes in "The Darkness of 'Passion,'" in sharing his view and voice in the episode's opening "we are immersed in the darkness with him." Ibid., 105.

31. Jowett, *Sex and the Slayer*, 158.
32. Drusilla echoes this scarlet shade in her costumes for "Innocence" and "Passion," the shade reflecting her status as both killer and lover and rhyming with Buffy and the latter's association with red.
33. The episode "Buffy vs. Dracula" (5.1) plays, both humorously and seriously, with Buffy's dark side through her interchanges with Dracula. In their dialogue he highlights her capacity for violence, while she dismisses his definition of her, with Dracula noting, "I came to see the renowned killer," and Buffy denying this identity, arguing, "Yeah, I prefer the term Slayer, you know killer just sounds so . . ." He fills in her blank with "Naked?" and she replies, "Like I paint clowns or something. I'm the good guy, remember?" For an analysis that focuses on this episode as a sustained treatment of "Red Riding Hood" tropes, see Kristopher Karl Woofter, "Little Red Riding . . . Buffy?: 'Buffy vs. Dracula' in Explorations of Intertextuality in Introduction to College English," in *Buffy in the Classroom: Essays on Teaching with the Vampire Slayer*. Edited by Meghan K. Winchell and Jodie A. Krieder (Jefferson, NC, and London: McFarland, 2010), 169–185.
34. As Wilcox notes, Buffy's darkness is explored through the characters of Faith and Spike. Setting up a discussion of Buffy and Faith against the background of the work of psychiatrist and psychoanalyst Carl Jung, she notes, "To quote a very simple expression of the idea by Jung, 'the realm of the shadow. . .is. . .the negative side of the personality' (147). The dark-haired, violent, promiscuous Slayer Faith is Buffy's Shadow figure." Wilcox, *Why Buffy Matters: The Art of Buffy the Vampire Slayer* (London: I.B.Tauris, 2005), 81.
35. Wilcox argues that through Buffy/Faith "simple dualism is not allowed—virgin/whore, devil/angel, hero/villain. Buffy and Faith are both aspects of each other and complex characters in their own right. Either of them might be capable of killing; and the ones they kill are not simply monsters. Killing is not cheap in this world." Wilcox, "'Who Died and Made Her the Boss?': Patterns of Mortality in Buffy," *Fighting the Forces*, 16.

14

Horror and the Last Frontier: Monstrous Borders and Bodies in *Firefly* and *Westworld*

Karen Herland

The dual frontiers of the American West and outer space have long symbolized the "universal" desire to discover, tame, and ultimately claim, the unknown. Joss Whedon's *Firefly* (2002–2003) and Jonathan Nolan and Lisa Joy's *Westworld* (2016–present) mine the intersections of these two rich genres—using a mythical future to explore the borders of culture and of humanity. The Western notion of frontier is revisited in both series, with a Gothic twist. Just as Gothic narratives diverge from archetypal representations, these frontiers do not fulfill the "promise" of settler expansion and conquest. Instead, the borders of the worlds depicted present "a conflict between the inscripted history of civilization and the history of the other, somehow immanent in the landscape of the frontier."[1] *Firefly* and *Westworld* offer dark, complex stories that complicate the border between human and monstrous bodies: those manufactured as hosts in *Westworld*, and those deconstructed as the cannibalistic, mutilated/ing Reavers lurking on the edges of *Firefly*'s 'verse. *Westworld*'s uncanny hosts are built by Delos Corporation to offer the ultimate "authentic" experience for affluent human guests who exploit these disposable bodies for their own pleasure—raping, torturing, or murdering at whim. *Firefly* focuses on a small group of smugglers, beneath the interests of the Alliance, until they take on two passengers, a doctor, Simon Tam, and his sister, River, who he has rescued from Alliance laboratories, but not before the government had inadvertently buried its secrets inside her. Whedon's crew is contained within a territory fringed by Reavers, terrifying figures tied to the legacy of the Alliance's domination. Whedon's observation that "[*Firefly*] is set 500 years in the future, but humans are still acting worse than any monster,"[2] could easily apply to either series. The capitalistic, cultural excesses of today are magnified in both futuristic settings. Jeffrey Jerome Cohen argues the monster is "an embodiment of a certain cultural moment—a time, a feeling, a place ... The monstrous body is pure culture, A construct and a projection."[3] By blending elements of speculative science fiction, the myth of the western frontier and horror's reflection of the monstrous within human behaviour, *Firefly* and *Westworld* consider how bodies are both driven and bound by borders and the expectation to conquer, and defined by a simplistic definition of humanity. Both series weave challenges to contemporary manifestations of power into their dystopian futures, mapping the mobility, integrity, and agency of the bodies travelling in their worlds. While the corporate, colonialist roots of these manifestations of power are evident, this paper also seeks to trace the masculinist assumptions driving the worlds presented in both series.[4] In many ways, the Gothic tendency to use "the body of the monster to produce race, class, gender and sexuality within narratives about the relation between subjectivities and certain bodies," in contemporary horror[5] unmasks the banalized horror of the rapacious nature of toxic masculinity itself.

Genre mash-ups challenge familiar tropes by blending traditional frames in unexpected, and, ideally, innovative ways. In *Firefly* and *Westworld*, science fiction and westerns collide in a manner that, additionally, evokes the uncanny characteristics of the horror and the Gothic traditions. *Firefly* ran for a truncated season (only eleven of fourteen episodes were aired—out of order—in 2002) and returned as a film, *Serenity*, in 2005. Jonathan Nolan and Lisa Joy's *Westworld* in 2016[6] is a reboot of Michael Crichton's 1973 film, with a key distinction (discussed further down), reflecting, as Cohen suggests, the different cultural moments of their respective productions. Both series function as classic speculative science fiction, taking current social trends and hurtling them into the future to demonstrate their constructed, and therefore mutable, nature.[7] They also generate unease around agency and the vulnerability of bodies, which become a figurative "monstrous" frontier themselves.

When Whedon flung *Firefly*'s band of outlaws and rebels several centuries into the future, he was not revisiting the same frontier that *Star Trek*'s optimistic crew had boldly travelled before. The small crew on the dubiously named spaceship *Serenity*, are not exploring the outer limits of society on behalf of the ruling Alliance, so much as seeking freedom *from* the control and oversight of the government.[8] Whedon's outlaw crew is marked by their uneasy relationship to the Alliance, a proto-corporate government both Captain Mal Reynolds and First Officer Zoë Washburne had actively fought to defeat. *Firefly*'s handful of characters are literally and figuratively peripheral, staying amongst the scattered planets, moons, and outposts on the Outer Rim of the 'verse. In contrast, *Westworld* shifts focus between all those with a stake in its microcosmic theme park. The series alternates between the machinations of the Delos Corporation's development of the cyborg technology used to generate the park's hosts (and for hinted-at paramilitary purposes), the park's impact on several guests, and charts the apparent emerging self-consciousness of a handful of the hosts. Comparable in its ubiquity to the Alliance, Delos Corporation's meticulous control of its theme park in *Westworld* is evident in multiple scenes of developers and security agents using holographic scale images to surveil, or reconfigure, various elements within it. In a similar gesture of wholesale mastery over both citizens and resources, the Alliance terraforms distant planets rich in resources necessary for its survival. Living conditions on these planets are insecure, and their populations are exploited to extract those resources. As has been noted by Jocelyn Sakal Froese and Laura Buzzard, this relationship is strictly unidirectional. The Alliance values these bodies only to the degree that their extracted labor benefits the central core, not bothering to offer any material help when their populations are threatened.[9] This Neoliberal commodification of bodies and resources is mirrored in *Westworld*, where the cyborg hosts exist to fill the coffers of the Delos Corporation by serving the whims of the guests. In both cases, a constructed frontier exists as a resource to be exploited by ruling powers, not as a site of collaboration or opportunity. The Alliance and Delos Corporation thus function as a source of dread in both their monstrous immanence and their corrupt ethics.

The mythology of the western frontier as a site of possibility depends on it being an unoccupied territory to be claimed—something that has never actually existed. These spaces are always already occupied, and the mythology's strength depends on demonizing and/or dehumanizing those occupants. If anything unites the western, science fiction, and horror genres, it is their potential monsters patrolling the frontier. "The safety originally promised by the empty landscape has metamorphosed into a revelation of hidden perils symbolized by the malevolent inhabitants of that landscape."[10] Traditional westerns pit homesteaders against violent, savage "Indians." These beings, always incomprehensible in both language and motivation—albeit uniformly cruel and vicious—make convenient villains: "[r]epresenting an anterior culture as monstrous justifies its displacement or extermination by rendering the act heroic."[11] As Agnes B. Curry notes, the Reavers serve as these classic monsters of *Firefly*. "Faithful to conventions of both the space epic and the Western," she writes, "*Firefly* and *Serenity* depend on the lurking presence of frontier savages to create narrative tension and moral order."[12] The Reavers represent senseless, chaotic, boundless violence, monsters who will "rape us to death, eat our flesh, and sew our skins into their clothing," warns Zoë when they approach Reaver territory in the *Firefly* episode, "Bushwhacked" (1.2), adding, "And if we're very, very lucky, they'll do it in that order."[13] Whedon explicitly acknowledged parallels between the Reavers and Hollywood Indians, noting, "Every story needs a monster. In the stories of the old west it was the Apaches," only to deny the connection in the 'verse he created, claiming his savages were not racialized.[14] Whether or not Whedon's Reavers escape racial stereotypes has been debated. J. Douglas Rabb and J. Michael Richardson argue that Whedon's intentions and deliberate decision to represent Reavers in rapid intercut flashes in which their individual features—including gender and race—are impossible to identify, challenges traditional and racialized representations of "savage Indians."[15]

Later, in Whedon's follow-up film *Serenity*, it is revealed that the Reavers are the result of a failed Alliance effort at biocontrol. When G-23

Paxilon Hydrochlorate, or "Pax" (a gas intended to keep Rim-dwellers compliant) was released, the vast majority of those exposed literally died of passivity. Reavers represent the ten per cent who went in the opposite direction, becoming uncontrollably violent after exposure. Whether or not Whedon's Reavers escape racial stereotypes has been debated.[16] Evoking Freud's concept of the uncanny, *Serenity*'s Reavers are figured as a monstrous primitiveness buried below the surface within each of us (see Figure 14.1).[17] The Reavers' behavior is not racially motivated, but instead, the legacy of the colonizer, a key point for arguing that they serve as "a metaphor for colonial oppression via racial stereotypes."[18] As such, their representation through a number of "tribal" tropes is troubling. Curry challenges Rabb and Richardson's argument that "it is necessary to present such stereotypes in order to deconstruct them,"[19] noting far too many parallels to Hollywood Indians (warpaint on their ships, drumbeats as they appear on screen) for them to be read against that particular trope in any meaningful way. Specifically, she argues:

> when stereotypical elements operate without foregrounding, at the edge of awareness, with no critical space opened up by emotional investment in the characters being stereotyped, they run a greater risk of merely triggering pre-existing schemas. And I think this is the case with Reavers and stereotypical Indians.[20]

If indeed, the Reavers serve as a metaphor for the violence of colonization, *Firefly* centres settler guilt as more compelling than the experiences of

Figure 14.1 A Reaver, as they appear in *Serenity* (2005).

265

those destroyed by it. The controlling, "meddling" actions of the Alliance are regularly criticized by *Serenity*'s crew, and by the time the Reavers' connection to Pax is revealed, it is clear that much of River's suffering is due to her buried awareness of their origins. This reading is reinforced by the fact that the Reavers are reduced to symbolic threats, with no apparent self-consciousness. For those on *Serenity*, "[t]hese characters, which cannot be identified as human, become the inhuman, the non-human."[21] Mal speculates that if they ever were men, that was so long ago, that "now, they're just nothing."[22] In the series, the Reavers function as silent boogeymen, a mythology designed to discourage frontier exploration.

In *Westworld* the role of threatening "savages" is filled by a band of Comanche-styled hosts known as Ghost Nation, who ambush and plunder on the edges of the park (see Figure 14.2).[23] They also serve the role of border patrol:

> The monster prevents mobility (intellectual, geographic or sexual) delimiting the social spaces through which private bodies may move. To step outside this official geography is to risk attack by some monstrous border patrol or (worse) to become monstrous oneself"[24]

These figures are so peripheral to the story that their sporadic appearances are simply used to signal "danger," as in *Firefly*; none of them have any real

Figure 14.2 Members of the border-patrolling Ghost Nation in *Westworld*.

role, dialogue, or individual backstory throughout season 1. They are dehumanized not merely as hosts, but also as symbols within the pageantry of *Westworld*, as ephemeral (albeit menacing) as their name implies.

While the Reavers' violence may have been biologically engineered, the Alliance requires inhumanity from its agents. In contrast to these unspeakable monsters, the Alliance's iron-fisted control is presented as cold, cruel, and calculated, particularly as embodied by their single-minded Operative, a government assassin featured in *Serenity*: "I'm a monster," he explains dispassionately to Mal. "What I do is evil. I have no illusions about it, but it must be done."[25] Ultimately, the Operative and *Serenity*'s crew members are all self-consciously aware of their own marginal, and monstrous, attributes. The Reavers are denied such self-knowledge and agency, maintaining them more at the level of caricature than metaphor.

This question of agency in the face of top-down control becomes critical in considering the monstrous within *Firefly*, and its reflection in *Westworld*. Sarah Corsie describes the Reavers' violence as "seemingly motivated only by the sheer pleasure of inducing the suffering of others without moral consequence."[26] Meanwhile, the human guests of Westworld pay $40,000 per day for the same pleasure. As the showrunners told *The Hollywood Reporter*, "There's this idea of the Vegas rule in a space where you can do whatever you want and there are no repercussions or consequences."[27] The guests can rationalize their behavior because the hosts are cyborgs, not-quite human since they combine biological and technological parts. Again, turning to Cohen, "the monster always represents the disruption of categories, the destruction of boundaries and the presence of impurities."[28] LeiLani Nishime reinforces this observation, "Cyborgs are hybrids of humans and machines, a mix of organic and inorganic. They are boundary crossers that inspire fascination and dread. They are, in the words of Donna Haraway, 'monsters'."[29] In the economy of *Westworld*, the hosts can be exploited because they are not "real" (purely human) even as their effectiveness depends on them appearing as real as possible. Like those dwelling on the Rim, the hosts' very existence is shaped by their capacity to be exploited. As one of the characters muses:

> You used to be beautiful. When this place started, I opened one of you up once. A million little perfect pieces. And then they changed you. Made you this sad, real mess. Flesh and bone, just like us. They

said it would improve the park experience. But you know why they really did it? It was cheaper. Your humanity is cost-effective. So is your suffering.[30]

In numerous scenes, especially in the first few *Westworld* episodes, lab technicians tinker with the park's naked hosts in glass-walled rooms to remind both employees and viewers alike that the hosts deserve none of the respect, privacy, or dignity accorded human bodies. Yet, even as technicians program the hosts, they also sneak intimacies, a practice ostensibly frowned upon but fairly widespread within Delos. The hosts' own programmers are both desensitized to the naked bodies around them and simultaneously willing to overlook their inauthenticity when it serves their own interests. When first-time guest William is offered the services of an intake hostess before he enters the park, he asks her if she is real and she replies, "Well, if you can't tell, does it matter?"[31]

Nishime draws a parallel here to racism, as in white Western culture, a mixed-race body reflects the same dangerous hybridity as a cyborg. Whiteness in this context equates to humanity and is defined by (and limited to) the absence of any "other" blood. Anyone revealed to have any non-white blood is immediately tainted (and thus rejected) as "other," as monstrous.[32] This "taint" justifies subsequent exploitation and dehumanization, and this same strict binary between human/not human is what marks *Firefly*'s Reavers as irredeemable "savages," and *Westworld*'s hosts as disposable machines. Hosts are produced, then made responsible for the deception they embody. However human their appearance, reactions, and behavior might be, they are ever always misleading and inauthentic because of their mechanical parts.[33] While the Reavers' lost humanity was catalyzed by the Alliance's introduction of Pax, it is *Westworld*'s guests who are more insidiously dehumanized; they are aware of the lines they cross, but they cheerfully pay dearly to transgress. However, the series does not simply imply that the truly monstrous rests in humanity, itself, the human monstrous is gendered as toxically masculine. This toxic masculinity is, in large part, the foundation for the park itself. Many critics have pointed out the series (through the park) takes a decidedly masculine point of view, treating male fantasy as a default setting, presuming that video-game style shoot-'em-ups and endless lines of eager sexual partners (or the conquest of unwilling ones) are universal pleasures.[34] The park is constructed to facilitate, even domesticate this macho posturing. As Zoe E. Seaman-Grant argues in her feminist reading of *Westworld* and *Ex Machina*: "even the masculine fantasy offered by Westworld is a mere simulacrum of 'true' masculinity. The androids are programmed to always lose fights with the visitors and the violence is never a true threat."[35] The thrill is to emerge victorious from a lopsided playing field, with no responsibility for the carnage left behind.

This moral murkiness also points to the key (and telling) distinction previously mentioned between *Westworld's* 2016 reboot and the original film. The film's tension is created by the Man in Black, played by a fierce-faced Yul Brynner, a cyborg who turns on the guests, embodying the fears of those who believe the machines will take over (fears reflected in hybrid science-fiction/horror films ranging from *2001: A Space Odyssey* [1968], to the *Stepford Wives* [1975], to *Robocop* [1987]). Cohen reminds us that "(t)he body that scares and appalls changes over time, as do the individual characteristics that add up to monstrosity, as do the preferred interpretations of monstrosity."[36]

In the series, the Man in Black is a frequent park guest whose exposure to Westworld sends him on a rampage during which he violates, tortures, and murders hosts repeatedly over the next three decades, searching for some secret he can unlock to make the experience "real." The big twist (both for the series and in comparison to the violent cyborg Man in Black of its earlier iterations), rests on his fragile masculinity. Although he entered the park as William, a white-hatted innocent, his realization that Dolores, the host he falls in love with, seduces others in the park with the same (programmed) gestures she used with him, transforms him into the Man in Black. Like a thousand Johns before him, he pays for a lavish experience, only to be crushed when he learns that he wasn't "special" and simply received exactly what he paid for. His resulting violent tantrum is not presented as diminishing in any way. Both in and outside of the park, bullies reign supreme (the Man in Black has become a key shareholder in the Delos Corporation, indulged by those in charge. When an employee expresses concern after the Man in Black slaughters every host in a small town, his boss shuts him down with "That gentleman gets whatever he wants"[37]). In discussing the everyday horror of masculinity, Imran Siddiquee observes of the powerful: "if something leads them to feel more masculine, those ends will always justify the means. And it's this single mindedness — this obsessive desire to overpower — which continues to be the scariest force in our society."[38]

This violent masculinity depends on a particular construction of femininity to be effective. And, both series unpack how that femininity is constructed. In *Westworld* female hosts bridge the divide between the (masculine/programmed) technology they are, and the (soft, malleable) hyperfemininity they represent.[39] Both Dolores, the innocent farmer's daughter, and, Maeve, the no-nonsense brothel madam, are literally built to exploit their feminine wiles to seduce guests in the park, though through vastly different tactics. Dolores's allure lies in her virginal, untested nature (disturbing for viewers because they know she has no memory of the multiple and most-often traumatic sexual encounters she has experienced), and Maeve's in the seductive self-confidence she exudes as she struts through her brothel. Unsurprisingly, as Seaman-Grant points out, these assignments are not arbitrary, Dolores is blonde and blue-eyed, while Maeve embodies the trope of "Black woman as intrinsically un-innocent."[40] In contrast, many of the flesh-and-blood women representing Delos Corporation are presented as coldly putting profit before their personal lives (executive Theresa Cullen displays zero emotion both when she ends her affair with scientist and host-programmer Bernard Lowe, and later when she fires him). Thus Dolores and Maeve's femininity, not necessarily shared by flesh-and-blood women, points to gender as ultimately performative[41] and not innate. The hybrid, monstrous bodies of the female hosts are threatening even as their femininity makes them vulnerable. As Lianne McLarty observes, "Contemporary horror seems doubly dependent on images of the feminine for its postmodern paranoia: it simultaneously associates the monstrous with the feminine and communicates postmodern victimization through images of feminization."[42]

Thus, viewers are encouraged to both fear the feminine, and punish it. The hosts' femininity (attractiveness and vulnerability) is further instrumentalized as a tool to garner viewer sympathies through extreme discomfort with graphic violence. *Westworld*'s female hosts are regularly, and brutally, sexually assaulted. These violations reinforce their vulnerability and humanity for the viewer,[43] while gesturing to "a disembodied spirit that can reside in either human or machine."[44] These assaults offer no opportunity to further the plot or the characters, and just as the hosts simply have these experiences wiped from their memories each night when they are reset, viewers are not encouraged to have an emotional response to these events. This construction ensures that guests need feel no remorse for assaulting fictional beings considered machines (a situation that parallels the experience of Actives in Whedon's *Dollhouse* [2009]). Yet, this doubled monstrous/fragile femininity is crucial within these horror tropes (Rieser quotes Hitchcock's "torture the women" as a genre blueprint).[45] Slasher films famously ensure that sexually active women are swiftly punished by becoming the first victims of whoever is wielding the blade, a practice so utterly normalized that it "conveniently conceal[s] that normative masculinity itself is the source of the monstrous,"[46] even while it is centred as the norm. *Firefly* and *Westworld* dovetail on this point. Kaylee Frye, *Firefly's* gifted mechanic, is portrayed as a cheerful, unsophisticated young woman who atypically has a flawless instinct for maintaining *Serenity's* engine in good working order. It is worth noting that only women are given nontraditional roles (mechanics, or soldiers) and "there are no unfamiliar masculinities in S/F that function in a similarly critical way."[47] Thus, the future in which women behave non-traditionally is a future in which women adopt the skills and behaviors of men.

In *Firefly's* "Out of Gas" (1.5), we learn that Kaylee became the ship's mechanic when she effectively diagnosed and fixed a problem on the ship after being discovered having sex with the ship's soon-to-be-former mechanic. In no way shamed by being caught in a carefree romp, she managed to scramble up and repair the engine before her partner could find his pants. Kaylee's position as a "natural" mechanic is not far from the hybridity embodied in the female cyborg. Yet, her assurance and ability can be easily destablized. In "Objects in Space" (1.10), Kaylee finds herself frozen in fear, at the mercy of a bounty hunter who has boarded *Serenity* and threatens her with a gruesome rape, "Ain't nothing but a body to me, and I can find all unseemly manner of use for it. Do you understand?" he hisses in her ear.[48] The risk of rape serves as a plot point, a shorthand about vulnerability and excess. "It seems that to evoke the feminine is the most economical means of demonstrating postmodern paranoia toward both the social world and its horrific effects on us."[49]

This becomes most evident when considering the character of Inara Serra, who uses a shuttle on *Serenity*, as a home base for her work in the sex trade. Her occupation as a Companion is presented as a status position that lends legitimacy to the ship's crew and activities. Whedon has said: "Inara's character originally was a whore, something very *Deadwood*. My wife said, 'Why not do something more in the style of a geisha and make her the most educated person on the ship, instead of just an oppressed, pathetic creature?'"[50] Certainly, Whedon's previous efforts presenting women as warriors seem a more satisfying challenge to feminine stereotypes than suggesting that all whores aren't pathetic. Whedon himself seems ambivalent about presenting Inara positively. While she clearly controls the terms of her labor, and refuses to be belittled or bullied, Inara's Companion status does not protect her from derision, even from her own clients (notably in "Shindig" [1.6]), nor from Mal's "endearing" insistence on calling her a whore at every opportunity. Despite Mal's obvious distaste for Inara's profession (and his repeated violation of her clearly articulated boundaries around being cast as a whore) he is obviously in love with her, and she him. This ambivalence is best captured in a plot line that, while never shot, has been often described by producer Tim Minear as the way Whedon first sold him on the show. This mythical episode opens with Mal dismissing Inara as a whore. Later, she is kidnapped by Reavers. *Serenity*'s crew learns Inara has a serum to make those who rape her die instantly. When Mal finds her, she is battered and broken, the only survivor amongst numerous dead Reavers. Later, he makes a point of kissing her hand, and calling her a lady.[51] Besides this scenario being the classic "female rape in the service of male character development," the scene also speaks volumes about representations of consent and agency. Inara is a whore insofar as she chooses to be sexual, and a lady when that consent is violated.[52] This misrepresentation of consent in the context of sex work might be traced to Whedon's ongoing support of Equality Now. (Over the years, he has used screenings of the film *Serenity* to fundraise hundreds of thousands of dollars for them.)[53] Equality Now's campaigns explicitly equate sex trafficking with consensual sex work. They advocate for an end-demand model, which sex trade workers themselves have vociferously rejected, arguing it keeps them within a criminalized context. A clear distinction between trafficking and sex work turns on the question of agency, a distinction Whedon blurred more deliberately in *Dollhouse* (2009–10). He seems less certain how to demonstrate Inara's independence. Inara's ongoing secret desire to settle down with Mal and live happily ever after neutralizes the challenge her position as a sex worker makes to monogamous heteronormativity,[54] and belies Inara's presumed sexual autonomy. This disconnect is most clearly evidenced in her reaction after discovering that Mal has slept with her friend, Nandi, in "Heart of Gold." She dismisses Mal's discomfort at being caught leaving Nandi's quarters, only to be seen weeping uncontrollably on the floor of her room when she's alone.[55] Not long after, she informs Mal she'll be leaving *Serenity* for good. As Dee Amy-Chinn rightly argues, "(r)ather than challenge the audience to re-conceptualize their response to a character who is a whore, Whedon re-writes whoredom to circumvent any challenge the profession might offer to the heteronormative matrix."[56] While it is not entirely fair to judge Whedon's intentions on the basis of an unproduced episode, questions of consent and violation remain unresolved in his framing of female bodies in resistance.

Even as bodies are violated, and their autonomy/fragility exploited, their mental integrity is also threatened. In *Westworld*, as in Whedon's *Dollhouse*, some of the more monstrous implications rest with the moral and ethical transgressions of meddling with the mind, and especially in the erasing of experience that might help one to find agency and community. In principle, the hosts have no knowledge of their programming, and believe themselves to be people in the Old West.[57] Although each encounter is new, the hosts are programmed on loops that trigger a set of pre-arranged responses, regardless of who they meet (hence Dolores' automatic flirtation, designed to engage whoever crosses her path). They live what they believe to be authentic lives even as viewers become familiar with stock phrases and gestures in various hosts, repeated as circumstances require. *Westworld* introduces us to the ghost-in-the-machines, Dr. Robert Ford, who has spent decades building and improving the park's hosts. The series' clearest character parallel to the mad scientist of 1930s horror, Ford has become preoccupied with trying to improve the hosts' memory and consciousness. Early in the series, he introduces a subprogram called "reverie," which triggers random memories in the hosts when they repeat a simple gesture. This is later blamed for a growing number of hosts glitching outside of their predetermined loops, frightening the guests with their erratic behavior. From the point of view of the hosts themselves, these programming hiccups allow glimpses into the repetitive routine of their lives, sometimes presented as nightmare flashbacks. After a shootout in "Dissonance Theory" (1.4), a glitch causes brothel madam Maeve to remain conscious as she watches Hazmat-suited Delos employees cleaning up the debris and collecting hosts for reprogramming. She quickly sketches one of the alien figures, so out of place in her Wild West brothel, and goes to hide the sketch under the floorboards. There, she finds dozens of similar sketches, shuffling through the evidence that she has lived through (and forgotten) this terrifying experience many, many times. This collapse of the strange and familiar surfaces in the series to create a sense of the uncanny for both the character and the viewer, who will remember the repeated trauma. The cycle is reminiscent of the Actives in Whedon's *Dollhouse*, who, each time they awaken from their memory wipes uncannily ask: "Did I fall asleep?" Later, Ford reveals that his former partner had taught him that the hosts behave more "humanly," and appear closer to developing consciousness when they experience suffering. Thus, each host's backstory includes a painful, unalterable memory—the seeding of a trauma—programmed to encourage the very sentience their treatment in the park discounts. These backstories are specific to whatever role the host plays, but the host's entire role/backstory can be changed at any time to suit a new narrative. As such, the series shows us several instances in which hosts interact with dear friends, family members, or lovers without any acknowledgement that the model has been changed and the person bears no resemblance to their previous embodiment. The effect is uncanny—the familiar is here made disconcertingly strange. *Westworld* has been constructed as a wonderland filled with disposable toys, and those toys must feel in order to remain convincing, even as that renders their disposability horrifying. This lack of memory is connected to the cyborg's lack of humanity; they cannot mourn, regret, or learn from past mistakes. This is what the hosts' dubious authenticity rests on, while they can suffer and feel both physical and emotional pain, these experiences leave no trace. As such, these hollow forms are, Barbara Creed suggests, as terrifying as zombies and vampires—bodies without souls.[58]

While *Firefly* does not have a technological character grappling with what it means to be consciously human, Simon's sister River presents the same hybridity in reverse—a human programmed to do the bidding of an institutional power, and inadvertently "storing" some of its darkest secrets as subconscious memory. Through Simon, the viewer learns that, as a supremely brilliant child, River became the object of Alliance interest and experiments, in programming her to be a weapon. Although it is unclear whether these efforts involved physical, chemical, or psychological interventions, River "is a product of their manipulation and, in their attempt to enhance her mental capacities for their own gain they have stripped her of her original identity, leaving her marked as an unidentifiable 'other'."[59] Her behavior is unpredictable, alternating between impulsive and violent outbursts, a childlike sense of playfulness and curiosity, and moments of perception, clarity, and genius. "River's reality is unique to that of the rest of the crew," writes Corsie, "resulting in her inability to communicate, both verbally and behaviorally, in a way that they can understand."[60]

Her transformation—and her very name, "River"—echoes that of the Reavers, also the result of Alliance manipulation. The experiments have introduced technology into River in ways that have tipped her from the human into the cyborg: she has at least partially lost her origins, her bearings and, it is implied, her humanity. River is emotionally traumatized by her inability to control her behaviour and, filter her own conceived thoughts from those that are somehow imposed upon her. Simon remains as both her protector and the embodiment of her past, the only one who remembers what she was like "before." In the film *Serenity*, it becomes clear that River learned of the Reavers' origins while under Alliance control, and as such represents a huge liability. Her presence on the ship is a double threat: she is dangerously unpredictable, having attacked a crew member without warning in "Ariel" (1.8), and her status as walking archive of government secrets will attract Alliance interference. River is first presented fragile and naked, huddled in a fetal position, smuggled in Simon's luggage. While *Westworld*'s hosts are naked to demonstrate (both to the viewer and to their programmers) their lack of humanity, River's reinforces her physical and psychological vulnerability. And yet, reinforcing the female body as simultaneously helpless and monstrous, as a programmed assassin, her abilities are extraordinary. In "War Stories" (1.9), she shuts her eyes and kills three advancing soldiers with a single bullet. In "Objects in Space" (1.10), she taunts a bounty hunter, the same villain who threatened Kaylee, suggesting the body he has come to claim has disappeared altogether is communicating through *Serenity*'s intercom system: "I am not on the ship, I am the ship," with an assurance that makes it difficult for the viewer to believe otherwise.[61] She then proceeds to work both ship and enemy to her advantage.

In *Westworld*, the female hosts diverge more frequently from their loops as the series progresses, perhaps developing the consciousness that Dr. Ford hopes they will achieve. Dolores's naïve farm girl is offered a pair of pants and a gun in a difficult situation in "Contrapasso" (1.5). She suddenly becomes a lethal sharp-shooter, leaving a trail of bodies in her wake. "You said people come here to change the story of their lives," she says. "I imagined a story where I didn't have to be the damsel."[62] Later on, in "The Adversary" (1.6), Maeve is made more aware of the constructed nature of her existence, when during a protracted, eerie tour of the Delos labs, she wanders through the hallways, seeing the people she interacts with every day as empty, naked bodies staring blankly from behind glass walls. Maeve is forced to recognize herself as such, as she watches a screen image of her programming type out each word of her reaction to the technology, as she utters it. She also sees an image of herself onscreen with a little girl and realizes that in a previous *Westworld* narrative, she was a homesteader with a daughter. These disturbing encounters with multiple selves create much-needed awareness of her situation, so that, eventually, she is able to force two Delos employees to help her plot her escape from the park, including an upgrade of her programmed intelligence, strength, and abilities. In an echo of Dolores's earlier comment, she announces: "Time to write my own fucking story."[63] Yet, although Maeve seems far more sure of herself and her plans than Dolores, it is never entirely clear whether either character's self-awareness and rebellion are their own, or an elaborately programmed means to someone else's ends. Dolores ends the season in a violent shootout, killing Ford, along with numerous Delos officials, but it is evident that Ford himself planned this cyborg-assisted suicide (echoing the death of his former partner). Meanwhile, Maeve's successful breakout from the park, aided by her increased abilities and a handful of host allies, is also a useful distraction for Delos security forces who might have stopped Dolores had their attention not been elsewhere. Thus, Ford might have had a puppet-master's hand in that awakening as well. In the final scenes of the show's first season, Maeve makes a decision to return to the park to seek out her daughter, a scene intended to reinforce her "human" instincts. Maeve's superhuman strength, intricate planning, and seamless success are reversed here by her impulsive return to reunite with a daughter she is aware she never had. Haraway has observed that cyborgs are characterized by a lack of history or origin.[64] This choice by Maeve suggests a nostalgic desire for the cyborg to claim an origin its manufactured status denies, again suggesting uncanny parallels to "real" human frailties and obsessions.[65] It also subverts the classic frontier narrative—instead of heading off to explore new horizons, she returns to retrace steps that were never authentically her own.[66]

While the masculine will-to-power, through corporate and technological means looms in both series, it is its presence within the female resistance to it that is most unsettling. McLarty traces a progressive path away from the merely monstrous feminine to locate "the monstrous in a mind representative of patriarchal social practices rather than in a female body that resists them."[67] In both series, that patriarchal power-over guides the action in myriad ways. River does extraordinary things at the bidding and programming of others, her implied "real" strength buried beneath manipulations of her mind and body by monstrous forces. River, Dolores, and Maeve—framed as heroes by their respective series—are oddly like *Firefly*'s Reavers: monsters created by monsters. And therein lies the real horror of both series, dressing up a fatalistic determinism in a froth of superhuman ability and intention.

Notes

1. David Mogen, Scott P. Sanders, and Joanne B. Karpinski, *Frontier Gothic: Terror and Wonder at the Frontier in American Literature* (Rutherford Fairleigh, NJ: Dickinson University Press, 1993), p. 17.
2. Emily Nussbaum, "Must-See Metaphysics," *The New York Times Magazine*, September 22, 2002. Available at www.nytimes.com/2002/09/22/magazine/must-see-metaphysics.html (accessed July 5, 2017).
3. Jeffrey Jerome Cohen, *Monster Theory: Reading Culture* (Minneapolis: University of Minnesota Press, 1996). p. 4.
4. As I write this chapter, revelations about the disconnect between Joss Whedon's woke feminist persona, and his rationalization of his serial betrayal of his wife, Kai Cole, through multiple affairs as a manifestation of cultural expectations on men seem to reinforce many of my observations in this chapter, while also complicating the context in which they were produced. (Whedon, quoted by Cole: "In many ways I was the HEIGHT of normal, in this culture. We're taught to be providers and companions and at the same time, to conquer and acquire — specifically sexually — and I was pulling off both!"). Kai Cole, "Joss Whedon is a "Hypocrite Preaching Feminist Ideals,' Ex-Wife Kai Cole Says" (Guest Blog), *The Wrap*, (20 August, 2017), www.thewrap.com/joss-whedon-femi nist-hypocrite-infidelity-affairs-ex-wife-kai-cole-says/ (accessed September 26, 2017).
5. J. Halberstam, *Skin Shows: Gothic Horror and the Technology of Monsters* (Durham, NC: Duke University Press, 1995). p. 6.

6. This chapter focuses on the first season of *Westworld*, aired in 2016. Subsequent seasons may enhance or complicate this initial reading.

7. Christina Rowley, *"Firefly/Serenity*: Gendered space and gendered bodies," *The British Journal of Politics and International Relations*, Vol. 9 (2007): p. 318.

8. Jocelyn Sakal Froese and Laura Buzzard, "'I Mean for Us to Live. The Alliance Won't Have That'": New Frontierism and Biopower in *Firefly/Serenity*," *Slayage: The Journal of Whedon Studies* (13.2 [42], Summer 2015) paragraph [5], www.whedonstudies.tv/uploads/2/6/2/8/26288593/froese_and_buzzard.pdf (accessed July 21, 2017).

9. Ibid., [10].

10. James K. Folsom, "Gothicism in the Western Novel," *Frontier Gothic*, p. 29.

11. Cohen, pp. 7–8.

12. Agnes B. Curry, "'We don't say "Indian': On the paradoxical construction of the Reavers", *Slayage: The Journal of Whedon Studies*, 7.1 [1] Available as pdf at www.whedonstudies.tv/uploads/2/6/2/8/26288593/curry_slayage_7.1.pdf.

13. "Bushwhacked," *Firefly*, Tim Minear/Tim Minear (2002, Los Angeles: 20th Century Fox Television/20th Television, 2003) (DVD).

14. Curry [2].

15. J. Douglas Rabb and Michael Richardson. "Reavers and redskins: Creating the frontier savage." *Investigating Firefly and Serenity: Science Fiction on the Frontier*, Rhonda V. Wilcox and Tanya Cochran, eds (New York, NY: I.B.Tauris and Co. Ltd., 2008).

16. Amy H. Sturgis, "'Just Get Us a Little Further": Liberty and the Frontier in *Firefly* and *Serenity*." In *The Philosophy of Joss Whedon*, edited by Kowalski, Dean A. and Kreider S. Evan (Lexington, KY: University Press of Kentucky, 2011). Sturgis summarizes some of this debate in a footnote on p. 37.

17. Sarah Corsie, "You know, you ain't quite right: Humanity and the monstrous 'other'," Watcher Junior 8.2 (Fall 2015) [1] www.whedonstudies.tv/uploads/2/6/2/8/26288593/corsie_watcherjunior_8.2.pdf) (accessed July 21, 2017) [2].

18. Froese and Buzzard [19].

19. Curry, quoting Rabb and Richardson. Similar connections are discussed by Froese and Buzzard, ibid.

20. Curry [15].

21. Corsie [1].

22. "Bushwhacked."

23. Viewers quickly learn that *Westworld* is designed to increase the horror/danger the further from of the park's centre a guest wanders.

24. Cohen, p. 12.

25. *Serenity*, Joss Whedon/Joss Whedon (California: Universal Pictures 2005).

26. Corsie [5].

27. Joanna Robinson, "In the *Westworld* Premiere, HBO Stares Back into Its Own Void." *Vanity Fair*, 2 October, 2016 Available at www.vanityfair.com/hollywood/2016/10/westworld-premiere-recap-season-1-episode-1-the-original (accessed July 21, 2017).

28. Cohen, p. 27.
29. LeiLani Nishime, "The Mulatto Cyborg: Imagining a Multiracial Future," *Cinema Journal*, 44:2, (Winter 2005), p. 34.
30. "Contrapasso," *Westworld*, Johnny Campbell/Lisa Joy (2016, Los Angeles: 20th Century Fox Television).
31. "Chestnut," *Westworld*, Richard J. Lewis/Jonathan Nolan and Lisa Joy (2016, Los Angeles: 20th Century Fox Television).
32. Nishime, ibid.
33. Zoe Seaman-Grant, *Constructing Womanhood and the Female Cyborg: A Feminist Reading of Ex Machina and Westworld*, Honours Thesis. Bates College, 2017, p. 58.
34. Emily Nussbaum, "The Meta-Politics of Westworld," *The New Yorker*, Oct. 24, 2016. Available at www.newyorker.com/magazine/2016/10/24/the-meta-politics -of-westworld (accessed July 22, 2017) [8].
35. Seaman-Grant, p. 69.
36. Cohen, p. 8.
37. "Chestnut."
38. Imran Siddiquee, "The Everyday Horror of Masculinity" *Medium* October 31, 2014. Available at https://medium.com/@imransiddiquee/the-everyday-horror-of-masculinity-d1d51288198b (accessed July 15, 2017).
39. Seaman-Grant, p. 1.
40. Ibid., p. 78.
41. Judith Butler, *Gender Trouble: Feminism and the Subversion of Identity* (London: Routledge Classics 1990).
42. Lianne McLarty, "'Beyond the Veil of the Flesh': Cronenberg and the Disembodiment of Horror," *The Dread of Difference: Gender and the Horror Film*, Barry Keith Grant, ed., University of Texas Press: Austin, 2nd Ed. 2015, p. 262. Also stressed by Klaus Rieser, "Masculinity and Monstrosity Characterization and Identification in the Slasher Film." *Men and Masculinities*, Vol. 3 No. 4, (April 2001) pp. 370–392.
43. Seaman-Grant, p. 75.
44. Nishime, p. 37.
45. Rieser, p. 375.
46. Ibid., p. 390.
47. Rowley, p. 322.
48. "Objects in Space," *Firefly*, Joss Whedon/Joss Whedon (2002, Los Angeles: 20th Century Fox Television/20th Television, 2003) (DVD).
49. McLarty, pp. 262–63.
50. Rowley, p. 321.
51. "*Firefly*: Browncoats Unite" (Science Channel Pangolin Pictures, 2012) Available at www.dailymotion.com/video/xvedx1 (accessed July 12, 2017).
52. This point has been made in multiple fan posts on websites; for instance, see Prozacpark, "The Rape of Inara: On heroines, consent, and women's sexuality" (2011), Dreamwidth, available at https://prozacpark.dreamwidth.org/111215.

html (accessed July 18, 2017). This also parallels the "brutalized Other as opportunity for settler character development" presented in *Firefly* through the Reavers.

53. Equality Now, "A just world for women and girls 'Joss Whedon for Equality Now'," available at www.equalitynow.org/content/joss-whedon-behalf-equality-now (accessed July 22, 2017).

54. Dee Amy-Chinn, "'Tis Pity She's a Whore: Postfeminist Prostitution in Joss Whedon's Firefly," *Feminist Media Studies*, Vol. 6 (2) (June 2006) p. 7.

55. Ibid., p. 7.

56. Ibid., p. 8.

57. Seaman-Grant, pp. 25–26.

58. Barbara Creed, "Horror and the Monstrous-Feminine: An Imaginary Abjection," in *The Dread of Difference*, p. 41.

59. Corsie [7].

60. Corsie [6].

61. Objects in Space.

62. "Contrapasso."

63. "Trace Decay," *Westworld*, Stephen Williams/Charles Yu and Lisa Joy (2016, Los Angeles: 20th Century Fox Television).

64. Donna Haraway, "Cyborg Manifesto: Science, Technology, and Socialist-Feminism in the Late 20th Century," J. Weiss et al. (eds), *The International Handbook of Virtual Learning Environments* (2006), p. 118.

65. Nishime.

66. David Mogen, "Wilderness, Metamorphosis, and Millennium: Gothic Apocalypse From the Puritans to the Cyberpunks," *Frontier Gothic*, p. 105.

67. McLarty, p. 260.

15

The Half-Lives of Horror: The Differential Embodiments of *Dollhouse*

Alanna Thain

"Ever wonder how a set of gestures and expressions can take over a whole sector of the population? When a society gives rise to scores of apparent replicants — through entertainment culture and media — it's hard to distinguish the doll from the cunning and conscious actor."

— Lesley Chow, "A Thousand Blooms: Inside Joss
Whedon's *Dollhouse*"[1]

Dispossession's horror marks Joss Whedon's work, explored through vampires, clones, aliens, robots, and biotechnologies whose violence enacts a mind/body split as a mechanism of control.[2] Dispossessed bodies reflect wider cultural concerns with the increasing fragmentation, serialization, and recirculation of human materials and images of the self that act in contexts beyond our own making in the digital age. Whedon rarely seeks a simple restoration of corporeal integrity, sovereignty, and autonomy; his work daringly explores affect, ambivalence, vulnerability, and the necessity of relation as fully part of human embodiment.

This paper takes a feminist horror studies approach to Whedon's "cultured images" of clones through *Dollhouse* (2009 – 10), Whedon's series set in a post-Fordist technology-assisted brothel. "Volunteers" sign up for a period of indentured servitude; fitted with "active architecture," they become "tabula rasa" known as Dolls or Actives. Their personalities and memories are wiped, supplanted with a set of basic stimulus responses designed to keep them passive and physically fit. Although Dolls are physically discrete, while non-implanted they are largely indistinct personalities, killing time with yoga, showering, and affirming their complacent servitude with statements like, "I try to be my best." On assignment, they are recoded with and embody completely the data pattern of another personality. At completion they are "wiped," waking up to ask as a Pavlovian pattern of call and response, "Did I fall asleep?" supposedly retaining no memory of their work. Their contract completed, they are paid out handsomely and their original personality is restored from date of incarceration. Set in LA, *Dollhouse* takes up reality TV's paradigm of perpetual performance under surveillance as a source of entertainment in exchange for money and social media's feedback loop of attention. While aware they have passed a period of not being themselves, there is no record in a Doll's memories. Throughout, a tension exists between imprints as an uploaded set of skills, as in *The Matrix* (the Wachowskis, 1999), and uploading a personality. Most of the time in *Dollhouse*, personality is just another word for affective labor: extractable, quantifiable, and circulatable, without concern for the host's somatic and emotional experience.

Cultured images emerge between biotechnologies and visual culture, demanding that we understand media as an experimental laboratory for novel corporeal forms. Today, media *are* reproductive technologies, and images the new automatons. Ambivalently positioned between science fiction and technological fact, cultured images are fabulations of sensible flesh. I draw on two concepts from Gilles Deleuze—the Lazarean body and the society of control—to explore the cultured images of *Dollhouse* as a novel take on cloning, to read the horror of resurrection and reanimation for feminist ends.[3] *Dollhouse* starts with a familiar cliché of the clone as a replacement body for an existing consciousness (for oneself or as a replacement object of desire). Gradually, the series centers on Echo, who functions as a *diagram* of virtual potential. I consider clones first via two categories of signs central to thinking of audio-visual specificity and media culture—Charles Peirce's index and icon—and then suggest a third term—

the diagram—which Deleuze and Guattari modify from Peirce's account, to best identify the clone's potential as cultured image.[4] Echo is a diagrammatic figure of feminist potential.

The first season centers on the question "who is Echo, really?," meaning "who was the person (Caroline) wiped to make way for Echo?" She attracts the attention of an FBI agent, Paul Ballard (Tahmoh Penikett), determined to rescue her from the Dollhouse. Their failed romance of missed connection is part of the series' critique of patriarchal salvation, relentlessly unavailable to the show's female protagonists who develop their own, alternative models of care or die trying, as with Mellie's (Miracle Laurie) suicide in "The Hollow Man" (2.12). When the record of Caroline's implant is damaged at the end of the first season, restoration makes way for Echo's story arc as a disjunctive synthesis of multiple personalities/ experiences. Echo becomes a new kind of clone, increasingly showing signs of retaining memories post-wipe through glitches, headaches, physical twitches, and inappropriate behavior, what Deleuze terms a Lazarean disturbance of sensory-motor habits.[5] Through Dolls, who rise repeatedly from the living death of new age crypts, endless yoga, Bonsai pruning, and bad art classes to reanimate other minds, *Dollhouse* treats the Lazarean body as a biotechnological clone. How do these glitchy bodies transmute horror into alternative modes of life? *Dollhouse*'s dark vision of the creeping horror of social control does not fully realize a resistant vision, but its forms of resistance (including to clichés of what reads as horrific or as salvation) make this minor series in Whedon's oeuvre a suggestive primer for living in the everyday apocalypse of control, rerouting horror's affective force into a body genre for the control society and a media ecological sublime.

Bad Visions

All modern biotechnological horror stories evoke Mary Shelley's *Frankenstein* (1818), written against the romantic backdrop of the sublime. The story begins and ends in the apocalyptic Arctic as the end of the world, an imaginatively unlivable space to Shelley's contemporaries, where only the monster can survive. The sublime speaks to what exceeds the boundaries of the self, frequently figured as Nature, overwhelming our senses and capacity for reason. *Dollhouse* modulates the sublime through evocations of *Frankenstein* in the everyday of Doll embodiment. By "A Spy in the House of Love" (1.9), the audience has repeatedly been exposed to images that viscerally display and then immediately undercut the physical challenge and pain of wiping by erasing identity and creating a synthesized life form, compliant and ready to work. These "treatments" in some ways fail to register in the viewer as horrific, in part because they fail to enter into the memory of Dolls, who contort in pain then instantly return to total comfort. It is thus shocking to finally see the horror of the procedure presented affectively in a manner that *works* to make us feel it. Until now, empathy with Dolls is undercut by their changeable personalities, making the direct apperception of their physical horror less mimetically impressionable. In contrast, the wiping of Mr Dominic (Reed Diamond), ironically a villain indifferent to the Dolls as living beings, is graphically presented as horror. This episode not only draws on horror clichés, it also uses Echo's obscure form of perception. I use cliché in a double sense, both as horror convention and in Deleuze's sense in *Cinema 1*, of *cliché* as a snapshot.[6] Much like the frozen profiles—snapshots of personality—reanimated in the Dolls, viewers reanimate these horror clichés to sometimes-unexpected ends, through the affectively contradictory ways that they play out.

"A Spy" unmasks Mr Dominic as an undercover NSA spy tasked with surveillance and supporting the Dollhouse's controlled dissemination of mind-wipe technology. When the LA Dollhouse director Adele De Witt (Olivia Williams) finds out, she decides to send him to the Attic. His mind wipe is like nothing we have seen before. Although Echo anxiously witnesses Sierra's tissue mapping in "Ghost," (1.1), the effects fade quickly for her and us. Mr Dominic's wipe is a Gothic drama, an unrelieved animalistic struggle, horrific both to internal and external witnesses. The episode opens with abstract images inside the treatment room, darkened and lit only by flashes of electric light that partially reveal bodies wrestling and some kind of violent operation taking place.[7] Echo and Sierra, strolling through the common area below, look up and mildly wonder at the bursts of light coming from above. The episode then flashes back twelve hours earlier.

The entire episode revolves around muted perception and unequal access. We constantly see Echo surveilling the anxious management of the spy's discovery, her signature head tilt modeling curiosity. The camera's positioning signals that she observes from a distance; we often know more than her yet but not what she knows, or how she feels. The episode foregrounds the warp in her perception, occluding it via non-diegetic effects. This does not suggest it is partial, but that Echo sees in a way we cannot. Much of the series mobilizes an affective gap between the Dollhouse's all-encompassing surveillance system, and knowledge that allows for resistant ideas to take hold. In a long sequence, Echo observes Mr. Dominic establishing a lockdown in the Dollhouse, while the surrounding noise is muffled and muted save a few sonic leaks of mysterious dialogue. A slow, tinkling, anempathetic soundtrack plays against the urgency of the situation.

The episode works largely as a suspense thriller whose big reveal is not the spy's identity, but Echo's distributed ability to act. Discovering the spy's identity does nothing to resolve the tension, siphoning it instead into the final act's tremendous horror. Dominic, calmly philosophical while riding back to the Dollhouse with Echo, suddenly fights back. We have never seen anything like this—a roving, spasmodic camera, flashes of light, and utter chaos as Dominic meets his fate. The scene explicitly evokes media adaptations of *Frankenstein*, particularly James Whale's *Frankenstein* (1931) and *Bride of Frankenstein* (1935), which typically render Shelley's reanimation scene by spectacularizing electricity's transduction of lightening through machinery to energy, transformation, power, and labor. Surrounded by doctors and technicians, rather than the Frankenstein monster's lone creator, the chaotic, violent scene of Dominic's wipe brings home the corporeal horror of being erased, that previous wipes only hinted at. Close-ups of faces seek an affective purchase on the action. The references to Whale's *Frankenstein* movies highlights Dollhouse's complicated refashioning of reanimation's ethics. In *Bride of Frankenstein*, for instance, the bride's animation cross-cuts close-ups of Henry Frankenstein and Dr Pretorius with the monster's murder of assistant Hans, so ethical responsibility moves transversally between both scenes of life and death.[8]

In *Dollhouse*, even when Dominic is finally incapacitated, the lights continue their Gothic flashing. When it is over, Topher brings out Dominic's brain on a drive like a dead rat. Topher and De Witt realize that Echo, "still evolving," has successfully taken out her enemy. [9] Why is Dominic's boxing rendered in such classic horror terms while other, equally dramatic and violent bodily modifications have their horrific force immediately modulated into oblivion: why do we witness the Dolls feeling fine?

The sublime staged the mind-boggling horrors of the individual's relation to an ecology that surpasses them. If Shelley's *Frankenstein* is the urtext of modern biotechnological horror, something new has displaced the horrific force of the sublime as Nature here today: information. In today's media ecology, where the nonstop mood-modulation onslaught of social media has radically shifted the question of self/other relations, the ecological sublime has become profoundly banal, framed in a relation of individual and nature. How does one access the horror of a social media ecology? How does *Dollhouse* mobilize tropes of double vision and the dispossession of affect on the viewer's part to restage the ethical problem of *Frankenstein* as the question: how to be together?[10] *Dollhouse's* horror is a failure of care networks (one of Shelley's feminist insights) here reinscribed in social media, weak ties, online dating and ghosting, and an ecological crisis so huge it produces only helpless responses. *Dollhouse* modifies Linda Williams' categorization of horror as a body genre that makes you scream to one that makes you sigh or shrug.[11] The viewer becomes dreadfully comfortable with modulation itself.

In "True Believer" (1.5), Echo goes undercover as a blind woman infiltrating a religious cult. Her imprint successfully makes Echo experience blindness; in a double theft of vision, the Rossum Corporation, working with the FBI, implants cameras in her retina to see through her. The worried conversation around this risky procedure ends in an image that encapuslates Carol Clover's (1990) "assaultive gaze of horror": a needle descends into her eye, held open and widening in terror.[12] We cut to commercial, and when we return, Echo seems none the worse for wear in her new personality, eyes vacantly open, occupied by an other. The sheer, visceral terror of the optical assault becomes hard to remember when she doesn't. In the blink of an eye, she is back to work, and we work to sustain a sense of disgust in the face of the plot's exigencies.

Dollhouse employs the modulations of its story and of TV to undercut horror. It is made for the society of control, where sustaining feeling against the plastic force of constant modulation is difficult. *Dollhouse's* potential is the horror of going with the flow, and the queasy ease of a status quo. Echo's miraculous adaptation to blindness and, her successful embodiment obscures the visceral image of her body's possession.

The series hesitates between rape and slavery as its dominant parallel, but its avoidance of fully actualizing the horror (except in Sierra's storyline, crucial because of her vulnerability as a racialized migrant outside normative labor and citizenship) does and should raise ethical hesitations. Does the show simply exploit the entertainment potential of rape and slavery because there is an appetite for it amongst spectators? Or does this tactic of quickly resolving what is explicitly horrific effectively stage what it is like to live as a vulnerable body in a world where vulnerability is a normalized condition of life for those who don't have the protective privilege of whiteness, masculinity, heteronormativity or wealth?

The show undercuts horror's spectacularization, making us question how we understand what we see. It holds a mirror up to a society endlessly producing the self, a society that "substitutes for the individual or numerical body the code of a 'dividual' material to be controlled."[13] The show doesn't seek to restore Echo's vision; it takes us deep into her refractive perceptions, mediated by more than forty imprints that attune to collective and non-clichéd forms of relation. It stages a new horror spectatorship for the society of control, working not via shock but through modulation's queasiness, and finally through the fragile compositional and diagrammatic force of Echo. *Dollhouse* deploys familiar genre tropes of horror repeatedly, but makes them banal because the Dolls can be reset; they fail to register. In *Dollhouse*, it takes time for things to sink in, because only through time can resistance be formed. Confronted with the imprint of Caroline ("Omega" (1.12)), Echo tells her Echo is "nobody, I'm just the porchlight, waiting for you."[14] Neither inside nor out, Echo is a lonely access point. Against the brilliant life-or-death flashes of Frankenstein's monster, Echo's sad metaphor becomes the sustaining support for something else. *Dollhouse* demonstrates the horror of the control society's demands for constant flexibility, integrated auto-surveillance, and the unliveability of constant availability.

The Society of Control

Gilles Deleuze's control society describes contemporary society's transition from what Michel Foucault called the disciplinary society, modeled on the prison, to one in which the object of social and political control is life itself.[15] The disciplinary society is figurally represented by the Panopticon, a model prison. Designed so that prisoners were always on display, and yet never knew when they were being watched, the Panopticon gained its disciplinary force not via direct bodily intervention, but by training bodies to incorporate surveillance. This structure of relation explains how surveillance is disseminated in society to reproduce citizens, displacing the need for actually existing panopticism. Instead, contemporary subjects, Foucault argues, act "as if" they were under surveillance at all times. The Panopticon induces "in the inmate a state of conscious and permanent visibility that assures *the automatic functioning of power.*"[16]

The Panopticon crucially dissociates the seeing/being-seen dyad, thus also dissociating direct and reciprocal relation between people. Foucault describes how disciplinary societies create "docile" bodies as useful (manipulable) and intelligible (analyzable), both dimensions exploited in the functioning of the Dollhouse. "A body is docile that may be subjected, used, transformed and improved."[17] The Dolls' mantra is of course, "I try to be my best." Discipline both "increases the forces of the body (in economic terms of utility) and diminishes those same forces (in political terms of obedience)".[18] Power is dissociated from the body, visually rendered in the Dollhouse as the electricity that powers the Dolls' transformation.

As featured in the opening credits, the Dolls sleep in illuminated crypts built into the floor. Arranged around an absent centre, the crypts iconically call to mind the Panopticon's design. Here, however, the surveillance's physical structure is mapped onto living in the space of death, the biopolitical space of the society of control. In the episode "Needs" (1.8), the main Dolls wake up with their original personalities intact, part of an experiment to resolve glitches of retained memory many Dolls seem to display.[19] In classic horror form, Echo in her crypt wakes up as Caroline, vividly experiencing the horror of being buried alive, but her panicked reaction is affectively distant to us as spectators—we know she is in no danger. Deleuze argues that while Foucault has been understood as the theorist of the disciplinary society, he in fact marks the shift from disciplinary societies towards a contemporary model, the "society of control," in which power is no longer centralized and mobilized within institutions, but where the breakdowns of these "confinements" allows power and discipline to flow through the body itself via "continuous control" and "instant communication."[20] Control is integrated into the body, much as the crypts/beds become the final space of safety at the end of the series, an imbrication of control, environment, and embodiment.

The society of control is marked by modulation or flexibility; rather than all individuals conforming to a single model, such as the ideal soldier, post-Fordist production demands constant retraining and the ability to shift at whim. Flexible adaptation is key; business and late capitalism become the hegemonic model. As Deleuze describes this: "control man undulates, moving among a continuous range of different orbits. Surfing has taken over from all the old sports."[21] Power becomes dispersive, networked, and connected, and the object of policing is life itself. The clone is the monster of the control society, the ultimate cultured image of how the individual is "dividual" or matter to be reworked. *Dollhouse* articulates the consequences of the reorientation of sovereign power away from the individual to "life itself," and to human society as a whole, from taking to making life and from killing to letting die. With characters constantly undergoing resurrection through wipes and implants, the biopolitical setting of *Dollhouse* is manifest. Echo's Lazarean body, its sensory motor disturbances repeatedly linked to a power to see, are also the site of her resistance to the constant modulation demanded by control society, where life as an active was the only "alternative" to life as a prisoner.

The Clone as Cultured Image

In the early 1990s there was a wave of interest in retracing the entwined roots of moving image technologies and medical imaging technologies, articulating Foucauldian genealogies, feminist film theory and critiques of science, a new availability and acceptance of reproductive and genetic biotechnologies and of visual tools such as ultrasounds, and critical work that sought to explore how these representations reproduced social norms. Cultured images are ambivalently positioned between science fiction and technological fact, giving them a fabulative quality. In "ethico-aesthetical" terms, to borrow Guattari's concept, this moves us away from interpreting "representations" to thinking images as creative sites of experimental activity.[22] Cultured images are onto-genetic, mutant reproductions, provoking us to think about our actions and habitual responses as immediately (re)creative of the world. An ethico-aesthetical approach might also be described as a pragmatics of sensibility, a sensible flesh. The power of these images is in the affective hesitation of response that allows us to feel our scope for action widening in the face of uncertain but intense response. To render flesh sensible might be the work of the biotechnological horror as body genre.

In his peculiar version of media effects theory in the *Cinemas* books, Deleuze describes figures that gain in their power to see what they lose in their ability to act. These "seers" "do not even have the consolation of the sublime ... they are rather given over to something intolerable which is simply their everydayness itself."[23] This visionary impotence occurs when actuality overwhelms our ability to respond through habitual cliché, and is often accompanied by physical pain and debility. One such example is the Lazarean body. For Deleuze, death marks the passage from a zero-degree of intensity to a new state of affective intensity. As such, death is the most common experience in the unconscious, because it takes place in every becoming.[24] Death is "the last form of the problematic, the source of problems and questions," the "exhaustion of a certain state of being that makes way for a new mode of becoming."[25] A Lazarean body is marked by this problematic of death. A character is "Lazarean precisely because he returns from death, from the land of the dead; he has passed through death and is born from death, *whose sensory-motor disturbances he retains*."[26] Deleuze means that the Lazarean body is not a smoothly functional new embodiment, or a reanimation of a body as it was before. Rather, it exhibits a breakdown of the sensory-motor schema, the habitual actions that allow us to function in the world, the marker of a differential embodiment. Note how often clones in popular culture exhibit such sensory motor disturbances: stuttering, breakdowns, and homicidal tendencies. The promise of the Dollhouse is that reanimated Actives, once they have served their term, will NOT be Lazarean figures. They will retain no memory of their servitude, and will be freed from the debilitating trauma that initially brought them there. Victor (Enver Gjokaj), for example, is a soldier with PTSD. The Dollhouse's twisted version of neo-liberal care simply has his carceral time replace the therapeutic rehabilitation owed to him by an indifferent state war machine. But what Echo makes clear from the start, via her relentless glitchiness, is that no one gets out alive. Instead, her very being bears ongoing witness to the horror of dispossession, and the flipside horror of clinging too tightly to individuality. A brief culture history of cloning since the 1990s indicates what makes *Dollhouse*'s take on cloning so disturbing and yet full of potential.

The clone's cultured image is a Lazarean body found across sci-fi and horror today, the zombie's companion species with an inverted relation to technologies of visibility. New media theorist Anna Munster calls the clone the "millennial figure of technological wonder," who conceals her artifice like a Baroque automaton.[27] While the clone re-emerged in the 1990s cultural imaginary with the "successful" cloning of animals, it also has special relevance for image culture. In 1996, when the famous clone, Dolly the sheep, was born, it unleashed a wave of speculation and fantasy. Dolly was not a perfect copy; these are already found in nature, in identical twins, and had been made artificially through embryo splitting. Dolly—named for Dolly Parton, in an adolescent snicker—is an example of somatic cell cloning, cloned from an adult sheep's mammary cell—a perfect copy of an already-independently-existing creature. Relation itself was thrown into doubt.

Science writer Gina Kolata claims that "events that alter our very notion of what it means to be human are few and scattered over the centuries. The birth of Dolly is one of them."[28] The technogenetic figure of this sheep, named after a media figure of notably technologically enhanced assets, speaks to the confounding nature of the clone as cultural figure. Cloning's opponents argue that the application of the industrial model to reproduction strikes at the heart of what makes us human: our individuality. *Dollhouse*'s production line has the side-effect of making even sympathetic figures treat the Actives as less-than-human, like animals or children.

Cloning provokes anxious interrogation of our own identity and our origins. The popular face of cloning suggests clones will be essentially mindless; the source for a "clone army," à la *Star Wars*, or spare body parts. "Haunted" (*Dollhouse* (1.10)) plays with this when Echo is implanted with the memories of a wealthy woman, recently murdered, who wakes up in Echo and casually adapts to her temporary form without much grief.[29] It is as if the clone's confoundingly novel and spectacular embodiment reinscribes a mind/body distinction, with the clone "all body" and even pure image, endlessly reduplicated. What makes *Dollhouse* such an unusual and sustained exploration of cloning is the show's insistence that minds and personalities are also reproducible, and its exploration of what the effects are when minds (are) matter.

Clones today are doubly embodied as matter and image, troubling this distinction. What kind of images are clones? As signs, clones seem suspended between index and icon. The clone is uncanny because it evokes a literal double: the mirror image; it is iconic, defined by resemblance and seriality. As Munster notes the clone "offers us the full promise of what digital code will offer—repetition."[30] Beyond iconicity lies the potential for a differential embodiment:

> if the clone is emblematic of a completely integrated body-technology symbiosis, then it can only stand as such by forgetting the genealogy of mutations, fluctuations and failures that constitutes its serial history.[31]

Clones "raise the specter of their others, the series of difference from which they were born."[32] This loads materiality back into serial reproduction, disrupting the icon's atemporality. *Dollhouse* exploited this through its actors' serial performances: Doll identities were often only vaguely sketched out in contrast with their imprints' "bigger than life" personalities. One reason the show was not successful could be viewers' difficulty emotionally investing in such inconstant characters, something the show exploits as the ethics of horror. We are not immune from the logic of erasure and invisibility (of the material, acting body) that the corporation uses to make itself successful.

Simultaneously, the clone is fascinating because it is an indexical image or a trace.[33] It literalizes the material connection between an originating moment and its pointing record. In clones this is popularly understood as DNA, or genetic code, making visible the trace of its making, and reminding us of our own origin in DNA, and the signs of our embodiment particularly via medical imaging technologies that reveal without resemblance. *Dollhouse* presciently applies DNA's coding to algorhythmic culture, where personalities are mapable and transferable between platforms, both mediatic and somatic. Airing two years after the first iPhone launched, *Dollhouse* predicted the intensification of social media and the dominance of algorhythmic culture as a mode of surveillance and control, but with the body as platform, rather than the phone. Clones confront us with the indexical image of what we barely recognize as ourselves (DNA, maps of brain functions, our Google search history, ads like uncanny mirrors in our social media feed).

It is as another kind of image—the diagram—that Echo is able to open a crack in modulation's closed circuit under a Control society that limits the clone to resemblance of reference, instead of creative fabulation. In this shift, the informational body of the clone provokes a differential embodiment, distorting both iconicity and indexicality. As Munster suggests, in the encounter of information technologies and embodiment: "we occupy and produce relations of differentiation and integration between the corporeal and the informatic, such that converging and diverging series of machine body events begin to map themselves out."[34] What then is the differential of the clone, beyond the model of a good copy? As Topher says of Alpha, a composite of different imprints: "He's not a person, he's like Soylent Green. He's people."[35]

The diagram, for Peirce, is a subtype of the icon, namely an icon of intelligible relation, but Deleuze distinguishes diagrams from icons, and raises the diagram to a differential force. Unlike the icon's resemblance, diagrams "never function in order to represent a persisting world but produce a new kind of reality, a new model of truth [...] unmaking preceding realities and significations, constituting hundreds of points of emergence or creativity, unexpected conjunctions or improbable continuums."[36] Diagrams provoke new articulations in an existing social field by abstracting an already co-present virtual potential. While much clone drama revolves around free will, the diagram draws on a different sense of freedom, not the recognition of self-consciousness, but remapping the present in terms of "free or unbounded points of creativity, change and resistance."[37] A tension emerges between self-identified caretaker characters in *Dollhouse* who feel that the Actives' "autonomous" choice to enter into a contractual agreement respects their subjectivity, and others who insist, like Echo in "Omega," that no one can "sign a contract to become a slave."[38] But rather than restoring individuality, Echo's creative evolution (initially "forced" by Alpha kidnapping her and uploading multiple imprints to make himself a monstrous mate—a trope from *Frankenstein*) exists between people, between her own imprints and experiences, between relations of care and concern, as the contagious force of her accumulative experience. Part of *Dollhouse*'s horror is that there seems to be no place in its world for such a diagrammatic view of personhood and its transformative relations of care. In the end, all Echo can do is retreat underground when the world restores people to individuality.

By virtue of her uniqueness, Echo becomes a transversal inducer of mutation, as we frequently see in Whedon's work, which, more than most television, explores the potential of what Guattari would call "collective assemblages of enunciation."[39] Echo's uniqueness, in first retaining traces of previous imprints, is only partially explained by her unique genetic make-up. A critical component of her ability to negotiate multiplicity is the body—particularly in physical training sessions, which are both appropriate and excessive to her status. One of the running jokes of the series is that the Los Angeles Dollhouse constantly features Dolls performing yoga, a dig at cultural conformity and California's hippy-dippy consumerism. Yet this dimmed potential of mind-body yoga is slyly rearticulated via a sensible flesh emergent amongst the Dolls. All that self-care slowly pays off into collective concerns! Although Echo makes it her mission to "rescue" the Dolls once she starts becoming self-aware, other Dolls are already sensitized, particularly Sierra and Victor who "remember" their love and physical attraction for one another. In myth, Echo loved Narcissus, and as the damaged witness to his exclusive specularity, was denied selfhood and wasted through desire into an incorporeal voice. In *Dollhouse*, Echo is initially such a figure, a receptacle for the narcissism of those who hire her to stage their own fantasies. But what makes *Dollhouse* intriguing is the abandonment of a typical sense of coming into consciousness. If, as Chow points out, "it's hard to distinguish the doll from the cunning and conscious actor," that is because Echo is insistently both, and seeks to live within this dispossession.[40] Echo remembers not simply her past as Caroline, but fragments of all her experiences defined increasingly as a set of actions. Very early on, Echo's individuation occurs in her glitchiness. That is, it is via an ongoing sensible flesh that she becomes a person, not by asserting or reclaiming her prior subjectivity, or by rejecting the condition of multiplicity in which she finds herself. The diagram is an image of topological transformation, unraveling signification in the name of a real yet to come. To read Echo as a diagram is to turn icon into a mode of differential embodiment—to move into potential from a frozen cliché. We begin the show expecting an answer to the question "who is Echo?" in terms of who she was (the past), but its Lazarean disturbances offer a different problematic. When Lazarus awakens, it is into a set of deranged temporal relations—what is the future for a reanimated corpse?—echoed through the wiping technologies' profound rewiring of normative temporal relations. But while this can be read in terms of dispossession's loss—losing one's memories, the suspended and unregistered eternal present of inactive Dolls, and the leapfrogging of a future paid for in lost time—through such temporal derangements a certain freedom takes hold. Against restoration's logic, the series explores the body's capacity for what I call "anotherness," or the intimate experience of a body in time.[41] Echo's failure to smoothly integrate her experiences is paradoxically a strength that holds open an (albeit) uncertain future.

Beyond trace, beyond resemblance, Echo is a diagram in Peirce's sense of a map of intelligible relations; she is all the personalities uploaded into her simultaneously.[42] But more importantly, she is a diagram as a differential embodiment of information, a transversal inducer of potential. At the end of *Dollhouse*, the radical sensory motor disturbances of these Lazarean bodies are literally re-buried. As the rest of humanity heads into the light to launch a global wipe that will restore people to who they were before becoming Dolls, Echo, Sierra, and Victor stay behind. Victor and Sierra do so because reverting to their old selves would mean losing each other and their son, and Echo does so because her work is not yet done. But also it is implied that the world is not yet renewed, simply reset, and the Dolls' radical potential holds open an ambivalent uncertainty. Whedon's mind clones reorient questions around the biotechnological image of the clone. Deleuze describes a contemporary society built on the image of an acentered brain, one in a topological relation to the world, or what he calls the "noosphere." Here, memory is stored not in discrete, spatialized locations, like a hard drive, but in the gap or leap between synapses, small suspensions of time full of potential. Deleuze cites Antonin Artaud as inspiration for this image. Artaud wrote that the brain, with its antenna turned towards the invisible, has a capacity to resume a resurrection from death.[43] In *Dollhouse*, Echo's sensible flesh, which includes the accentered brain, is such an embodiment. *Dollhouse* takes a different approach to horror, rerouting clichés to different ends. A diagrammatic spectatorship asks us to think transversally, across the limits of characters and embodiment; it holds onto the possibility that Echo's reanimations can lay claim to futurity.

Notes

1. Lesley Chow. "A Thousand Blooms inside Joss Whedon's Dollhouse." *Bright Lights Film Journal* 68 (2010).

2. For works that explore the biotechnological in relation to *Dollhouse*, see, for example, Bronwen Calvert's *Being Bionic: The World of TV Cyborgs*. London, I.B.Tauris, 2017, and Holly Randell-Moon's "'I'm Nobody': The somatechnical construction of bodies and identity in Joss Whedon's *Dollhouse*," Feminist Media Studies (2011) 12:2, 265–280.

3. For a relevant discussion of *Dollhouse* via Deleuze's notion of the assemblage, see Michael Starr's "I've watched you build yourself from scratch: the assemblage of Echo." In Sherry Ginn, Alyson R. Buckman, and Heather M. Porter, eds, *Joss Whedon's Dollhouse: Confounding Purpose, Confusing Identity*. Lanham, MD: Rowman & Littlefield Publishers, 2014.

4. Peirce's notions of index and icon are discussed via Deleuze's use of these terms in *Cinema 1* (1986) and *Cinema 2* (1989). The concept of the diagram is largely drawn from Deleuze's book *Foucault* (Gilles Deleuze and Seaán Hand, *Foucault*. Minnesota: University of Minnesota Press, 1994b) and from Deleuze and Guattari's *A Thousand Plateaus*, in particular the chapter "On Several Regimes of Signs" (Gilles Deleuze and Félix Guattari, *Anti-Oedipus: capitalism and schizophrenia*. Minneapolis: University of Minnesota Press, 1983).

5. Gilles Deleuze, Robert Galeta and Hugh Tomlinson. *Cinema 2: The Time-Image*. Minneapolis: University of Minnesota Press, 1989, 207.

6. Gilles Deleuze, Hugh Tomlinson, and Barbara Habberjam. *Cinema 1: the movement-image*. Minneapolis: University of Minnesota Press, 1986, 208.

7. Editor Kristopher K. Woofter points out that this scene is especially evocative of the James Whale versions of *Frankenstein* (1931) and *Bride of Frankenstein* (1935), two works that established a visual iconography for "Frankenstein" as a cultural entity that has frequently eclipsed the novel in the popular imaginary.

8. Thanks to Kristopher Woofter for pointing out these parallels.

9. "A Spy in the House of Love" (1.9).

10. For a discussion of double vision as an affective modality of cinema, see Alanna Thain, *Bodies in Suspense: Time and Affect in Cinema* (Minnesota: University of Minneapolis Press, 2017), for example pp. 4–15.

11. Linda Williams, "Film Bodies: Gender, Genre, and Excess," *Film Quarterly* 44, no. 4 (1991): 2–13, 4.

12. Clover, Carol. *Men, Women, and Chainsaws*. Princeton, NJ: Princeton University Press, 1992, 204.

13. Gilles Deleuze, "Postscript on the Society of Control," Negotiations, 1972–1990, Columbia University Press, 1995a, 177–82, 182.

14. "Omega" (1.12), *Dollhouse*, written and directed by Tim Minear (2009; Burbank, CA: 20th Century Fox Home Entertainment, 2009), DVD.

15. See Deleuze 1995a and Gilles Deleuze, "Control and Becoming," in Gilles Deleuze *Negotiations* (169–76). New York: Columbia University Press, 1995b, and Michel Foucault, *Discipline and punish: the birth of the prison*. New York: Vintage Books, 1995.

16. Foucault, 1995, 201.

17. Ibid., 136.

18. Ibid., 138.
19. "Needs" (1.8), *Dollhouse*, directed by Felix Alcalá and written by Tracy Bellomo (2009; Burbank, CA: 20th Century Fox Home Entertainment, 2009), DVD.
20. Deleuze, 1995b, 174.
21. Ibid., 180.
22. See Félix Guattari, Paul Bains, and Julian Pefanis, *Chaosmosis: an ethico-aesthetic paradigm*. Sydney: Power Publications, 2006.
23. Deleuze, 1989, 41.
24. Deleuze and Guattari, 1983, 330.
25. Gilles Deleuze, *Difference and Repetition*. New York: Columbia University Press, 1994a, 112.
26. Deleuze, 1989, 207–208.
27. Anna Munster, *Materializing new media: embodiment in information aesthetics*. Hanover, NH: Dartmouth College Press, 2006, 27.
28. Gina Bari Kolata, *Clone: the road to Dolly, and the path ahead*, New York: William Morrow & Co., 1999, 5.
29. "Haunted," *Dollhouse*, directed by Elodie Keene and written by Jane Espenson, Maurissa Tancharoen and Jed Whedon, 2009, Burbank, CA: 20th Century Fox Home Entertainment, DVD.
30. Munster, 2006, 26.
31. Ibid., 28.
32. Ibid.
33. In photography, a photograph is indexical as the trace of the light hitting the emulsion at a specific point in time.
34. Munster, 2006, 31.
35. Chow, 2010.
36. Deleuze, 1994, 35.
37. Ibid., 44.
38. "Omega" (1.12).
39. Gilles Deleuze and Félix Guattari, *Kafka: Towards a Minor Literature*. Minneapolis: University of Minnesota Press, 1986, 81.
40. Chow, 2010.
41. Thain, 2017, 25–39.
42. Charles S. Peirce and Carolyn Eisele, *The New Elements of Mathematics: Vol.: 4.: Mathematical Philosophy*. The Hague: Mouton Publishers, Humanities Press, 1976, 315.
43. Deleuze, 1989, 218.

APPENDIX I

The Work of Joss Whedon and the Horror Tradition: A Selected Bibliography

Compiled by Alysa Hornick

This bibliography is comprised of work published or presented in English that focuses on the work of Joss Whedon and his collaborators within the traditions related to horror. At the point of writing, many studies locating Whedon's work within horror refer back to literary traditions; thus existing scholarship tends to be weighted slightly toward the Gothic tradition, followed by a focus on "body horror."[1] Because the critical discourses in horror trade on topics related to alienation and "othering" based upon race, gender, and sexuality, the list also includes work on these issues. Other horror-related topics of interest covered in the list include (but are not limited to) generic hybridity, postmodernism, folkloric and mythological traditions, monstrosity (particularly vampires and witch-craft), science fiction, eroticism, abjection, cult television and films, comics, feminism, apocalypticism, reality television and teen television, and uncanny spaces, places, and architecture.

On a final note—and in the interest of comprehensiveness and encouraging developing scholars—we are proud that this selected bibliography includes PhD dissertations, master's theses, bachelor's theses, and undergraduate work published in the Whedon Studies Association's

Appendix I

journal of undergraduate studies, *Watcher Junior*.[2] It is our hope that this selected bibliography on the work of Joss Whedon and collaborators within the horror tradition will be a helpful resource and a source of inspiration for future scholarship in the field.

—Alysa Hornick and Kristopher Karl Woofter

Abbott, Stacey. "'Creeped Out and Comforted at the Same Time?': The Generic Hybridity of *Angel*." In *Angel*, 27–43. Detroit: Wayne State University Press, 2009.

———. "'Does Giant Tentacle Spew Come out with Dry Cleaning?': *Angel* and TV Horror." In *Angel*, 44–62. Detroit: Wayne State University Press, 2009.

Alderman, Naomi and Annette Seidel-Arpaci. "Imaginary Para-Sites of the Soul: Vampires and Representations of 'Blackness' and 'Jewishness' in the Buffy/Angelverse." *Slayage: The Online International Journal of Buffy Studies* 3, no. 2 [10] (2003).

Amy-Chinn, Dee. "Good Vampires Don't Suck: Sex, Celibacy and the Body of Angel." In *Vampires: Myths and Metaphors of Enduring Evil, Conference Proceedings, Budapest, Hungary, May 22–24 2003*, edited by Carla T. Kungl, 115–20. Oxford: Inter-Disciplinary Press, 2003.

Anderson, Devon. "Echoes of *Frankenstein*: Shelley's Masterpiece in Joss Whedon's *Dollhouse* and Our Relationship with Technology." *Slayage: The Journal of Whedon Studies* 14, no. 1 [43] (2016).

Barbaccia, Holly G. "Buffy in the 'Terrible House.'" *Slayage: The Online International Journal of Buffy Studies* 1, no. 4 [4] (2001).

Battis, Jes. "Demonic Maternities, Complex Motherhoods: Cordelia, Fred and the Puzzle of Illyria." In *Blood Relations: Chosen Families in* Buffy the Vampire Slayer *and* Angel, 112–33. Jefferson, NC: McFarland, 2005.

Blouin, Michael J. "American Horror, Global Commons, and *The Cabin in the Woods*." In *Magical Thinking, Fantastic Film, and the Illusions of Neoliberalism*, 139–68. New York: Palgrave Macmillan, 2016.

Bridges, Elizabeth. "Grimm Realities: *Buffy* and the Uses of Folklore." In *Buffy Meets the Academy: Essays on the Episodes and Scripts as Texts*, edited by Kevin K. Durand, 91–103. Jefferson, NC: McFarland, 2009.

Bryce, Devon Elizabeth. "Surviving the Change: the Domestication of the Vampire in Literature, Film, and Television." Master's thesis, University of Alberta, 2009.

Burr, Megan. "Manifesting Monsters: Metaphor and Genre in *Buffy the Vampire Slayer*," in "Our Corner of the Whedonverse [The Whedon Issue]," special issue, *Watercooler Journal* 2, no. 3 (2014). http://watercoolerjournal.com/issue-index/.

Burr, Vivien. "'Oh Spike, you're covered in sexy wounds!': The Erotic Significance of Wounding and Torture in *Buffy the Vampire Slayer*." In *Sex, Violence, and the Body: The Erotics of Wounding*, edited by Vivien Burr and Jeff Hearn, 137–56. New York: Palgrave Macmillan, 2009.

Callander, Michelle. "Bram Stoker's Buffy: Traditional Gothic and Contemporary Culture." *Slayage: The Online International Journal of Buffy Studies* 1, no. 3 [3] (2001).

Calvert, Bronwen. "Inside Out: Motherhood as Demonic Possession in *Angel*." *Slayage: The Journal of the Whedon Studies Association* 12, no. 2/13, no. 1 [40–41] (2014–2015).

———. "'Who Did They Make Me This Time?': Viewing Pleasure and Horror." In *Joss Whedon's Dollhouse: Confounding Purpose, Confusing Identity*, edited by Sherry Ginn, Alyson R. Buckman, and Heather M. Porter, 113–26. Lanham, MD: Rowman & Littlefield, 2014.

Canavan, Gerry. "'Something Nightmares Are From': Metacommentary in Joss Whedon's *The Cabin in the Woods*," in "'We Are Not Who We Are': Critical Reflections on *The Cabin in the Woods* (2012)," edited by Kristopher Karl Woofter and Jasie Stokes, special issue, *Slayage: The Journal of the Whedon Studies Association* 10, no. 2/11, no. 1 [36–37] (2013–2014).

Cardow, Andrew. "Everyman with Fangs: The Acceptance of the Modern Vampire." Department of Management and International Business Working Paper Series, no. 6 (2007). Auckland, NZ: Massey University, 2007. http://hdl.handle.net/10179/651.

Chandler, Holly. "Slaying the Patriarchy: Transfusions of the Vampire Metaphor in *BtVS*." *Slayage: The Online International Journal of Buffy Studies* 3, no. 1 [9] (2003).

Cole, Phillip. "Rousseau and the Vampires: Toward a Political Philosophy of the Undead." In *Zombies, Vampires, and Philosophy: New Life for the Undead*, edited by Richard Greene and K. Silem Mohammad, 183–96. Chicago: Open Court, 2010.

Cooper, L. Andrew. "Judith Halberstam's *Skin Shows* and Joss Whedon's *Buffy the Vampire Slayer*." In *Gothic Realities: The Impact of Horror Fiction on Modern Culture*, 86–93. Jefferson, NC: McFarland, 2010.

Corsie, Sarah. "'You Know, You Ain't Quite Right': Humanity and the Monstrous 'Other' in Joss Whedon's *Firefly*." *Watcher Junior: The Undergraduate Journal of Whedon Studies* 8, no. 2 [12] (2015).

Coulombe, Renée T. "'I Had It All Wrong': New Vampires, Grrrl Heroes and the Third Wave Body in *Buffy the Vampire Slayer*." In *Nostalgia or Perversion?: Gothic Rewriting from the Eighteenth Century until the Present Day*, edited by Isabella van Elferen, 206–22. Newcastle upon Tyne: Cambridge Scholars Publishing, 2007.

Cover, Rob. "(Re)Cognising the Body: Performativity, Embodiment and Abject Selves in *Buffy the Vampire Slayer*." *Aesthethika: International Journal on Culture, Subjectivity and Aesthetics* 2, no. 1 (2005): 68–83.

Davis, Robert A. "*Buffy the Vampire Slayer* and the Pedagogy of Fear." *Slayage: The Online International Journal of Buffy Studies* 1, no. 3 [3] (2001).

Day, Deanna. "Toward a Zombie Epistemology: What it Means to Live and Die in *Cabin in the Woods*," in "Feminist Science Fiction," edited by Alexis Lothian, special issue, *Ada: A Journal of Gender, New Media, & Technology* 3 (2013). http://adanewmedia.org/2013/11/issue3-day/.

Diehl, Laura. "Why Drusilla's More Interesting Than Buffy." *Slayage: The Online International Journal of Buffy Studies* 4, no. 1/2 [13–14] (2004).

Duda, Heather L. *The Monster Hunter in Modern Popular Culture*. Jefferson, NC: McFarland, 2008.

Appendix I

Edelson, Cheryl D. "Siting Horror: Place and Space in American Gothic Fiction." PhD diss, University of California – Riverside, 2007.

Edwards, Lynne Y. "'The black chick always gets it first': Black Slayers in Sunnydale." In *Joss Whedon and Race: Critical Essays*, edited by Mary Ellen Iatropoulos and Lowery A. Woodall III, 37–50. Jefferson, NC: McFarland, 2017.

Edwards, Lynne Y., Elizabeth L. Rambo, and James B. South, eds. *Buffy Goes Dark: Essays on the Final Two Seasons of* Buffy the Vampire Slayer *on Television*. Jefferson, NC: McFarland, 2009.

Elliott, Tara. "The Use of Count Famous in 'Buffy vs. Dracula.'" *Journal of Dracula Studies* 8 (2006): 14–19.

Evusa, Juliet. "Witchy Women: Witchcraft in *Buffy* and in Contemporary African Culture." In *The Truth of* Buffy: *Essays on Fiction Illuminating Reality*, edited by Emily Dial-Driver, Sally Emmons-Featherston, Jim Ford, and Carolyn Anne Taylor, 173–84. Jefferson, NC: McFarland, 2008.

Fletcher, Lawson. "'Is She Cold?': Telaesthetic Horror and Embodied Textuality in 'The Body.'" *Slayage: The Journal of the Whedon Studies Association* 9, no. 1 [33] (2011).

Free, Anna. "Re-Vamping the Gothic in *Buffy the Vampire Slayer*." *Screen Education* 46 (2007): 138–44.

Freedman, Eric. "Television, Horror and Everyday Life in *Buffy the Vampire Slayer*." In *The Contemporary Television Series*, edited by Michael Hammond and Lucy Mazdon, 159–80. Edinburgh: Edinburgh University Press, 2005.

Gölz, Peter. "Fear and Laughing in Sunnydale: Buffy vs Dracula." *Journal of Dracula Studies* 11 (2009).

Gray, Emily. "Writing 'lesbian, gay-type lovers': *Buffy*, Postmodern Gothic and Interruptions to the Lesbian Cliché." In *New Directions in 21st-Century Gothic: The Gothic Compass*, edited by Lorna Piatti-Farnell and Donna L. Brien, 132–45. New York: Routledge, 2015.

Hadyk-Delodder, Gareth and Laura Chilcoat. "'See What's Inside': Understanding the Reavers' Posthuman Identity and Role in *Firefly* and *Serenity*." In *Firefly Revisited: Essays on Joss Whedon's Classic Series*, edited by Michael Goodrum and Philip Smith, 37–52. Lanham, MD: Rowman & Littlefield, 2015.

Hallab, Mary Y. "Alternative Lives: *Buffy* and *Angel*." In *Vampire God: The Allure of the Undead in Western Culture*, 122–8. Albany, NY: SUNY Press, 2009.

Hammond, Mary. "Monsters and Metaphors: *Buffy the Vampire Slayer* and the Old World." In *Cult Television*, edited by Sara Gwenllian-Jones and Roberta E. Pearson, 147–66. Minneapolis: University of Minnesota Press, 2004.

Harbin, Leigh. "'You Know You Wanna Dance': *Buffy the Vampire Slayer* as Contemporary Gothic Heroine." *Studies in the Humanities* 32, no. 1 (2005): 22–37.

Harper, Steven. "Dark Fears: Madness in Gothic and Supernatural Drama." In *Madness, Power and the Media Class, Gender and Race in Popular Representations of Mental Distress*, 115–16. New York: Palgrave Macmillan, 2009.

Hastie, Amelie. "The Epistemological Stakes of *Buffy the Vampire Slayer*: Television Criticism and Marketing Demands." In *Undead TV: Essays on* Buffy the

Vampire Slayer, edited by Elana Levine and Lisa Parks, 74–95. Durham, NC: Duke University Press, 2007.

Hemstrom, Cassie. "What's at Stake? The Use of Simulacra to (Re)Construct Identity in *Buffy the Vampire Slayer*." In *Buffy Conquers the Academy: Conference Papers from the 2009/2010 Popular Culture/American Culture Associations*, edited by U. Melissa Anyiwo and Karoline Szatek-Tudor, 48–59. Newcastle upon Tyne: Cambridge Scholars Publishing, 2013.

Herman, Caroline. "*Buffy the Vampire Slayer* and Dichotomy of Self: A Study in the Shadow Selves of Buffy and Spike." *Watcher Junior: The Journal of Undergraduate Research in Buffy Studies* 1, no. 1 [1] (2005).

Hills, Matt and Rebecca Williams. "*Angel*'s Monstrous Mothers and Vampires with Souls: Investigating the Abject in 'Television Horror.'" In *Reading* Angel: *the TV Spin-off With a Soul*, edited by Stacey Abbott, 203–17. New York: I.B.Tauris, 2005.

Hollis, Erin. "Revisiting the Gothic: *Buffy the Vampire Slayer* and *Angel* as Contemporary Gothic." In *Critical Insights: Good & Evil*, edited by Margaret Sönser Breen, 238–52. Ipswich, MA: Salem Press, 2012.

Horrocks, Adrian. "The First Horror Soap: The Innovative Genre Mix of *Buffy the Vampire Slayer*." *Necronomicon: The Journal of Erotic and Horror Cinema* 5 (2007): 7–20.

Jackson, Kimberly. "Meta-horror and Simulation in the *Scream* Series and *The Cabin in the Woods*." In *Technology, Monstrosity, and Reproduction in Twenty-First Century Horror*, 11–30. New York: Palgrave Macmillan, 2013.

Jarvis, Christine. "School is Hell: Gendered Fears in Teenage Horror." *Educational Studies* 27, no. 3 (2001): 257–67.

Jobbling, J'annine. "The Good and the Monstrous: *Buffy the Vampire Slayer*: 'From Beneath You, It Devours.'" In *Fantastic Spiritualities: Monsters, Heroes, and the Contemporary Religious Imagination*, 168–88. London: Clark, 2007.

Joplin, Benjamin. "New Breed, Old Blood: Gothic Horror in Contemporary Fiction and Film." PhD diss, State University of New York – Buffalo, 2006.

Jowett, Lorna. "*Buffy*, Dark Romance and Female Horror Fans." In *Fan Phenomena*: Buffy the Vampire Slayer, edited by Jennifer Kate Stuller, 90–101. Chicago: Intellect, 2013.

——. "Masculinity, Monstrosity, and Behaviour Modification in *Buffy the Vampire Slayer*." *Foundation: The International Review of Science Fiction* 31, no. 84 (2002): 59–73.

Jowett, Lorna and Stacey Abbott. *TV Horror: Investigating the Dark Side of the Small Screen*. New York: I.B.Tauris, 2013.

Kane, Tim. "The Sympathetic Cycle (1987–): *Buffy the Vampire Slayer*." In *The Changing Vampire of Film and Television: A Critical Study of the Growth of a Genre*, 112–16. Jefferson, NC: McFarland, 2006.

Karras, Irene. "The Third Wave's Final Girl: *Buffy the Vampire Slayer*." *thirdspace: a journal of feminist theory & culture* 1, no. 2 (2002). http://journals.sfu.ca/ thirdspace/index.php/journal/article/view/karras.

Kellner, Douglas. "Teens and Vampires: From *Buffy the Vampire Slayer* to *Twilight*'s Vampire Lovers." In *Kinderculture: The Corporate Construction of Childhood*, edited by Shirley R. Steinberg, 55–72. 3rd ed. Boulder, CO: Westview Press, 2011.

Appendix I

Key, Kristina Pope. "'There will be Others. . . . Like me': The Legacy of Otherness in *Tales of the Slayers*." In *The Comics of Joss Whedon: Critical Essays*, edited by Valerie Estelle Frankel, 82–92. Jefferson, NC: McFarland, 2015.

Kind, Amy. "The Vampire with a Soul: Angel and the Quest for Identity." In *The Philosophy of Horror*, edited by Thomas Fahy, 86–101. Lexington, KY: University Press of Kentucky, 2010.

Knowles, Claire. "Sensibility Gone Mad: or, Drusilla, Buffy and the (D)evolution of the Heroine of Sensibility." In *Postfeminist Gothic: Critical Interventions in Contemporary Culture*, edited by Benjamin A. Brabon and Stephanie Genz, 140–53. New York: Palgrave Macmillan, 2007.

Krimmer, Elizabeth and Shilpa Raval. "'Digging the Undead': Death and Desire in *Buffy*." In *Fighting the Forces: What's at Stake in* Buffy the Vampire Slayer, edited by Rhonda V. Wilcox and David Lavery, 153–64. Lanham, MD: Rowman & Littlefield, 2002.

Kungl, Carla T. "Fears and Femininity at the Fin-de-siecle: of Vampires and Vampire Slayers." In *Vampires: Myths and Metaphors of Enduring Evil, Conference Proceedings, Budapest, Hungary, May 22–24 2003*, edited by Carla T. Kungl, 109–14. Oxford: Inter-Disciplinary Press, 2003.

Laskari, Isabelle. "'My emotions give me power': Radcliffean Sensibility and Female Gothic Anxieties in *Buffy the Vampire Slayer*." *Watcher Junior: The Undergraduate Journal of Whedon Studies* 7, no. 1 [9] (2014).

Lipsett, Joseph. "'One for the Horror Fans' vs. 'An Insult to the Horror Genre': Negotiating Reading Strategies in IMDb Reviews of *The Cabin in the Woods*," in "'We Are Not Who We Are': Critical Reflections on *The Cabin in the Woods* (2012)," edited by Kristopher Karl Woofter and Jasie Stokes, special issue, *Slayage: The Journal of the Whedon Studies Association* 10, no. 2/11, no. 1 [36–37] (2013–2014).

Little, Tracy. "High School is Hell: Metaphor Made Literal." In *Buffy and Philosophy: Fear and Trembling in Sunnydale*, edited by James B. South, 282–93. Chicago: Open Court, 2003.

Lockett, Christopher. "'We are not who we are': Lovecraftian Conspiracy and Magical Humanism in *The Cabin in the Woods*." *Horror Studies* 6, no. 1 (2015): 121–39.

Luria, Rachel. "Nothing Left but Skin and Cartilage: The Body and Toxic Masculinity." In *Sexual Rhetoric in the Works of Joss Whedon: New Essays*, edited by Erin B. Waggoner, 185–93. Jefferson, NC: McFarland, 2010.

McClelland, Bruce. "By Whose Authority?: The Magical Tradition, Violence, and the Legitimation of the Vampire Slayer." *Slayage: The Online International Journal of Buffy Studies* 1, no. 1 [1] (2001).

McCracken, Allison. "At Stake: Angel's Body, Fantasy Masculinity, and Queer Desire in Teen Television." In *Undead TV: Essays on* Buffy the Vampire Slayer, edited by Elana Levine and Lisa Parks, 116–44. Durham, NC: Duke University Press, 2007.

Magistrale, Tony. "Vampiric Terrors: *Dracula, The Hunger, Interview with the Vampire, Bram Stoker's Dracula, Buffy the Vampire Slayer*." In *Abject Terrors: Surveying the Modern and Postmodern Horror Film*, 37–56. New York: Peter Lang, 2005.

Martens, John W. "The Apocalyptic Vision in Film and Television: Traditional Apocalyptic Films." In *The End of the World: The Apocalyptic Imagination in Film & Television*, 130–7. Winnipeg: Shillingford, 2003.

Metz, Jr., Jerry D. "What's Your Fetish?: The Tortured Economics of Horror Simulacra in *The Cabin in the Woods*," in "'We Are Not Who We Are': Critical Reflections on *The Cabin in the Woods* (2012)," edited by Kristopher Karl Woofter and Jasie Stokes, special issue, *Slayage: The Journal of the Whedon Studies Association* 10, no. 2/11, no. 1 [36–37] (2013–2014).

Meyer, Jenna. "'You're a Vampire. Was That an Offensive Term? Should I Say "Undead American"?': The Evolution of the Vampire in Popular Culture." Master's thesis, State University of New York – Buffalo, 2010.

Molloy, Patricia. "Demon Diasporas: Confronting the Other and the Other Worldly in *Buffy the Vampire Slayer* and *Angel*." In *To Seek Out New Worlds: Science Fiction and World Politics*, edited by Jutta Weldes, 99–122. New York: Palgrave Macmillan, 2003.

Morehouse, Lyda. "Romancing the Vampire and Other Shiny Bits." In *Whedonistas!: A Celebration of the Worlds of Joss Whedon by the Women Who Love Them*, edited by Lynne M. Thomas and Deborah Stanish, 100–106. Des Moines, IA: Mad Norwegian Press, 2011.

Mukherjea, Ananya. "'When you kiss me, I want to die': Gothic Relationships and Identity *Buffy the Vampire Slayer*." *Slayage: The Online International Journal of Buffy Studies* 7, no. 2 [26] (2008).

Murphy, Bernice M. "'Ah, But Underneath.': *Buffy the Vampire Slayer* and *Desperate Housewives*." In *The Suburban Gothic in American Popular Culture*, 166–92. New York: Palgrave MacMillan, 2009.

Nelson, Andrew Patrick. "*Trick 'r Treat*, *The Cabin in the Woods* and the Defense of Horror's Subcultural Capital: A Genre in Crisis?" in "'We Are Not Who We Are': Critical Reflections on *The Cabin in the Woods* (2012)," edited by Kristopher Karl Woofter and Jasie Stokes, special issue, *Slayage: The Journal of the Whedon Studies Association* 10, no. 2/11, no. 1 [36–37] (2013–2014).

Nuttall, Alice. "'I Am the Monster Parents Tell Their Children About at Night': The Marvel Films' Loki as Gothic Antagonist." *Gothic Studies* 18, no. 2 (2016): 62–73.

Nuzum, Eric. "I May Be Dead, but I'm Still Pretty." In *The Dead Travel Fast: Stalking Vampires from Nosferatu to Count Chocula*, 186–216. New York: Thomas Dunne Books, 2007.

Oliver, Ashley. "Queer Sex Gods or Patriarchs with Fangs?: Gender and Sexuality in Modern Vampire Narratives *Buffy the Vampire Slayer*, *True Blood*, and *Twilight*." Bachelor's thesis, Colby College, 2012. http://digitalcommons.colby.edu/honorstheses/636/.

Ono, Kent A. "To Be a Vampire on *Buffy the Vampire Slayer*: Race and ('Other') Socially Marginalizing Positions on Horror TV." In *Fantasy Girls: Gender in the New Universe of Science Fiction and Fantasy Television*, edited by Elyce Rae Helford, 163–86. Lanham, MD: Rowman & Littlefield, 2000.

Overstreet, Deborah Wilson. "Welcome to the Buffyverse: Vampires, High School, and the Hellmouth." In *Not Your Mother's Vampire: Vampires in Young Adult Fiction*, 109–26. Lanham, MD: Scarecrow Press, 2006.

Appendix I

Pender, Patricia J. "'From Beneath You It Devours': Andrew and the Homoerotics of Evil." In *I'm Buffy and You're History: Buffy the Vampire Slayer and Contemporary Feminism*, 119–32. London: I.B.Tauris, 2016.

Potvin, Jacqueline M. "Pernicious Pregnancy and Redemptive Motherhood: Narratives of Reproductive Choice in Joss Whedon's *Angel*." *Slayage: The Journal of Whedon Studies* 14, no. 1 [43] (2016).

Raha, Maria. "Angels, Aliens, and Ass-Kicking." In *Hellions: Pop Culture's Women Rebels*, 214–16. Berkeley, CA: Seal Press, 2008.

Rambo, Elizabeth L. "'Queen C' in Boys' Town: Killing the Angel in Angel's House." *Slayage: The Online International Journal of Buffy Studies* 6, no. 3 [23] (2007).

Rein, Katharina. "Archives of Horror: Carriers of Memory in *Buffy the Vampire Slayer*." In *Undead Memory: Vampires and Human Memory in Popular Culture*, edited by Simon Bacon and Katarzyna Bronk, 131–56. Bern, Switzerland: Peter Lang, 2013.

Renner, Karen J. "Generational Conflict, Twenty-first Century Horror Films and *The Cabin in the Woods*." In *The Millennials on Film and Television: Essays on the Politics of Popular Culture*, edited by Betty Kaklamanidou and Margaret Tally, 110–25. Jefferson, NC: McFarland, 2014.

Rose, Anita. "Of Creatures and Creators: *Buffy* Does *Frankenstein*." In *Fighting the Forces: What's at Stake in* Buffy the Vampire Slayer, edited by Rhonda V. Wilcox and David Lavery, 133–42. Lanham, MD: Rowman & Littlefield, 2002.

Rose, Susanne. "Nothing Normal about the Monsters: Postmodern Monstrosity in *Buffy the Vampire Slayer*'s 'Normal Again.'" *Watcher Junior: The Undergraduate Journal of Whedon Studies* 7, no. 1 [9] (2014).

Rutkowski, Alice. "Why Chicks Dig Vampires: Sex, Blood, and Buffy." *Iris: A Journal about Women* 45 (2002): 12–20.

Santos, Jennifer Marie. "Anxieties of Audience: A Study of Gendered Gothic Reception." PhD diss, Arizona State University, 2008.

Saulnier, Katie. "From Virtuous Virgins to Vampire Slayers: The Evolution of the Gothic Heroine from the Early Gothic to Modern Horror." *Watcher Junior: The Journal of Undergraduate Research in Buffy Studies* 4, no. 1 [4] (2009).

Sayer, Karen. "'This Was Our World and They Made It Theirs': Reading Space and Place in *Buffy the Vampire Slayer* and *Angel*." In *Reading the Vampire Slayer: An Unofficial Critical Companion to* Buffy *and* Angel, edited by Roz Kaveney, 132–55. 2nd ed. New York: I.B.Tauris, 2004.

Segura, Allison. "Perfect Creatures: A Social and Cultural Interpretation of Vampires in Fiction and Film." PhD diss, University of Louisiana – Lafayette, 2008.

Shapiro, Paul D. "Someone to Sink Your Teeth Into: Gendered Biting Patterns on *Buffy the Vampire Slayer*: A Quantitative Analysis." *Slayage: The Online International Journal of Buffy Studies* 7, no. 2 [26] (2008).

Skwire, Sarah E. "'Whose Side Are You On, Anyway?': Children, Adults, and the Use of Fairy Tales in *Buffy*." In *Fighting the Forces: What's at Stake in* Buffy the Vampire Slayer, edited by Rhonda V. Wilcox and David Lavery, 195–204. Lanham, MD: Rowman & Littlefield, 2002.

Spooner, Catherine. "Teen Demons." In *Contemporary Gothic*, 87–123. London: Reaktion, 2006.

Stadler, Jane. "Becoming the Other: Multiculturalism in Joss Whedon's *Angel*." *Flow TV: A Critical Forum on Television and Media Culture* 7, no. 4 (2007).

Stasiak, Lauren. "'When You Kiss Me, I Want To Die': *Buffy the Vampire Slayer* and Gothic Family Values." In *Goth: Undead Subculture*, edited by Lauren M.E. Goodlad and Michael Bibby, 307–15. Durham, NC: Duke University Press, 2007.

Stein, Atara. "Conclusion: The Vampire with the Face of an Angel." In *The Byronic Hero in Film, Fiction, and Television*, 213–18. Carbondale, IL: Southern Illinois University Press, 2009.

Stephenson, Sophie. "Deconstructing the Gaze and Desensitisation in *The Cabin in the Woods*." PhD diss, Edinburgh Napier University, 2013.

Stommel, Jesse James. "I'm Not a Dead Body; I Just Play One on TV: *Buffy the Vampire Slayer* and the Performativity of the Corpse." *Slayage: The Journal of the Whedon Studies Association* 8, no. 1 [29] (2010).

Tonkin, Boyd. "Entropy as Demon: Buffy in Southern California." In *Reading the Vampire Slayer: An Unofficial Critical Companion to Buffy and Angel*, edited by Roz Kaveney, 83–99. 2nd ed. New York: I.B.Tauris, 2004.

Vetere, Lisa M. "The Rage of Willow: Malefic Witchcraft Fantasy in *Buffy the Vampire Slayer*." In Buffy *Conquers the Academy: Conference Papers from the 2009/2010 Popular Culture/American Culture Associations*, edited by U. Melissa Anyiwo and Karoline Szatek-Tudor, 76–88. Newcastle upon Tyne: Cambridge Scholars Publishing, 2013.

Wagner, Katherine A. "Haven't We Been Here Before?: *The Cabin in the Woods*, the Horror Genre, and Placelessness," in "'We Are Not Who We Are': Critical Reflections on *The Cabin in the Woods* (2012)," edited by Kristopher Karl Woofter and Jasie Stokes, special issue, *Slayage: The Journal of the Whedon Studies Association* 10, no. 2/11, no. 1 [36–37] (2013–2014).

Weyant, Curtis A. "Exploring Cabins in the Whedonverse Woods," in "Joss in June: Selected Essays," edited by K. Dale Koontz and Ensley Guffey, special issue, *Slayage: The Journal of the Whedon Studies Association* 11, no. 2/12, no. 1 [38–39] (2014).

Wilcox, Rhonda V. "Death: They're Going to Find a Body: Quality Television and the Supernatural in 'The Body.'" In *Why Buffy Matters: The Art of* Buffy the Vampire Slayer, 174–90. London: I.B.Tauris, 2005.

———. "Fear: The Princess Screamed Once: Power, Silence, and Fear in 'Hush.'" In *Why Buffy Matters: The Art of* Buffy the Vampire Slayer, 146–61. London: I.B. Tauris, 2005.

Williamson, Milly. "The Predicament of the Vampire and the Slayer: Gothic Melodrama in Modern America." In *The Lure Of The Vampire: Gender, Fiction And Fandom From Bram Stoker to* Buffy, 76–96. New York: Wallflower Press, 2005.

———. "Spike, Sex and Subtext: Intertextual Portrayals of the Sympathetic Vampire on Cult Television," in "The Vampire Spike in Text and Fandom: Unsettling Oppositions in *Buffy the Vampire Slayer*," edited by Dee Amy-Chinn and Milly Williamson, special issue, *European Journal of Cultural Studies* 8, no. 3 (2005): 289–311.

Appendix I

———. "Vampire Transformations: from Gothic Demon to Domestication?" In *Vampires: Myths and Metaphors of Enduring Evil, Conference Proceedings, Budapest, Hungary, May 22–24 2003*, edited by Carla T. Kungl, 101–107. Oxford: Inter-Disciplinary Press, 2003.

Wilson, Dominique Beth. "Willow and Which Craft?: The Portrayal of Witchcraft in Joss Whedon's *Buffy: The Vampire Slayer*." In *The Buddha of Suburbia: Proceedings of the Eighth Australian and International Religion, Literature and the Arts Conference 2004*, edited by Carole M. Cusack, Frances Di Lauro, and Christopher Hartney, 146–58. Sydney: RLA Press, 2005. https://openjournals. library.sydney.edu.au/index.php/SSR/issue/view/41/showToc.

Wirth, Sarah. "Horror and Fairy Tale Elements in the *Buffy the Vampire Slayer* Episode 'Hush.'" *Slayage: The Journal of Whedon Studies* 15, no. 1 [44] (2017).

Woofter, Kristopher Karl. "Watchers in the Woods: Meta-Horror, Genre Hybridity, and Reality TV Critique in *The Cabin in the Woods*." In *Reading Joss Whedon*, edited by Rhonda V. Wilcox, Tanya R. Cochran, Cynthea Masson, and David Lavery, 268–79. Syracuse, NY: Syracuse University Press, 2014.

Woofter, Kristopher Karl and Jasie Stokes. "Once More into the *Woods*: An Introduction and Provocation," in "'We Are Not Who We Are': Critical Reflections on *The Cabin in the Woods* (2012)," edited by Kristopher Karl Woofter and Jasie Stokes, special issue, *Slayage: The Journal of the Whedon Studies Association* 10, no. 2 / 11, no. 1 [36–37] (2013–2014).

Notes

1. Initially a term used to refer to the work of David Cronenberg (e.g., *Shivers* [1975], *Rabid* [1977], *The Brood* [1979]), "body horror" is now used more broadly to signify films, or aspects of films, that fix the site of repulsion and desire in the abject body.

2. *Watcher Junior*, along with *Slayage: The Journal of Whedon Studies*, both maintained by the Whedon Studies Association, can be found online at www. whedonstudies.tv/journals.html (other URLs are provided throughout the selected bibliography where appropriate). Please note that *Slayage* has had several changes to its subheading over its sixteen years in existence, an indication of the expanding nature of Whedon studies; the entries reflect these changes.

APPENDIX II

Foundational Works in Horror and Related Scholarship

This selected bibliography lists essential scholarship in (or translated into) English as a resource for students and scholars conducting research in the horror tradition. While it is by no means comprehensive, it has been compiled with the goal of providing the researcher with a primary survey of horror and related studies that have been central to the development of horror scholarship. Works are listed alphabetically within the historical period or decade in which they appeared in English.[1]

1900–1969

Artaud, Antonin. *Collected Works: Volume Three*. London: Calder & Boyars (1958) 1972.[2]

Benjamin, Walter. *The Work of Art in the Age of its Technical Reproducibility and Other Writings on the Media*. Cambridge, MA: Harvard University Press, 2008.[3]

Clarens, Carlos. *An Illustrated History of the Horror Film*. New York: Putnam, 1967.

Epstein, Jean. "Le cinéma du diable." (1947) *Jean Epstein: Critical Essays and New Translations*. Trans. Franck Le Gac. Ed. Sarah Keller and Jason N. Paul. Amsterdam: Amsterdam University Press, 2012, 317–26.

Freud, Sigmund. "The Uncanny." (1919) *The Standard Edition of the Complete Psychological Works of Sigmund Freud*. Ed./Trans. James Strachey. London: Hogarth Press, 1948.[4]

Jentsch, Ernst. "On the Psychology of the Uncanny." (1906) *Angelaki: A New Journal in Philosophy, Literature and the Social Sciences* (2.1, 1995), 7–16.[5]
Lovecraft, H.P. *The Annotated Supernatural Horror in Literature.* (1927) Ed. S.T. Joshi. New York: Hippocampus Press, 2012.
Otto, Rudolph. *The Idea of the Holy: An Inquiry into the Non-Rational Factor in the Idea of the Divine and Its Relation to the Rational* (1917). Trans. John W. Harvey. Oxford: Oxford University Press, 1980.[6]

1970s

Mulvey, Laura. *Visual and Other Pleasures.* Gordonsville: Palgrave Macmillan, 2009.
Pirie, David. *A New Heritage of Horror: The English Gothic Cinema* (1973). London: I.B.Tauris, 2009.
Siegel, Joel E. *Val Lewton: The Reality of Terror.* New York: Viking Press, 1973.
Todorov, Tzvetan. *The Fantastic: A Structural Approach to a Literary Genre.* Trans. Richard Howard. Ithaca, NY: Cornell University Press, 1975.
Wood, Robin, Andrew Britton, and Richard Lippe, Eds. *American Nightmare: Essays on the Horror Film.* Toronto, ON: Festival of Festivals, 1979.

1980s

Brophy, Philip. "Horrality – The Textuality of Contemporary Horror Films." *Screen* 27 (Jan/Feb 1986): 2–13.
Clover, Carol. "Her Body, Himself: Gender in the Slasher Film." *Representations* 20 (Special Issue: Misogyny, Misandry, and Misanthropy, Autumn 1987), 187–228.
Ferguson Ellis, Kate. *The Contested Castle: Gothic Novels and the Subversion of Domestic Ideology. The Gothic* (1989) Ed. Gilda Williams. Documents of Contemporary Art. Cambridge, MA: MIT Press, 2007.
Grant, Barry Keith and Christopher Sharrett. *Planks of Reason: Essays on the Horror Film* (1984). Lanham, MD: Scarecrow Press, 2004.
Gunning, Tom. "The Cinema of Attraction(s): Early Film, Its Spectator, and the Avant-Garde." (1986) *The Cinema of Attractions Reloaded.* Ed. Wanda Strauven. Amsterdam: Amsterdam University Press, 2006, 381–8.
———. "An Aesthetic of Astonishment: Early Film and the [In]Credulous Spectator." *Art and Text.* Fall 1989.
Heller, Terry. *The Delights of Terror: An Aesthetics of the Tale of Terror.* Urbana and Chicago: University of Illinois Press, 1987.
Jackson, Rosemary. *Fantasy: The Literature of Subversion.* London: Methuen, 1981.
King, Stephen. *Danse Macabre.* (1981) New York: Pocket Books/Simon and Schuster, 2011.
Kristeva, Julia. *Powers of Horror: An Essay on Abjection* (1980) Trans. Léon S. Roudiez. New York: Columbia University Press, 1982.
Reynolds, David S. *Beneath the American Renaissance: The Subversive Imagination in the Age of Emerson and Melville.* New York: Knopf, 1988.
Sedgwick, Eve Kosofsky. *The Coherence of Gothic Convention.* New York and London: Methuen, 1986.

Stewart, Susan. "The Epistemology of the Horror Story." *The Journal of American Folklore.* 95.375 (Jan–Mar 1982): 33–50.

Tudor, Andrew. *Monsters and Mad Scientists: A Cultural History of the Horror Movie.* Oxford: Basil Blackwell, 1989.

Varma, Devendra P. *The Gothic Flame: Being a History of the Gothic Novel in England: Its Origins, Efflorescence, Disintegration, and Residuary Influences.* Lanham, MD: Scarecrow Press, 1988.

1990s

Benshoff, Harry M. *Monsters in the Closet: Homosexuality and the Horror Film.* Manchester, UK: Manchester University Press, 1997.

Carroll, Noël. *The Philosophy of Horror, or Paradoxes of the Heart.* New York: Routledge, 1992.

Clover, Carol J. *Men, Women and Chainsaws: Gender in the Modern Horror Film.* Princeton, NJ: Princeton University Press, 1997.

Cohen, Jeffrey Jerome. "Monster Culture (Seven Theses)." *Monster Theory: Reading Culture.* Ed. Jeffrey Jerome Cohen. Minneapolis: University of Minnesota Press, 1996, 3–25.

Creed, Barbara. *The Monstrous Feminine: Film, Feminism, Psychoanalysis.* London and New York: Routledge, 1993.

Botting, Fred. *Gothic.* New York: Routledge, 1996.

Grant, Barry Keith. *The Dread of Difference: Gender and the Horror Film* (1996). Austin, TX: University of Texas Press, 2015.

Halberstam, J. *Skin Shows: Gothic Horror and the Technology of Monsters.* Raleigh, NC: Duke University Press, 1995.

Martin, Robert K. and Eric Savoy, Eds. *American Gothic: New Interventions in a National Narrative.* Iowa City: University of Iowa Press, 1998.

Pinedo, Isabel Cristina. *Recreational Terror: Women and the Pleasures of Horror Film Viewing.* Albany, NY: State University of New York Press, 1997.

Punter, David. *The Literature of Terror, Volume 1: The Gothic Tradition.* Essex, UK: Pearson/Longman, 1996.

———. *The Literature of Terror, Volume 2: A History of Gothic Fictions from 1765 to the Present Day.* Essex, UK: Pearson/Longman, 1996.

Sconce, Jeffrey. "'Trashing' the Academy: Taste, Excess, and an Emerging Politics of Cinematic Style." *Screen* 36 (4) 1995.

Shaviro, Steven. *The Cinematic Body. Theory Out of Bounds* (1993). Minneapolis and London: University of Minnesota Press, 2011.

Skal, David J. *The Monster Show: A Cultural History of Horror* (1993). New York: Faber and Faber, 2001.

Williams, Anne. *Art of Darkness: A Poetics of Gothic.* Chicago: University of Chicago Press, 1995.

Williams, Linda. "Film Bodies: Gender, Genre, and Excess" (1991). *Film Theory and Criticism.* Ed. L. Baudry and M. Cohen. New York: Oxford University Press, 2004, 727–41.

Appendix II

2000s

Bergland, Renée L. *The National Uncanny: Indian Ghosts and American Subjects.* Hanover, NJ: University Press of New England, 2000.

Cherry, Brigid. *Horror.* New York and London: Routledge, 2009.

Curtis, Barry. *Dark Places: The Haunted House in Film.* London: Reaktion Books, 2008.

Freeland, Cynthia. *The Naked and the Undead: Evil and the Appeal of Horror.* Boulder, CO: Westview Press, 2000.

Hand, Richard J. and Michael Wilson. *Grand-Guignol: The French Theatre of Horror.* Ed. Richard J. Hand and Michael Wilson. London: University of Exeter Press, 2002, 1–78.

Hawkins, Joan. *Cutting Edge: Art-Horror and the Horrific Avant-Garde.* Minneapolis: University of Minnesota Press, 2000.

Hills, Matt. *The Pleasures of Horror.* London and New York: Continuum, 2005.

Jancovich, Mark. *Horror: The Film Reader.* London: Routledge, 2002.

Lowenstein, Adam. 2005. *Shocking Representation: Historical Trauma, National Cinema, and the Modern Horror Film.* New York: Columbia University Press.

Marks, Laura U. *The Skin of the Film: Intercultural Cinema, Embodiment, and the Senses.* Durham: Duke University Press, 2000.

Modleski, Tania. "The Terror of Pleasure: The Contemporary Horror Film and Postmodern Theory." *Film Theory and Criticism.* Eds Leo Braudy and Marshall Cohen. Oxford: Oxford University Press, 2004. 764–73.

Royle, Nicholas. *The Uncanny.* London and New York: Routledge, 2003.

Salomon, Roger B. *Mazes of the Serpent: An Anatomy of Horror Narrative.* Ithaca, NY: Cornell University Press, 2002.

Sobchack, Vivian. *Carnal Thoughts: Embodiment and Moving Image Culture.* Berkeley: University of California Press, 2004.

Wheatley, Helen. *Gothic Television.* Manchester, UK: Manchester University Press, 2006.

Worland, Rick. *The Horror Film: An Introduction.* London: Blackwell, 2007.

2010s

Jowett, Lorna and Stacey Abbott. *TV Horror: Investigating the Dark Side of the Small Screen.* London, UK: I.B.Tauris, 2013.

Ligotti, Thomas. *The Conspiracy Against the Human Race: A Contrivance of Horror.* New York: Hippocampus Press, 2010.

Lowenstein, Adam. "Spectacle Horror and *Hostel*: Why 'Torture Porn' Does Not Exist." *Critical Quarterly* 53 (1) (2011): 42–60.

Massumi, Brian. *Politics of Affect.* Cambridge: Polity Press, 2015.

Reyes, Xavier Aldana. *Horror Film and Affect: Towards a Corporeal Model of Viewership.* London: Routledge, 2016.

———. "Beyond Psychoanalysis: Post-Millennial Horror Film and Affect Theory." *Horror Studies* 3 (2) (2012): 243–61.

Wheatley, Helen. *Spectacular Television: Exploring Televisual Pleasure.* London: I.B.Tauris, 2016.

Notes

1. Thanks to Mario DeGiglio-Bellemare for helping to flesh out this list.
2. The first English translation of Artaud's work, *Le Théâtre et son double* (1938), appeared in 1958.
3. The first English translation of Benjamin's 1936 essay, *Das Kunstwerk im zeitalter seiner technischen reproduzierbarkeit*, appeared in Hanna Arendt's edited volume *Illuminations* in 1968.
4. The first English translations of Freud's works were in 1924–1925, by a group of scholars led by Strachey.
5. According to translator Roy Sellars, Jentsch's 1906 essay was not translated into English until Sellars' own 1996 translation in the journal, *Angelaki* (2.1) 1995. See also Forbes Morlock's "Doubly Uncanny: An Introduction to 'On the Psychology of the Uncanny'" (*Angelaki*, 2.1 [1995]), 17–21. We list the work here in the period of its original German publication date because the work has been referred to and "known" by scholars since Freud took issue with Jentsch's theorization.
6. The first English translation of Otto's study was in 1923.

About the Contributors

Stacey Abbott, PhD, is a Reader in Film and Television Studies at the University of Roehampton. She is the author of *Undead Apocalypse: Vampires and Zombies in the 21st Century* (2016), *Celluloid Vampires* (2007), *Angel: TV Milestone* (2009), and co-author, with Lorna Jowett, of *TV Horror: The Dark Side of the Small Screen* (2013). She is the editor of *The Cult TV Book* (2010) and *Reading Angel: The TV Spin-off with a Soul* (2005).

Cynthia Burkhead, PhD, is Associate Professor and Chair of the Department of English at the University of North Alabama. She is the author of *Dreams in American Television Narratives: From Dallas to Buffy* (2014) and co-editor of *Joss Whedon: Conversations* (2011). Her publications also include essays on the programs *Lost*, *The Sopranos*, and *Carnivale*, and on television finales.

Bronwen Calvert, PhD, is an associate lecturer at the Open University in the North of England, UK. Her research looks at embodiment in fantasy and science fiction narratives, with particular focus on cyberpunk fiction, horror, and versions of the television action hero. She has published work on various television series, most recently on *The X-Files* (2013), *Fringe* (2014), and *Dollhouse* (2014), and in her book *Being Bionic: The World of TV Cyborgs* (I.B.Tauris, 2016).

Mario DeGiglio-Bellemare, PhD, is a "monster kid" who teaches courses on genre cinema, grotesque traditions, embodiment, and monster ethics in the Humanities department of John Abbott College. He is presently finishing a book linked to the history of the Parisian Grand-Guignol theatre, entitled *Sinister Tableaux: Grand-Guignol Cinema, Corporeality and the Senses*. His most recent publication is an article on Jean Rollin for the book, *Global Fear: International Horror Directors* (2017). He is Co-Editor of *MONSTRUM*, and Co-Director of the Montreal Monstrum Society.

Clayton Dillard is a PhD Candidate in Screen Studies at Oklahoma State University. He is a contributor to the three-volume *Race in American Film* (2017) and has been published in *The European Journal of American Studies* and *The Journal of American Culture*. He is also a staff film critic for *Slant Magazine* and a member of the Online Film Critics Society.

Erin Giannini, PhD, received her PhD in television studies from the University of East Anglia, and has written on new technology and product placement on American scripted television programs and their impact on a cultural, televisual, and economic level, as well as shifts in definitions of television programs brought about by new technology and new platforms. She has also published and presented work on religion, socioeconomics, technology, and corporate culture, and, if pressed, could probably name every Buffy episode in order, which only comes in useful for trivia games or combating boredom while waiting in line.

Anne Golden, MFA, teaches film courses in the Media Arts Department at John Abbott College in Montreal. She has an MFA from Concordia University. Her writing has appeared in the magazines *Fuse, Canadian Theatre Review*, and the anthology *Recovering 1940s Horror: Traces of a Lost Decade* (2015). She is also an independent video artist, curator and writer whose programs have been presented at Musée National du Québec, Edges Festival, and Queer City Cinema among others. Golden is Artistic Director of Groupe Intervention Vidéo (GIV). She published her first novel *From the Archives of Vidéo Populaire* in 2016.

Stephanie Graves completed her MA in English at Middle Tennessee State University, where her concentration was film and television studies. Stephanie's research interests include horror, the grotesque, the southern gothic, postmodernism, and gender and queer studies. She has presented her research at various conferences, including PCAS and the *Slayage* Conference on the Whedonverses. She is currently a PhD student at Georgia State University.

Karen Herland, MA, teaches courses on cultural constructions of gender, sexuality at Concordia University's Simone de Beauvoir Institute, as well as at McGill University, Carleton University, and the University of Ottawa.

About the Contributors

She is a regular lecturer at the Montreal Monstrum Society, and published "'Always Hearing Voices, Never Hearing Mine': Sound and Fury in *The Snake Pit*" in *Recovering 1940s Horror Cinema: Traces of a Lost Decade* (2015). Her research on sex work, queer identities, and horror is concerned with how expectations and representations of those on the margins serve to inscribe and contain difference. Her work has appeared in *POV* magazine, *The Journal of Canadian Studies*, and *No More Potlucks*.

Alysa Hornick, MLIS, has maintained *Whedonology: An Academic Whedon Studies Bibliography* (hosted by the Whedon Studies Association: www.whedonstudies.tv), since 2005, and has served on the editorial board of *Watcher Junior: The Undergraduate Journal of the Whedon Studies* since 2010. She has a BA in Comparative Literature from New York University, and an MLIS from Long Island University. She has published in the collection, *Joss Whedon: The Complete Companion: the TV Series, the Movies, the Comic Books and More* (2012), and is the co-editor of *The Vampire in Folklore, History, Literature, Film, and Television: A Comprehensive Bibliography* (2015). She lives and works in New York City.

Jerry D. Metz, Jr., PhD, is an independent scholar and translator of Brazilian Portuguese. He received his PhD in History from the University of Maryland, College Park, with a dissertation on mid- to late twentieth-century regional dynamics in Brazil's national carnival festival. His areas of research and publication include Brazilian popular culture, folklore and the culture industry, popular music, soundtrack and film scores, horror cinema and television, and the horror genre in (inter)national socio-cultural and historical contexts. His essay on *The Cabin in the Woods* appeared in *Slayage: The Journal of Whedon Studies* (Fall 2013/Winter 2014).

Selma A. Purac, PhD, is an Assistant Professor in the Faculty of Information and Media Studies at Western University in London, Ontario, Canada. Her work in word-image relations allows her to bridge her interests in literary theory, art history, and cultural studies. Selma's most recent publication, "Undercutting Arcadia: Banville, Espionage, and Poussin," is an extension of her work on contemporary manifestations of the *paragone* in media as varied as literature, film, and music videos.

Alanna Thain, PhD, is Associate Professor of World Cinemas and Cultural Studies at McGill University, and Director of the Institute for Gender, Sexuality and Feminist Studies. She also directs the Moving Image Research Laboratory, devoted to the study of the body in moving image media. Her book, *Bodies in Suspense: Time and Affect in Cinema* (2017) looks at how films that explore strange experiences of time give us insight into the body's power of changing in time, or the experience of "anotherness" in works by David Lynch, Alfred Hitchcock, Christian Marclay, Rian Johnson, and Lou Ye. Her current project, "Anarchival Outbursts," looks at dance in post digital cinema as a key technique for negotiating the complicated forms that embodiment takes in a digital world, through work by William Kentridge, Lynch, Bjork, Pipilotti Rist, and more.

K. Brenna Wardell, PhD, is an Assistant Professor of film and literature at the University of North Alabama. Her research, published in venues such as *The Cine-Files,* focuses on gender and sexuality, aesthetics, and issues of place/space in media and literary texts. Recent publications include an article on Joss Whedon's acting ensemble for *Slayage: The Journal of Whedon Studies,* and a piece on Alfred Hitchcock's film *Frenzy,* published in *Critical Insights Film: Alfred Hitchcock* from Salem Press (December 2016).

Index

Index

319

Index

Index

Freud, Sigmund, 8, 23, 81, 82, 107,
  239n.16, 265, 308, 312n.4, 312n.5
Friday the, 13th (1980 film), 22
Friday the, 13th, Part, 2 (1981 film), 20
Friday the, 13th, Part VI: Jason Lives
  (1986 film), 27
Friday the, 13th franchise, 126, 132,
  134, 135
Friedkin, William, 37, 78
Fright Night (1985 film), 145t.8.1, 149,
  150, 151, 158
frontier, 10, 154, 220, 225, 228, 261,
  262, 263, 264, 266, 276
Fury, David, 173, 191

Garland, Judy, 75
gaze (*see also* male gaze), 26, 168, 201,
  252–5, 259n.27, 259n.28, 286
Geena Davis Institute on Gender in
  Media, 204
gender, 17, 18, 22–4, 27–9, 31, 33n.21,
  103n.2, 125, 158, 166, 178, 201–4,
  206–8, 210–11, 213–15, 244–5,
  247, 252, 256, 262, 264, 268,
  270, 298
genre (*see also* excess; horror genre),
  1–12
  negotiation, 22, 24, 27, 28, 31, 36,
    126, 128,
  as process, 5, 90
ghost, ghosts, 1, 2, 4–6, 82, 83, 86, 106,
  108, 113, 114, 114f.6.1, 177, 202,
  218n.51, 222, 266, 266f.14.2, 273
Ghost Nation *see Westworld*
ghosting, 286
Goddard, Drew, 2, 8, 89, 106, 123, 124,
  127, 128, 130, 131, 133, 134f.7.1,
  135, 137, 163–5, 171, 178, 205
gore, 22, 164, 165, 167, 174, 177, 183,
  184, 185, 193
Gothic (tradition), the, 1, 5, 8, 10, 17,
  27, 54, 56, 79, 107, 108, 110, 112,
  113, 166, 168, 181, 182, 183, 184,
  185, 195n.6, 209, 215n.7, 218n.53,

220, 221–9, 237, 238n.8, 238n.12,
  239n.14, 250, 261, 262, 284, 285,
  298
Grand Guignol, Grand-Guignol, 27, 28,
  31, 311
Green, Bruce Seth, 167
Greenwalt, David, 167, 179n.14,
  197n.37, 214, 254
grief, 53, 65, 68, 172, 173, 232, 291
Grossman, David, 173
Guattari, Félix, 283, 289, 294, 296n.4
guilt, 7, 94, 95, 97, 101, 170, 190, 236,
  250, 252, 265
Gunning, Tom, 57, 65, 66, 69, 73, 309

Hagen, Jean, 75
Hallab, Mary Y., 155, 301
Halloween (1978 film), 7, 17–33,
  25f.1.1, 134, 148, 152, 155, 170,
  171, 253, 259n.28
Halloween (holiday), 76, 183, 243
Haraway, Donna, 267, 276
Hauer, Rutger, 147–8
haunted house, 1, 9, 76, 106–8,
  110–11, 115, 118, 202, 311
hauntology, hauntological, 10, 222, 228,
  238n.12
Hayworth, Rita, 87
Heathers (1988 film), 148, 152–5, 157
Hellraiser (1987 film), 38, 132, 135, 152
Herrmann, Bernard, 67
heterogeneity, heterogeneous, 28, 54, 56
heteronormativity, 23, 87, 201, 272,
  273, 287
Hill, Debra, 22
Hills Have Eyes, The (1977 film), 21, 135
Hitchcock, Alfred, 66, 67, 72n.44, 112,
  170, 252, 271
Holbein, Hans, 62, 63f.3.2, 64, 67
horror genre, the, 2, 6, 123–40
  conventions, 2, 3, 4, 7, 8, 11, 23, 28,
    35, 36, 37, 41, 42, 68, 74, 77, 86, 96,
    98, 102, 126, 127, 128, 129, 131,
    132, 133, 136, 137, 138, 149, 150,

Index

Index

Index

226, 230, 247–9, 252, 254, 258n.14, 259n.28, 270, 271
victim-hero *see* female
Videodrome (1984 film), 58
villain, 19, 21, 37, 38, 43, 119n.13, 148, 151, 155, 161n.31, 233, 234, 255, 260n.35, 264, 275, 284
virtual reality, 117, 129
virtuality, 115
voyeur, voyeurism, 105, 136, 166, 201

Walking Dead, The (2010–present TV series), 9, 166, 172, 180n.19, 197n.43
Walters, Charles, 91n.17
Way to Shadow Garden, The (1954 film), 81
WB Network, 24, 174, 185, 194, 196n.30, 197n.42
Weinstock, Jeffrey, 226
Westworld (1973 film), 262, 269
 characters
  Man in Black (Yul Brynner), 269
Westworld (2016–present TV series), 10, 261–80, 266f.14.2
 characters
  Ghost Nation, 266, 266f.14.2
  Man in Black (Ed Harris), 269
 episodes
  "The Adversary" (1.6), 276
  "Chestnut" (1.2), 279n.31, 279n.37
  "Contrapasso" (1.5), 276
  "Dissonance Theory" (1.4), 273
  "Trace Decay" (1.8), 280n.63
Weird (tradition), the, 10, 220, 222, 226, 229–30, 233, 236–7
Western (genre), the, 5, 11, 89, 261, 264
western frontier, the, 262, 264
Whedon, Joss
 as brand, 1–13, 143–62, 167, 178, 191, 220, 243, 252, 263, 264–5, 271–3, 277n.4, 94–5

as feminist, 10, 11, 20, 22, 24, 31, 147, 201–18, 277n.4
 quoted in interviews/commentary, 1, 6, 7, 18, 19, 22, 30, 32n.14, 34, 36, 37, 38, 41, 95, 144, 151–2, 154, 248, 259n.24, 262, 264, 271–2
 and revisionism, 1–13, 19, 23, 24, 25, 28, 31, 128, 130, 131, 133, 135, 137, 164, 165, 170, 244–5, 254
 as writer/director/producer/auteur, 17, 18, 20–2, 26, 28, 29, (32)n.14, 35–6, 37, 38, 41, 43, 45, 48, 53, 54, 61–7, 81, 83, 89, 93–5, 107, 123, 124, 127, 143, 146, 163, 167, 172, 177, 191, 219, 220, 221, 226–7, 248, 251, 281, 283, 294
Whedon Studies Association, 13n.24, 202, 298
Whedonesque (weblog), 11, 13n.22
Whedonverse, 1, 6, 7, 93, 171, 172, 182, 186, 187, 188, 191, 219
Wilcox, Rhonda, 37, 58–9, 75, 77, 252, 255, 259n.22, 259n.23, 259, n.26, 259n.30, 260n.34, 260n.35, 306–7
Williams, Linda, 12n.13, 286, 310
Wings of Desire (1987 film), 186
Wizard of Oz, The (1939 film), 75
WLVI-56 Boston (*see also* "Creature Double Feature"), 55
Wonder Woman (1975–9 TV series), 207
Wonder Woman (unproduced Whedon screenplay), 215n.1
Wood, Robin (character) *see Buffy the Vampire Slayer*
Wood, Robin (scholar), 8, 58, 75, 92, 95, 103n.2, 107, 180n.19, 238n.12,
Woofter, Kristopher K., 5, 10, 106, 127, (140)n.55, (260)n.33, (296)n.7, 307

Index